PUBLIC DUTY AND PRIVATE CONSCIENCE IN SEVENTEENTH-CENTURY ENGLAND

GERALD AYLMER

PUBLIC DUTY AND PRIVATE CONSCIENCE IN SEVENTEENTH-CENTURY ENGLAND

Essays Presented to
G. E. Aylmer

Edited by
JOHN MORRILL
PAUL SLACK
and
DANIEL WOOLF

CLARENDON PRESS · OXFORD
1993

Oxford University Press, Walton Street, Oxford OX2 6DP
Oxford New York Toronto
Delhi Bombay Calcutta Madras Karachi
Petaling Jaya Singapore Hong Kong Tokyo
Nairobi Dar es Salaam Cape Town
Melbourne Auckland
and associated companies in
Berlin Ibadan

Oxford is a trade mark of Oxford University Press

Published in the United States
by Oxford University Press, New York

British Library Cataloguing in Publication Data
Data available

Library of Congress Cataloging in Publication Data
Public duty and private conscience in seventeenth-century England:
essays presented to G. E. Aylmer / edited by John Morrill, Paul
Slack, and Daniel Woolf.
p.   cm.
Includes bibliographical references.
1. Great Britain—Politics and government—1603–1714.
2. Political ethics—England—History—17th century.   3. Ethics,
Modern—17th century.   I. Morrill, J. S. (John Stephen)   II. Slack,
Paul.   III. Woolf, D. R. (Daniel R.)
DA375.P85   1993
942.06—dc20   92-32519
ISBN 0–19–820229–6

Filmset in Garamond by
Selwood Systems, Midsomer Norton
Printed and bound in
Great Britain by Biddles Ltd.,
Guildford and King's Lynn

PREFACE

THIS book represents a tribute to Gerald Aylmer by just a few of his friends, colleagues, and former students. It is presented to him with the affection and admiration they all share for his selfless devotion to the craft of history, and for the generosity which he has shown to all who have sought out his counsel and his deep knowledge of the period.

Gerald's interests have always been unusually broad, extending far beyond the seventeenth century. In recent years, for example, much of his teaching in Oxford has been of American colonial history. But there is no doubt that his first love has been for seventeenth-century English history, and within that for the shaping of political attitudes in times of acute stress. His monumental analyses of the civil services of Charles I and of the Interregnum stand as two of the most enduring of all works produced in his time.

Gerald has not only been preoccupied with the relationship between public duty and private conscience as a theme in history. He is also notably a man who has striven to live his own public life in accordance with his high principles. The choice of theme for this volume represents, then, a double tribute to a man whose integrity and scrupulosity of conscience are so much admired. But we hope that the book also has its own integrity as a set of essays on a theme of central importance in a period of perennial fascination to scholars and students.

The editors have sought to bring together essays by those who have collaborated with Gerald, who have been long-standing colleagues, and who have been his students. Whichever of the categories they are in, they have all benefited from his friendship. They dedicate this book to him, with affection.

John Morrill
Paul Slack
Daniel Woolf

1 January 1992

CONTENTS

ABBREVIATIONS

BIHR	*Bulletin of the Institute of Historical Research*
BL	British Library
Bodl.	Bodleian Library
Cal. SP Dom.	*Calendar of State Papers, Domestic Series*
CJ	*Journals of the House of Commons*
DNB	*Dictionary of National Biography*
Ec. Hist. Rev.	*Economic History Review*
EHR	*English Historical Review*
HLRO	House of Lords Record Office
HMC	Historical Manuscripts Commission, Reports
P&P	*Past and Present*
PRO	Public Record Office
RO	Record Office
TLS	*Times Literary Supplement*
TRHS	*Transactions of the Royal Historical Society*

Unless otherwise stated, all works cited were published in London. In dates the old style has been retained, except that the year is taken to begin on 1 January.

I

Gerald Aylmer at Balliol

CHRISTOPHER HILL

GERALD AYLMER came up to Balliol from Winchester College in 1944, as a Domus Exhibitioner. He was then 18, and remained in College only for the summer term before departing for three years in the navy. We have a brief glimpse of him at Winchester in the early years of the war. Thomas Hinde, a contemporary Wykehamist, writes, 'after my parents, Gerald Aylmer is certainly the person who most changed my life', though he is not specific about the direction of the change. His description of Gerald anticipates many later comments. 'He has a hyper-active conscience, and though he may reject [school] ritual *on principle*, he will never evade it secretly.' He 'continually says things which widen my world'. And with a note of proper awe Hinde adds, '*Horizon* is his light reading."[1] At his interview for admission to Balliol Gerald was described as 'pink', which probably refers to his complexion rather than to his politics.

After the war had ended we have a rather full sketch of the nautical Gerald just before and after his twenty-first birthday, in George Melly's *Rum, Bum and Concertina*. Melly recalls his shipmate's 'deep booming voice and magnificent laugh'. Gerald was the 'prototype WASP', with 'a kind of dogged nobility about him, an admirable probity'. But this austere picture is modified by 'a love of gossip, a delight in alcoholic excess, and a shared enthusiasm for . . . W. H. Auden'. Gerald spent a night in a Spanish prison cell after being arrested trying to crawl across the border from Gibraltar, in a state of mild inebriation. Melly was puzzled that, although Gerald seemed a natural for promotion to commissioned rank, he chose to remain a rating. Melly concluded that 'it was because he was a convinced socialist'.[2]

I am most grateful for help to Alan Montefiore, Donald Pennington, Professors Archie Duncan, Peter Marshall, Paul Rolo, Hugh Stretton, and John Taylor. But they are not responsible for anything.

[1] Hinde, *Sir Henry and Sons: A Memoir* (1980), 144–5.
[2] Melly, *Rum, Bum and Concertina* (1977), 118–19, 132, 142.

One story shows Gerald in a particularly agreeable light. Melly had got himself put on a charge of subversion, not only for possessing a large number of Anarchist pamphlets, but for confessedly intending to distribute them among other members of the crew. It could have been a very serious matter. Gerald helped Melly in the preparation of his defence. His recommendation was to begin on a note of high seriousness, recalling that the object of the recently concluded war had been 'to ensure freedom of thought and expression to all, including those holding minority opinions, even those which might appear repulsive to many people'. Melly, again on Gerald's advice, combed the works of G. B. Shaw, collecting passages parallel to those in the pamphlets most likely to outrage naval authority. After reading them out, he pointed out that Shaw's works were in the ship's library, freely available to the entire ship's company. Fortunately the officer hearing the case had a sense of humour, and those were relaxed post-war days, before the cold war had started. Melly got off very lightly.[3] The story shows Gerald putting his knowledge to practical use.

He returned to Balliol in October 1947. Paul Rolo recalls how when he started as a Balliol history lecturer in 1946, he apologized to his first pupils for being a little rusty after years of wartime absence. 'Don't worry,' they said, 'we saw Christopher Hill through that phase last year.' So by 1947 I hope I was able to cover up my ignorance when faced with Gerald, a formidable pupil from the start. From his first term his tutors' termly reports were invariably excellent—'mature, scholarly, massive orderly mind, good judgement, original' were standard phrases. 'Already alpha' in his first year, 'first-class work' is the norm after that. One phrase stands out, which I am pleased to note was mine: 'a sledge-hammer mind'.

Gerald's undergraduate contemporaries stood in some awe of him. His commanding height gave him an advantage over everybody else in the room. When I tried to collect reminiscences of him from his contemporaries, I found that he was not a man around whom anecdotes gathered. 'Gerald frightened all of us,' wrote a future Scottish professor, adding as the supreme tribute, 'He was perhaps the only one of us whom Brian Manning respected.'[4] He was 'exceptionally, even unnaturally judicious in demeanour', recalls

[3] Ibid. 173–5.
[4] Author of *The English People and the English Revolution* (Harmondsworth, 1976).

another. Tutorials shared with him were 'memorable occasions', but he was regarded as a worrying tutorial partner because of his omniscience and indefatigability. There was 'a measured ruthlessness' in his approach to his work: 'there were times and days when it took precedence.' One pleasing recollection is that, in those days of post-war austerity, 'Gerald appeared to sustain himself on an endless supply of boiled sweets,' which he generously offered to any friend who called. His closest friends knew that he was 'firmly rooted in a radical tradition'. 'He had thought through his position on most issues.' He 'resembled the early Auden, whom he often quoted'—as in the navy. The awe was based on real respect for 'the most remarkable person I met among my contemporaries in Balliol'. Yet together with this Gerald had 'a very judicious sense of humour', 'a capacity for friendship, and a tolerance of other people's eccentricities'.

The solemn dedication to academic work was balanced by equally serious relaxation. One fellow reveller recalls him on the morning after a Balliol ball, still drinking champagne—out of a pint mug. Another unacademic occasion was his appearance in a College production of Noel Coward's *Hands Across the Sea*, together with *Disordered String*, an extravaganza co-written for the occasion by Paul Rolo, who was also the producer. The cast included two don's wives, two future professors, and one future newspaper editor. Despite that, I recall only two things clearly from what was a riotously successful evening. One was the College organ thumping out, fortissimo, 'There's no business like show business'. We were more accustomed to hearing Handel and hymn tunes played on that sacred instrument, but Paul Rolo had somehow wangled College approval. The other memorable event was Gerald's performance as Lt.-Commander Alastair Corbett, RN (retd.) in *Hands Across the Sea* and as Mr Burton (a business magnate) in *Disordered String*.[5]

In November 1949 Gerald Aylmer won the College Kington Oliphant Prize for an historical essay, and of course he got his First without difficulty in 1950. After a year at Princeton as Visiting Fellow he returned to Balliol as a Junior Research Fellow of the College (1951–4). My recollections of Gerald as undergraduate and Fellow are of a self-contained, slightly reserved, hard-working colleague who—everybody recognized—would go far. He was a

---

[5] I am very grateful to Paul Rolo for refreshing my memory here.

member of an extremely lively group of young men and women, including many future academics and civil servants, who taught one another far more than they learnt from their tutors. Gerald early became a sort of elder statesman in their group. It was enriched by the presence of Ursula Nixon, then College Secretary at next-door St John's, whom Gerald was to marry in 1955. It was the cleverest and most fortunate thing even he ever did.

One personal recollection may tell us something about Gerald. In 1949 Edmund Dell (later Labour cabinet minister and Rt. Hon. and I jointly edited and published *The Good Old Cause*, an anthology of documents intended to illustrate 'the causes, course and consequences of the English Revolution'. Three years later this was panned by a reviewer in *History*. It was, he said, a book whose purpose was 'not historical but propagandist', bearing 'suspiciously close resemblance to the historical technique of the speeches of Adolf Hitler'.[6] I was a bit taken aback, not to say depressed; but that was at the height of the cold war, when such outbursts were not uncommon. But Gerald, then a Junior Research Fellow, was outraged. Without a word to me, he wrote a long and carefully documented letter to *History*, protesting. Rather unexpectedly, *History* published it in the next number.[7] Gerald made it clear that he did not agree with all the ideas of ours which the reviewer had criticized, and he was far from sharing our political views at that time, which clearly had caused the reviewer's hostility. It was enough for Gerald that he thought injustice had been done, and he wished to register his protest against it. Gerald was 26 at the time. For a young man who had not yet held a permanent teaching job, it might have been a very imprudent step. I do not suppose Gerald thought about that for a moment. It was a demonstration of the integrity and independence which he has always shown. The reviewer did not attempt to answer Gerald's arguments; instead, in a curt note, he wrote with supreme condescension, 'When your correspondent has devoted a lifetime to Stuart history, as Gardiner did, and has made himself conversant with Gardiner's austere view of the duties of an historian, his charge that Gardiner was tendentious and question-begging may carry more weight.' (The reviewer had objected to our use of 'the Good Old Cause' as 'equivalent to what they refuse to call "the Puritan" Revolution',

---

[6] *History*, NS 37 (1952), 244–5.   [7] Ibid. NS 38(1953), 94–5.

and Gerald had ventured to suggest that this was not indefensible.)
Well, Gerald has reached the years of discretion now. He has
devoted a lifetime to the austere duties of the historian, and his
name today means rather more to scholars than that of the reviewer
who so patronizingly dismissed him. I am glad to have this occasion
of recalling Gerald's bold and memorable gesture, and to thank
him not only for his defence of us but also for his stand on the
principle of fair comment in reviewing, as against political innuendo
and slander.

In the days when Gerald was undergraduate and a Junior
Research Fellow, the study of seventeenth-century English history
was in an even more cantankerous state than it is today. Gerald
did the Commonwealth and Protectorate Special Subject for History
Schools, so he was well versed in these controversies. He was
fortunate in obtaining R. H. Tawney as his supervisor for his
ambitious research project, ultimately published in 1961 as *The
King's Servants: The Civil Service of Charles I, 1625–1642*. Tawney was a
very great historian, and a very humane person, who deplored the
virulence with which arguments about the seventeenth century
were conducted in the 1950s. He was also a man whose radical
outlook must have appealed to Gerald.

Until the 1950s seventeenth-century studies were dominated by
Tawney's wide-embracing thesis of 'the rise of the gentry', which
amplified and complemented Harrington's seventeenth-century
argument that the Civil War was caused by an upset in the balance
of property through the transfer of land from Church, Crown, and
aristocracy to 'the people', by whom Harrington meant those
people who had enough money to buy land, those 'people' whom
the House of Commons represented.[8] In 1953 the young Hugh
Trevor-Roper, pursuing a vendetta against Lawrence Stone, tried
in a savage onslaught to stand Tawney's thesis on its head by
attributing the Civil War not to the rise but to a decline of a
section of the gentry, 'the mere gentry'.[9] He confidently advanced
the thesis that holding State office was a major source of income

---

[8] 'The Rise of the Gentry, 1558–1640', *Ec. Hist. Rev.* 11 (1941), 1–38, and *Harrington's
Interpretation of his Age* (Raleigh Lecture, 1941). Cf. L. Stone, 'The Anatomy of the Elizabethan
Aristocracy', *Ec. Hist. Rev.* 18 (1948), 1–53.

[9] *The Gentry, 1540–1640* (Ec. Hist. Rev. Supp. 1; 1953); cf. 'The Elizabethan Aristocracy: An
Anatomy Anatomized', *Ec. Hist. Rev.* 2nd ser., 3 (1951), 279–98; 'Oliver Cromwell and his
Parliaments', in R. Pares and A. J. P. Taylor (eds.) *Essays Presented to Sir Lewis Namier* (1956),
1–48.

for English gentlemen, many of whom were undergoing financial difficulties in consequence of inflation. Those gentry who were weathering the storm were not improving estate-managers but Court office-holders. The Civil War alignment was in significant part a conflict between 'ins', and 'outs' trying to get in. It seems difficult to believe it now, but Trevor-Roper's thesis was advanced so confidently and so stridently that for a short time it appeared to hold the field.

It is largely because of Gerald Aylmer's *The King's Servants* that it is now forgotten. His is, of course, the exact opposite of a polemical work. Its scholarly apparatus is impeccable and formidable, analysing in minute detail the finances of some nine hundred royal servants. But two simple sentences, based on eighty-nine statistical tables, undermined the whole Trevor-Roper edifice: 'it is impossible to identify the rising with the office-holding gentry. . . . Wealth changed hands via office under the Crown, but office did not create wealth.'[10] Court office was profitable for the lucky few, but Aylmer's careful statistics show how very few they were, and how much it cost to establish oneself as a courtier. Many might be bankrupted in the search for remunerative office.

Five years later Gerald was equally authoritatively trenchant in his dismissal of Peter Laslett's *The World We Have Lost*. 'Mr. Laslett's 17th-century England is one which I have great difficulty in recognizing and which, I believe, would have surprised most contemporaries—though it would have delighted some of them.'[11] With typically balanced justice, Gerald compensated by (rightly) praising Laslett's Introduction to his edition of Sir Robert Filmer's *Patriarcha and Other Political Works* (Oxford, 1949), which did contain novel and interesting ideas. (In all fairness I should perhaps add that there have been occasions on which Gerald has hinted—indeed more than hinted—that I too have carried an argument further than he thinks the evidence will bear. I spare myself the details.)

Meanwhile Gerald during the last two years of his Junior Research Fellowship had been Junior Dean—an office whose occupant must be *persona grata* with both senior and junior members

[10] *The King's Servants*, 333–4.
[11] G. Aylmer, 'Caste, ordre (ou statut) et classe dans les premiers temps de l'Angleterre moderne', in R. Mousnier (ed.), *Problèmes de stratification sociale* (Paris, 1968), 146. (I have retranslated from the French.)

of the College. In 1954 he left Oxford for an assistant lectureship in history at Manchester University (promoted to full lecturer in 1957). In 1963 he became the first Professor of History at the new University of York, and an exceptionally successful one. Here he remained until he was elected Master of St Peter's College, Oxford, in 1978. None of his tutors or undergraduate contemporaries would have been in the least surprised at this recognition by the outside world of what they had always seen as Gerald's inescapable destiny. We all learnt much from him, not only about history.

2
Gerald Aylmer in Manchester and York
GORDON LEFF

I FIRST came to know Gerald when we were assistant lecturers and lecturers together, in Manchester, for nearly seven years—from the mid-1950s until Gerald went to York at the end of 1962 to become founder and first head of the new history department there. I subsequently spent a further thirteen years with him in York before he left in 1978 to be Master of St Peter's College, Oxford. Over those twenty years, not to mention the succeeding thirteen years at St Peter's, Gerald, for me, has remained entirely true to the person whom I knew in the beginning. From assistant lecturer, in Manchester, to professor, in York, and beyond, there have been the same overriding concern for justice, and the integrity to try to see that it is done, joined to a no less remarkable modesty and recognition and appreciation of others. If they combine to make Gerald incapable of mere self-interest or pretence, he is anything but a plaster saint. Conscience and public duty, which are so much his traits, can be awkward companions, even when exercised with his self-restraint. The awkwardness was less evident in York than in Manchester, where conscience tended to predominate in inverse proportion to the much more limited scope for public service. The difference in emphasis broadly corresponded to the difference between Gerald's time in Manchester and York.

The university in Manchester, in the 1950s and into the 1960s, was still a largely closed academic society, where professors ruled and non-professors had little or no voice outside their own departments and faculties, and very limited powers within them. Professorial control, which originated at Manchester and at other civic universities with the formation of the university, extended to most facets of academic life, including the courses to be taught. Although it did not invariably mean autocracy, professorial jurisdiction within a department was unaccountable and ultimately unchallengeable. There was no other machinery for internal government; the only departmental meetings were the three annual examiners' meetings, to allocate the setting of the examination papers, to scrutinize the papers when set, and to determine the examination results when taken, with no provision for any other kind of business or consideration of wider issues. Teaching was predominantly by lectures and, for honours students, weekly essay classes, usually of six, which militated against the individual contact found at Oxford and Cambridge, and accentuated the sense of lack of community within a department, experienced by most of those coming from the older universities, like Gerald. It was not mitigated by any wider sense of community within the university at large or the city.

The university, like most civic or redbrick universities, was essentially a daytime and weekday institution, on the edge of the city centre, and ringed by what then seemed slums. Its buildings were still mainly Victorian and inter-war. Some, like the administrative building and the neo-classical arts building, constructed immediately after the First World War, had a certain style; but their dreary setting, begrimed exteriors, and bare, dark, institutional interiors, almost entirely devoid of any furnishings, made them uninviting as well as impracticable for any kind of social interchange. Apart from the usually overcrowded staff house, the only place where we could converse during hours was in our shared teaching rooms in the recent extension to the arts building: in those days, as lecturers, we did not have telephones. Apart from meetings, or the need to work in the library, there was little to detain us after hours; many of us returned home after teaching was done, in time to miss the rush hour.

There was not much compensation to be found in the life of the city at that time. The period of post-war affluence and 'renewal' was a decade away; and Manchester still displayed many of the scars of nineteenth-century northern industrialism—although not itself an industrial city, as Sheffield then was—with seeming unending acres of blackened terrace houses and dreary streets, which extended into the traditional university residential enclaves of Withington and Didsbury, in south Manchester and beyond, and led to the growing exodus into the satellite towns of north Cheshire: Cheadle, Bramhall, and Wilmslow. There was, it is true, quite a vigorous cultural life; but it could not be an adequate substitute for the lack of any continuing university life after working hours, which was a feature of civic universities, separated by increasing distances from where most of their members, senior and junior, lived. Nor did a salary of £650 a year, at the top of the assistant-lecturer scale, leave much over for outside diversions, even in a period of negligible inflation. Straitened finances were a central fact of our lives; they went with the indigence around us, to be seen in the harsher physical surroundings, meagre shops (except in the city centre), and generally poorer quality of life and amenities than further south.

These circumstances had a dispiriting effect, at least initially, esecially upon those who came from the more favoured and liberal dispensations of Oxford and Cambridge, Gerald among them; but, in his case, more, I think, because of the university as an institution than the physical ambience, although the large gloomy flat in Fallowfield, about two miles south of the university, in which he and Ursula lived during term, after they were married, could not have raised the spirits. He reacted characteristically, not by withdrawing into his own work—though it is hardly necessary to say that he pursued it—but by concerning himself with some of the more glaring defects which he saw in the university, notably, the lack of individual teaching and attention to students, and the absence of any effective voice for non-professors in either departments or other sectors of the university and, crucially, of any representation on the main university bodies. There was also the continuing irritant for many assistant lecturers in their late twenties and into their thirties of having to wait three years before being eligible for promotion to lecturer, which compounded their late academic start because of military service.

Gerald was not alone in these concerns, either in the history department or in the wider university. Some of them he and others resolved by their own efforts, such as teaching in smaller numbers, not always approved by other colleagues, and by having more direct contact with students, including joint cider parties, to loosen their reserve, the shared expenses for which Gerald computed by dipping a graduated stick—reminiscent of a medieval sheriff's tally—into the cider barrel, to measure how much had gone, and then dividing the amount to be paid. Other concerns they sought to raise at examiners' or faculty meetings and in general discussion. Gerald went further and wrote on university government and representation in the *Universities Quarterly*, which in some quarters gained him the reputation of being a revolutionary. He was also a visible member of the Association of University Teachers, when it was not very prominent or fashionable; and he became chairman of the local assistant lecturers' group, where he helped to begin a survey of their average age, presented to the Vice-Chancellor by his successors.

All this, though, was uphill work and made little real impression on the university. It continued in much the same way until it was caught in the general movement for reform after Gerald had left. Neither he nor most of those who sought reform was remotely a political activist; and for Gerald these were only some among a considerable number of other activities: in the university, attending staff seminars and lectures, both in history and outside departments, notably Politics, where he had a close rapport with several of its members. The university, for all its institutional rigidity, was also an intellectually vital place in a number of fields, and had a high reputation. Academically, even if not constitutionally, the staff enjoyed very favourable conditions and good facilities, in some respects at the expense of the students, who at that time were under-attended to.

There was also life beyond the university, in personal and social contacts, which were probably more intense in the absence of a visible university life; certainly Manchester was where some lasting friendships were made. Gerald and Ursula have always had a wide circle of friends, then, as now, not confined to the history department or academics. Nor were Gerald's interests narrowly historical; they extended to most of the areas covered by the social sciences, including political and social theories and the theoretical aspects of history, an interest which found expression in the Discipline of History course at York. He also had a keen sense of constitutional niceties, developed, no doubt, by his own work, which, with his disposition to questioning one's meaning, could have made him an effective lawyer, a suggestion which he disclaimed on the grounds that he was not quick-witted enough. In his case, it was not adversarial, but represented a genuine interest in what other people had to say and in their work, whether an expert or contemporary or a first-week-old undergraduate. It was exemplified in his accessibility to both students and staff at York, and the endless trouble to which he would go to help them, not to mention Ursula's and his unfailing hospitality. That openness to other people's ideas and needs went with a genuine diffidence about himself, though he was never afraid to give his own opinion or to disagree. The one place where he was less receptive to different standpoints was Conservative politics. Gerald was at that time a committed but undogmatic supporter of the Labour Party; he had no time for Conservatism; and in those days he could react disconcertingly to support for Conservative views by falling silent for a considerable period. He took a strong interest in politics, including developments in Africa, some of whose nationalist leaders he knew; to those of us who formed our opinions from a superficial reading of the daily and weekly Press, he could appear and indeed was dauntingly well informed.

Politically, the 1950s came to life, if that is the right word, with the invasion of Suez and the suppression of the Hungarian uprising, both in the autumn of 1956. They led, among other things, to the emergence of the New Left, which Gerald followed closely, without becoming actively associated with it. But the catalyst was the formation of the Campaign for Nuclear Disarmament, in 1958, which rapidly became a national movement, drawing in thousands of previously unpolitical individuals. In Manchester its high point became the annual series of public meetings in May, which for the first few years filled the Free Trade Hall. Gerald and especially Ursula were closely involved in its organization, under direction of Donald Pennington, one of Gerald's closest friends in the university. Gerald's activities included addressing local meetings and distributing leaflets in the centre of Manchester. But by the time Gerald left Manchester the great days of CND were past.

Absorbing as these activities might be, they were only a part of the part of Gerald's life spent in Manchester in term; the rest was spent away from it engaged in his own work. But Gerald, I think, never found a satisfying academic life in Manchester. He was not alone in chafing at the prospect of remaining there indefinitely. The opportunity for change came for him, as for many others, with the founding of six new universities and the expansion of existing ones at the beginning of the 1960s.

Gerald was among the youngest professors of history (36) when he went to York. In moving to York he came into his own. His almost over-active conscience about Manchester's shortcomings was put to public service in York. The scope for it was almost limitless, in the creation not only of a new department, but also of a new university. As one of the founding members of the second, Gerald was hardly less involved with it than he was with the first. The sense of being engaged in a great enterprise was greatly enhanced by the conception of the university as an integrated community, with a collegiate structure and social life, which Manchester left out. With that went a minimalist institutional hierarchy of autonomous departments, which were their own boards of studies with no faculties above them: just a general academic board of elected members, drawn from all the academic staff. The only element of hierarchy was a professorial board, whose powers fell well short of the traditional university senates.

Although the character of departments varied with the character of their individual heads, their very considerable independence gave free rein to Gerald's reforming proclivities. They were undoubtedly reinforced by his experiences in Manchester; but they also expressed his own beliefs about history as a subject and how it should be taught. Throughout his fifteen years in the department he remained its head, responsible for its finances, appointments, and promotions, and giving it its vision. But at the end of the first three years, the chairmanship, concerned with the day-to-day running and teaching, which he had also initially held, became a rotating office, usually for two years. The other offices, such as for admissions and examinations, were similarly rotating and for set periods, invariably by individual agreement and not by imposition from above. That was equally true of all the informal arrangements for specific activities, like convening meetings of those involved in a course or potential participants in a new course, and also of the setting of the examination papers, which, in contrast to Manchester, was left to those concerned. Again, in contrast to Manchester, there were regular departmental meetings, as well as additional ones to consider special issues, which, in Manchester, would have been the prerogative of professors, such as the area of the course most in need of new appointments, or, more commonly, had not been raised at all, such as syllabus reform. Since every member of the department was eligible to take part in whatever was happening, and also free to propose new projects, with only the chairmanship, because of its responsibilities, confined to more senior members, there was usually no need for elections in what was in effect a full participatory democracy of some twenty members. From the outset, then, the department was run by its staff members; later, there was also student representation. The success of staff involvement can be gauged from the willingness to undertake the multifarious duties;

in nearly a quarter of a century I knew of no occasion when there was not a volunteer for something which had to be done, however onerous or unattractive. There was also the opportunity for regular meetings with colleagues, largely missing in Manchester, principally at lunch in one of the college common rooms, a feature of all departments, producing a very different life.

Gerald's main innovations in the degree course, compared with the traditional courses in history at the majority of English universities, were, first, a departure, to some extent already made in Cambridge, from the emphasis upon English constitutional and political history. Second, there was an attempt to get away from the conventional division between medieval and early modern history at around 1500, and to treat a span of about one hundred and fifty years each side of that date as a single period, not as accomplished fact, but in the form of an open question, of what kind of period it represented. On that, as on many other questions, the jury remains out. Third, there were new kinds of courses, like the discipline of history and comparative or thematic special subjects, in addition to the more traditional ones, including longer period courses, which, unlike a number of the new universities, were retained at York, without treating them as old-fashioned outline courses. Fourth, there was the inclusion of a wider range of different kinds of history, notably intellectual and religious history, in addition to the more staple political and economic history, and not restricted to Britain and Europe; that was in keeping with encouraging individual members of the department to teach their own interests and devise their own courses within the framework of the syllabus, as well as participating in other courses. Fifth, and as a consequence, there were joint courses, taught together by several members of staff, beginning, at that time, with the first two terms' introductory courses, and also extending to the combined degree courses with other departments, which were a feature of the new universities. Finally, instead of exclusive reliance upon the closed three-hour examination paper, and perhaps one longer piece of writing, other methods of examining were used, principally open papers which could be taken away and done privately over a longer period ranging from one day to three weeks. They were not all equally successful, and some courses were not suitable for open papers, but they have continued to coexist with conventional three-hour papers. Throughout Gerald's time in York pressure for some kind of continuous assessment was resisted—in my view, rightly. Few of these features were exclusive to York, and most of them have become common practice. But their combination in the construction of the course was the achievement of Gerald; they show a degree of imagination and boldness at the time which came from searching thought about the nature of history and how best to teach it, that was in part the fruit of his experience in Manchester. There were some lacunae and weaknesses in the course. There was perhaps not enough attention to the rigours of traditional constitutional history, and no place within the syllabus for political thought; nor was there anyone who taught the history of science. The university emphasis upon tutorials and seminars as integral methods of teaching, undoubtedly beneficial and rewarding as they were, tended to relegate the lectures to a subsidiary role, in the department of history at least, where, except in certain courses, they did not have the same more general function which they had in civic universities. But to those of us who lived under both regimes, there could scarcely be any doubt about which was to be preferred. For beyond York's greater conceptual and historical range, Gerald created a self-regulating society, capable of almost indefinite adaptation and development.

That capacity was in existence from the outset, in the open nature of the department, which in one aspect was a continuing forum of opinion, with the opinion of the most junior equally to be heard with the opinion of the most senior, who was Gerald. And it survived Gerald; or, more accurately, he established it by his own example. Although, so long as he remained, his authority was unquestioned, and he continued to be head of department, it was essentially a personal authority, derived from his own personal qualities. He had set the tone of full and free discussion, when he was chairman, departmental meetings often lasting so long that they had to be resumed later. The most celebrated occasion of open-ended discussion was a weekend meeting at the Spa Hotel, in Ripon, in December 1969, to discuss the future shape of the department, where the fact that nothing was decided was secondary to the participation of everybody in the process of making decisions. By that time Gerald was no longer chairman; and, apart from having organized the weekend, with characteristically a scale of charges according to academic rank, merely participated in the meeting as one more departmental member. As chairman, Gerald was endlessly patient, allowing every view, while not attempting to impose his own, and trying to avoid Mill's tyranny of the majority by closing a discussion only when, if possible, every disquiet had been met, and without having to take a vote. Once no longer chairman, he only intervened as the occasion arose, and far less frequently than the regulars, who were considerably his juniors. For much of a meeting Gerald would sit with his tall frame hunched low in his chair, his head bent towards the ground, all but motionless, and, except that we all knew him, the most inconspicuous person in the room. The contrast with most heads of department was patent; any stranger coming into the room in search of the head would have been pressed to have identified him with Gerald. When he did speak, everyone listened because of the person he was—someone who listened to everyone else and only spoke when he had something to say.

That special standing was not confined to the history department. The first Vice-Chancellor, Lord James of Rusholme, in a farewell speech to mark Gerald's departure for Oxford, said that the time when he really worried about having made a wrong decision was when Gerald disagreed with him. In both Manchester and York, Gerald was a presence who could not be ignored; and those of us who have known him and enjoyed his friendship have been the better, if not always the easier, for the experience.

3
Gerald Aylmer as a Scholar
AUSTIN WOOLRYCH

GERALD AYLMER is one of a select band of historians who made a considerable reputation in his field before he published so much as an article. Soon after he submitted his doctoral thesis in 1954, word began to spread that, despite its modest title—'Studies in the Institutions and Personnel of English Central Administration, 1625–1642'—and its thoroughly immodest length, one needed to read it; for there was much in it to make us think again, not only about early Stuart government but about the causes and the very nature of the English Revolution (as we nearly all called it then). In the sheer scale and depth of the research that it embodies and in the boldness of its reappraisals, it still seems a formidable achievement for a young historian to have completed in a year at Princeton and three years as a Junior Research Fellow of Balliol. Naturally enough, early readers tended to be most interested in its bearing on the arguments then raging over the role of rising or declining gentry in the genesis of the Civil Wars, especially since Gerald had enjoyed the supervision of both R. H. Tawney and Christopher Hill. Collective studies were just beginning to make their vital contribution to our knowledge of seventeenth-century England; Gerald completed his thesis very shortly after Douglas Brunton and Donald Pennington—stars (like Gerald himself after leaving Balliol) in the galaxy of young scholars in Manchester University's history school in the 1950s—published their *Members of the Long Parliament*, with an introduction by Tawney himself. Both works were naturally much concerned with the gentry controversy; both did much to shake the rasher hypotheses on either side, and both looked well beyond that now grass-grown battlefield.

At a time before we all grew wise to the dangers of hindsight, Gerald never let his awareness of the upheavals of the 1640s throw a distorting shadow across his investigation of Charles I's civil service. His central interest was in how government worked and (still more) in the sort of men who operated it. His field of vision stretched back to Tout's classic studies in medieval administration, took substance from Sir Geoffrey Elton's work in Tudor institutions (though without being persuaded of a 'Tudor revolution in government'), and stretched forward even then to the shaping of the modern Civil Service. What distinguished his own work from the start was an equally keen interest in the social history of his administrators collectively and in their characters, wherever recoverable, as individuals. He took his time in fashioning *The King's Servants* (1961) out of the copious material of his thesis, meanwhile staking his claim to his field in a series of articles. Two of these—on 'Attempts at Administrative Reform, 1625–1640' (1957) and 'Office Holding as a Factor in English History, 1625–42' (1959)—were in the nature of summaries or surveys (and the latter in particular has been a lasting boon to students); others— on 'The Last Years of Purveyance 1610–1660' (1957), 'Charles I's Commission on Fees, 1627–1640' (1958), and 'Officers of the Exchequer, 1625–42' (1961)—developed specialized offshoots from the main study.[1] *The King's Servants*, when it eventually appeared, was a book of fine proportions and exemplary clarity, so meticulously researched and carefully considered that when a second edition was called for a dozen years later it needed only minor amendment. Indeed there have been few works on seventeenth-century England so obviously built to last since the classic writings of Gardiner and Firth. Its methodology has proved as fruitful and original as its findings. It sets forth with countless examples the various combinations of patronage, patrimony, and purchase whereby places of profit were acquired under Charles I, and it shows how far the practice of selling not only offices but first, second, and even third reversions to offices came to compromise the royal administration and weaken the Crown's freedom of appointment. It not only expounds in detail the bewildering variety of means, official and unofficial, by which the king's servants were remunerated; it also makes a heroic effort to estimate the entire income that office-holders in the royal Household, the central administration, and the judiciary derived collectively from their places. By showing approximately to what extent the Court in the largest sense redistributed wealth among the landed classes, by relating this to their even more approximate collective income from land and other sources, and by establishing how small a proportion of

---

[1] For details of publications, see Chapter 16 below.

them were office-holders, *The King's Servants* dealt a damning blow to the thesis that Court service or the lack of it was the main factor in the rise or decline of gentry families. Still more strikingly, it demonstrated (by a sophisticated sampling technique) how very limited a correlation there was between the pre-war Court and Royalism from 1642 onward. Below the level of privy councillors and peers, only a minority of the King's servants sided actively with him in the Civil War, and a surprising number became Parliamentarians. But the book's eighty-nine tables and abundant statistics are only part of its achievement. It is given humanity by its constant recourse to illustrative biographical examples, which not only render apparent inconsistencies of behaviour intelligible but keep reminding us of the limits of generalization where human choice comes into play.

Gerald has always been a great taxonomist, and it is certainly more fruitful to consider his work by categories than chronologically. In *The State's Servants: The Civil Service of the English Republic, 1649–1660* (1973) he took on an even more formidable challenge than in his first book. In contrast with Charles I's peacetime years, there were frequent and drastic changes of regime, not only between 1649 and 1660 but between 1642 and 1649; moreover, many of the Commonwealth's administrators were more obscure in their origins than the king's servants had been, and hence more resistant to the biographer. Gerald clears the ground with a wonderfully clear and concise account of the whole institutional structure, executive, financial, legal, military, and naval, through all its metamorphoses from the outbreak of the first Civil War to the Restoration. He recognizes the improvisatory character of many of the administrative arrangements, and through his profound knowledge of the political circumstances in which they evolved he makes their intricacies intelligible. He finds a good deal more continuity than the textbook picture of a series of abrupt ruptures would suggest, and he challenges conventional wisdom on a number of points, questioning, for instance, the over-simple view of the Cromwellian Protectorate as a conservative reaction: 'It can also be thought of as the long-delayed and grossly overdue return to normality after the protracted but essentially temporary expedients of a wartime and then post-war regime' (p. 46). His treatment of the manner in which the Commonwealth's officials were appointed, and of their pay and tenure and terms of employment, benefits

enormously from the comparisons that he is able to draw with the
early Stuart regime, and also (as in *The King's Servants*) with the
bureaucracies of the major continental monarchies. Both books
handle the questions of corruption and self-enrichment judiciously,
with a realistic sense of the standards of the time but without
sliding into a facile moral neutralism.

More than a third of *The State's Servants* is devoted to the social
biography of the Commonwealth's officials. Their sheer number,
nearly 1,200 by Gerald's sensible criteria, impelled him to a further
refinement of his sampling technique. For purposes of analysis he
picked two hundred at random, without regard to their importance
in the system or the availability of biographical sources; then he
separately selected a hundred who did hold important positions
(though not at the very top) and about whose personalities and
careers something significant was known or discoverable. Heroic
labour on the lives and opinions of these 284 men (there is a small
overlap between the two samples) has yielded a wealth of statistical
data and tables, but what crowns the whole exercise is a sequence
of about fifty case histories, each a page or two in length.
Ostensibly they exemplify various types among the Rump's and the
Protectorate's officials, but Gerald's delight in rescuing interesting
individuals from obscurity and probing the springs of their action
keeps taking over, to the reader's great pleasure. How intriguing,
for instance, to meet Robert Spavin, secretary to Cromwell when
he was only 25, fluent in the language of the saints, and heading
for a bright future until he was caught forging his master's signature
and misusing his seal in order to sell letters of protection to ex-
Royalists—and that is only one of the riddles surrounding him. A
memorable 'collective biography' rounds off this long and splendid
section. Finally, in an attempt to offset the tendency (acknowledged
by Gerald) for administrative history to be written from the point
of view of the governors rather than the governed, a long chapter
attempts to assess the impact of the regimes of 1649–60 on the
population at large—a most difficult exercise in view of the
sketchiness of the sources, but carried through with his typical
blend of learning, judgement, and disciplined historical imagination.
For this reader, *The State's Servants* marks the summit of his
achievement to date, and it is good to know that he is extending
his study of English bureaucracy into the post-Restoration period.
Several shorter pieces have demonstrated over the years his

continuing interest in the wider context of his subject. In 1965 he addressed the Royal Historical Society on 'Place Bills and the Separation of Powers: Some Seventeenth-Century Origins of the "Non-Political" Civil Service' (1965). A concise but stimulating paper, given in Florence in 1978, surveyed 'Office-Holding, Wealth, and Social Structure in England' over the whole period from *c.* 1580 to *c.*1720. Still wider-ranging is his highly enjoyable Prothero Lecture on 'From Office-Holding to Civil Service: The Genesis of Modern Bureaucracy' (1980), which identifies six principal characteristics of 'the old administrative system', and deploys an impressive knowledge of eighteenth-century practices and of still longer-term changes in mentalities to account for their extraordinarily long persistence in England. He was, of course, the obvious man to contribute a general chapter on bureaucracy to the companion volume to the *Cambridge Modern History* (1979); surely no one else could have done it with such authority. The contribution that his specialist knowledge can make to social as well as political history is developed in an essay on 'Crisis and Regrouping in the Political Élites: England from the 1630s to the 1660s', contributed to a symposium which compared *Three British Revolutions: 1641, 1688, 1776* (1980). Of the two most recent articles that stem from his central interest in bureaucracy and administration, one on 'The Peculiarities of the English State' (1990) continues to explore its wider implications, while that on 'Buckingham as an Administrative Reformer' (1990)—not a role in which one would have instinctively cast the royal favourite—returns fruitfully to the area of his first researches.

Before turning to his other particular interest, it is time to acknowledge what a considerable part of his published output arises from his role as a teacher of undergraduates or supervisor of postgraduate research, and how valuable it has been to students and tutors alike. *The Struggle for the Constitution, 1603–89* (1963) was written out of his eight years' experience at Manchester, and had a long innings as quite the best narrative textbook of moderate length on seventeenth-century England. Its splendid opening sentence conveys something of Gerald's own qualities as a teacher: 'The first question to ask about any period is what matters most in it and why.' It shows great skill in avoiding over-simplification and in making complex events and concepts clear to readers with no previous knowledge of the period, while at the same time it

manages to keep them constantly aware of differences and difficulties in interpretation. It shows its age very little, and where it
occasionally does so it is through the inevitable advance of knowledge on specific points rather than because its judgements look
dated. The same clarity, concision, and judiciousness are found
twenty-three years later in *Rebellion or Revolution? England 1640–1660*
(1986), which is written as much for the general reader as for the
student, and is arguably the best brief introduction to the period
for either. 'I hope to live long enough to see this book superseded
in its turn,' says Gerald in the preface. He must be looking forward
to a very ripe old age.

On a smaller scale, his Historical Association pamphlet *The
Personal Rule of Charles I, 1629–40* (1989) is a shrewd and helpful
survey of a decade that is still the subject of much controversy.
Its interim judgements, though offered with characteristic modesty,
look likely to stand the test of time. A broader survey, forming
the first chapter of a collective volume on *the Age of Milton* and
sketching 'The Historical Background' from Elizabeth I's reign to
Charles II's (1980), is admirably calculated to meet the needs of
students of literature whose historical knowledge is limited. Indeed
Gerald's contributions to collective works have always been carefully thought out and well matched to their likely readership.

He has put students and fellow historians alike in his debt by
his work as editor as well as author. *The Interregnum: The Quest for
Settlement 1646–1660* (1972) is one of the best volumes in a distinguished series, its topics exceptionally well conceived and its
contributors all giving of their best, thanks not a little to his care
and advice. The book was instrumental in restoring the 1650s to
the attention that the decade deserved, after a lengthy spell of
relative over-concentration on the 1640s. Briefer, but at least as
great a boon to tutors and students, is *The Levellers in the English
Revolution* (1975), an excellent selection of excerpts from Leveller
texts, each with a model brief introduction. It is prefaced by an
essay of nearly fifty pages which is quite simply the best short
account of the Leveller movement to be found anywhere. While
avoiding the adulatory tone of some of the Levellers' latter-day
admirers, it is nevertheless profoundly sympathetic. Those who
have not penetrated beyond the benignly patrician front that Gerald
presents to the world—and I am not referring only to his elegant
and fastidious prose style—may be slightly surprised by the warmth

of his feeling for seventeenth-century radicals. It is a spontaneous response, uncoloured by any ideological commitment, and not uncritical. It shines clearly through the third of his presidential addresses to the Royal Historical Society (1988), which will be noticed shortly. He has also written memorably about 'The Religion of Gerrard Winstanley' (1984), and published a hitherto unknown pamphlet by Winstanley (1968) from an apparently unique copy that he discovered in the Clarke Collection in Worcester College library. A brief but cogent communication on 'Gentlemen Levellers?' (1970) helped to correct over-simple generalizations about the movement's social origins and leadership. Gerald has also investigated the radical offshoot of the Fronde in Bordeaux known as the Ormée and described its links with the Levellers in England (1979). His contribution to Christopher Hill's festschrift was a learned and thoughtful essay on 'Unbelief in Seventeenth-Century England' (1978), which demonstrates his sensitivity to attitudes that went so far against the grain of their time that few dared to express them. As so often in his work, he finds the key to unlock a difficult problem in an identification and definition of different types of unbeliever. He has also delivered what seems to the present writer the soundest judgement on a recent attempt to write the Ranters—another feared and hated group—out of history, and he has done it with the fine courtesy that he always shows to those with whom he feels compelled to disagree (1987).

He has always been generous with his time in placing his profound knowledge of seventeenth-century sources at the service of fellow scholars. A colleague on the editorial board has described him as a leading spirit in an ambitious project to reprint in facsimile the bulk of the Thomason Collection of pamphlets and newspapers in the British Museum. This enterprise got as far as publishing thirty-four volumes of fast-day sermons preached to the Long Parliament and nineteen of the newspaper *Mercurius politicus* before it succumbed to the microfilm revolution. Gerald went on to edit the microfilm edition, seventeen reels of it, of all Sir William Clarke's manuscript collection in Worcester College, Oxford. The booklet in which he introduces and comments on this wonderful archive is a model of its kind. In the same year as that appeared, he, in collaboration with John Morrill, published *The Civil War and Interregnum: Sources for Local Historians* (1979), which not only furnishes an excellent brief guide to the various manuscript repositories, both national and local, and to the printed sources and other aids, but describes the principal topics which currently interest serious local historians. He and Morrill have also collaborated in editing for publication the collected papers of J. P. Cooper, after the latter's untimely death (1983).

A more personal part of Gerald's output is linked to the spirit of place or to the institutions in which he has made his career. It was a publisher in his native Dorset who persuaded him, early in that career, to edit the diary which William Lawrence, a Gloucestershire worthy, kept intermittently between 1662 and 1681 (1961). He has delved deeply in his county of adoption to answer the question 'Who was ruling in Herefordshire from 1645 to 1661?' (1972), a piece which suggests what a powerful contribution he could have made to regional history if he had chosen to specialize in that field. More recently he responded to a request from the editor of a volume celebrating his old school's sixth centenary with a substantial thirty pages on 'Seventeenth-Century Wykehamists' (1982).

But it is appropriately York and Oxford, the places to which he has given most as a scholar, teacher, and administrator, that have inspired the most substantial of his studies with a local bearing. For most of a decade he was engaged, in partnership with Reginald Cant, in editing *A History of York Minster* (1977), whose handsome production is worthy of the distinguished team of contributors whom he and Canon Cant enlisted. His own chapter, one of the longest in the book, is on 'Funeral Monuments and Other Post-Medieval Sculpture', but the title hardly conveys the pleasures that it has in store for the reader. It is at least as much a portrait gallery in words of the more notable people commemorated as an account of their effigies, and a lot more interesting and revealing than most of the latter. But Gerald's aesthetic interest is strongly engaged too, and his judgement is as refreshingly frank on the figure sculpture of the early seventeenth-century ('extraordinarily awkward and often technically incompetent') as on the drearier products of the Gothic revival. Of one of the latter he writes: 'Goodness knows what Mason [the good clergyman commemorated] would have made of it all; at least in this life he had a sense of humour.' And commenting on Grinling Gibbons's fine but somewhat unusual portrayal of the time-serving Archbishop Lamplugh as not recumbent but 'fully on his feet, as if anticipating the General Resurrection', he remarks: 'One can but hope such confidence is not misplaced.' As always, he cannot resist being drawn into a good story and a character with a touch of mystery; one of his best on both scores concerns Richard Fisher, the first of a dynasty of carvers whose work really did grace the Minster in the later eighteenth century. And contemplating with unconcealed dismay some of the war memorials from the 1890s to the 1940s, he remarks: 'It should surely be possible to honour the nation's dead . . . and yet avoid confusing Christian saints and angels with the gods of war, officers' swords with the Cross of Jesus'—a comment the more cogent for his own experience of active service in war.

His Oxford piece is a long chapter in volume iii of the new *History of the University of Oxford* on 'The Economics and Finances of the Colleges and University c.1530–1640' (1986). He took the task over from J. P. Cooper after the latter's death, when there was still much spadework to be done, and he broadened its scope considerably. Despite his generous acknowledgements of the contributions of others, it cost him heavy labour, and the shapeliness and lucidity of the final product bear his stamp.

Gerald was a distinguished President of the Royal Historical Society from 1985 to 1989. His four presidential addresses on the theme of 'Collective Mentalities in Mid-Seventeenth-Century England' deserve an even wider readership than they have received through the Society's *Transactions* (1986–9). Subtitled 'The Puritan Outlook', 'Royalist Attitudes', 'Varieties of Radicalism', and 'Cross Currents: Neutrals, Trimmers and Others', they embody his most mature reflections on the problems of motivation and allegiance among the various participants and non-participants in the Civil Wars. As in so much of his work, careful categorization is the key to successful analysis. The first two papers distinguish with rare penetration the different types of faith and temperament to be found among both Anglicans and Puritans—terms whose careful use Gerald sensibly defends, despite the one being unknown to contemporaries and the other used only pejoratively by them. The exploration in the third paper of the wide differences covered by that equally slippery term 'radicalism', and in the fourth of the scarcely less differing types of neutrals and side-changers, sharpens one's understanding of the whole conflict. Gerald would put both students and tutors still further in his debt if he could be persuaded to republish these addresses as a short book, perhaps coupled with his essay (already referred to) on 'Crisis and Regrouping in the Political Élites' (1980), which also addresses questions of allegiance, though within a narrower social band and over a slightly longer period.

Gerald's *œuvre* has been so large and varied that it has been impossible in the space allowed to mention all of it—and it is, of course, still in progress. Besides extending his study of administration and administrators into the post-Restoration period, one hears that he means to turn his hand to naval history, prompted by a strong naval tradition in his family and by his own experience of the service as a young man. He is still at the height of his powers, and one can be confident that retirement—another term which historians understand differently from most other mortals—will free him to concentrate on the work that he really wants to do. Meanwhile I ask his pardon for having left it so late to acknowledge his long and much valued service on the Historical Manuscripts Commission and as chairman of the editorial board of the History of Parliament Trust, and for not having mentioned so far his more recent participation in the European Science Foundation's project on the modern state, which presumably prompted his essay on 'The Peculiarities of the English State' (1990). I have also failed to find a slot for his searching article on 'The Meaning and Definition of "Property" in Seventeenth-Century England' (1980). Limitation of space has precluded consideration of his many scholarly reviews, which are always marked by the same scrupulous thoroughness and fairness that characterize his own work. What are the other Aylmer hallmarks? I would say a profound but never desiccated erudition; a special flair for cracking historical problems by means of exact categorization and the establishing of vital distinctions; exceptional impartiality and balance of judgement, stemming not from Olympian detachment but from the independence of a mind impervious to fashion and (still more) from a breadth of sympathy that gives him the entry into the minds of all parties to a conflict or controversy; an affectionate delight in the varieties and vagaries of human character; an enviable grace, precision, and clarity of style; and (not least) an unfailing courtesy towards both the living and the dead. Firm though his principles are, I always feel that Gerald would rather think well than ill of both.

4

Cases of Conscience in Seventeenth-Century England

KEITH THOMAS

Of all Divinity that part is most useful, which determines Cases of Conscience; and of all cases of Conscience the Practical are most necessary; as action is of more concernment than speculation; and of all Practical Cases those which are of most common use are of so much greater necessity and benefit to be resolved.

Joseph Hall, *Resolutions and Decisions of Divers Practicall Cases of Conscience in Continuall Use amongst Men* (2nd edn., 1650), sig. A3

Beloved, you live in a world wherein conscience is like to cost you dear; if you will own any such thing as conscience, or conscientious walking, you are like to smart for it.

R[ichard] A[lleine], *Vindiciae pietatis* (1663), 34

THE seventeenth century can justly be called the Age of Conscience. Certainly there has been no period in English history when men and women were subjected to so many religious and political conflicts of duty and allegiance or responded to them in so intensely scrupulous a fashion. For much of the century it was generally believed that conscience, not force of habit or self-interest, was what held together the social and political order. Every change in that order accordingly precipitated a moral crisis for its members. Every new oath of allegiance posed a dilemma for those who had sworn loyalty to the previous regime. Every attempt by the State

The casuistry of the early modern period has attracted a good deal of attention in recent years. Historians have studied its use by persecuted religious groups. Literary scholars have shown its influence upon poetry, drama, and the novel. Intellectual historians have examined its links with political thought. Philosophers have urged its revival as a philosophical technique. 'New historicists' have seen an affinity between its 'destabilizing' effect and the deconstructionist theory of language. I have profited from (almost all) these writings while drawing on my own reading in this brief attempt to evoke the general historical interest of the subject. As an offering to one who is unsurpassed for the scrupulousness with which he confronts dilemmas of conscience, whether in the seventeenth century or the twentieth, it is necessarily inadequate.

to prescribe the forms of religious doctrine and worship tested the consciences of those who believed it was their duty to obey the laws of the land but were also persuaded of the truth of a rival creed.

Outside the public arena, changing social and economic circumstances made many inherited rules of morality increasingly difficult to observe. The application of the Ten Commandments to daily life had never been a straightforward business; it did not grow easier with the passage of time and the emergence of conditions very different from those of ancient Israel. Traditional maxims about buying and selling or lending or borrowing appeared archaic as the economy diversified and credit became universal. The duties of parents and children, husbands and wives, and masters and servants needed constant redefinition in an age when people were encouraged to think for themselves and religious unity had disappeared. The complexities of human relationships had always been such that even the simplest prohibition, whether on killing people or on telling lies, could prove anything but simple to interpret in practice. In every sphere of life moral obligations could conflict and circumstances alter cases.

The generally accepted view was that any person unlucky enough to be caught in a dilemma which made it difficult to know how to act should follow the dictates of his or her conscience. This did not mean that individuals could do what they wished, provided their intentions were upright. For conscience was not a subjective matter, but an act of deliberate judgement, which could be mistaken. Following the example of Aquinas, most divines taught that conscience was the application to a particular case of a person's knowledge of right or wrong.[1] That knowledge was made up of two ingredients: the natural law of reason, or law of nature, which was universal to all human beings, and knowledge of the word of God, which required appropriate religious education. Many Calvinists, convinced of the depravity of man, tended to be sceptical about the value of the universal law of nature; they placed their emphasis not on this 'natural conscience', but on the 'renewed conscience', divinely enlightened in those born again. For them God's word, rationally interpreted, was the principal source of

---

[1] T. Wood, *English Casuistical Divinity during the Seventeenth Century* (1952), 67–72.

guidance.[2] But most commentators thought that both the law of nature and the law of God had a role to play in shaping conscience. Conscience, therefore, was presumed to have an objective basis. Good intentions were not enough; indeed it was a sin to act in accordance with an erroneous conscience. Unfortunately, it was also a sin to act against it, since that would involve disregarding what the individual took to be the law of God: 'This is a constant rule: we always sin when we disobey conscience.'[3] It is not surprising that the conscientious individual, confronted by these stern doctrines, should have felt the need for guidance.

In the Roman Catholic Church the provision of such guidance had long been a specialized function of the clergy. In the later Middle Ages, priests hearing confessions had needed to assess a penitent's degree of sinfulness in order to impose an appropriate penance. That need had stimulated the production of numerous confessors' manuals which classified human actions in a variety of circumstances and assessed the degree of sin involved. After the Reformation the composition of large works of casuistry became a Europe-wide phenomenon; and these volumes were as much concerned with prescriptions for future action in difficult circumstances as with the assessment of actions already committed.[4] Casuistry was the science of applying general rules of conduct to particular cases, particularly in instances where the rules appeared to conflict or where their application caused doubt or perplexity. The casuist might proceed by formulating general rules—for example, by teaching that when two opposed courses of action seemed open it was better to follow the safer one, that is, the one less likely to involve the individual in a sin. But the casuist also multiplied examples of so-called 'cases of conscience', real or hypothetical, and explored their nuances and intricacies with a view to arriving at a firm resolution. In the process he laid bare the

[2] e.g. I. Bourne, *The Anatomie of Conscience* (1623), 9; E. Huit, *The Anatomy of Conscience* (1626), 229–39; R. Bernard, *Christian see to thy Conscience* (1631), 241–88. Cf. N. Fiering, *Moral Philosophy at Seventeenth-Century Harvard* (Chapel Hill, NC, 1981), 61–2; J. S. Wilks, *The Idea of Conscience in Renaissance Tragedy* (1990), 5–6.

[3] W. Fenner, *The Souls Looking-Glasse* (Cambridge, 1643 edn.), 53. On this 'double bind', see L. Gallagher, *Medusa's Gaze* (Stanford, Calif., 1991), 111–12.

[4] There is a lively general account in A. R. Jonsen and S. Toulmin, *The Abuse of Casuistry* (1988). Much information can be found in *Dictionnaire de théologie catholique*, ed. A. Vacant *et al.* (3rd edn., Paris, 1930–72), s.v. 'casuistique', 'laxisme', and 'probabilisme'. R. Briggs, *Communities of Belief* (Oxford, 1989), ch. 7, offers an illuminating discussion of French seventeenth-century practice.

circumstances in which it might be pardonable to evade the strict letter of the moral law.

In England, with the abolition of the confessional at the Reformation, this type of casuistry was at first associated exclusively with the Roman Catholics. The persecution of the Elizabethan recusants created many acute dilemmas for Catholics who were basically loyal to the regime, but had no desire to forgo their religion, or who disliked telling lies, yet had no wish to betray themselves or the missionary priests. At seminaries on the Continent, pupil-priests were instructed in the ways and means by which they could, with a good conscience, equivocate or dissimulate in order to escape arrest when they came to England. Roman casuists taught the laity how to comport themselves when required to attend Protestant services or to take loyalty oaths or to answer questions about the whereabouts of the seminary priests. They also gave advice on cases of conscience relating to marriage, property, usury, and other problems arising in daily life.[5]

A spectacular example of the use which the Catholic laity could make of such clerical advice was provided in 1605, when it was discovered that the Gunpowder Plotter Robert Catesby had sounded out the Jesuit Henry Garnet on the morality of killing innocent persons, including unbaptized children, in pursuit of a just cause. He had done this by putting the case, not of the intended Plot, but of a hypothetical attack upon a fort during the war in the Low Countries. Garnet had conceded that the destruction of the innocent would be permissible if it was an unintended consequence of the attack, 'done as *per accidens*, and not as a thing intended by or for itself'. This was enough for Catesby; he related Garnet's opinion to his fellow conspirators, who dispelled their scruples by applying it to their own situation.[6]

Yet the Protestant layman was no less likely to be subject to

[5] E. Rose, *Cases of Conscience: Alternatives Open to Recusants and Puritans under Elizabeth I and James I* (Cambridge, 1975); P. J. Holmes (ed.), *Elizabethan Casuistry* (Catholic Rec. Soc., 67; 1981); Holmes, *Resistance and Compromise: The Political Thought of the Elizabethan Catholics* (Cambridge, 1982), chs. 8–10; J. P. Sommerville, 'The "New Art of Lying": Equivocation, Mental Reservation and Casuistry', in E. Leites (ed.), *Conscience and Casuistry in Early Modern Europe* (Cambridge, 1988), 159–84; P. Zagorin, *Ways of Lying: Dissimulation, Persecution, and Conformity in Early Modern Europe* (London and Cambridge, Mass., 1990), chs. 7–9.

[6] J. Morris (ed.), *The Condition of Catholics under James I* (1871), 65–8; S. R. Gardiner, *History of England from the Accession of James I to the Outbreak of the Civil War 1603–1642* (10 vols.; 1883–4), i. 273–4.

intense moral dilemmas and he too might seek expert advice. When Charles I shrank in 1641 from agreeing to the attainder of the Earl of Strafford, he turned to the bishops. Juxon told him that he should not consent to the Bill if he were unsatisfied in his conscience, but Archbishop Williams maintained that there was a distinction between the king's public and private consciences: Charles's public duty was to assent, in order to save the peace of the kingdom, even though his private conscience was against it. This was the advice the King followed, though he subsequently bitterly lamented doing so, it being 'a bad exchange to wound a man's own conscience, thereby to salve State sores'.[7] It was, however, neither the first nor the last time when the King turned to clerical casuists for the resolution of his own problems. Archbishop Laud records mysteriously in his diary for 20 March 1631 that 'His Majesty put his great case of conscience to me, about, &c; which I after answered. God bless him in it.'[8] It was Laud who recommended Robert Sanderson to the King because of his casuistical learning. Charles put many cases of conscience to Sanderson and took him on as his permanent adviser; during his subsequent imprisonment in the Isle of Wight, he is even said to have translated Sanderson's Latin lectures on the obligation of oaths. The King seems to have gone from one crisis of conscience to another.[9] Pressed in 1646 to agree to abandon episcopacy, he fell back on the doctrine of mental reservation; in a letter to Juxon he asked whether he would condone 'some kind of compliance with the iniquity of the times . . . which at another time were unlawful', demanding specifically 'whether I may with a safe conscience give way to this proposed temporary compliance, with a resolution to recover and maintain that doctrine and discipline where I have been bred'. Juxon and his fellow bishop Brian Duppa agreed that he could.[10]

---

[7] Gardiner, *History of England*, ix. 365; *Eikon Basilike, or the King's Book*, ed. E. Almack (1904), 7–9; *The Works of Robert Sanderson*, ed. W. Jacobson (6 vols.; Oxford, 1854), vi. 304.
[8] *The Works . . . of William Laud*, ed. W. Scott and J. Bliss (7 vols.; Oxford, 1847–60), iii. 213.
[9] *Works of Sanderson*, vi. 296; i, pp. x–xii.
[10] *State Papers Collected by the Earl of Clarendon* (3 vols.; Oxford, 1767–86), ii. 265–8. The King subsequently put the same issue to Sanderson (*Works of Sanderson*, v. 139–41; vi. 304). An unsolicited answer had already been supplied by the Puritan John Geree in his *A Case of Conscience Resolved: Wherein it is Declared that the King may without Impeachment to his Oath . . . consent to the Abrogation of Episcopacy* (1646). To this, Edward Boughen replied with *Mr. Geree's Case of Conscience Sifted* (1648).

Cases of conscience were not peculiar to monarchs or plotters, but were liable to confront anyone. For that reason they figured largely in the theological literature of the period. A representative definition was that of William Ames: a case of conscience was 'a practical question concerning which the conscience may make a doubt'.[11] It was a 'case' because it fell or happened in the course of a person's life; and it was a 'case of conscience' because the nature of the decision taken would affect the actor's soul. Many worldly dilemmas were, therefore, not cases of conscience at all. Conversely, many cases of conscience related not to action in the world but to the individual's state before God. Much Protestant casuistry concerned problems of grace and assurance of salvation. In particular, Puritan casuists sought to drive away despair, and to indicate ways by which the soul could be saved. For William Perkins, the greatest case of conscience 'that ever was' was *How a man may know whether he be the child of God or no?*[12] The casuist was thought of as a physician or healer, who brought 'peace and a quiet mind', relieved troubled consciences, and allayed needless doubts.[13] His primary objective was less the resolution of some immediate difficulty than the long-term health of the patient's soul; and for this the individual's relationship to God was more important than any practical problem in the world. 'Duties towards God are the great object of conscience, but duties towards man are the secondary.'[14] Of Richard Greenham it was related that 'unto one that asked his advice in outward things, who as yet stood in greater need to be instructed in inward, he said, "If you first will confer with me and establish yourself in things concerning faith and repentance, then ask me and I will advise you freely for the outward state." '[15] The good casuist was like a doctor who refuses to treat some particular malady until the patient has first agreed to reform his whole way of life.

Yet the casuist's main task was to give advice, 'sound direction'

[11] W. Ames, *Conscience with the Power and Cases thereof* (n.p., 1639), ii. 1. Cf. E. Dublanchy, 'Cas de conscience', *Dictionnaire de théologie catholique*, ii (2), cols. 1815–20.

[12] *The Workes of . . . William Perkins*, (Cambridge, 1608). i, sig. 004.

[13] *The Whole Works of . . . Jeremy Taylor*, ed. R. Heber and C. P. Eden (10 vols.; 1847–54), ix, p. xvi; M. Sampson, 'Laxity and Liberty in Seventeenth-Century English Political Thought', in Leites (ed.), *Conscience and Casuistry*, 99.

[14] *The Morning-Exercise at Cripplegate: Or, Several Cases of Conscience Practically Resolved* (4th edn., 1677), 4.

[15] Rose, *Cases of Conscience*, 203.

as to what was to be done, whether towards God or man.[16] The scope of such advice was immense, for there was 'not any one article of faith or duty prescribed as a part of piety or righteousness about which questions may not be moved and cases propounded wherein the conscience may seek satisfaction'.[17] To be effective, the casuist was expected to be learned in Latin, Greek, and Hebrew, educated in the arts and sciences, knowledgeable in law, skilled in reasoning, and well versed in the literature of his subject. For the application of God's laws to the world was a complex matter. As Francis Bacon put it,

It is an easy and compendious thing to call for the observation of the Sabbath-day, or to speak against unlawful gain; but what actions and works may be done upon the Sabbath, and in what cases; and what courses of gain are lawful, and what not; to set this down, and to clear the whole matter with good distinctions and decisions, is a matter of great knowledge and labour, and asketh much meditation and conversation in the Scriptures, and other helps which God hath provided and preserved for instruction.[18]

Age and experience were also important. No young man was fit to write cases of conscience, thought Charles I; at the age of 77, Bishop Barlow modestly claimed that 'I am, or ought to be, in some measure a competent judge of such cases.'[19]

Of course, in a Protestant country the casuist's role could be only advisory. His conclusions were based not on his own authority or that of the popes and the Roman councils, but on Scripture and reason. The client was expected to know the principles on which the judgement rested: 'It is a pastor's duty, not to captivate to his own authority the mind and conscience of his flock, not magisterially to determine, but with humility and modesty to declare what he judges most agreeable to the will of God; above all, he ought to see that his judgment be as well-grounded as possible.'[20] Nevertheless, it was a widespread assumption that the solving of

---

[16] T. Pickering, 'Epistle Dedicatorie', to W. Perkins, *The Whole Treatise of the Cases of Conscience*, in *Workes of Perkins*, ii (Cambridge, 1617).

[17] D. Dickson, *Therapeutica sacra* (Edinburgh, 1664), 10.

[18] *The Letters and the Life of Francis Bacon*, ed. J. Spedding (7 vols.; 1861–74), i. 92. Cf. *Works of Sanderson*, vi. 358; *The Genuine Remains of . . . Dr. Thomas Barlow* (1693), 2; J. La Placete, *The Christian Casuist*, trans. B. Kennett (1705), 372–3.

[19] *Works of Sanderson*, vi. 304; T. Barlow, *Several Miscellaneous and Weighty Cases of Conscience* (1692), ii. 14.

[20] La Placete, *The Christian Casuist*, 254.

cases of conscience was a matter of expertise, not impossible for an uneducated layman, but very difficult. 'Ignorant persons', thought the Elizabethan Thomas Cartwright, should 'hunt and seek out some discreet and learned minister of God's word . . . and require at his mouth the knowledge of the Law of the Lord.'[21] Others agreed that few men were wise or good enough to be their own casuists. 'If their case be . . . involved', ruled Jeremy Taylor, they needed 'a spiritual guide to untie the intrigue and state the question, and apply the respective rules to the several parts of it'. The perplexed should defer to the 'authority of learned men' and the 'example and judgement of the sagest and soberest persons'. 'Learned counsel' was as necessary for advice on moral dilemmas as for legal ones.[22]

The generally accepted ideal in post-Reformation England, accordingly, was of 'able ministers over the land, applying themselves in every case of conscience, as godly casuists unto all the distressed in mind'.[23] The Prayer Book encouraged communicants to repair to the curate for 'ghostly counsel, advice and comfort'; and the Anglican Church preserved the possibility of voluntary private confession to a minister.[24] Many of the Puritan clergy in Elizabethan times gave extensive advice to their flock in personal consultations and 'comfortable letters'.[25] Throughout the seventeenth century, the Church's leaders maintained that the handling of cases of conscience was one of the clergy's most essential functions. 'If we would do our duty as we ought,' ruled Bishop Stillingfleet, 'we must inquire into, and be able to resolve cases of conscience.' Bishop Sprat agreed: it was 'a most excellent qualification' to be 'a sound and well-experienced casuist', and highly desirable 'to have some good, sound body of casuistical divinity . . . always at hand'.[26] Even the Erastian John Selden accepted that the study of casuistry was one of the things a minister should 'be at'.[27]

[21] *Cartwrightiana*, ed. A. Peel and L. H. Carlson (1951), 92–4.
[22] R. B. Schlatter, *The Social Ideas of Religious Leaders, 1660–1688* (1940), 207; *Whole Works of Jeremy Taylor*, ix, p. xx (and ix. 102); *Works of Sanderson*, iii. 125; *Workes of Perkins*, ii. 139.
[23] W. Loe, *Vox clamantis* (1621), 30.
[24] K. Thomas, *Religion and the Decline of Magic* (Harmondsworth, 1978 edn.), 186–8.
[25] P. Collinson, *The Elizabethan Puritan Movement* (1967), 435–7; B. Brook, *The Lives of the Puritans* (3 vols.; 1813), ii. 193.
[26] Edward [Stillingfleet], *Ecclesiastical Cases Relating to the Duties and Rights of the Parochial Clergy* (1698), 58; Wood, *English Casuistical Divinity*, 31–3.
[27] J. Selden, *Table Talk*, ed. Sir F. Pollock (1927), 80.

But where was this casuistry to be found? In 1589 Francis Bacon had lamented that the teachings of the Puritans were cast in too general terms:

The word (the *bread of life*) they toss up and down, they break it not. They draw not their directions down *ad casus conscientiae*; that a man may be warranted in his particular actions whether they be lawful or not. Neither indeed are many of them able to do it, what through want of grounded knowledge, what through want of study and time.[28]

Throughout the following century it was a recurring complaint that English casuistic effort had gone into sermons, private conferences, and advice to pious persons, but not into print; there was little published casuistical divinity and what there was seemed intellectually inadequate. Relatively few authors completed a systematic treatment of the whole subject comparable to the work of their Jesuit or Lutheran contemporaries. On the Puritanical wing there were the great works of William Perkins, William Ames, and Richard Baxter. On the Anglican side there were the writings of Robert Sanderson and Jeremy Taylor.[29] Some other, equally ambitious, projects came to grief. Richard Greenham did not live long enough to produce the casuistical compendium which others had hoped for. Ralph Cudworth, father of the Platonist, informed James Ussher in 1617 that he had 'begun a long work, The Cases of Conscience, in the three societies, of family, church and commonwealth', beginning with the first, 'where the perplexed questions concerning marriage, contracts, divorce, &c, are to be discussed'. He later told Joseph Hall that he had completed it, but it never saw the light of day.[30] Samuel Clarke began a similar treatise, handling all cases of conscience alphabetically, but the published version never got beyond the letter 'C'.[31] In the 1630s John Dury, Samuel Hartlib, and a group of London ministers had asked Archbishop Ussher to supervise a scheme to produce 'a Complete Body of Practical Divinity', to be translated for the

---

[28] *Letters and Life of Bacon*, i. 92; also *The Works of Francis Bacon*, ed. J. Spedding, R. L. Ellis, and D. D. Heath (14 vols.; 1857–9), iii. 489.

[29] Wood, *English Casuistical Divinity*, 143–4, lists the main works. An earlier casuistical publication from a Reformed viewpoint was P. Martyr, *Common Places*, Eng. trans. A. Marten (1583).

[30] S. Clarke, *The Lives of Two and Twenty English Divines* (1660), 16–17; *The Whole Works of the Most Rev. James Ussher*, ed. C. R. Elrington and J. M Todd (17 vols.; Dublin, 1847–64), xvi. 347; J. Hall, *Resolutions and Decisions* (2nd edn., 1650), sig. T10ᵛ.

[31] S. Clarke, *Medulla theologiae* (1659).

benefit of German Protestants. Dury urged in 1642 that the project be advanced by establishing professors in the subject at the universities and in London; and the scheme was again resurrected during the Protectorate, but without success. Baxter's *Christian Directory* (1673) was a belated answer to this call.[32] In 1649 Bishop Hall published a selection of highly practical cases which was commended by the licenser as 'profitable, necessary and daily useful' and went into five editions in ten years. Hall later confessed that he had been pressed to make up 'a complete body of case-divinity', so as to fill that 'great defect in our language', but he was approaching 80 and felt unequal to the task.[33]

At the end of the century, another bishop, Thomas Barlow, who had himself resolved numerous cases, concluded that 'for Protestants, there is no part of divinity which has been (I know not why) more neglected; very few have writ a just and comprehensive tract of Cases of Conscience'. By contrast, European Catholics since the Council of Trent had put out over six hundred volumes of casuistry, containing tens of thousands of cases.[34] It is not surprising that some English divines consulted the Roman handbooks *faute de mieux*, being forced, in a much-quoted analogy, to sharpen their ploughshares in the forges of the Philistines.

Yet the relative shortage of full-scale works of casuistical divinity should not be allowed to conceal the ubiquity of casuistical thinking in seventeenth-century England. Only a few brave spirits attempted to give rules for resolving all the cases of conscience which might conceivably arise in the course of a person's life, but there were innumerable published works of guidance on specific dilemmas. It was usual to present some current controversy as a 'case of conscience' crying out for resolution. Discussions of individual cases or batches of them were regularly put out by divines, on every subject from witchcraft to swearing.[35] In addition, there were

[32] G. Westin, *Negotiations about Church Unity, 1628–34* (Uppsala, 1932), 18, 158–9 n., 240–1; N. Bernard, *The Life and Death of . . . James Usher* (1656), 83; J. Minton Batten, *John Dury, Advocate of Christian Reunion* (Chicago, 1944), 52–3, 92, 131; *Reliquiae Baxterianae*, ed. M. Sylvester (1696), i. 122; *The Practical Works of Richard Baxter* (1707), i, p. xx; ii. 481. Dury's conception of 'practical divinity' is set out in his *An Earnest Plea for Gospel-Communion* (1654).

[33] Hall, *Resolutions and Decisions*, sigs. T9–10.

[34] *Remains of Thomas Barlow*, 46; H. Hurter, *Nomenclator literarius theologiae Catholicae* (5 vols.; 3rd edn., Innsbruck, 1903), iii and iv *passim*.

[35] An idea of their frequency can be gained from a perusal of the short-title catalogues of Pollard and Redgrave and of Wing, as well as the British Museum catalogue of the Thomason Tracts. Other collections survive in manuscript.

expositions of the Catechism, commentaries on the Decalogue, discourses on 'relative duties', biblical commentaries, sermons and casuistical 'exercises', letters of advice and exemplary biographies, all offering reflections on moral duties and guidance on the resolution of specific moral dilemmas. As Bishop Fleetwood observed of his *Relative Duties* (1715), 'to make these discourses more useful, there is something casuistical in most of them'. Protestant casuistry was not confined to works written specifically about the conscience; it could be found almost anywhere, in drama and poetry as well as in religious writing.[36]

In the universities casuistical themes were regularly handled in formal disputations. Could one emigrate to avoid persecution? Was equivocation ever allowable? Could children marry without the consent of their parents? Was it permissible to fight a duel? These and similar issues were all debated at Oxford at the beginning of the seventeenth century.[37] It was a form of education which did much to disseminate the habit of casuistical thinking.

Many of the clergy seem to have put this education into vigorous practice, settling cases of conscience for their parishioners and providing advice, both oral and written, to all comers. There were celebrated Puritan 'oracles', like Richard Greenham at Dry Drayton or William Whately at Banbury or James Horrocks of Dean in Lancashire.[38] Many kept regular surgeries, meeting weekly to confer about 'wholesome cases of conscience'. Robert Bolton and James Ussher were sent enquiries from abroad.[39] During the Commonwealth, John Norman, the Presbyterian minister of Bridgwater,

---

[36] W. Fleetwood, *The Relative Duties of Parents and Children, Husbands and Wives, Masters and Servants* (1705), sig. A3. Cf. R. L. Greaves, *Society and Religion in Elizabethan England* (Minneapolis, Minn., 1981); C. H. and K. George, *The Protestant Mind of the English Reformation* (Princeton, NJ, 1961); Schlatter, *Social Ideas of Religious Leaders*; W. E. Houghton, jun., *The Formation of Thomas Fuller's Holy and Profane States* (Cambridge, Mass., 1938), ch. iv; G. A. Starr, *Defoe and Casuistry* (Princeton, NJ, 1971); C W. Slights, *The Casuistical Tradition in Shakespeare, Donne, Herbert, and Milton* (Princeton, NJ, 1981); Gallagher, *Medusa's Gaze*.

[37] *Register of the University of Oxford, ii. 1571–1622*, ed. A. Clark (Oxford Hist. Soc.; 1887–8), pt. 1, 194–217.

[38] Rose, *Cases of Conscience*, 201–5; S. Clarke, *The Marrow of Ecclesiastical History* (2nd edn., 1654), 931; *The Rev. Oliver Heywood . . . his Autobiography, Diaries, Anecdote and Event Books*, ed. J. Horsfall Turner (4 vols.; Brighouse and Bingley, 1882–5), i. 43. For others, see Brook, *Lives of the Puritans*, iii. 167; S Clarke, *The Lives of Sundry Eminent Persons* (1683), 144, 189; *The Life and Times of Anthony Wood*, ed. A. Clark (5 vols.; 1891–1900), i. 460; K. L. Sprunger, *The Learned Doctor William Ames* (1972), 155–66.

[39] S. Torshell, *The Hypocrite Discovered and Cured* (1644), 50; *Reliquiae Baxterianae*, i. 83; Clarke, *Marrow of Ecclesiastical History*, 926; Bernard, *Life of James Usher*, 83.

displayed 'a scholastical dexterity, able to tie and untie Gordian knots, and no mean casuistical faculty'; while in Oxford a regular session for the satisfaction of doubtful consciences held in 1646 by a group of Presbyterian divines was known irreverently as 'the scruple-house'.[40] Yet it was not only Puritans who applied themselves to practical cases of conscience. Lancelot Andrewes was 'a man deeply seen in all cases of conscience and in that respect ... much sought unto by many, who ever received great satisfaction from him in clearing those doubts which did much perplex them'. John Donne kept written copies of the cases of conscience that had concerned his friends, 'with his observations and solutions of them'. Archbishop Williams was often asked to resolve cases of conscience; and 'when he thought the doubting person would not be contented with discourse, he gave them his resolutions, very long and laborious, in writing, which, gathered together . . . would have made an handsome tractate'.[41] Sanderson resolved the perplexities of many private individuals during the 1650s, while Barlow, Burnet, and other later seventeenth-century bishops gave extensive written advice to prominent laymen, including Robert Boyle, whose repeated consultations have recently been admirably documented.[42]

It is likely that the overwhelming proportion of these consultations were with individuals like Boyle whose religious scruples were highly developed; and it is impossible to determine how extensive was the recourse to clerical casuists by the population at large. Published works of casuistry were probably read more by the clergy than by the laity; and when laymen were addressed it was usually assumed that they were employers rather than servants: the readers of Baxter's *Christian Directory* were intended to include 'the more judicious masters of families'.[43] The clergy were not the

[40] J. Norman, *Cases of Conscience Practically Resolved* (1673), sig. A3ᵛ; *A True Relation of the Late Conference held at Oxford* (n.p., 1646).

[41] L. Andrewes, *Two Answers to Cardinal Perron and other Miscellaneous Works* (Library of Anglo-Catholic Theology, Oxford, 1854), vii; A. E. Malloch, 'John Donne and the Casuists', *Studies in English Literature, 1500–1900*, 2 (1962); John Hacket, *Scrinia reserata* (1693), ii. 61–2.

[42] *Works of Sanderson*, vi. 320; Barlow, *Several Cases of Conscience, passim*; T. E. S. Clarke and H. C. Foxcroft, *A Life of Gilbert Burnet* (Cambridge, 1907), 173–6; M. Hunter, 'Casuistry in Action: Robert Boyle's Confessional Interviews with Gilbert Burnet and Edward Stillingfleet, 1691', *Journal of Ecclesiastical History*, 43 (1992); Hunter, 'The Conscience of Robert Boyle' (unpublished paper). I am grateful to Dr Hunter for letting me read his two excellent articles in typescript.

[43] *Practical Works of Baxter*, i, p. xx; *Reliquiae Baxterianae*, i. 122.

only advice agency; for every person who, like Ben Jonson's Morose, may have 'run out o'door in's nightcaps, to talk with a casuist about his divorce', there was another who consulted a friend or an astrologer.[44] Richard Baxter admits that his own wife, Margaret, was 'better at resolving a case of conscience than most divines that ever I knew in all my life . . . she would lay all the circumstances presently together, compare them, and give me a more exact resolution than I could do'.[45] Other women could be equally independent of clerical expertise. The obstetrician Percival Willughby recalled how some divines were consulted during a particularly difficult labour when it became necessary to decide whether to save the mother or the child. 'Several women frowned upon some of these divines, and, upon the women's dislikes, they turned their coats, and changed their opinions.'[46]

For many people the very idea of a case of conscience was ill developed. John Downame thought that dilemmas seldom occurred to 'ignorant and simple people, whose consciences, through defect in knowledge and want of understanding . . . do seldom check them for anything they do, unless it be so grossly wicked that even the light of nature doth discover and condemn it'.[47] There were numerous profane persons with 'a dead and cauterized conscience', whose normal retort was that 'conscience is hanged a great while ago'.[48] There were those who made easy excuses, like tradesmen, who, according to Perkins, used 'many practices of fraud and injustice, and that upon a persuasion that they have a charge and family which must be maintained'.[49] There were libertines, who made it 'their chief happiness and perfection to have the sense of sin extinguished', and there were religious hypocrites, who, according to Samuel Torshell, invoked conscience as 'a cover' for baser motives, for example, by finding good reasons why they should not give money to beggars.[50] The political history of the seventeenth century suggests that a large proportion of the

[44] B. Jonson, *Epicoene, or the Silent Woman*, Act IV, sc. v. Cf. Thomas, *Religion and the Decline of Magic*, ch. 10, sect. 4.
[45] J. T. Wilkinson, *Richard Baxter and Margaret Charlton* (1928), 127.
[46] P. Willughby, *Observations in Midwifery*, ed. H. Blenkinsop (1863; East Ardsley, 1972), 125.
[47] J. Downame, *The Christian Warfare* (4th edn., 1634), 1109.
[48] Bourne, *Anatomie of Conscience*, 17; Fenner, *Souls Looking-Glasse*, 25.
[49] *Workes of Perkins*, ii. 315.
[50] Ames, *Conscience*, i. 41; Torshell, *Hypocrite Discovered*, 20.

population was, by repeated compliance and accommodation, able to circumvent with apparent ease what other, more scrupulous, persons saw as intolerable dilemmas of conscience.

Nevertheless, the huge mass of surviving cases of conscience and their written resolutions gives some idea of the extent of this kind of thinking in seventeenth-century England. They also indicate the areas of life in which moral perplexity was most likely to arise; and this is what makes them of such interest to the social historian. Of course, they are not a wholly reliable guide to contemporary preoccupations, since works of casuistry were shaped by literary models as ancient as Cicero's *Offices* and the Roman law. Jeremy Taylor kept his distance from topical issues, and his baroque construction, *Ductor dubitantium*, was more a product of the study than of experience. Perkins and Ames conspicuously failed to address some of the most immediate practical issues confronting the godly ministers of their day.[11] Yet, on the whole, the casuists learnt through experience to identify 'those questions ... in which the conscience useth most to doubt'.[12]

If we set aside the (very numerous) problems relating to faith, assurance, and other spiritual matters, and concentrate upon those which concerned life within the world, it is not difficult to identify the contexts in which cases of conscience most frequently arose.

The first concerned political and religious allegiance. Here the essential issue was whether human laws were binding on the conscience. That, said Jeremy Taylor, was 'the greatest case of conscience in this whole matter': was it a matter of conscience as well as of prudence to conform to the law of the land?[13] In his view, and that of many of his fellow casuists, it unquestionably was. The commands of a lawful authority in indifferent matters were to be obeyed. Only if those commands were directly against the law of God could they be ignored; and even then active resistance was unlawful.[14] But what was a lawful authority and what were matters indifferent? And did not the very law of nature concede an ultimate right of self-defence? It was by asking such questions that one could deny the duty of Puritans or Dissenters

---

[11] Rose, *Cases of Conscience*, 200.
[12] Ames, *Conscience*, sig. A4.
[13] *Whole Works of Jeremy Taylor*, x. 4.
[14] Taylor ruled that 'no man who can think it lawful to fight against the supreme power of his nation can be fit to read cases of conscience' (ibid. x. 186).

to conform to the worship of the Anglican Church, justify Parliamentary resistance to Charles I, and require citizens to pledge
their support to the Commonwealth government. As has been
justly written of the controversialists of the 1640s,

> the Civil War presented itself to them as the most colossal case of
> conscience with which they had ever to contend, and their assumption
> was that the solution could be found if men kept their tempers and
> honed their arguments to ever finer distinctions.... casuistry provided
> the main support for the remonstrances, declarations, ordinances, and
> answers in which the parties' practical measures were put forward.[55]

The titles of the political pamphlets which proliferated in the 1640s
and 1650s transparently reveal their casuistical origin: *Conscience
Puzzel'd; Conscience Caution'd; Conscience Satisfied; A Case of Conscience
Concerning Flying in Times of Trouble; A Resolution of a Seasonable Case
of Conscience; Certain Considerable and Most Materiall Cases of Conscience;
Seven Cases of Conscience; Nineteen Cases of Conscience; The Grand Case
of Conscience Stated.*[56] The list could be greatly extended, for there were
innumerable 'Cases' and 'Resolutions', 'Queries' and 'Questions',
'Problems Propounded' and 'Scruples' or 'Doubts'. No wonder
that at the very beginning of the war an anonymous Welsh
Royalist called for a national synod to decide the pressing cases of
consciences which, in his view, threatened people's souls even
more than violence threatened their bodies.[57]

Casuistical debate was intensified by the ever-increasing recourse
to loyalty oaths. The successive imposition of the Protestation
(1641), the Solemn League and Covenant (1643), and the Engagement to the Commonwealth (1650) created acute dilemmas about
the compatibility of each with its predecessor and of all with the
Oaths of Allegiance and Supremacy to the Crown. In the process
all the old 'Jesuitical' doctrines about equivocation, mental reservation, and dissimulation, supposedly unique to papists, were
resurrected and strenuously employed against those who took a
more rigorist view of such obligations; and much was made of the
linguistic indeterminacy of all verbal agreements. The efforts of

[55] J. M. Wallace, *Destiny his Choice* (Cambridge, 1968), 10.
[56] The sixth item was published at Oxford in 1645. The others can be found in BL
Thomason Tracts (E. 585 (7); E. 341 (7); E. 97 (7); E. 250 (3); E. 1812 (2); E. 989 (21); E.
986 (16); E. 530 (45)).
[57] *Pro-Quiritatio Παραινετικη or, a Petition to the People* (1642), sig. A2 (anonymous, but its
references to the 'Welsh nation' and, possibly, its verbosity suggest its author's provenance).

some Puritan clergy to reconcile their consciences with the King's command to read the Book of Sports had generated a good deal of accommodating casuistry in the pre-Civil War period, but it was as nothing to what now occurred. Casuistry became a supple means of enabling contemporaries to adjust to new political realities without incurring an undue burden of guilt. A Royalist in 1650 denounced 'new state chaplains', like the indefatigable John Dury, who had become 'tutors . . . in . . . the black art of breaking all sacred bonds and obligations whatsoever, and that under the notion of satisfying the consciences and resolving the scruples of such who cannot swallow down this camel of perjury as easily as themselves'.[58] Dury indeed saw most of the Interregnum's problems as casuistical, and busily compiled resolutions to cases of conscience on every subject from the Engagement and the political role of clerics to Protestant reunion and the readmission of the Jews.[59]

The Restoration gradually reduced the spate of casuistical pamphleteering, but in the 1680s the process started all over again. The Anglican Church unsuccessfully attempted to win over the Dissenters by staging a series of lectures, subsequently published as a collection of cases of conscience, designed to show that conformity in matters indifferent was a binding duty.[60] The 1688 Revolution brought up once again all the old questions about allegiance, resistance, and the sacred inviolability of oaths; and in the ensuing torrent of publication they received the same casuistical treatment.[61]

Recent scholarship has made it abundantly clear that it was casuistry which provided the context for some of the most crucial developments in seventeenth-century political thought. Grotius,

---

[58] *A Pack of Old Puritans* (1650), sig. A3; Bodl. MS Tanner 71, fos. 186–7 (for ingenious reasoning on the Book of Sports). Cf. W Prynne, *Concordia discors* (1659); C. Hill, *Society and Puritanism in Pre-Revolutionary England* (1964), 395, 410; Wallace, *Destiny his Choice*, 49–53; Sampson, 'Laxity and Liberty', 111–12; A. Snider, 'By Equivocation Swear, *Hudibras* and the Politics of Interpretation', *The Seventeenth Century*, 5 (1990); Zagorin, *Ways of Lying*, ch. 10.

[59] Batten, *John Dury*, 119–24, 142–3, 147. Cromwell's conference of 1655 on Jewish readmission was intended to arrive at 'some clearing [of] the case, as to conscience'; unfortunately, the ministers present disagreed, leaving the Protector doubtful; [H. Jessey], *A Narrative of the Late Proceedings at Whitehall Concerning the Jews* (1656), 9. Cf. Barlow, *Several Cases of Conscience*, pt. v.

[60] *A Collection of Cases and Other Discourses Lately Written to Recover Dissenters to the Communion of the Church of England by some Divines of the City of London* (1685).

[61] M. Goldie, 'The Revolution of 1689 and the Structure of Political Argument: An Essay and an Annotated Bibliography of Pamphlets in the Allegiance Controversy', *Bulletin of Research in the Humanities*, 83 (1980).

Ascham, Filmer, and Locke can all be better understood when
fitted into the casuistical tradition.[62] So, even, can Thomas Hobbes.
The immediate object of *Leviathan* was to resolve the acute dilemma
which confronted ex-Royalists in 1651: 'I find by divers English
books lately printed that the Civil Wars have not yet sufficiently
taught men in what point of time it is that a subject becomes
obliged to the conqueror.'[63] But Hobbes's casuistical preoccupations
went further than that. When he tells us that the laws of nature
'oblige *in foro interno* . . . but *in foro externo* . . . not always', he is
invoking the age-old distinction between matters appropriate for
the confessional and matters which concern the Church courts.
When he claims that his science of the laws of nature is 'the true
and only moral philosophy', he signals his intention to supersede
those 'innumerable and huge volumes of ethics' with which lax
casuists had confirmed 'wicked men in their purposes'.[64] *Leviathan*
abounds in solutions to traditional casuistical dilemmas: do covenants made under force oblige? must one keep faith with heretics?
are poor men justified in stealing in order to keep alive? is revenge
lawful? what excuses for crimes are allowable? may a soldier
flee from the field of battle? what can Christians do to escape
persecution?[65]

Of course, Hobbes's solutions to such problems were often
unconventional: he brushed aside the vast literature on the binding
force of oaths by remarking tartly that an oath adds nothing to an
obligation, though it may make subsequent non-performance more
dangerous.[66] Even more brutally, he rejected the notion that every
individual is the judge of good and evil and entitled to follow his
own conscience. This, he thought, could only lead to anarchy; in
the commonwealth, the sovereign's law was the public conscience
of everyone.[67] Yet Hobbes was far from jettisoning all earlier
teachings about conscience and its importance. On the contrary,

---

[62] Wallace, *Destiny his Choice*; Sampson, 'Laxity and Liberty'.

[63] Thomas Hobbes, *Leviathan*, ed. R. Tuck (Cambridge, 1991), 484 (Review and Conclusion);
Q. Skinner, 'Conquest and Consent: Thomas Hobbes and the Engagement Controversy',
in G. E. Aylmer (ed.), *The Interregnum: The Quest for Settlement 1646–1660* (1972), 94–7.

[64] *Leviathan*, 110 (ch. 15).

[65] Ibid. 97–8 (ch. 14); 103 (ch. 15); 208 (ch. 27); 106–7 (ch. 15); ch. 27; 151–2 (ch. 21);
343–5 (ch. 42).

[66] Ibid. 100 (ch. 14); *The Elements of Law*, ed. F. Tönnies (1889), 81.

[67] *Leviathan*, 223 (ch. 29); 236 (ch. 30). Ralph Cudworth thought the notion of a public
conscience 'nonsense and ridiculous' (*The True Intellectual System of the Universe* (3 vols.; 1845
edn.), iii. 514).

he agreed that what was done against conscience was always a sin. In the state of nature, conscience was the individual's only guide; and, in the civil state, it still governed the sovereign.[68] Hobbes shared the belief of earlier casuists that the common people and those without leisure needed moral guidance from their superiors.[69]

Next to politics and religion, the most persistent source of cases of conscience was to be found in the domestic sphere. Most of the cases brought to John Williams related to 'matrimonial scruples'. Over a third of those published by Sanderson concerned marriage; and the subject filled a quarter of Joseph Hall's collection. Jeremy Taylor thought 'matrimonial questions' so large a subject as to require a separate treatise, though he never wrote it: such questions were 'very material and very numerous', he thought, 'and of all things have been most injured by evil and imperfect principles and worse conduct'.[70] So long as the law of marriage allowed an informal contract without banns or a priest to create a binding union, it was inevitable that moral ambiguities about the status of the affianced parties should subsequently arise; and the situation was further complicated by the temporary suspension of the Church courts during the Interregnum and the short-lived introduction of civil marriage.[71] As bishop of Exeter, Joseph Hall was frequently approached by well-to-do parents seeking the annulment of irregular marriages made by their children without their consent. John Angier told a young minister in 1654 that he could not marry without his prospective mother-in-law's agreement, despite her notorious ungodlinesss: to proceed without the parent's consent was 'at best . . . not a clear case, but dark and doubtful'.[72] Hall encountered many cases of unintended incest, for the precise extent of the prohibited degrees was much debated and far from clear to all the laity.[73] Jeremy Taylor remarked that the problem of how wives should comport themselves towards their adulterous hus-

---

[68] *Leviathan*, 223 (ch. 30); 202 (ch. 27); 244 (ch. 30).

[69] Ibid. 233–5 (ch. 30); *Behemoth*, ed. F. Tönnies (1889), 144.

[70] Hacket, *Scrinia reserata*, ii. 61–2; *Works of Sanderson*, v (cases iv, v, viii, and x); Hall, *Resolutions and Decisions*, 285–423; *Whole Works of Jeremy Taylor*, x. 500.

[71] M. Ingram, *Church Courts, Sex and Marriage in England, 1570–1640* (Cambridge, 1987), 133, 154; L. Stone, *Road to Divorce: England 1530–1987* (Oxford, 1990), 67–80.

[72] Hall, *Resolutions and Decisions*, 286; O. Heywood, *Life of John Angier of Denton*, ed. E. Axon (Chetham Soc., 1937), 104–7.

[73] Hall, *Resolutions and Decisions*, 383; Ingram, *Church Courts, Sex and Marriage*, 246.

bands was 'a case which now-a-days happens too frequently'.[74] Another painful issue was that of whether a barren union could be dissolved to enable the husband to remarry and secure an heir. The law was unyielding on this point, but one of Bishop Burnet's youthful indiscretions was to produce for the Earl of Lauderdale a *Resolution of Two Important Cases of Conscience*, in which he affirmed, with Charles II and Catherine of Braganza in mind, that a wife's barrenness was just grounds for divorce and that, in any case, polygamy was lawful under the gospel.[75] In 1648 Philip Nye cited the case of the gentleman cast into Newgate to be executed for having two wives and who pleaded it was 'a case of conscience'. An Irish cleric George Pressicke bombarded his bishop in 1661 with arguments as to why he should be allowed to remarry because his wife had deserted him. Throughout the century, marriage, divorce, and sexual morality remained areas of debate, uncertainty, and conflicting opinion.[76]

So did business ethics. Long ago, in one of this century's greatest historical works, R. H. Tawney gave an unforgettable account of the process by which economic life was emancipated in mid-seventeenth-century England from the constraints of conscience and left with no moral rule save the letter of the law. But it is clear that Tawney exaggerated the speed of this process, for, until the end of the seventeenth century, churchmen continued to regard usury, business contracts, buying and selling, and the relationship between master and servant as a domain in which there were ethical standards to be observed beyond those prescribed by the law.[77] As Sanderson put it in 1660:

human laws cannot be the adequate measure of moral duty in the judgment of any reasonable man ... the laws being finite and fixed, but the circumstances of men's actions, on which their lawfulness and unlawfulness chiefly dependeth, various and infinite. The laws allow ... many things to be done, which an honest man would be loath to do; and afford sundry advantages, which one that feareth God, and maketh conscience of his ways, ought not to take.[78]

[74] *Whole Works of Jeremy Taylor*, ix. 240.

[75] Clarke and Foxcroft, *Life of Gilbert Burnet*, 103–4.

[76] A S. P. Woodhouse, *Puritanism and Liberty* (1938), 146; G. Pressicke, *A Case of Conscience Propounded* (n.p., 1661).

[77] Schlatter, *Social Ideas of Religious Leaders*, 226–7. Cf. R. H. Tawney, *Religion and the Rise of Capitalism* (West Drayton, 1938), 23–4.

[78] *Works of Sanderson*, v. 208.

Casuists therefore continued to discuss the extent to which trad-esmen could sell for the highest price or take advantage of their customers' ignorance, even if the tradesmen themselves may have been less ready to proffer their scruples to the casuist. As Daniel Defoe later remarked, 'If our yea must be yea, and our nay nay, why, then, it is impossible for tradesmen to be Christians.'[79]

Another area in which cases of conscience regularly appeared was that of actions which involved the taking of life. Casuists incessantly debated such subjects as war, killing in self-defence, duelling, suicide, and the destruction of infants in childbirth in order to save their mothers. Hall found that 'too many of the weaker sex' were 'grossly culpable in matters of willing abortion', terminating pregnancies by 'over-vehement motion or unwhole-some medicine'.[80] Equally controversial was the status of obligations which individuals had unwisely undertaken, only to regret sub-sequently. Rash vows, fraudulent contracts, and promises extracted by force were much debated; and the differences between a promise, a vow, and an oath carefully defined.[81]

Litigation was another perplexing area, for many moralists clung to the notion that going to law was something to be avoided if possible and were suspicious of the conventions of advocacy. Ames regarded the art of pleading as 'nothing but sophistical and pernicious, and made up of guile, deceit, sleights, cavils, snares, captiousness, entrappings, tricks, windings, and circumventions'.[82] Dress, rec-reations, and conventional social usages also created moral problems: mixed dancing, gambling, lotteries, alms-giving, health-drinking, and polite courtesies could all generate cases of conscience. Could boys dress as women on the stage in defiance of the biblical prohibition on cross-dressing? Could one eat black puddings? Was it wrong to offer dinner guests a second helping? What if one's physician advised that it was 'wholesome to be drunk sometimes'?[83]

---

[79] Daniel Defoe, *The Complete English Tradesman* (2 vols.; Oxford, 1841), i. 184. Similar sentiments are expressed in J. Downame, *A Treatise against Lying* (1636), 7–11, 164–5.

[80] Hall, *Resolutions and Decisions*, 89.

[81] e.g. *Works of Sanderson*, v. 88–90. In 1691 William Sherlock resolved a case of conscience for a correspondent who had rashly vowed to forsake his trade; item 116 in catalogue 39 (Apr. 1976) of Hofmann and Freeman, booksellers.

[82] Ames, *Conscience*, iii. 288. Cf. Downame, *Treatise against Lying*, 5–6; *Whole Works of Jeremy Taylor*, x. 144.

[83] [John Dod and Robert Cleaver], *A Plaine and Familiar Exposition of the Ten Commandements* (18th edn., 1632), 269; *Practical Works of Richard Baxter*, i. 294, 307; [Thomas Barlow(?)], *The Trial of a Black-Pudding* (1652).

There was, in short, no sector of seventeenth-century life where moral problems might not arise. Broadly speaking, cases of conscience were most likely to be generated when the application of human or divine law to a particular case was not straightforward, either because the circumstances were unusual or because the human law seemed incompatible with the Ten Commandments (as in the case of the Book of Sports) or with the teachings of the New Testament (as in the case of warfare, litigation, and private property). The dilemmas multiplied when the laws were obscure (as with marriage and divorce) or conflicted sharply with the values of a particular social group (as in the case of duelling) or with their religious principles (as with nonconformity). Baxter thought that 'one of the commonest difficulties among cases of conscience' was 'to know which duty is the greater and to be preferred'.[84] Changing social conditions, such as the growth of business and industry, the development of a national poor law, and the emergence of new habits of personal consumption, made the application of traditional principles seem inappropriate; and an over-scrupulous conscience could be relied upon to find difficulties where none had previously existed.[85]

The amount of compromise, accommodation, and complaisance required to make any human society run smoothly has always placed a heavy strain on those who believe it is necessary to follow an upright course. Even if the period had not been one of rapid social change and turbulence, the application of moral rules to particular instances could never have been an easy business. Why then did casuistry, the science of this application, disappear so rapidly from public view in England after the seventeenth century, vanishing off the theological map with what one authority calls 'almost incredible speed'? By the mid-eighteenth century the subject seemed as archaic as baroque art, which, in its detailed complexity and tortuous striving to reconcile incompatibles, it greatly resembled.[86] For Hanoverian philosophers, casuistry, with all its 'endless subtleties and intricacies',[87] had no intellectual interest.

[84] *Practical Works of Richard Baxter*, i. 32.
[85] As John Locke remarked (*Two Tracts on Government*, ed. P. Abrams (Cambridge, 1967), 139–40).
[86] H. R. McAdoo, *The Structure of Caroline Moral Theology* (1949), 66; Jonsen and Toulmin, *Abuse of Casuistry*, 145–6.
[87] D. Hartley, *Observations on Man* (2 vols.; 1749), ii. 293; Gallagher, *Medusa's Gaze*, 1–3.

Some religious writers, particularly nonconformists, maintained the tradition in their works of moral guidance, but among the general public 'cases of conscience' were becoming objects of satire.[88] It used to be thought that the main reason for the change was that Pascal's *Lettres provinciales* (1656–7; English translation 1657), with their damning exposure of Jesuit laxity, discredited the whole casuistical tradition. By the end of the seventeenth century Pascal's polemic was said to be as well known in English taverns and coffee houses as Foxe's *Martyrs* and to enjoy equal authority.[89] There is no doubt that Pascal did much to popularize the view of casuistry as a perverse and over-ingenious device for evading all unwelcome moral obligations. Horace Walpole would remark that casuistry was never needed for the observance of an oath, only for the breach of it; while Sir Henry Maine later declared that casuistry had so distorted human moral instincts, 'that at length the conscience of mankind rose suddenly in revolt against it'.[90] Yet Catholic casuistry had been associated with equivocation, mental reservation and other departures from conventional morality since late Elizabethan times. So, for that matter, had much of its Protestant counterpart.[91] These defects persuaded many of the need for a more rigorous casuistry which would be less accommodating to human weakness, but they did not constitute an argument against casuistry as such. Jeremy Taylor, Samuel Clarke, and Richard Baxter continued to labour on their own case-divinity in full knowledge of what Pascal had written.

Nevertheless, Pascal's influence can be seen in the increasing tendency of Anglican divines to maintain that moral problems were

---

[88] S. Pike and S. Hayward, *Some Important Cases of Conscience Answered* (1755 and frequently reissued), the writings of Isaac Watts and Philip Doddridge, and the numerous reissues of *The Whole Duty of Man* contrast with such squibs as *Oxford Honesty: Or, a Case of Conscience . . . whether one may take the oaths to King George; and yet, consistently with honour, and conscience, and the fear of God, may do all one can in favour of the Pretender?* (2nd edn., 1750).

[89] [Gabriel Daniel], *Les Provinciales: Or, the Mysterie of Jesuitisme* (1657); *Discourses of Cleander and Eudoxe* (1704), sig. a5; and see Sampson, 'Liberty and Laxity', 73–85. D. Clarkson, *The Practical Casuistry of the Papists discovered to be destructive of Christianity* (1676), extended the attack to non-Jesuit casuistry.

[90] [Horace Walpole], *A Catalogue of the Royal and Noble Authors of England* (2 vols.; Strawberry Hill, 1758), i. 37; Sir Henry Sumner Maine, *Ancient Law* (1920 edn.), 361–2. According to Viscount St Cyres, in a spirited article on 'casuistry' in *Encyclopaedia Britannica* (11th edn., 1913), casuistry was 'swept away by the rising tide of common-sense'.

[91] G. L. Mosse, *The Holy Pretence* (Oxford, 1957); Zagorin, *Ways of Lying*, ch. 10; and Burnet's comments on Oliver Cromwell in his *History of My Own Time* (6 vols.; Oxford, 1823), i. 78, 135–6.

essentially simple and that it was only the desire to gratify appetites without formally breaking God's law which had generated so much learned effort. Religion is a plain thing, said the Marquess of Halifax, but interest is a subtle casuist.[92] Impatience with casuistry had long been shown by those who believed that an honest desire to serve God would take care of most difficulties; as early as 1626 Ephraim Huit lamented the practice of loading the conscience 'full of cases to be resolved, about the disquisition whereof much time is spent that might have been better employed'.[93] In the eyes of Restoration satirists, Puritan casuistry had proved a disreputable tool of adjustment and accommodation.[94] By the 1690s Archbishop Tillotson, Archbishop Sharp, and others were suggesting that, in doubtful cases, an individual should simply follow his own best instincts, rather than search for the most 'correct' rule and method by exploring a body of accumulated opinions. 'When all is done, much must be left to the Equity and Chancery of our own breasts.' Prolonged doubt was a likely sign of weakness, and elaborate casuistry a way of eroding moral responsibility: a person's first impulses were usually correct.[95]

What was involved here was a shift from a conception of morality as the application of divine laws to human affairs to the idea of it as the simple love of God and pursuit of goodness. Instead of thinking of life as made up of a series of discrete problems, each to be solved separately in accordance with the rule-book, theologians were increasingly inclined to place their emphasis upon the formation of an individual's general moral character. As John Preston had stressed long before, no one should be judged on the basis of one or two particular actions: 'the only measure to esteem ourselves or others is the continued tenor of the course and actions. This proceeds from inward principles and from the frame of the heart.'[96] Moreover, churchmen no longer saw it as

---

[92] *The Works of George Savile Marquis of Halifax*, ed. M. N. Brown (3 vols.; Oxford, 1989), iii. 325. Cf. Schlatter, *Social Ideas of Religious Leaders*, 208; J. Sharp, *The Theological Works* (5 vols.; Oxford, 1829), i. 187–8.

[93] Huit, *Anatomy of Conscience*, 259.

[94] e.g. *The Godly Man's Legacy . . . Exhibited in the Life of . . . Mr. Stephen Marshall* (1680), 4, 25–6, Cf. Snider, 'By Equivocation Swear'.

[95] *The Morning-Exercise at Cripplegate*, 198; Sharp, *Theological Works*, i. 188–9; ii. 92; *Whole Works of Jeremy Taylor*, i, p. ccxxiv.

[96] *An Abridgment of Dr. Preston's Works*, ed. W. Jemmat (1648), 243. See E. Leites, 'Casuistry and Character', in Leites (ed.), *Conscience and Casuistry*, 119–33.

their task to create by preaching and cure by casuistry the tormented, afflicted consciences to whom the Puritan clergy had
ministered. Bishop Burnet declared robustly that 'the greater part of
those that are troubled in mind' were 'melancholy hypochondriacal
people'; they needed medicine, not spiritual advice.[97]

The process by which Protestant theologians shifted from maintaining that it was sinful to follow an erroneous conscience to uphold-
ing the view that all that mattered was sincerity of intention has yet
to be fully documented. Yet this transition, it has been rightly said,
was the origin of the modern, more secular, belief that, whatever we
do, we retain our moral integrity so long as we obey our consciences.[98]
Nowadays a wartime tribunal for conscientious objection decides
not whether the objection is well founded, but whether it is con-
scientiously held. This notion, so alien to the thinking of most Jacobean divines, was foreshadowed in the attitude of those Protestant
sectaries who claimed that the spirit, or the conscience, was superior
even to Scripture.[99] It was also expressed by Hobbes, who maintained
that in the state of nature, and also in the civil State, so far as
concerned those matters left undetermined by the sovereign, 'every
man (is) his own judge, and accused only by his own conscience, and
cleared by the uprightness of his own intention. When therefore his
intention is right, his fact is no sin.'[100]

The eighteenth century would see the triumph of the proto-
Romantic belief in the authenticity of individual sentiment. Once
sincerity became more important than correctness, there was no
room for casuistry. As Adam Smith put it, 'nice and delicate
situations' could not be resolved by a formula; they should be left
to 'the man within the breast'. The mistake of the casuists had
been to try 'to direct by precise rules what it belongs to feelings
and sentiment only to judge of'. Books of casuistry were there
fore 'generally as useless as they are commonly tiresome'.[101]

---

[97] Gilbert [Burnet], *A Discourse of the Pastoral Care* (1692), 199. Cf. Hunter, 'Casuistry in Action'.

[98] E. Leites, 'Conscience and Moral Ignorance', *Journal of Chinese Philosophy*, 2 (1974–5), 71. Cf. Fiering, *Moral Philosophy*, 94, 191–2; J. Tully, 'Governing Conduct', in Leites (ed.), *Conscience and Casuistry*, 64–5.

[99] G. F. Nuttall, *The Holy Spirit in Puritan Faith and Experience* (Oxford, 1946), 37; C. Hill, *The World Turned Upside Down* (1972), 66–7, 76, 297–8.

[100] Hobbes, *Leviathan*, ed. Tuck, 202 (ch. 27).

[101] A. Smith, *The Theory of Moral Sentiments*, ed. D. D. Raphael and A. L. Macfie (Oxford, 1976), 339.

So long as the idea prevailed that a single right answer existed for every moral dilemma, then the notion of moral expertise had made sense. It was in that spirit that Charles I's parting advice to Robert Sanderson had been that he should 'betake himself to writing cases of conscience for the good of posterity'.[102] But when a sincere intention was what mattered most, the need for experts dwindled. By the end of the seventeenth century the role of the clerical adviser was on the wane. One could still take legal problems to lawyers and medical problems to doctors, but the demand for professional experts in morality was shrinking, as it became increasingly common to maintain that individuals, being responsible for their own spiritual state, could and should take their own moral decisions for themselves.[103] This was only pushing to its logical conclusion the priesthood of all believers which had been implicit in the Protestantism from the start. The century after the Reformation, when clergymen sought to resolve individual cases of conscience, appears in retrospect as an essentially transitional period, during which, as Christopher Hill puts it, ministers 'tried to help men to take moral decisions for themselves, and yet at the same time tried to preserve some sort of control over the workings of the consciences of individuals, to prescribe courses of action for every possible occasion'.[104] The clergy did not subsequently lose their advisory role, of course, but it became increasingly confined to purely spiritual matters.

For the effect of the mid-seventeenth-century upheaval had been that the moral dilemmas of politics and economics had been largely taken over by laymen. As moral theology was overtaken by moral philosophy and political casuistry by political theory, the clergy found themselves moved to the sidelines of the debate.[105] Moreover, the way in which these matters were discussed became increasingly secular. Economics in the hands of the political arithmeticians was

---

[102] *Works of Sanderson*, vi. 304.

[103] E. Leites, 'Conscience, Casuistry and Moral Decision: Some Historical Perspectives', *Journal of Chinese Philosophy*, 2 (1974–5), is an excellent discussion. See also Leites, 'Casuistry and Character'.

[104] Hill, *Society and Puritanism*, 398. For reluctance to be ruled by the clergy in matters of conscience, see *Practical Works of Richard Baxter*, ii. 399.

[105] This is the theme of Margaret Sampson's outstanding article, 'Laxity and Liberty'. For a defence of clerical claims, see H. Ferne, *The Resolving of Conscience* (2nd edn., Oxford, 1643), sig. A2ᵛ.

not a subject which generated many moral problems.[106] Law was
the business of lawyers, who were increasingly hostile to the
view that any casuistry other than their own was necessary to
resolve legal dilemmas. John Selden scornfully observed that
some had tried to make it a case of conscience as to whether
one could keep a pigeon-house, since the birds would pillage
the crops of neighbours; that was a legal question, he snorted,
and there was an end to the matter. 'If once we come to ...
pretend conscience against law, who knows what inconveniency
may follow?'[107]

Moral philosophy, as treated by the natural lawyers of the
later seventeenth century and the 'moral-sense' philosophers of
the early eighteenth, no longer looked first to Scripture for
guidance on moral duties; instead the source of obligation was
to be discovered by human reason and the study of human
nature. God's law, which had traditionally been the first criterion
for making a conscientious judgement, now took second place.[108]
Political obedience similarly became for Hobbes, Locke, and
their contemporaries a matter less of conscience and more of
convenience, interest, and self-preservation. In the eighteenth
century it would be recognized that most subjects obeyed the
government, not out of conscience or even fear, but from what
Burke called 'imperceptible habits and old custom'.[109] The loyalty
oaths which had kept the casuists so busy during each political
upheaval of the seventeenth century fell into increasing disrepute
because of the equivocation and downright perjury which they
had evoked. Conscience did not become irrelevant to political
conduct, but, in the age of Walpole, its role was less central
than it had been a hundred years earlier.[110]

Meanwhile many of the problems which had caused painful
moral dilemmas in the seventeenth century had evaporated after

---

[106] Tawney, *Religion and the Rise of Capitalism*, 24, 194.
[107] Selden, *Table Talk*, 35.
[108] As was noted by W. Paley, *The Principles of Moral and Political Philosophy* (2 vols.; 13th
edn., 1801), i, pp. xv–xvi. Cf. I. Rivers, *Reason, Grace and Sentiment*, i (Cambridge, 1991), 207,
224; Fiering, *Moral Philosophy*, 6, 49–50.
[109] *The Works of the Right Honourable Edmund Burke* (6 vols.; Bohn edn., 1854–70), ii. 33;
Tully, 'Governing Conduct'; G. M. Straka, *Anglican Reaction to the Revolution of 1688* (Madison,
Wis., 1962), 124.
[110] Hill, *Society and Puritanism*, 413–18; S. Staves, *Players' Scepters* (Lincoln, Neb., 1979), ch.
4; Snider, 'By Equivocation Swear'.

the 1688 Revolution and the coming of religious toleration. The Non-Jurors and Jacobites were the last groups to have crises of conscience about allegiance, while Protestant and Catholic Dissenters were freed from many of the conflicting pressures of earlier times. As the Church courts fell into abeyance, public control over private morality diminished. Dress, recreation, and the consumption of goods were largely left to the market; and only some dissenting congregations continued to regulate their members' conduct in this area. Finally, with Hardwicke's Act of 1753, some of the most blatant deficiencies in the law of marriage were remedied and the scope for matrimonial dilemmas markedly reduced.

Because of all these circumstances, the discussion of 'cases of conscience', so characteristic of seventeenth-century England, ceased to be so conspicuous a feature of the cultural landscape. Of course, moral dilemmas continued. Many were taken by worried individuals to the columns of the newspapers, like the *Athenian Mercury*, whose founder John Dunton hit on the brilliant idea of encouraging individuals to put their queries anonymously.[111] Questions about oaths, restitution, and marriage vows poured in. Others were ventilated in the pages of that new literary genre, the novel.[112] From time to time people complained that the old-style casuistry was still needed, for example to deal with the pressures men of honour found themselves under to observe the duelling code, or to resolve that eternal problem of the eighteenth-century employer, whether or not to give a truthful testimonial for an unreliable servant seeking new employment.[113] Heterodox clergy used laxist casuistry to justify their continuing subscription to the Thirty-nine Articles.[114] But philosophers tended to turn their back on the resolution of particular cases. In the famous words of F. H. Bradley, they held that it was not the business of moral philosophy to tell us what in particular we are to do.[115] Only in very recent years have philosophers returned to the analysis of the

---

[111] Starr, *Defoe and Casuistry*, 9–33, and, more recently, J. P. Hunter, *Before Novels* (New York, 1990), 289.

[112] Starr, *Defoe and Casuistry, passim.*

[113] *The Collected Writings of Thomas de Quincey*, ed. D. Masson (14 vols.; Edinburgh, 1889–90), viii. 338–40, 357–9; *Uncollected Writings of Thomas de Quincey*, ed. J. Hogg (2 vols.; 1892), ii. 64–112; Paley, *Principles of Moral and Political Philosophy*, i. 170.

[114] [Francis Blackburne], *The Confessional* (1766).

[115] F. H. Bradley, *Ethical Studies* (rev. 2nd edn., Oxford, 1988), 139. A strong case for the continuing utility of casuistry is made by Jonsen and Toulmin, *Abuse of Casuistry*.

practical dilemmas which individuals may face, whether in cases of abortion, genetic engineering, or the treatment of animals. But the terms in which such issues are nowadays discussed and the criteria invoked are very different from those to be found in the Protestant casuistry of seventeenth-century England.

5

Public Duty, Conscience, and Women in Early Modern England

PATRICIA CRAWFORD

HISTORIANS have recently become interested in the areas of the public and private, and some attention has focused on the concepts of public duty and conscience in early modern times. The gender dimension of these concepts has been less examined. Historians have usually associated public duty with citizenship and men, although they recognize that contemporaries thought that the voice of conscience was to be heeded by all.

Questions of gender were central to discussions of public duty and the exercise of conscience in early modern England. Everyone knew that difference of sex affected the social experiences of men and women. Thus this chapter argues three main points: first, that the public and private in early modern England were permeable concepts in thought, and slippery concepts in practice—both the public and the private were constantly under negotiation and debate; secondly, that the public sphere was not an entirely male space, and that some females shared responsibility for the discharge of public duties; and, thirdly, that women used religious beliefs and arguments about conscience to justify action in the public sphere. Axiomatic to this discussion is the view that gender—the social construction of difference of sex—affected the ways in which people thought and acted. Conscience and duty were not the same things for men and for women, and part of the purpose of this chapter is to show how gender complicated contemporary behaviour and thought.

My warmest thanks to Gerald and Ursula Aylmer for their friendship and kindness over many years, from 1965, when I first went to York to talk of matters seventeenth century. I am extremely grateful to Colin Davis, Sara Mendelson, John Morrill, Lyndal Roper, Kevin Sharpe, and Paul Slack for their comments on this chapter.

THE CONCEPTS OF PUBLIC AND PRIVATE

In pre-industrial societies where gender roles were rigid and the public and private were separated, women were relegated to the private sphere. Thus in ancient Greece and Rome women were excluded from citizenship, and the contrast between the public and private was enshrined in Roman law.[1] The public was open, subject to scrutiny. The private was hidden, secret. Virtue was public, vice was private. Ideally, public duty took precedence over any private interests. The classical example for emulation was that of Brutus, whose devotion to public justice was such that he denounced his own sons for plotting to restore the previous regime. However, in medieval times, when the boundaries between the public and the private were less rigid, women were able to participate in a wider range of activities. For example, when government emanated from the king's household, queens consort and other women in the chamber were able to participate in politics. Public and private were not exclusive categories.

Although Habermas argues that by the mid-sixteenth century the public and the private were more rigidly separated, the private designating exclusion from the sphere of state apparatus, his concepts seem somewhat anachronistic in early modern England.[2] Contemporary thinkers saw their society ideally as an organic whole, a world in which every individual would seek the common good. As Kevin Sharpe has explained, there were forces in England undermining this ideal, but, while contemporaries recognized the tension, they continued to idealize a harmonious, loving whole. In so far as there were private interests, these were to be subordinated to common purposes. As Sharpe concludes, 'What we would separate as private and public interest, the individual and the state, were harmonized in the concept of the commonweal.'[3]

---

[1] R. K. Sinclair, *Democracy and Participation in Athens* (Cambridge, 1988). Men required Athenian parentage in the female as well as the male line in order to be accepted as citizens (p. 24). Noble women had enjoyed higher status before the advent of the city state (M. Saliou, 'The Process of Women's Subordination in Primitive and Archaic Greece', in S. Coonz and P. Henderson (eds.), *Women's Work. Men's Property: The Origins of Gender and Class*, (1986), 192–3).

[2] J. Habermas, *The Structural Transformation of the Public Sphere.* (1962; trans., Cambridge, Mass., 1989), 11.

[3] K. Sharpe, 'A Commonwealth of Meanings: Languages, Analogues, Ideas and Politics', in K. Sharpe, *Politics and Ideas in Early Stuart England: Essays and Studies* (1989), 13.

Yet there was a distinction in early modern society, as there is in every society, between the public and the private. To talk of the public and the private in early modern England was part of the attempt to redefine the gender order consequent upon the Reformation changes in belief.[4] Changes in the gender order had an impact on the ways in which the public and the private were discussed. The revival of classical learning encouraged the development of civic virtue, which jostled with and interpreted Christian notions of godly citizenship. Increasingly, the citizen was a responsible adult man, head of his household, with duties to his country, his prince, and his God. Ideally, a woman was a good wife and mother. She did not belong in the public sphere because her weakness incapacitated her for public duties.[5] Contemporaries commended the picture of the woman as a snail, 'signifying that the wife was to abide at home, and indeede it is a very uncomely thing for women to frequent markets, as many doe'.[6] The public world belonged to men, while the private world, the household, was the sphere to which women were to be confined. Reformers in England from the mid-sixteenth century onwards stressed the family responsibilities of women. Ideally, there was no place outside the household for the single woman. The Elizabethan Statute of Artificers, which endeavoured to ensure that all unmarried women between 12 and 40 were placed in employment in a household, under the authority of a master, affected women more than men, because in practice the justices disliked women setting up in independent trades.[7]

In practice the rulers of England did not view the distinctions between the public sphere of men and the private sphere of women as absolute. Boundaries were always shifting, constantly being redrawn as men and women contested the definitions of the gender order. The household could never be an entirely private sphere, because it was the means by which women, a source of disorder, were controlled.[8] In marriage a woman was brought into subjection,

---

[4] For a discussion of the impact of the European Reformation on gender relations, see L. Roper, *The Holy Household: Women and Morals in Reformation Augsburg* (Oxford, 1989).

[5] I. Maclean, *The Renaissance Notion of Woman: A Study in the Fortunes of Scholasticism and Medical Science in European Intellectual Life* (Cambridge, 1980), 43.

[6] F. Dillingham, *Christian Oeconomy*, (1609), fo. 10.

[7] *An Act . . . for Artificers*, 5 Eliz. c. iv.

[8] Maclean, *Renaissance Notion of Woman*, 28–46; N. Davis, 'Woman on Top', in N. Davis, *Society and Culture in Early Modern France* (Stanford, Calif., 1975).

under the government of a husband. The Elizabethan homily on marriage, which was regularly read in parish churches, explained that one of the pains of marriage for women was that 'they relinquish the liberty of their own rule'.[9] Since the household was always open to public scrutiny, men at home were not in a private world. Men's behaviour there was, in the first instance, under the observation of their neighbours, who would remonstrate with the man who seemed unduly violent towards his wife.[10] Sexual disorders were publicly mocked, and men as well as women could be called to account for their private sexual acts.[11] Instructions about good behaviour extended even to the matter of headwear in bed: ministers were advised that a black silk nightcap was most suitable.[12] Masters of families were answerable for what happened in the households under their authority. For example, legally men were responsible for the debts of their wives, for the religious behaviour of their households, and for maintaining good order. A husband was both king and priest in his family. Order in a man's household was a microcosm of the order desired in the world.

For the majority of women the household could never be a private sphere isolated from the world. First, contemporaries recognized that women had roles which took them into the public arena.[13] In pursuit of their domestic tasks, women were forced to go abroad. They went out for wood, for water, and to market. Secondly, women knew that what they did in their households was open to the public. As William Gouge explained, for a good wife 'a conscionable performance of household duties . . . may be accounted a publike worke'.[14] Wives were open to public censures as well as to the private rebukes of their fathers, husbands, or masters. To receive a man 'in secret and private places' led to 'greate and strong suspicion of publique fame' of sexual immorality.[15] Thirdly, certain public behaviour was expected of women, such as attendance at church, and thanksgiving for a safe delivery

[9] Church of England, *Certain Sermons or Homilies* (1908), 540.
[10] For one example, Guildhall, Archdeacon's Court, 1566–7, MS 9056, fos. 16ᵛ–21ᵛ.
[11] The records of the Church courts and the quarter session records contain many cases relating to sexual reputation and bastardy.
[12] G. Meriton, *The Parson's Monitor* (1681), 13.
[13] D. Willen, 'Women in the Public Sphere in Early Modern England: The Case of the Urban Working Poor', *Sixteenth-Century Journal*, 19 (1988), 559–75.
[14] W. Gouge, *Of Domesticall Duties* (1622), 18.
[15] Glos. RO, Court papers, GDR B 4/1/64.

in childbirth 'in the Publique church'.[16] Thus, in practice, the categories of public and private were permeable in early modern England. Public duties could conflict with private beliefs, and men argued about the dichotomy. For example, King Charles I agonized in 1641 over whether he should sign the Act of Attainder thus condemning the Earl of Strafford to death when he had promised the Earl that he should suffer neither in life nor fortune if he came to the King's aid.[17] Charles was persuaded by the argument that, as a matter of public duty, he must sacrifice his private conscience: 'I never met with a more unhappy conjuncture of affaires . . . when between My owne unsatisfied-nesse in Conscience, and a necessity (as some told me) of satisfying the importunities of some people.' Charles later regretted his decision bitterly, praying 'never suffer me for any reason of State, to goe against my Reason of Conscience'.[18] He repented of more than his unkindness to Strafford, for he recognized his error in conceding a difference between the private person and the public office of the king. The distinction which Charles initially accepted between his personal and his public self was one which allowed Parliament to wage a war to rescue him from his evil counsellors. The dilemma of the king's two bodies was inherent in political life, and ultimately there would be a separation. While Charles was, perhaps, atypical, his was a classic example of conflict between conscience and duty.

Since most European jurists believed that women were debarred by their sex from public office, no conflict between public duty and conscience was envisaged.[19] Ideally, women's sole public duty was obedience to fathers or husbands. In practice, female public duties were more extensive.

---

[16] Guildhall, Churchwardens' presentments, MS 9583/2/pt. 5, fo. 13.

[17] S. R. Gardiner, *History of England from the Accession of James to the Outbreak of the Civil War, 1603–1642* (10 vols.; 1883–4), ix. 365–7; *The Earl of Strafford's Letters and Despatches*, ed. W. Knowler (2 vols.; 1739), ii. 418; J. Hacket, *Scrinia reserata*, (1693), ii. 161; *The Whole Works of the Most Rev. James Ussher*, ed. C. R. Elrington and J. M. Todd (17 vols.; Dublin, 1847–64), i. 210–17.

[18] Charles I, *Eikon Basilike* (1648), 7–11.

[19] Maclean, *Renaissance Notion of Woman*, 77.

WOMEN AND PUBLIC DUTY

All the women who were queens in early modern England—
Mary Tudor, Elizabeth I, Mary II, and Anne—had public duties.
The history of their conflicts between duty and conscience has yet
to be written, but one example, that of Queen Elizabeth and the
execution of Mary, Queen of Scots, indicates possibilities of an
analysis which brings gender into the equation between conscience
and duty.

In 1586 Queen Elizabeth faced a conflict between her conscience
and what her Parliament and Council told her was her public
duty—to consent to the execution of Mary, Queen of Scots. In
her private person, Elizabeth pointed out that, as a woman, and
'a maiden Queen', she was under special obligation to be true to
the feminine stereotype of compassion. Further, she was obliged
to Mary by bonds of kinship. What would her enemies say (and
what, we may read, would she say to her conscience) 'that for the
safety of her life a maiden Queen could be content to spill the
blood even of her own kinswoman?'[20] To Parliament, she pleaded
Mary's sex as a reason for sparing her,[21] which was an argument
for mercy any prince might have used, but without the force of
the special obligation imposed on Elizabeth as a woman ruler.
Elizabeth was trying to exploit expectations about gender in order
to find a way out of her dilemma other than shedding Mary's
blood, but the members of Parliament were determined. MPs
argued that, as Mary was guilty, the Lord's vengeance would fall
upon the kingdom should they spare her.[22]

Although there was a wide range of public offices in the service
of the monarch and of the Church for which women were ineligible,
nevertheless there were some offices for women. At the royal
Court, aristocratic ladies held positions. Service in the household
of the monarch was originally seen as a private duty, but by the
sixteenth century some places at Court were public offices, in that
courtiers were paid salaries and had specified duties in attending
their sovereign. In the reign of Elizabeth, the women officers of
the chamber played an even more significant role in the transaction

[20] Quoted in J. E. Neale, *Elizabeth I and her Parliaments*, (2 vols.; 1965), ii. 127, 277, 24
Nov. 1586.
[21] S. D'Ewes, *The Journals of all the Parliaments during the Reign of Queen Elizabeth* (1682), 402.
[22] Ibid. 401.

of certain suits and business.[23] During the early modern period there were also female officers in the households of the kings, of the queens consort, and of royal children. All female officers, even down to laundresses, were sworn to their duties and received a salary.[24]

As executrixes of wills, women had public responsibilities. As widows of royal accountants, women were required to present the accounts of the business for which their husbands were responsible. For example, in 1701 Lady Mary Howard, executrix, swore the account of Lord Thomas Howard, Master of the Robes to James II. In 1660 Richard Waring and Elizabeth Herring, widow of Michael Herring, swore accounts for the huge sum of £1.6 million for delinquents' and recusants' lands.[25]

Some of women's public duties had diminished at the Reformation. No longer were there female churchwardens or wardens of women's guilds collecting money for their parish churches.[26] Nor were midwives authorized to baptize babies in imminent danger of death. However, a range of civic duties was discharged by those below the level of gentry. There were instances of women serving in the public office of parish constables during the seventeenth century, not necessarily in their own persons, but being called on to provide substitutes.[27] Similarly, there were female tithingmen.[28]

Some kinds of work took women into the sphere where public duty could conflict with private conscience. Midwives had public duties. Early modern casuists discussed the case of the midwives of Egypt whose duty to God required disobedience to the rulers' command. In Exodus 1: 19 the story was told of the midwives who were commanded to kill any sons born to the Israelites. The

---

[23] P. Wright, 'A Change in Direction: The Ramifications of a Female Household, 1558–1603', in D. Starkey (ed.), *The English Court from the Wars of the Roses to the Civil War* (1987).

[24] G. E. Aylmer, *The King's Servants: The Civil Service of Charles I, 1625–1642* (1961), 474–5, lists female officers in the households of the Queen and royal children. For an example of the range of female officers at the Court, see Book of Warrants (Charles II), PRO LS 13/252. I am grateful to Gerald Aylmer for this reference.

[25] PRO E351/2838, E351/440. Thanks to Sybil Jack for this information and references.

[26] See, e.g., *The Accounts of the Wardens of the Parish of Morebath, Devon, 1520–1573*, ed. J. E. Binney (Exeter, 1904); R. Graham, 'The Civic Position of Women at Common Law before 1600', in R. Graham, *English Ecclesiastical Studies* (1919), 371–4.

[27] Ibid. 376; J. R. Kent, *The English Village Constable, 1580–1642* (1986), 58–9.

[28] Devon RO, Quarter Sessions Order Book, 1, 1625–1633, fo. 6. Elizabeth Attwill, widow, was ordered 'to execute the office of a tithingman by her deputy for this yeare'.

midwives refused to murder, but, when questioned, lied to the King, saying that the women were all delivered before they got there. The comment in the Geneva Bible of 1560 was that 'their disobedience herein was lawful, but their dissembling evil'.[29] In 1593 the famous divine William Perkins concluded that they were commended for their faith, not for any lying.[30] There was thus a general sense that, in performing the public office of midwife, women should put their duty to God before any other issue, but that they should be clear in their consciences about telling the truth.

Midwives had duties in courts in cases relating to the consummation of marriages, and the births and paternity of children. They examined women verbally and physically and swore details about the virginity of women, the paternity of children, and monstrous births.[31] In the notorious case of the annulment of the marriage of Frances Howard and the Earl of Essex in 1616, the midwives performed the examination of the Lady Frances in the presence of three ladies of high social status, who then presented the evidence to the commission. In this important case, the verdict depended on the testimony of women.[32] Midwives and other women were involved in witchcraft cases to search for signs of the devil's mark. For example, in 1664 six women were directed to search a suspect, and, in another case in 1699, to examine the corpse of a suspected witch.[33] At the Assizes, a jury of matrons was sworn to examine convicted women who pleaded pregnancy.[34] In all these instances, society expected that women's responsibility to tell the truth, according to their office and licence, would override any moral obligation to other women.

Searchers for the plague in early modern society were largely female and were likewise sworn to the truth. Those employed were frequently poor women, who were dependent on the charity of

[29] Geneva Bible.

[30] [William Perkins], *A Direction for a Government of the Tongue* (1593), 21.

[31] *The Book of Oaths* (1689), 161–5 (Midwife's oath); 250 (oath of jury of women). See also D. Harley, 'Historians as Demonologists: The Myth of the Midwife-Witch', *Social History of Medicine*, 3(1990), 10–11.

[32] Folger Shakespeare Library, MS V b 211, 'The Proceedings … Touching the Divorcement', fo. 51.

[33] M. Hale, *The Tryal of Witches . . . 1664*, in *A Short Treatise Touching Sheriffs Accompts* (1683), 36; Harley, 'Historians', 10–11.

[34] See, e.g., J. S. Cockburn (ed.), *Calendar of Assize Records. Surrey Indictments, James I* (1982), 104, 165, 276, 299.

civic authorities. In 1646, a year of the plague in Reading, the mayor administered an oath to the searcher that she would faithfully examine the bodies of the dead, and declare if the cause were plague.[35] Whatever conflicts this caused between kinship or neighbourly obligation were not a matter for the civic record, but for the searcher's own conscience.

Women who served as matrons and nurses in hospitals such as St Bartholemew's London had defined responsibilities.[36] In 1682 the governors of the hospital ordered that no one who dissented from the Church of England could serve the hospital with any commodity, and all officers were to receive the sacrament. In 1684 Susannah Cook, the cook, confessed that she had not taken the Anglican communion within the last twelve months, nor would she do so. She sacrificed her employment for her conscience by her refusal to conform.[37] Similarly, in 1699 a widow who was the sister of one ward, was discharged from St Bartholemew's for Roman Catholicism.[38] Other poor women served as public employees dispensing poor relief.[39]

In the early seventeenth century, women did not accept that the division between the public and the private restricted them to the world of the household. Being female was not a total disqualification from citizenship. A few women were still voting in parliamentary elections in the sixteenth and earlier seventieth centuries: the last recorded vote by a woman I know of was in 1654, but there may well be other later records.[40] In 1641, when Parliament required an oath from the citizens to support the cause of true religion, these Protestation returns included—as Sara Mendelson has discovered—a few women's names.[41] No women were exempt from the public duty of witnessing in legal trials or in Church

[35] J. M. Guilding (ed.) *Reading Records* (4 vols.; 1892–6), iv. 201; see also T. S. Forbes, 'The Searchers', *Bulletin of the New York Academy of Medicine* (1974), 1031–8.
[36] *Orders and Ordinances for the Better Government of the Hospitall of Bartholemewe the Lesse* (1652), 52–3.
[37] N. Moore (ed.), *The History of St Bartholemew's Hospital* (2 vols.; 1918), i. 339, 341–2.
[38] Ibid. i. 350–1.
[39] Willen, 'Women in the Public Sphere', 559–75.
[40] See D. Hirst, *The Representative of the People? Voters and Voting in England under the Early Stuarts* (Cambridge, 1975), 18–19. For the reference to a woman voting in Bristol in the 1654 election, I wish to thank Sarah Jones.
[41] Sara Mendelson, 'Women and Politics in Seventeenth-Century England' (unpublished paper, 1988). 164 women took the Protestation at St Mabyn, 149 at St Tudy (T. L. Stoate (ed.), *The Cornwall Protestation Returns* (Bristol, 1974), 189–91, 195–7).

court cases. Collectively, women as compurgators testified to the character of other women in the Church courts.[42]

During the Civil Wars in particular, women exercised their rights to petition Parliament for justice, and to demonstrate.[43] According to common law, if women banded together 'for their own cause', such as to demand corn if they were starving, then they would not be punished for riot, provided no men had been involved.[44] In practice, female protests were not always viewed indulgently. In 1608 women and men in Lincolnshire who threw down hedges were prosecuted in Star Chamber.[45] In February 1642, as public affairs became contentious and war seemed likely, a group of gentlewomen and tradesmen's wives petitioned for peace. Recognizing that 'It may be thought strange, and unbeseeming in our sex, to shew our selves by way of Petition to this Honourable Assembly', the petitioners justified their action in religious terms. Christ had purchased women as well as men, so women too had the right to enjoy Christ. Further, as women shared in common calamities, including the unlimited power of the prelates 'to exercise authority over the Consciences of Women, as well as Men', then Scripture authorized female action. While not seeking equality with men, the petitioners claimed that they were discharging 'that duty we owe to God, and the cause of the church.'[46] When the petition was delivered by Mrs Anne Stagg, a gentlewoman, on 4 February 1642, John Pym's response was unsympathetic: 'We intreat you to repaire to your Houses, and turn your Petition . . . into prayer at home for us.'[47] Pym's view was not an isolated one. There are may examples of men in authority during the seventeenth century telling women that they would do better to direct their energies into prayer at home, or, more crudely, to 'look after your own businesse, and meddle with your huswifery'.[48] One MP told a

[42] R. A. Houlbrooke, 'Women's Social Life and Common Action in England from the Fifteenth Century to the Eve of the Civil War, *Continuity and Change*, i (1986), 174.

[43] P. Higgins, 'The Reactions of Women, with Special Reference to Women Petitioners', in B. Manning (ed.), *Politics, Religion and the English Civil War* (1973).

[44] W. Lambarde, *Eirenarcha, or of the Office of the Justice of the Peace* (1614), 180; M. Dalton, *The Country Justice* (1618), 196.

[45] R. B. Manning, *Village Revolts: Social Protest and Popular Disturbances in England, 1509–1640* (Oxford, 1988), 97.

[46] *A True Copie of the Petition of the Gentlewomen, Tradesmens-Wives, in and about the City of London* (1641[2]).

[47] Ibid. [7].

[48] *Perfect Occurrences*, no. 121 (20–7 Apr. 1649), 988.

gentlewoman who attended the House on 23 April 1649 with many hundreds of women petitioning for the release of the imprisoned Leveller leaders 'that it was not for women to petition, they might stay at home and wash their dishes'. The newsbook gave the last word to the woman: 'she answered, Sir, we have scarce any dishes left us to wash, and those we have we are not sure to keep them.'[49] While accepting her domestic and wifely role, she enlarged the household boundaries to include a responsibility for public action. Women could transform domestic duties into matters of public concern.

So there were several areas where some women claimed, and were recognized as possessing, formal public duties. Informally, highly placed ladies could tender political advice, as did the Countess of Westmorland over the Scots war in 1639. She apologized for her intervention—'to medle in things above us is dangerous'—but argued that her interest in 'the children unborne, inforceth me to utter my minde'.[50] Yet, although some women could participate in politics, others experienced their society as restrictive: Margaret Cavendish complained that 'we are never imployed either in civil nor marshall affaires . . . our counsels are despised, and laught at'.[51]

But there was one area where women claimed public duties for themselves which led to contention, namely, religion. In matters of belief and practice, women could be called upon to act in public. Everyone conceded the right of conscience to all believers. While women may have practised religion in private, faith was also a matter of public worship and profession. Some women's religious beliefs took them into the public sphere, where they challenged male authority.

PRIVATE CONSCIENCE AND PUBLIC DUTY

Religion was the main sphere in which women were called upon to answer for themselves. While they were not responsible for the public formulation of religious policy, they were expected to have religious beliefs, and to act upon their consciences. Conscience,

---

[49] *Mercurius militaris, or The People's Scout*, 17–24 Apr. 1649, 13.

[50] PRO SP 16/420, fo. 70, Countess of Westmorland to Secretary Windebanke, 6 May 1639.

[51] M. Cavendish, *The Philosophical and Physical Opinions* (1655), sig. B. v.

the individual's guide, was not in itself a gendered concept. The notion of conscience was constructed differently after the Reformation. Protestants abolished the Catholic practice of auricular confession by which clergy informed the laity of their duties. Instead, divines sought to guide individual consciences through sermons and advice. In 1603 William Perkins argued that conscience was 'a part of the understanding in all reasonable creatures'. Because he believed that it was 'a naturall power, facultie, or created qualitie', his arguments allowed that even those who were commonly thought to lack knowledge could be endowed with conscience. Conscience was not a matter of human law, but rather of God's law.[12] Human law was not binding in the same way as the word of God.[13]

Divines acknowledged that women had consciences and were responsible to them. One author dedicated his treatise on conscience to his sister in Queen Mary's time,[14] and Thomas Fuller dedicated his to the countess of Rutland in 1647.[15] Few of the Protestant casuists discussed specifically female dilemmas of conscience. However, they did, by implication, discuss the duties owed by women as well as men. For example, obedience to the ten commandments was a public responsibility for all Christians, and individuals were invited to examine their consciences under each head. A treatise of 1602 interrogated women about their breaches of the sixth commandment, thou shalt not kill: had they caused miscarriages by 'medicines, or labor, or dancing, or any other means', and had they tenderly nursed their babes?[16] Thomas Fenner in 1640 argued that no magistrates could bind the conscience when they commanded anything contrary to God's word, although, if the doctrine were pure, they might limit Christian liberty in the matter of eats, drinks, times, and garments.[17] Catholic casuists gave more detailed guidance. They permitted wives of non-Catholic husbands to maintain priests out of their husbands' property, since it was a husband's duty to provide priests. Confessors were to

---

[12] W. Perkins, *A Discourse of Conscience* (Cambridge, 1596), 1–3.

[13] Ibid. 40. See also Lord Brooke, *Two Speeches* (1642), 6–7.

[14] A. Kingsmill, *A Most Excellent and Profitable Treatise* (1585), preface by F. Mylles, sigs. Aii–Aiiii.

[15] T. Fuller, *The Cause and Cure of a Wounded Conscience* (1647).

[16] A. Gerardus, *The True Tryall and Examination a Mans Owne Selfe* (1602), 109–10.

[17] W. Fenner, *The Souls Looking-Glasse* (Cambridge, 1640), 299–300.

permit wives to prepare meat for their husbands on a fast day, no doubt to reduce domestic conflict.[58]

Contemporaries recognized praiseworthy examples of women whose conscientious beliefs led to their deaths. Martyrs for the Protestant cause were well known through the work of John Foxe. His *Acts and Monuments* offered powerful emotional examples of female disobedience for the sake of conscience, such as that of Anne Askew, a gentlewoman, who had discarded her husband's name after he evicted her from their home for her Protestant views. Askew was also defended by John Bale, who argued that a woman could depart from an unbelieving husband.[59] At the other end of the scale, a poor woman from Exeter, Agnes Priest, withstood her husband and children who were Catholic, as well as the bishop's court. She left her Catholic family and was earning her living by spinning, but they brought her home, and her neighbours accused her. Foxe told the story of the bishop asking her why she meddled with high matters, such as the body of Christ: 'Keep thy work, and meddle with what thou hast to do. It is no women's matters.' Berated as a bad wife, she said she would rather forsake her husband than Christ: 'I am contented to stick only to Christ my heavenly spouse, and renounce the other.' Foxe said that, although she was called 'an Anabaptist, a mad woman, a drunkard, a whore, a runagate', she continued to claim 'God is my Father, God is my Mother'.[60] Foxe's eulogy encouraged other Protestant women to defy earthly obedience for Christ.

In Catholic hagiography, Margaret Clitheroe, Anne Wiseman, and others, while not officially canonized, were revered as women who had died for their faith. During the Elizabethan period, many women who resisted alterations of faith pleaded their consciences. For example, a standard plea for a woman's non-attendance at the Anglican church before the ecclesiastical courts at York was 'because her conscience will not serve her', or 'she thinketh she should offend God'.[61] Straight lying could also be justified for the sake of faith. As Lady Throckmorton explained, Catholics could lie 'without touche of Conscience for our Englishe books where

[58] P. J. Holmes (ed.), *Elizabethan Casuistry* (Catholic Record Soc., 67; 1981), 29, 119.

[59] J. Foxe, *Acts and Monuments*, ed. J Pratt (8 vols.; 4th edn., 1870), v. 537–50; *Select Works by John Bale*, ed. H. Christmas (Parker Soc.; 1849), 180, 199.

[60] Foxe, *Acts and Monuments*, viii. 497–503.

[61] J. Morris (ed.), *The Troubles of our Catholic Forefathers* (3 vols.; 1872–7), iii. 248–59.

upon they should be sworne, were but the bookes of heritiques &
of no force before God'.[62]

In practice, the operation of conscience was affected by gender.
Later authors have not devoted much attention to the gender
dimension of casuistry.[63] Mosse, in his interesting study of the
conflicts between Christian ethics and the idea of reason of State,
used cases involving women for his general theme but did not
consider how gender affected contemporary debates or his own
arguments.[64] Yet contemporaries regarded female conscience as
more of a problem than male conscience because women, since
the time of Eve, had been led astray by wilfulness and carnal
reasoning. Female conscience was less reliable.

During the 1640s and 1650s the dangers of using individual
judgement as a guide to public duty were widely apparent. By the
end of the seventeenth century, educatèd men were suspicious of
conscience as a guiding principle. Locke saw conscience as 'nothing
else, but our own Opinion or Judgment of the Moral Rectitude
and Pravity of our own Actions'.[65] Individual judgement could
always be mistaken. This was an intellectual shift which dis-
advantaged the way in which the workings of female conscience
were viewed. Since women's knowledge and judgement were widely
thought to be weak, there was less tolerance of their pleas of
conscience when it was no longer an innate, natural, and human
quality. The difficulties over allowing pleas of conscience to justify
female insubordination were one reason why political thinkers
modified their views.

During the seventeenth century, conflicts between female conscience and wifely obedience worried contemporaries. Married
women were to be subject to their husbands, but contemporaries
were unsure of the extent to which a wife's conscience was in her
husband's keeping. In the Church courts before the Civil Wars,
one man, Edward Harding, was accused of refusing to allow his
wife and daughter to receive the sacrament. The indictment stated

---

[62] PRO SP 12/173/26(1), the examination of Joane Morley, 1584.

[63] e.g. T. Wood, *English Casuistical Divinity during the Seventeenth Century. With Special Reference
to Jeremy Taylor* (1952); E. Rose, *Cases of Conscience: Alternatives Open to Recusants and Puritans
under Elizabeth I and James I* (Cambridge, 1975); K. T. Kelly, *Conscience: Dictator or Guide? A
Study in Seventeenth-Century English Protestant Moral Theology* (1967).

[64] G. L. Mosse, *The Holy Pretence: A Study in Christianity and Reason of State from William
Perkins to John Winthrop* (Oxford, 1957).

[65] J. Locke, *An Essay Concerning Human Understanding* (Oxford, 1975), I. iii, 8.

'that you ye sd Edward Harding was Master of their consciences, and they should do what you thought fit'.[66]

The exercise of female conscience was central to a fundamental issue of English political life before the Civil Wars: what was the extent of the duty of obedience, and what was to be done if individuals entrusted with authority did not behave properly?[67] The difficulty facing those who approved of both the integrity of the individual and the conventional virtues of the ideal woman was to reconcile these two notions. How far did the duty of wifely obedience extend? Casuists wrestled with the problem posed by unbelieving husbands, as they did with the contradictory messages in Scripture about the duty of the citizen's obedience. Whereas Romans 13 affirmed the duty of unconditional obedience, Acts 5. 29 enjoined duty to God rather than to man.[68] Most contemporaries recognized that wives could do little about violent and immoral husbands, apart from remonstrating.[69] Gouge warned husbands not to abuse their authority so as to pit it against God's in the consciences of wives.[70] Religious unbelief was a more difficult matter. The conclusion of earlier commentators, that the duty to God overrode any duty to an unbelieving husband, was proving more vexatious when Protestantism was the established faith. Catholic wives of Protestant husbands were more common than the reverse, and some wives were attracted to religious separatism. To authorize wifely disobedience meant that women could leave their husbands' church to join what they believed, in their consciences, to be a true church. It was a dangerous licence. Thus, in 1608, the author of *Counsel to the Husband* was advising that, if a husband were neglecting his household religious duties, a wife might counsel him to amend, but do nothing more.[71] Around the same date, a wife's desire to leave her husband was being seen as a sign of psychic disturbance.[72] By the 1630s the dangers inherent

---

[66] Bodl. MS Rawl. 382, fos. 121–7. My thanks to Sara Mendelson for this reference.

[67] Sharpe, 'Commonwealth of Meanings', 16.

[68] C. Russell, *The Causes of the English Civil War* (Oxford, 1990), 66. See also below, pp. 113–14.

[69] S. Amussen, 'Gender, Family and the Social Order, 1560–1725', in A. Fletcher and J. Stevenson (eds.), *Order and Disorder in Early Modern England* (Cambridge, 1985), 201.

[70] Gouge, *Of Domesticall Duties*, 374.

[71] Quoted by Sharpe, 'Commonwealth of Meanings', 59.

[72] M. MacDonald, *Mystical Bedlam: Madness, Anxiety and Healing in Seventeenth-Century England* (Cambridge, 1981), 101–2.

in the difference of faith were so troubling that William Gouge published four pages in 1634 which had been suppressed in the 1622 and 1627 editions of *Of Domesticall Duties*, arguing that no woman should marry an unbeliever.[73] The marriage of Charles I to a Catholic wife was one prominent case where contemporaries thought that the King's insistence on more wifely obedience would further the cause of the true Protestant religion.

Heresiographers continually attacked wives who asserted independence of conscience. Ephraim Pagitt castigated an independent congregation who taught that a wife might put away her husband 'if he will not follow her in a new Church way which she pleaseth to imbrace'. Pagitt also cited with disapproval the case of Dorothy Traske, a wife whose conscience was not guided by her husband. The Traskes were imprisoned in 1618 for their sabbatarian views. Dorothy lived an ascetic life there, refusing her husband sexual relations, 'saying that they were committed to suffer'. When he recanted in 1620 and was released, she refused to alter her views, and remained in prison until her death in 1645. Contemporaries viewed her as a good Christian, but marred with 'a spirit of strange unparallel'd opiniativeness and obstinacy in her private conceits'. Pagitt argued strongly against the view that she would be justified by her strict asceticism and piety, for what he called 'true love' of Christ was the only way to salvation.[74]

More evidence about women's own views of their consciences has survived from the Civil War period. In the sects, the public and private boundaries were understood differently. The worship of God remained a public matter, but discipline and the admission of members were private Church business in which women as well as men participated.[75] Although women held no Church offices in the sects, they took responsibility for the public state of the Church. 'This was I moved to write to clear my conscience of thee,' declared the Quaker Anne Audland, later Camm, to the minister of Banbury.[76] Many women who published their writings in seventeenth-century England claimed that they published under com-

---

[73] Gouge, *Of Domesticall Duties* (1634 edn.), 193–6. The signatures of the 1622 edition between sig. N4 and sig. O3 indicate the suppression of the four pages.

[74] PRO SP 16/427/107; E. Pagitt, *Heresiography* (6th edn., 1661), 209–13; *Biographical Dictionary of British Radicals*, ed. R. Greaves and R. Zaller (3 vols.; Brighton, 1982), iii. 251–2.

[75] P. Crawford, 'Historians, Women and the Civil War Sects', *Parergon*, 6 (1988), 26.

[76] A. Audland, *The Saints Testimony Finishing through Sufferings* (1655), 29.

pulsion: 'The word of the Lord came unto me, saying write, and again I say write.'[77] A sense of public responsibility for warning the nation of the consequences of sin was particularly strong among Quaker women: 'This Warning and Reproof . . . I dare not with hold from this my Native Land,' declared Elizabeth Redford.[78] The basis for Quaker women's public action was that the Lord made no difference of sex. As Elizabeth Bathurst explained, 'That as Male and Female are made one in Christ Jesus, so Women receive an Office in truth as well as Men, and they have a Stewardship, and must give an account of their Stewardship to the Lord, as well as the Men.'[79]

Conscience could be an imperative to public action, as the Quaker, Dorcas Dole, explained in publishing a message in 1683: 'in true love to your Immortal Souls, have I cleared my conscience.'[80] Significantly, the large number of Quaker women—seven thousand, it was claimed—who petitioned against tithes in 1659 based the justification for their public action on the argument about blood guilt: should they not act, the Lord would hold them 'guilty of innocent blood'. While 'it may seem strange to some that women should appear in so public a manner as this of tithes', this, the author—probably Mary Forster—observed, 'was the work of the Lord'.[81] Less spectacularly, other Quaker women risked their livelihoods to witness to the truth. Barbara Blaugdone, a schoolteacher who adopted plain speech and dress after she was converted to Quakerism, found that she lost her pupils: 'when I went into their Publick Places and Steeple-houses to speak ... they took their Children away from me, so that I lost all my Imployment.'[82] Within the Quaker movement, there was limited tolerance of women's claim to speak 'in the power of the Lord', or with authority, as we might say. Martha Simmonds, who attempted to speak prophetically at meetings in 1656 and 1657, was abused by male Quaker leaders: 'This is the truth from ye Lord God concerning thee Martha Simons . . . ye are out of ye truth, out of ye way, out of ye power,

---

[77] D. White, *A Diligent Search* [1659], 1.

[78] E. Redford, *A Warning* [1696], 2.

[79] E. Bathurst, *The Sayings of Women* (1683), 23.

[80] D. Dole, *Once more a Warning* (1683), 19.

[81] M. Forster, *These Several Papers was sent to the Parliament* (1659), 3; P. Crawford, 'Charles Stuart, that Man of Blood', *Journal of British Studies*, 16 (1977), 41–61.

[82] *An Account of the Travels, Sufferings & Persecutions of Barbara Blaugdone* (1691), 6.

out of ye wisdom & out of the Life of God.'[83] James Nayler told her 'that she sought to have the dominion & charged her to goe home and follow her calling'.[84]

Quaker women were not the only ones to feel responsible for a church's religious policy. Anne Wentworth left a Particular Baptist congregation because 'they declared me an *heathen* and a *publican* for *matters of conscience* in which I was faithful to the teachings of God'. Commanded by the Lord to prepare a testimony 'for public view', she separated from the husband who endeavoured to stop her, and declared that she would return only if she had freedom to publish for 'the *peace of my own soul* and *of the whole nation*'.[85]

Yet female defiance on the basis of conscience was viewed differently from male defiance. Thus, in the dispute over singing in the Horsleydown Particular Baptist congregation in the 1690s, the pastor Benjamin Keach abused the women who objected to communal public singing as puppets who had no views of their own, only those of their husbands. 'You have learnt a fine peace of Relidgon ha'nt you,' he told Mary Leader, the wife of the leading male dissident. 'I confess I am troubled to see you that are but a Babe should pretend to such knowledge above others . . . and then turning to her Husband Bror Luke Leader he said you have finely dragg'd her up.'[86] Keach could not accept that women had independent consciences.

Although there were changes in the public esteem accorded to conscience during the seventeenth century, women did not cease to justify their religious behaviour in terms of conscience. Conscience itself was understood variously, according to the women's beliefs. Among Quaker women, it was to be true to the spark of the divine within them, to witness to the Lord. Since their faith involved an abnegation of self, of gender, and of class, it was the Lord who acted, not the individual.[87] They were unabashed by

---

[83] Friends House Library, Markey MS, p. 120, Edward Burrough to Martha Simmonds, [late May] 1656.

[84] FHL Caton MS, vol. 3, 364–5. For a fuller discussion of Martha Simmonds, see P. Crawford, *Women and Religion in Early Modern England* (forthcoming).

[85] A. Wentworth, *A Vindication*, printed in E. Graham *et al.*, *Her Own Life: Autobiographical Writings by Seventeenth-Century Englishwomen* (1989), 183, 188.

[86] Angus Library, Regent's Park College, MS 2/4/1, Maze Pond [Particular Baptist], 1691–1745, fos. 31–59.

[87] P. Mack, 'Gender and Spirituality in Early English Quakerism, 1650–1665', in E. Potts Brown and S. M. Stuard (eds.), *Witnesses for Change: Quaker Women over Three Centuries* (New Brunswick, NJ, 1989), 43–53.

allegations of wildness or bedlam-like behaviour.[88] Other Anglican women, such as Bathsua Makin, Mary Astell, and Anne Halkett, tried to see that women's judgements were better informed, so that they would have surer guides within themselves. Makin's whole plea for the education of leisured women was so that they should know God: 'the great end of Arts and Tongues is the better to enable us to know God in Jesus Christ, and our own selves, that we may glorifie and enjoy him for ever.'[89] These Anglican women hoped that the moral precepts of Christianity would shape women's judgements and so influence their behaviour.

A final example of a woman insisting upon what she called 'her little liberty of conscience' comes from the household of the Anglican minister, Samuel Wesley, the father of John and Charles. When Susannah, taking a Non-juring position, refused to kneel at her husband's family prayers for King William, Samuel swore divine vengeance on himself 'if ever he touched me more or came into a bed with me before I had begged God's pardon and his'. Samuel was unpersuaded by her arguments that his oath was unlawful, and that he ought not to deprive her of her liberty of conscience. He left her and their six children, determined to be a naval chaplain. The case was submitted to various persons, but Susannah insisted that she saw no reason for asking God's or her husband's pardon 'for acting according to the best knowledge I have of things of that nature'. Samuel was dissuaded from his determination by a fellow minister, but, given Susannah's intransigence, it is not clear on what terms the couple resumed sexual relations. Seven years later Susannah continued to believe that no king of England 'can ever be accountable to his subjects for any mal-administrations or abuse of power'.[90]

Although some women in the separatist churches developed resistance strategies based on their own conscientious beliefs, there was limited scope for independent action. Despite the fact that women usually outnumbered men around two to one in the separatist churches, there were no signs of them developing concerted resistance as women to the power of men. Although they could have had collective power, they did not perceive it, and

[88] A. Docwra, *An Apostate Conscience Exposed* (1699), 28–9.

[89] [Bathsua Makin], *An Essay to Revive the Antient Education of Gentlewomen* (1673), 15.

[90] R. Walmsley, 'John Wesley's Parents: Quarrel and Reconciliation', *Proceedings of the Wesleyan Historical Soc.*, 29 (1953), 50–7.

so did not use it. Instead, their responses were individual. Some thought that consciences should remain a private matter. Hannah Ellis, a Particular Baptist, when urged to think of the sufferings of the martyrs in Queen Mary's days, replied, 'theye were as wise yt keept themselues out of ye fire and kept there conscience to themselues'.[91]

Women experienced less conflict than men between public duty and conscience. With a few exceptions, women were not tied to the formal constraints of public office, and it can be argued that they were freer to follow their consciences than were men. but gender constrained women in other ways. Women's duties as wives and good women conflicted with their duties as good Christians, in a way that men's duties as husbands and citizens never did. In many cases the voice of religious conscience triumphed over mere earthly wifely obedience. Conscience, as a woman's inward decision with reference to her view of God, stilled other conflicting voices. While the duty of wifely obedience was strongly preached and enforced, the voice of conscience, experienced as the commands of the Lord, could impel some women into public action. MPs might expostulate with women petitioners that, since they had given an answer to their husbands last week, the women should go home and be satisfied. Some women believed that this was insufficient, for they too had responsibility for public affairs: it was, after all, the habit of the Lord to act by his weakest instruments. Empowered by God, no social constraints could be allowed to restrict them. Conscience for women was no private matter to be left to one side or squared with public duty; it justified some women's wifely disobedience and their participation in English social and political life.

[91] Guildhall, Turners' Hall Meeting, MS 20228/1A, 3 Jan. 1672/3.

6

Private Conscience and Public Duty in the Writings of James VI and I

KEVIN SHARPE

Conscience: 'a man cannot steal, but it acuseth him; a man cannot swear but it checks him; a man cannot lie with his neighbour's wife but it detects him. 'Tis a blushing shame fac'd spirit that mutinies in a man's bosom ...'

2nd Murderer, *Richard III*, i. iv. 133–9

Let not our babbling dreams afright our souls;
Conscience is but a word that cowards use,
Devis'd at first to keep the strong in awe.
Our strong arms be our conscience, swords
our law.

Richard III, v. iii. 308–11.

'PRIVATE conscience' and 'public duty' are in our usage terms that usually imply opposites. Though numerous events and controversies—politicians' sexual indiscretions, the publication of offensive books, the responsibility for riot and disorder—belie a simple distinction between them, we adhere to a belief in the separateness of private and public spaces. Indeed, commitment to that separateness and the idea of the ownership of the self are fundamental to both modern psychology and the modern state. Almost from the time that the word became respectable, the business of politics has been that of a negotiation between the individual and the State, private interests and public interests. Indeed, the acceptance and validation of a world of politics—of contest and party, lobby and propaganda—marked a recognition of the artificiality of the social state, and of a public morality that might differ from the ethical values that governed personal behaviour. Brave would be the historian who endeavoured confidently to assign an exact date to, or list of causes for, what were truly revolutionary developments. But we know that by the end of the seventeenth century, despite lingering pejorative associations, parties had become enshrined in the social and political life of the nation; that the Toleration Act signalled a degree of separation of Church and State; and that the language of 'interest' had gained respectability.[1] Such developments, it has been suggested, were inextricably linked with a new attitude to the autonomous individual and a sphere of self-determination.[2] By the end of the seventeenth century the conscience was defined as part of that sphere: as, in Locke's words, 'nothing else but our own opinion or judgement of the moral rectitude or pravity of our own Actions'.[3]

Before the Civil War, however, such distinctions were not so readily made and ideas of conscience were correspondingly different and less individualistic. The normative texts of politics were the works of Aristotle and the Bible. Following Aristotle, it was held that the State was an ethical community and there was no contradiction between the good person, the good citizen, and the good ruler. The concept of the commonweal precluded clear delineation of the public and the private. The human body and 'self' were as much a part of the public as the 'body politic' was anthropomorphized. Because it was natural, the commonweal united all in one interest. Because all were members of a Christian commonweal that shaped its laws and codes according to God's decrees, there should no more have been contention over the 'right course' in public action than in private.[4] There was one God, one Scripture, and therefore—in theory—one conscience for the commonwealth. Conscience was the inner law-giver, the 'deity within us', that element of knowledge of God that remained even in fallen man. Those who claimed God or Scripture spoke to them differently from the prescriptions of the commonweal were, it was held, betrayed by a false conscience or pretended to conscience, *as they themselves knew*, out of evil intent. Nor, in this model, was conscience at odds with duty. Both implied a moral obligation, that is an obligation to a shared morality. The Geneva Bible's translation of Eccles. 12: 13 enjoined: 'Feare God and keep his

---

[1] See S. Zwicker, 'Lines of Authority: Politics and Literary Culture in the Restoration', in K. Sharpe and S. Zwicker (eds.), *Politics of Discourse: The History and Literature of Seventeenth-Century England* (1987), 230–70; also pp. 5–7.

[2] M. McKeon, *The Origins of the English Novel, 1600–1740* (1987).

[3] J. Locke, *An Essay Concerning Human Understanding* (1824 edn.), 25.

[4] Cf. K. Sharpe, *Politics and Ideas in Early Stuart England: Essays and Studies* (1989), 11–14.

commandments: for this is the duty of man."[5] Among God's commandments was obedience to divinely instituted authority. As the conscience was God's lieutenant in the soul, so the king was God's lieutenant in the commonweal, responsible for guiding the *respublica Christiana* according to the divine decrees. Loyalty to the king was an act of conscience as well as a duty and an interest. Resistance to the ruler was rebellion not only against God but against the self, the rise of ignorance and passion against the knowledge and reason which distinguished men from beasts.

Such ideal prescriptions had perhaps always been compromised by observed human experience: theological controversy, popular and baronial revolt, conflicting loyalty to family and ruler. But the rent of Christendom massively exacerbated the tensions and bequeathed to the era between the Reformation and the age of toleration fundamental practical and theoretical problems which could not be resolved nor even fully conceptualized within the prevailing paradigms. Many of those problems and questions—the nature of 'true religion', the extent of obedience to the prince, the relation of man to God and his fellows, the ends and organization of society and the State—were intimately bound up with and revolved around issues of 'conscience'. As old vocabularies and value systems lived on in radically new circumstances, the very word conscience, once a symbol of unity, was deployed to defend violence, rebellion, and division. As a consequence a few thinkers, most notably Niccolò Machiavelli, advocated the radical course of freeing public life and government from religion and morality. But, to an age which still hoped for an ecumenical solution to the division of Christendom, Machiavelli's secular politics were anathema.[6] Faced, then, with the enduring ideals of Christian humanism and the experience of religious division and contest, rulers and citizens had to define—and redefine—their own conscience. It is hardly surprising that in doing so they faced contradiction—not only from others, but also within themselves.

Often in early modern England the theatre staged (and attempted to contain) those contradictions. As our opening quotations remind us, Shakespeare glaringly presents a world in which conscience both preserves some of its unifying moral authority and yet lies at

[5] *Oxford English Dictionary*, s.v. 'Conscience'.
[6] Sharpe, *Politics and Ideas*, 25–8; F. Raab, *The English Face of Machiavelli* (1964).

the mercy of 'Machiavels'—illegitimate princes—who would subject it to personal ambition and force. It is no coincidence that, in the works of Shakespeare and other Elizabethan and Jacobean dramatists, we encounter debates about conscience in plays self announcedly about kings.[7] For many of the tensions and contradictions in early modern English society were examined through a notion which had an 'important heuristic function in the period of transition from medieval to modern political thought': the concept of the king's two bodies.[8] On the one hand, in his mystical body, the king was the head, the reason, the conscience of the commonweal, exemplifying the oneness of private and public, duty and interest. On the other, in his natural body, the king was 'but a man as I am', as Henry V puts it, having but 'human conditions' and being subject to human frailties.[9] The virtuous king was he who harmonized his natural to his mystical body, who subjected his passions to his reason, and so through his own example of wholeness applied holistic medicine to the body politic. Yet, even in the case of Shakespeare's good king, questions and tensions remained. The virtuous quality of sincerity required that the king display his 'crystal heart' to his subjects, but diplomacy and discretion, in Henry V's case even intercourse with his subjects, necessitated disguise and deceit. Though the king was responsible for his subjects, yet 'he is not bound to answer the particular endings'.[10] Similarly the king might keep the conscience and command the duty of the realm, 'but every subject's soul is his own' and it was for every subject to 'wash every mote out of his conscience'.[11] As Professor Goldberg reminds us, even this most heroic monarch and mirror for princes appears to different observers—within and outside the play—differently; 'whether he is most Machiavellian or most pious has divided critical response to him'.[12]

---

[7] As well as *Richard III*, *Richard II*, *Henry V*, *Lear*, *Hamlet*, and *The Winter's Tale* are obvious texts in which the king's conscience both faces dilemmas and is yet central to the integrity of the realm.

[8] See E. H. Kantorovicz, *The Kings's Two Bodies: A Study in Mediaeval Political Theology* (Princeton, NJ, 1957), *passim* and p. 447.

[9] E. Forset, *A Comparative Discourse of the Bodies Natural and Politique* (1606); D. G. Hale, *The Body Politic* (The Hague, 1971); Shakespeare, *Henry V*, Act IV, sc. i.

[10] *Henry V*, Act IV, sc. i.

[11] Ibid.

[12] J. Goldberg, *James I and the Politics of Literature* (Baltimore, Md., and London, 1983), 161. I am grateful to Jonathan Goldberg for his brilliant insights both in this work and in discussion.

Historians have similarly been as divided over their characterization of Tudor and Stuart monarchs. Was Henry VIII a ruthless manipulator of circumstance, or a man who sincerely governed himself as well as the polity according to his conscience? Was Charles I genuine in his claim to rule only for the weal of his people, or did he act—in *both* senses—only to establish his power as absolute? The historiographical differences of interpretation of 'actual rulers', like the critical disagreements about Henry V and other kings represented on the stage, owe much to the self-contradictions of the age and so especially of its rulers, particularly over questions of conscience and duty.[13] In one case, we are fortunate to have a monarch who not only reigned during the period of the richest dramatic representations of these tensions, but also, in (what we would delineate as) both public and more private genres of writing, contributed to the debate of these issues. Indeed it was in 1599, the year of the first performance of *Henry V*, that James VI penned his own reflections on kingship, the *Basilikon Doron* or 'His Majesty's Instructions to his dearest son, Prince Henry'.

James VI and I's most public pronouncements on kingship, as well as the *Basilikon Doron*, *The Trew Law of Free Monarchies*, the *Apology for the Oath of Allegiance*, the *Remonstrance for the Right of Kings*, and the speeches to Parliament, have been easily available in C. H. McIlwain's *The Political Works of James I* since 1918. It is surprising that they have attracted little critical study as political theory or discourse.[14] Perhaps even more regrettably, no study has been made of James's letters, devotional tracts, commentaries on Scripture, and, especially, his poetry as self-examinations and as self-explications of the king's person and concept of office. Central to any such investigation must be an understanding of James's perceptions of conscience and duty—his own, and his subjects' in a Christian commonweal—and of the contradictions within them.

In his most public and avowedly political works, James outlined what conscience and duty meant to him. No more for his subjects than for himself could they be divided. It was the duty of the

---

[13] The historiographical disagreements are especially heated for early modern British history, not least because the period set itself contrary criteria of judgement.

[14] They find no place in Quentin Skinner's survey, *The Foundations of Modern Political Thought* (2 vols.; Cambridge, 1978). See, however, L. Avack, *La ragione dei re. Il pensiero politico di Giacomo I* (Milan, 1974).

people to obey their sovereign 'in all things except directly against God', and subjects were 'bound to obey their princes for conscience sake'.[15] 'The bond of conscience', James once wrote to James Hamilton in Scotland, was 'the only sure bond for tying of men's affections to them whom to they owe a natural duty'.[16] Herein, of course, lay the central problem of the early modern state: if conscience were the foundation of the duty of obedience to princes, yet conscience informed some subjects that the ruler acted 'directly against God', how could monarchy and the commonweal survive? James himself conceded that it was the duty of the clergy to encourage disobedience of commands contrary to God's—'it is always better to obey God than man'—yet continued to maintain that there was no conflict, rather a harmony, between faith and allegiance.[17] In part this seeming contradiction was resolved in theory by another: the notion of civil obedience. In the case of his Catholic subjects, the King separated their civil obedience from their conscience. Never believing that 'the blood of any man shall be shed for diversity of opinions in religion', James left them to their 'opinion', requiring only subscription to an oath of allegiance.[18] That oath he regarded as the solution to the pull between conscience and the duty of obedience: 'I never conceived the difference between real obedience and promise by subscription to obey.'[19] However, the promise involved in an oath itself rested on one's obligation and accountability to God—in other words on conscience.[20] In order to reconcile the conscience and duty of his Catholic subjects, James was forced to separate what he intrinsically believed should be inviolable—the civic and the religious.

For, whilst his defence of the Oath of Allegiance seemed to imply it, elsewhere James denied that the sphere of conscience could be separated as a personal realm outside the public. In *A Premonition to All Most Mighty Monarchs* he went so far as to refute the sacred secrecy of the confessional when the public interest was

---

[15] *The Trew Law of Free Monarchies*, in *The Political Works of James I*, ed. C. H. McIlwain (Cambridge, Mass., 1918), 61; *Apology for The Oath of Allegiance*, ibid. 72; HMC, *Salisbury*, XV. 300, James I to Thomas Parry, Nov. 1603.

[16] *The Letters of King James VI and I*, ed. G. P. V. Akrigg, (1984), 166–7.

[17] *A Remonstrance for the Right of Kings*, in *Political Works*, 213.

[18] *Letters*, 204; *Apology for Oath of Allegiance*, in *Political Works*, 72 and *passim*.

[19] *Letters*, 223.

[20] See R. Sanderson, *De juramento: Seven Lectures Concerning the Obligation of Promisory Oaths* (1655), a work revised by Charles I.

at stake.[21] Most of all he was at pains to deny the Puritan claim to personal conscience, that is to a personal interpretation of what God ordained. Parity of conscience, he realized, would soon lead to equality (and hence anarchy) in the commonwealth.[22] Conscience was not identical with mere opinion: sinners confused the dictates of conscience with those of appetite, and many did 'prattle of' a conscience they did not feel.[23] True conscience was not opinion but knowledge, 'the light of knowledge that God hath planted in man'.[24] 'Conscience not grounded on knowledge', James once put it, 'is either an ignorant fantasy or an arrogant vanity.'[25] Knowledge of God came to man through Scripture, the principal tutor to the conscience. Therefore, 'in making the Scripture to be ruled by their conscience and not their conscience by the Scripture', the Puritans subverted conscience no less than they did authority.[26]

In matters of dispute, of course, the interpretation of Scripture rested with the Church. So, though on occasions he appears to regard conscience as an individual's personal negotiation with God, for the most part James believed in a 'common quality conscience' in which all (himself included) shared, rather than 'distinct individual consciences'.[27] Perhaps, he saw that acceptance of the idea of individual conscience ultimately threatened not only diversity of religious sects but moral and religious relativism. What most upset James about the teachings of Conrad Vorstius was his contention that God had 'some kind of diversity or multiplicity in himself yea even a beginning of a certain mutability'.[28] Against Vorstius no less than Montaigne, James reasserted a theoretical axiom of the early modern polity: 'God is unity itself and verity is one.'[29] But, though necessary, the belief in a common conscience of the commonweal

[21] *Political Works*, 167.

[22] James I, *A Meditation upon The Lords Prayer* (1619), 18: 'trust not to that private spirit or Holy Ghost which our Puritans glory in, for then a little fiery zeal will make thee turn separatist.'

[23] *The Basilikon Doron of King James VI*, ed. J. Craigie (2 vols.; Scottish Text Soc.; Edinburgh, 1944–50) i. 40, 124.

[24] Ibid. i. 40.

[25] James I, *Flores regii, or Proverbes and Aphorismes . . . Spoken By His Majesty* (1627), 104–5.

[26] *Basilikon Doron*, i. 16.

[27] *OED*, s.v. 'Conscience', history of usage.

[28] *A Declaration Concerning the Proceedings with the States General of the United Provinces . . . in the Cause of D. Conradus Vorstius*, in *The Workes of The Most High and Mighty Prince James* (1616), 365.

[29] Ibid. 372.

was fraught with difficulties and inconsistencies. For in certain passages the King discerns the light of conscience in all men. God, he concludes in the second book of the *Basilikon Doron,* has 'imprinted in men's minds by the very light of Nature the love of all moral virtues' and an awareness of wrongdoing.[30] Even malefactors retained, like Richard III's murderer, a sense of their own evil, a residual conscience which, as James described it in his *Daemonologie,* 'haunted' them, until 'the purging of themselves by amendment of life from such sins as have procured that extraordinary plague'.[31] But, if such were the case, why could not a man's conscience be autonomous? How was it that Puritans professed a conscience that was false or pretended, if God planted the light of his knowledge in all? Or, to put the question simply and fundamentally, why did all not agree about the right course for a Christian commonweal?

At times James wants to claim that they did. 'You know in your conscience', he told Members of the House of Commons in 1624, 'that of all the kings that ever were . . . never was king better beloved of his people than I am.'[32] But there is a silent *ought to* implicit before that 'know', a silent phrase that alone can bridge the gap between the theory of common conscience and James's experience, not least with his Parliaments, of fundamental disagreement. Whatever should be, conscience was not common to all. Their conscience led the Puritans to become a 'sect', as James described them, whose members 'refuse to obey the law and will not cease to stir up a rebellion'.[33] Theirs led the Powder Plotters into 'denying the king to be [their] lawful sovereign or the anointed of God'.[34] God had his own ways of expressing the dictates of true conscience. When Catesby and others were wounded when the powder for their plot exploded on them, James thought they were 'wonderfully stroken with amazement in their guilty consciences, calling to memory how God had justly punished them with that same instrument which they should have used for the effectuating of so great a sin'.[35] Yet it was the role of the State to lend some assistance even to 'the wonderful

[30] *Basilikon Doron,* i. 160.
[31] James I, *Daemonologie,* in *Workes of Prince James,* 125.
[32] *Cobbett's Parliamentary History of England,* i (1806), 1376.
[33] *Basilikon Doron,* i. 16.
[34] *A Discourse of the . . . Discoverie of the Powder Treason,* in *Workes of Prince James,* 231.
[35] Ibid. 245.

power of God's justice upon guilty consciences'. Accordingly, Guy Fawkes was imprisoned (and, not mentioned, tortured) to help him to 'advise upon his conscience'.[36] Conscience may have been to James the foundation of his authority, but, paradoxically, his authority was an essential prop of a true conscience. To answer the cynic, then, who would dismiss the whole notion as a disingenuous disguise for power, we must look at how James interpreted conscience and duty when he turned to examine his own.

Too much that has been written about the King's theory of divine right has failed to grasp that James saw his position as God's lieutenant not as a power but as a duty—and an awesome duty, in the sense of religious observance as well as feudal obligation, at that. 'Being born to be a king,' he instructed Prince Henry, 'ye are rather born to ONUS than HONOS: not excelling all your people so far in rank and honour as in daily care and hazardous pains in the dutiful administration of that great office that God hath laid upon your shoulders.'[37] A king owned himself even less than private men. For the commonweal, James wrote in 1593, 'I am born more than for myself'.[38] Even as a parent, a king did not own his son. Henry was 'not ours only as the child of a natural father, but as an heir apparent to our body public in whom our state and kingdom are essentially interested'.[39] If the king's body and flesh were not his own, no more was his conscience. As in his mystical form he was head of the body politic, so the king's conscience was not only personal but the conscience of the realm. James was explicit about how his conscience was bound to the codes of the polity that it was his duty to rule—to law, justice, and equity. 'Certainly,' as he put it in *The Trew Law of Free Monarchies*, 'a king that governs not by his law can neither be countable to God for his administration.'[40] 'A King that will rule and govern justly', he told his parliamentary audience in March 1610, 'must have regard to conscience ... '[41]

Now, our cynic (or Dr Sommerville) might point out that justice was the king's justice and that the laws too were—James himself

[36] Ibid. 241.
[37] *Basilikon Doron*, i. 6–7.
[38] *Letters*, 25.
[39] HMC Salisbury, xv. 302.
[40] *Political Works*, 63.
[41] Ibid. 318.

used the possessive—'his'. The conscience of the king's mystical self was then one and the same with his personal conscience and so autonomous and untrammelled. James, however, had sworn a coronation oath to see law, justice, mercy, and truth maintained, and felt himself as bound to execute that promise as were the Catholics by the Oath of Allegiance.[42] It had been, he recalled in a speech of 1616, his principal care to keep his conscience clear in all points of his coronation oath.[43] For an oath was to God as well as to the other party and so, as Bishop Sanderson was to put it, 'not to be taken with a relucting and unsatisfied conscience'.[44] That conscience was inextricably part of the honour of the king, 'without which', James proclaimed in 1607, 'I have no being'.[45] Indeed, so much was the king's conscience the realm's as much as the king's own that at times, it would appear, he came close to subordinating his 'private conscience' for the sake of the commonweal. Where his policy towards the papists was concerned, for example, 'I must', James acknowledged in a speech in the Lords, 'put a difference betwixt mine own private profession of mine own salvation and my politic government of the realm for the weal and quietness thereof.'[46] He did so because, 'as I would be loather to dispence in the least point mine own conscience for any worldly respect than the foolishest precisian of them all; so would I be as sorry to straight the politique government of the bodies and minds of all my subjects to my private opinions ...'[47] In theory, of course, in the ideal commonweal there should have been no such disjuncture. The king's personal and public consciences should have accorded with each other and those of his subjects. The reality was otherwise. The reality of politics threatened the separation of the king's two bodies at a time when their conjunction was essential for—indeed was a device for—the cohesion of the body politic.[48] It was not least because he fully grasped that necessity that James struggled to reconcile and to harmonize all those consciences: to be (as we shall argue) the

---

[42] See *The Ceremonies, Form of Prayer and Services Used in Westminster Abbey at the Coronation of King James 1st* (1685).
[43] *Political Works*, 329.
[44] Sanderson, *De juramento*, 144, 197–8, 236, 269.
[45] *Political Works*, 298.
[46] Ibid. 274.
[47] Ibid.
[48] Cf. Sharpe, *Politics and Ideas*, 61–3, 68–9.

crystal mirror in and through which his subjects could come to a
shared knowledge of God.

In the first place, James went to some lengths to remove and
deny any barrier between his private and public selves. Kings, he
advised Prince Henry, should have no secret thoughts that they
were afraid publicly to avouch. A prince ought to keep 'agreeance
and conformity . . . betwixt his outward behaviour and the virtuous
qualities of his mind'.[49] 'By the outward using of your office . . .
testify the inward uprightness of your heart.'[50] 'I never with God's
grace', he once wrote to Cecil, taking his own counsel, 'shall do
anything in private which I may not without shame proclaim upon
the tops of houses.'[51] Because discourse was 'the true image' of
the king's mind (a 'testament' as he called the *Basilikon Doron*), it
was important that monarchs spoke and wrote what they meant.[52]
Accordingly James vowed to his Parliament that he would promise
nothing which he intended not to deliver.[53] His 'tongue should
ever be the true messenger of his heart'.[54] Today we would be
inclined to interpret this as a *claim* to sincerity—something we tend
to doubt in public figures, dismissing such talk as itself political
rhetoric or strategy. And this is the point. James was intending
more than to secure belief in his word. He was specifically opposing
those Machiavels who sought to justify deceit and disguise as
stratagems of power in an amoral political universe.[55] And his
counter-argument not only opposed Machiavellian premises; it
deployed to opposite purpose Machiavelli's own language. As a
king James spoke 'without artifice'; 'as a prince', he wrote to
Elizabeth, perhaps choosing his self-description carefully, 'it
becomes me not to feign'.[56] In 1621, subverting the metaphors of

---

[49] *Basilikon Doron*, i. 15.

[50] Ibid. i. 200.

[51] *Letters*, 192.

[52] *Basilikon Doron*, i. 21–2.

[53] *Political Works*, 305.

[54] Ibid. 280.

[55] Though Machiavelli was not available in English until 1640, *The Prince* was translated
into Scotch by W. Fowler, a Court poet, who contributed a celebratory verse to James's
own collections of poems. See *His Maiesties Poetical Exercises at Vacant Houres* (Edinburgh,
1591), sig. 4; *The Essayes of a Prentise in the Divine Art of Poesie* (Edinburgh, 1585), sig. 3v; *The
Poems of James VI of Scotland*, ed. T. Craigie (2 vols.; Scottish Text Soc.; Edinburgh, 1955–
8), i. xxii.

[56] *Commons Debates 1621*, eds. W. Notestein, F. H. Relf, and H. Simpson (7 vols.; New
Haven, Conn., 1935), v. 85; *Letters*, 162.

The Prince, he condemned orators who 'fox-like . . . seem to speak
one thing and intend another'.[57] The King's own discourse was
itself a denial of the new 'politics' and a reassertion of the
Aristotelian premiss that the good ruler and the good man were
one. Because the political reality was otherwise, and James was
a shrewd observer, that realization crept into his speech even
as he sought to deny it. He knew and evidently articulated that
'in civil actions he is the greater and deeper politic that can
make other men the instruments of his will and ends and yet
never acquaint them with his purpose'.[58] But knowing was not
accepting, and certainly not authorizing: James's use of 'politic'
here appears pejorative. Elsewhere he is forcefully condemnatory
of deceptions. It was a '*tyrant*', he told Cecil in 1604, who gave
'fair words till he had gotten his turn done, and then but have
kept his promise as he had thought convenient'.[59] A 'just king'
opened his mind 'freelier'. Whatever the politic might do, James
would swear: 'never shall I for compulsion either speak, promise
or write otherwise than I think and that which is honest.'[60]
And his subjects could then place trust in his meaning as 'ever
one and alike in all his royal resolutions'.[61]

James's denial of the rhetoric of artifice and dissimulation
had a purpose beyond a negation of Machiavellian politics—a
more constructive, or perhaps we should say *re*constructive,
purpose. In his written tracts and in speech after speech James
went to great lengths to display to his subjects, and to assure
them that he was displaying, 'the true image of my very mind'.[62]
He expressed his wish to Parliament 'that there were a crystal
window in my breast wherein all my people might see the
secretest thoughts of my heart'.[63] In 1610 he offered a 'rare
present', 'a fair and crystal mirror ... such a mirror or crystal
as through the transparentness thereof you may see the heart
of your king'.[64] In 1621 he delivered yet again 'a true mirror
of my mind'.[65] The recurrence and doubleness of the metaphor
is important. The word *crystal* had a dual meaning in early
modern England: the crystal was, as we understand it, transparent;
it was also another term for a mirror, which, of course, reflects.

---

[57] *Commons Debates 1621*, ii. 12.   [58] *Flores regii*, 125; cf. *Commons Debates 1621*, iv. 72.
[59] *Letters*, 240.   [60] Ibid. 68.   [61] HMC, *Salisbury*, xvi. 395.
[62] *Basilikon Doron*, i. 22.   [63] *Political Works*, 285.
[64] Ibid. 306.   [65] *Commons Debates 1621*, ii. 2.

James, I would suggest, intended both. In 1618, in *The Peace-Maker or Great Britain's Blessing*, he described honour as a rumour of virtuous action which redounded from the soul, to the world and, by reflection, on to ourselves.[66] Conscience, we have seen, was often coupled by James with his honour. Because the king was God's lieutenant, when the subject looked into the king's heart he looked as through a crystal at God's laws and decrees, the codes of his own conscience. When he looked at the mirror of the king's mind, he saw how his own conscience fell short of God's decrees as they were reauthorized (that is rewritten and revalidated) by the king. That is why James believed it 'necessary that a king should deliver his thoughts to his people'.[67] Mediating God's will and decrees as his lieutenant, the virtuous king might become an image of God and a pattern for men, acting like God, in 'wakening up their zeal' for the good.[68] This was the duty of authority, 'persuasion and example of life being more proper means to reclaim men's consciences than compulsion'.[69]

Kings most fulfilled their duty, then, when they not only acted according to, but enacted and transmitted, the will of God. As James put it in a speech in Star Chamber on 20 June 1616, 'No king can discharge his accompt to God unless he make conscience . . . to declare and establish the will of God.'[70] The king, in other words, was not only God's lieutenant; he was—both in actions and discourse—his exegete. We are familiar with the concept that the king as head was the reason of the body politic. But we do not always accord it the deep theological meaning that reason carried: the idea of acting divinely, according to the 'light of knowledge that God had planted in man', before the Fall, a light that still flickered in all and shone in the godly.[71] By acting as a representation of Christ, the king might kindle that light in his subjects. Prince Henry, therefore, was advised by his father in words that Christ had spoken: 'let it not be said that you command others to keep the contrary course to that which in your own person you practise.'[72] Following that counsel himself, James vowed

---

[66] *The Peace-Maker or Great Britain's Blessing* (1618), sig. D4.
[67] *Proceedings in Parliament 1610*, ed. E. R. Foster (2 vols.; New Haven, Conn., 1966), i. 45.
[68] *Daemonologie*, in *Workes of Prince James*, 126.
[69] *Commons Debates 1621*, v. 426.
[70] *Political Works*, 327.
[71] See above, n. 24.
[72] *Basilikon Doron*, i. 102.

to follow that 'alike Christian as politic rule to measure as I would be measured unto'.[73] 'Peace be with you', James took as the fit 'motto of a king' because 'the blessing of a God'.[74]

James's tracts, speeches, and letters contain constant applications of Scripture to issues and problems of State. Scripture was for him a text of State because the Christian and political realms were one and shared a discourse. 'Let our souls be bound for our bodies,' he urged in 1618, 'our bodies for our souls, and let each come in at the General Sessions to save his bail, where he shall find a merciful judge.'[75] No less than his actions, the King's words, his *Works*, were mediations of God's will', as revealed in Scripture. Their function, as Bishop Montagu saw it when he introduced them to their readers in 1616, was to operate on men's consciences so that they might be 'converted by them'.[76] James described his own *Basilikon Doron* as a 'discharge of our conscience'.[77] *Basilikon Doron* means the royal gift. James so described others of his works, dedicated to Prince Charles or the Duke of Buckingham. In a larger sense, they were, when published, gifts to all his subjects. For, by bringing readers closer to God, leading them to know him, James might indeed convert men by bringing them to the knowledge of God, which, when shared, united all in a Christian commonweal. The author (writer/authorizer) of the tag to the frontispiece to James's works was the earthly no less than the heavenly king: 'Ecce do tibi animum sapientem et intelligentem.'[78]

A king who saw it as his duty to be an apostle as well as a prince, to mediate God's word and will, faced an awesome responsibility to ensure the uprightness of his own conscience. And, in the main, he faced it alone. It may be the duty of MPs 'upon *your* consciences plainly to determine' for 'the weal both of your king and your country'.[79] And the king had his counsellors, bishops, and chaplains close to his bosom. But these were men chosen 'out of my own judgement and conscience' who owed loyalty and service to their

---

[73] *Letters*, 181.
[74] *The Peace-Maker*, sig. A4.
[75] Ibid. sig. E4ᵛ.
[76] *Works . . . of Prince James*, epistle to the Reader.
[77] *Basilikon Doron*, i. 22.
[78] *Serenissimi Potentissimi Principis Jacobi . . . Opera* (1619), motto at foot of frontispiece depicting the figures of Religion and Peace.
[79] *Political Works*, 288.

master.[80] The acclaim of others could not be relied upon as a mark of the king's virtuous courses. Reputation, James once wrote, was but other men's 'opinion'—and for that a prince should not risk his soul.[81] Ultimately the keeper of the nation's conscience was alone—with his own, before God. In his epistle to the Reader of 'His Majesty's Instructions to his . . . son', James explained his resolution 'ever to walk as in the eyes of the Almighty, examining ever so the secretest of my drifts, before I gave them course, as how they might some day bide the touchstone of a public trial'.[82] Kings had, he put it in the *Trew Law*, 'the count of their administration' to give to God.[83] Not only was that an account more strict than that any other servant owed his master; it was a count of each and every word and deed. Justice demanded of kings that, 'as we reign by [God's] grace ... we should turn all our energies and thoughts to His glory'.[84] This was not rhetoric. Every day, James commanded his son, he should take the reckoning with himself, his conscience, and his God:

remember ever once in the four and twenty hours, either in the night or when ye are at greatest quiet, to call yourself to account of all your last days actions, either wherein ye have committed things ye should not, or omitted the things ye should do, either in your Christian or kingly calling: in that account let not yourself be smoothed over with that flattering $\Phi i \lambda a \mu \tau i a$ ... but censure yourself as sharply as if ye were your own enemy.[85]

Never, he concluded 'ever wilfully or willingly . . . contrare your conscience'. The king more than any must fear as well as serve God.[86] 'Let hell afright thee', he advised his fellow rulers, 'and let thy conscience describe it to thee'.[87] When alone taking the count of his obedience and service to God, the king needed only to turn to Scripture—'the statutes of your heavenly king'—to determine whether he had acted (as good kings should) as a true subject of *his* sovereign.[88] 'Would ye then know your sin by the law? read the books of Moses . . . Would ye know . . . Christ? looke the

---

[80] *Letters*, 261.
[81] *The Peace-Maker*, sig. D4.
[82] *Basilikon Doron*, i. 12.
[83] *Political Works*, 54.
[84] *Letters of the Kings of England*, ed. J. O. Halliwell (2 vols.; 1848), ii. 68.
[85] *Basilikon Doron*, i. 44.
[86] Ibid. 5, 'The Argument'.
[87] *The Peace-Maker*, sig. C2. [88] *Basilikon Doron*, i. 5.

Evangelists.'[89] With Scripture, especially the books of Kings and Chronicles, James told his son, he should be familiarly acquainted: 'for there will ye see yourself (as in a mirror) either among the Catalogues of the good or evil kings.'[90] Self-knowledge, conscience, the same as the knowledge of God, came from meditation upon *His* word, as in turn the King's *Works* written and enacted were the mirror in which subjects saw their God and themselves.

It is in this context that we must glance specifically (if briefly) at the more neglected of James I's writings: the king's own exegeses of and commentaries on scriptural texts. James called them 'paraphrases' and 'meditations'. And they stand, indeed, as evidence of his personalizing the Scriptures, meditating upon their message to himself and communicating their meaning to his subjects. The King's *Paraphrase upon the Revelation* is an exegesis, a decoding of that most complex of biblical books and a specific application of its symbolic figurations to his own and his contemporaries' world. James deconstructs, as we would now say, the visions of Chapter 10, explaining how Christ was the Angel foretold and how the rainbow signified His covenant with his elect. Similarly the woman of Chapter 12 represents the Church, he explains, and the twelve stars stand for the prophets and the patriarchs.[91] Throughout, James puts his own words as if they were spoken by St John and so joins, as if in a dialogue, the text of Revelation and his reflections upon it. As a consequence it is no less the King's than the apostle's words we read when he writes 'and [God] said unto me, Write and leave in record what thou hast seen'.[92] James saw much that was for the edification of himself. He read again, as Scripture in many places showed him, that 'the hearts of the greatest kings as well as of the smallest subjects are in the hands of the Lord'. The book of the last things forcefully urged him: 'Be watchful then and sleep no longer in negligence and careless security . . . revive your zeal and fervency.'[93] His discursive dialogue with Scripture sharpened his conscience. As he turned to meditate on some verses of the fifteenth chapter of the first book of Chronicles (which he

---

[89] Ibid. i. 34.
[90] Ibid.
[91] *Paraphrase upon The Revelation*, in *Workes of Prince James*, esp. pp. 13–14, 19–21, 36–9, 63–4, 78.
[92] Ibid. 65.
[93] Ibid. 11, 56.

had, we recall, recommended to Prince Henry), he was reminded clearly of the first duty of kings.[94] David after his victory over his enemies immediately translated the ark of the Covenant to his house, 'whereof *we* [sic] may learn first that the chief virtue which should be in a Christian prince . . . is a fervency and constant zeal to promote the glory of God'.[95] James applied his text closely to his place, comparing the elders of the Chronicles to the barons and burgesses of his kingdom and underlining his own responsibility for 'choosing good under-rulers'.[96] At all points the 'opening up of the text' was the basis for examining 'how pertinently the place doth appertain to us and our present estate', guiding the king, for example, on the lawfulness of Sunday sports.[97]

James's meditations on Scripture were a form of self-counsel, a didactic engagement with the commands in Scripture as a means of tutoring conscience. And not only his own. The meditation on the twentieth chapter of Revelations reads also like a sermon. Introducing his meditation upon the first book of the Chronicles, James expressed his desire that 'these meditations of mine may after my death remain to the posterity and a certain testimony of my upright and honest meaning . . .'.[98] Like the overtly *Political Works* (as McIlwain defined them) from which they have been artificially separated, James's paraphrases and explications of Scripture were a discharge of his conscience, an image of the king, at once a crystal and a mirror for all men as well as for magistrates.

Perhaps we see their public and, as well as personal, heuristic function most clearly in two little-studied works, the *Meditation upon The Lords Prayer* of 1619 and the *Meditation upon the . . . XXVII Chapter of St Matthew* of 1620. The first, though dedicated as a New Year's gift to the Duke of Buckingham, was 'written by the King's Majesty for the benefit of *all* his subjects, especially of such as follow the court'.[99] The meditation was a plea for Christian unity at a time of mounting tension and division; as in *The Peace-Maker* of 1618 James had called on the 'monarchical bodies of many

---

[94] *A Meditation upon the XXV, XXVI, XXVII, XXVIII, XXIX Verses of the XVth Chapter of The First Book of The Chronicles of The Kings*, in *Workes of Prince James*, 81–90; see p. 92.

[95] Ibid. 82.

[96] Ibid. 83.

[97] Ibid. 86–7.

[98] Ibid. 81.

[99] *Meditation upon The Lords Prayer*. The full title includes this address.

kingdoms' to 'be one mutual Christendom',[100] so he now urged all
his subjects to join in the fellowship of the sacraments and prayer.
The Arminians, he wrote, sought to rob God of his secret will; at
the 'other extremity', 'some puritans . . . make God author of
sin'.[101] Exposition of the prayer taught by Christ warned all to
'trust not to that private spirit which our Puritans glory in' but to
remember, through the words 'Our Father', that 'every one of us
is a member of a body of a church that is compacted of many
members'.[102] James commends confession to churchmen for the
clearing of the conscience and, through reflection on the Lord's
Prayer, finds the 'true visible church . . . now in this kingdom' the
best hope for salvation.[103]

The *Meditation upon St Matthew* began, James informed his son
Charles, as a private reading 'to myself the passion of Christ'.[104]
But, as he thought on the crown of thorns, James contemplated
'the thorny cares which a king . . . must be subject unto as (God
knowes) I daily and nightly feel in mine own person'.[105] As he
meditated further, 'I apprehended that it would be a good pattern
to put inheritors to kingdoms in mind of their calling by the form
of their inauguration' and 'whom can a pattern for a king's
inauguration so well fit as a king's son and heir being written by
the king his father and the pattern taken from the king of all
kings'. And so the work became for Charles what the *Basilikon
Doron* had been for Henry, James's gift of knowledge of God to
his son. Indeed, James informed the reader of his meditation that,
if God gave him days and leisure, he intended to expand it to
cover 'the whole principal points belonging to the office of a
king'.[106] Meantime, the *Meditation upon . . . St Matthew* was a
forewarning of the heavy burden of kingship: 'make it therefore',
he instructed the prince, 'your vade mecum'. As he laid out for
his son the verses describing Christ's crowning with plaited thorns
and mock coronation with sceptre of reed and the soldiers' laughing
'obeisance', James detailed the cares and duties of the prince who

[100] *The Peace-Maker*, sig. B1.
[101] *Meditation upon The Lords Prayer*, 42, 116–17.
[102] Ibid. 18, 22.
[103] Ibid. 62, 66, 15.
[104] *Two Meditations of the King's Maiestie* (1620), Epistle dedicatory.
[105] *A Meditation upon the . . . XXVII Chapter of St Matthew or A Pattern for a King's Inauguration*
(1620), Epistle dedicatory.
[106] Ibid. Advertisement to the Reader.

was to take his 'pattern' from Christ. The thorns, he explained, made a king remember 'that he wears not that crown for himself but for others'; the reed sceptre instructed a ruler to correct gently and govern 'boldly yet temperately'. In general, Christ's crowning passion reminded kings that they were 'mixtae personae . . . bound to make a reckoning to God for their subjects' souls as well as their bodies'.[107] 'In a word,' James concludes, 'a Christian king should never be without that continual and ever wake-riffe care of the account he is one day to give to God of the good government of his people and their prosperous estate both in souls and bodies, which is a part of the health of his own soul.'[108] As often with James, it was counsel to himself as well as to his son. Just as Pilate proclaimed Christ King of the Jews in Hebrew, Greek, and Latin, so 'upon St George's day and other high festival times the chief Herald Garter . . . proclaims my titles in . . . Latin, French and English'.[109] We can almost hear James meditating with himself as he tells Prince Charles that the purple robe of office was to remind him 'to take great heed of his conscience, that his judgements may be without blemish or stain'.[110]

Our final texts of the king's conscience have all but rested unexamined by historians—doubtless, not least, because they are poetry. James, however, was a major influence on the Renaissance poetry of Scotland, and both his poems and treatise on poetry are rich in evidence of his values and ideals. Like his paraphrase of Revelations, James's verse translations of the Psalms of David were a form of meditation on Scripture, by means of absorbing its meaning into his own words—a placing 'before thy holy throne this speech of mine'.[111] Translation, James decreed, did not license reinterpretation of Scripture; those who adulterated Holy Writ with their own opinions were accursed.[112] The translator was a glass through which Scripture could be read, and poetry might be the instrument by which it was read most clearly.[113] So the King of

[107] Ibid. 25, 50, 124, and *passim*.
[108] Ibid. 125–6.
[109] Ibid. 78–80.
[110] Ibid. 120.
[111] BL Royal MS 18 B xvi, fo. 9; *Poems of James VI*, ii. 11. James's father-in-law, the King of Denmark, had written too a manual of selected psalms which 'was his continual vade mecum' (*Meditation upon The Lords Prayer*, 96).
[112] *Paraphrase upon The Revelation*, 72.
[113] Bodl. MS 165 fo. 20.

Scotland, through David, the King of Israel, addressed, as in prayer, his heavenly King, a 'king that last for ever shall quaire all the nationis perish & decayes'.[114] Through David, James learnt (as he taught) that the Lord was a lord of justice, that he abominated the 'creuell and bloodthristie tyran' and those false princes who 'speake with pleasant lippes and dowble myndis'.[115] He read that the Lord preserved his anointed king and bestowed his grace on the virtuous, 'thaim of conscience iust & pure'.[116] James therefore prayed for protection from his enemies without and from temptations of wickedness within; he asked 'lett all my judgement ay proceid from thy most holy face'.[117] Urging, as he was to do in the *Basilikon Doron*, 'all princes sonnes yield to the lorde', he vowed to place his trust 'in Iehova's might'.[118] Trust here meant not only his confidence but his responsibility, his kingdom. In the exercise of his office James, with David, knew the Lord would guide and 'counsaile me', as in turn he would give account to God how he had heeded His counsel:

> the lorde doth iustice give unto the nationis sure
> then judge me lorde according to my iustice great & pure[119]

James's Psalms, *The Psalmes of His Maiestie* as they were titled, were not his only poetical exercises that we should consider as medi-tations on God and self-examination of the royal conscience. Only when we recall James's admonition to his son to reflect upon God and take his reckoning with himself at quiet moments free from worldly business may we understand the significant epithet in *His Maiesties Poeticall Exercises at Vacant Houres*. In his translation of 'divine' Du Bartas's *The Furies*, a poem about the Fall, James advised that the reader (and reader/writer) might 'see clearly, as in a glass, the miseries of this wavering world: to wit, the cursed nature of mankinde and the heavie plagues of God. And especiallie | heere maye thou learne not to flatter thyselfe, in cloaking thy odious vices with the delectable coulour of vertue ...'.[120] In *The Furies*, we read how authority had once been natural and kings could rule,

---

[114] *Psalmes of His Maiestie*, in *Poems of James VI*, ii. 20.
[115] Ibid. ii. 11, 23.
[116] Ibid. ii. 42.
[117] Ibid. ii. 21, 26, 27.
[118] Ibid. ii. 9, 36.
[119] Ibid. ii. 14, 26.
[120] *Poems of James VI*, i. 98; James I, *Workes of Prince James*, 328.

like Adam over beasts, not by force but with a wink or a nod. But disobedience to God had as its consequence the collapse of all natural hegemony, as well as the disintegration of order and harmony into chaos. The animals now formed 'rebellious bands' against Man:

> Man in rebelling thus against
> The soveraigne great, I say,
> Doth feele his subjects all enarm'd
> Against him everie way ... [121]

Wolves, leopards, and bears now challenged the lion, king of beasts:

> Most jealous of the right divine
> Against their head conspire.[122]

Even kings themselves were stained by the Fall:

> The King of beasts ... of himselfe
> Is not the maister now.[123]

Yet poetry, Sir Philip Sidney, had claimed, could bring fallen man closer again to God. As James himself summarized him: 'a breath divine in Poets breasts doth blow.'[124] Through *The Furies*, therefore, James learnt and taught the emptiness of man's 'outward show', the illegitimacy of princes who advanced themselves 'by false contracts and by unlawfull measures', and the wisdom of those who had 'the feare of God | Imprinted deepely ...' and who obeyed his will.[125] Similarly, from his verse account of the battle of Lepanto we know James learnt and taught the duty of kings: to be God's generals against the devil, to prefer the 'honour of the Lord' before all else, and to be 'volunteers of conscience' in the Lord's ranks.[126]

In and through his poetry, which awaits a critical/political reading, James, as the poet Gabriel Harvey put it, 'read a . . . lecture to himself'.[127] He did more than tutor his own conscience,

[121] *The Furies*, ll. 224–7, in *Poems of James VI*, i. 126.

[122] Ibid. ll. 381–2, (i. 134).

[123] Ibid., ll. 1359–60 (i. 184).

[124] *Poems of James VI*, ii. 68.

[125] *The Furies*, u. 1167–8, 1451–2, 1461–2 (i. 175, 190).

[126] 'The Lepanto of James The Sixth', ll. 283, 317–18, in *Poems of James VI*, i. 216–18, and *passim*.

[127] *Poems of James VI*, i. 274. Cf. Goldberg, *James I*, 17–28. I am preparing an essay on 'The Politics of James VI and I's Poetry'.

however. The 'heavenly furious fire' of poetry, he believed, might reignite the embers of conscience and knowledge of God in all men.[128] Poets are 'Dame Natures trunchmen, heavens interprets trewe'.[129] So James offered instruction in the art of poetry as he penned advice on the art of kingship. And, in his *Essayes of a Prentise in the Divine Art of Poesie*, he prayed that he, as poet and king, might have the power to represent the wind, the seas, and the seasons, nature—the created works of a living God whom men through verse may come to know and follow:

> For as into the wax the seals imprent
> Is lyke a seale, right so the Poet gent
> Doeth grave so vive in us his passions strange,
> As makes the reader, halfe in author change
> For verses force is sic that softly slydes
> Throw secret poris and in our sences bydes
> As makes them have both good and eville imprented
> Which by the learned works is represented.[130]

David, Job, and Solomon had been poets as well as kings. The poet like the good king prayed to his God 'That I thy instrument may be', so that, as *The Furies* concludes, 'this worke which man did write' also 'by the Lord is pend'.[131] Poetry for James VI and I, like his devotional works, was a meditation with himself and God and a representation to his subjects of himself and God— his purest crystal. In purifying his own conscience, he equipped himself to teach; by teaching, he learnt. So the wise poet of *Uranie* was told:

> In singing kepe this order showen you heir,
> Then ye your self, in feeding men shall leir
> The rule of living well ...[132]

And, thus, the King published rules for poetry as well as for government, that 'reading thir rules ye may find in yourself such a beginning of Nature ...'. In the words of the sonnet to the reader, 'Sic docens discans'.[133]

---

[128] *Poems of James VI*, ii. 70.
[129] James VI, *The Essayes of a Prentise in the Divine Art of Poesie*, ed. E. Arber (1869), 29.
[130] Ibid. 29.
[131] *The Furies*, ll. 29, 1515–16 (i. 114, 192).
[132] *Essays of a Prentise*, 37.
[133] James VI, *An Schort Treatise Conterning Some Reulis ... to be Observed ... in Scottis Poesie*, ed. E. Arber (1869), Preface to the reader, p. 55, Sonnet of the author, p. 56.

In early modern Europe, as circumstances challenged traditional beliefs, all rulers faced difficult choices. Either they accepted the realities and were forced to compromise long-held beliefs and codes, or they fought to reassert the paradigms and to reconstruct a shattered world. Even though faced with the obvious fact of religious wars in Europe and theological wrangles at home, James VI and I pursued hopes of, and policies towards, an ecumenical resolution to the divisions of Christendom. He endeavoured to make the Church of England a platform for the reunification of a truly Catholic church, a *unum corpus* of which all Christians could be members. In his own countries he sought to minimize dispute over theology and ceremony. And we now see that, as an essential part of his ambitious designs, he sought to lead his subjects to a knowledge of God's dictates, so that all might partake of a common conscience, as well as be members of one church and commonweal. He faced, inevitably, inconsistencies in his own exposition of his ideal, because the means to obtain his goal (a coincidence of private and public belief) were the goal itself. His only answer to the new challenges was the reassertion of the old ideals. James, however, went beyond reassertion; his *Works* were a strategy of reenactment. By his own example, he attempted to demonstrate that conscience was neither mere opinion, nor, as the 'politics' would have it, a disguise, nor yet the inevitable victim of force. And he tried to heal the divisions in the commonwealth, by resolving the disjunctures in himself—between his natural and mystical body, his person and office—ruling his own conscience and his kingdom, as he claimed, according to Scripture.

In the public sphere it is clear that he failed: religious differences and even moral positions continued to polarize. The King perforce took political decisions which accorded uneasily with his conscience. Furthermore, even in his own person James exemplified not only the ideals but also the failings he discussed, to the point that he became a microcosm of the human frailties that always threatened a Christian society. In his quest for the English Crown after Elizabeth's death, the young James acquiesced in his mother's execution, for all his formal protest, and so failed in the filial devotion he believed was owed to parents.[134] Similarly, for all his

---

[134] See *Letters*, 81–2; *Letters of Queen Elizabeth and King James VI of Scotland*, ed. J. Bruce (Camden Soc.; 1849), 46; Goldberg, *James I*, 14–17.

injunctions to honesty, it would appear that he was prepared to mislead about his willingness to convert to Rome.[135] More tragically still, the king who thundered against the vices of intemperance, drunkenness, and especially sodomy (a crime he exempted from pardon and which, he told Henry, 'ye are bound in conscience never to forgive') was a drunkard and homosexual.[136] How, then, could James counsel his son not to commend what he did not practise or boast—as, in 1616, that 'both our theorique and practique agree well together'?[137] The simple answer would be that James was a straightforward hypocrite, but it would be too simple an answer. For James's denunciations of what were also his own sins were part of his meditations, and may have been a form of the confession that he recommended to others, for 'amendment of life'. We cannot know how, in his private moments, James faced his God and himself. But knowing, as he told his son, that Christ did not come for the perfect, he found 'in the religion we profess . . . so much comfort and peace of conscience'.[138]

[135] *Letters*, 308.
[136] Ibid. 315; *Basilikon Doron*, i. 64, 102, 122, 136, 168.
[137] James I, *Workes of Prince James*, 379.
[138] HMC, *Salisbury*, xv. 302.

7
Divine Rights in the Early Seventeenth Century
CONRAD RUSSELL

IT is perhaps superfluous to set out to prove that many people have thought that the fact that James I believed in the divine right of kings was one of the major reasons why he had quarrels with his House of Commons: this is something which every schoolboy knows. However, like many other things which every schoolboy knows, it is false. It is a proposition which is so deep in our historical consciousness that it has been more often asserted than argued, since it has been assumed not to stand in need of proof. These, of course, are precisely the propositions which historical research must continually test. When this proposition is tested, it turns out to be surprisingly difficult to supply evidence for it.[1]

In fact, the argument that belief in divine right was not controversial and did not necessarily imply any particular view of the extent of the king's power, is not particularly novel. J. W. Allen said that 'belief in the King's divine right implied no particular belief as to the extent of a king's rights in England or elsewhere. . . . Quite certainly none of the resounding stock phrases above referred to implied any belief in "royal absolutism".' Professor Margaret Judson, who anticipated more of the revisionism of the 1970s than she has yet been given credit for, wrote in 1949 that

right up to the moment when the civil war broke out, the leaders of the Parliamentary opposition and Puritan preachers joined with royalist supporters and Anglican clergy in preaching the divine origin and sanction of kingly authority, and the superiority of the monarchical form of government to other forms. The Parliamentary opposition did not talk

---

This is a revised version of the Hayes Robinson Lecture, delivered at Royal Holloway and Bedford New College on 28 November 1990. I would like to thank the College for inviting me to give the lecture, and members of the audience for their helpful comments.

[1] For one of the sources of 'what every schoolboy knows', see J. R. Tanner, *Constitutional Conflicts of the Reign of James I* (repr. Cambridge, 1960), 4–9.

of resistance until 1642, and at that late date, they insisted they were not resisting the person of the King.

'To believe in both the divine right of kingly authority and at the same time in its limited nature was perfectly natural and consistent for many excellent seventeenth century minds.' Professor Owen Chadwick wrote that

the dogma that Kings rule by divine right was common ground to everyone who used his Bible. How far a citizen might engage in resistance and rebellion, and under what conditions, if any, a king might lose the allegiance of his subjects by his tyranny, were widely and urgently canvassed; but the doctrine that the secular power is of God was common to everyone.[2]

Yet, though this approach has a long history, it has never succeeded in dispelling the contrary belief, and has not yet achieved general acceptance. Professor Johann Sommerville, in 1986, reasserted a traditional Whig view when he referred to 'the theory of royal absolutism, or, to give it its traditional title, the divine right of kings'. Professor Sommerville still believes that Englishmen in the reign of James did not share a single political outlook and that major differences in political ideas are part of the long-term causes of the Civil War. For him, the doctrine of the divine right of kings is one of these ideas.[3] It is his work which makes it necessary to reassert ideas I learnt from Margaret Judson when I was a postgraduate, and whose truth everything I have read since seems to me to have confirmed.

Belief in divine right of course took many forms, and was applied to many different types of authority: Professor Owen Chadwick's phrase that 'the secular power is of God' is deliberately worded to be applied not only to kings, but to all forms of duly constituted authority that might be covered by the injunction of Romans 13: 1: 'let every soul be subject unto the higher powers. For there is no power but of God: the powers that be are ordained of God.' Among these 'powers that be', the one which gave rise to the greatest dispute seems to have been, not the divine right of

---

[2] J. W. Allen, *English Political Thought, 1603–1660* (1938), 97–99; M. A. Judson, *The Crisis of the Constitution* (repr. New York, 1971), 19–20; O. Chadwick, *The Reformation* (1964), 391. For some remarks by James which not every schoolboy knows, see S. R. Gardiner, *History of England from the Accession of James I to the Outbreak of the Civil War 1603–1642* (10 vols.; 1883–4), i. 291.

[3] J. P. Sommerville, *Politics and Ideology in England, 1603–1640* (1986), 9, 3 ff.

kings, but the divine right of husbands: William Gouge, in his *Of Domesticall Duties*, complained that, among all those of whom the Holy Ghost required subjection, 'wives for the most part are the most backward in yeelding subjection to their husbands'. According to Daniel Rogers, many women said most men had so many defects it was impossible to be subject to them.[4] Since the overwhelming majority of political discourse was carried on by men, of whom a large majority were husbands, this gave most of them a vested interest, as well as an intellectual conviction, in defending the notion of divine right.

When applied to government, the statement that it was of divine right was a tautology: if it was not of divine right, it was not government. The statement that authority was of divine right did not answer the question whether it existed by a patriarchal pattern rooted in nature, or whether it acquired its title to divine right by human consent. The claim to divine right did not answer the question whether the ruler was like a father, whose subjects were born in subjection, or like a husband, whose authority depended on his wife's consent. Fathers and husbands enjoyed different types of authority, but both equally ruled by divine right and by a pattern rooted in nature, and James VI and I indiscriminately compared his authority to both. Nor, indeed, did the statement that government was by divine right necessarily answer the question of what type of government should exist. When Bulstrode Whitelocke, in the Westminster Assembly, said that 'no government in perticular was so cleer to be *jure divino* as government in the generall', he was attacking Scottish Presbyterians, but the point could equally well have been made against claims to exclusive divine right for bishops or kings. It was a perfectly sound divine-right point.

By this line of reasoning, a government might hold power by election, and at the same time enjoy divine right. This point was conceded by James VI and I himself. In discussing 1 Sam. 8: 18, which described how, because the Israelites had chosen a king, God would not hear them when they complained against him, he combined divine right, election, and non-resistance in a way reminiscent of the Roman *lex regia*. He wrote that God would say: 'although you shall grudge and murmure, yet it shal not be lawful

[4] W. Gouge, *Of Domesticall Duties* (3rd edn., 1634), 24. D. Rogers, *Matrimoniall Honour* (1642), 260.

to you to cast it off, in respect it is not only the ordinance of God, but also your selves have chosen him unto you, thereby renouncing for ever all priviledges by your willing consent out of your hands.'[5]

Any doctrine which is held all the way across the political spectrum is likely to be held with a series of different emphases and shadings. The central proposition which held all these beliefs together was the belief that God was the only source of legitimacy: either authority existed by divine right, or it was no authority. A certain John Hodges, who incepted MA in 1631, took as one of his questions for disputation: 'is there any power which is not from God? No.' The *Homily of Obedience* said that 'he that resisteth or withstandeth common authority, resisteth or withstandeth God'.[6] Divine right, like democracy today, covered a multitude of sins because it was the basic currency of legitimacy. When Yelverton, in the Parliament of 1604, commented on James's message on the *Goodwin* v. *Fortescue* case that 'the prince's command is like a thunderbolt; his command upon our allegiance, like the roaring of a lion: to his command there is no contradiction',[7] he was no doubt using flowery language, but he meant only what members of the House of Lords now mean when they say: 'we must give way to the elected chamber'; he was invoking the basic principle of legitimacy.

It is in this sense that the doctrine of divine right was accepted all the way across the political spectrum. It was used by all those who, in the course of day-to-day politics, annoyed the King most, and was often used for purposes he found uncongenial. We can perhaps hear, in a series of quotations, some of the variation in the purposes for which the idea was used. Sir Edward Coke, giving the charge at Norwich Assizes in 1606, said that 'to kings, rulers, judges and magistrates, this sentence is proper, *vos dii estis*, you are Gods on earth: when by your execution of justice and judgement, the God of heaven is in your actions represented'. In the Parliament of 1621, after being sacked from the Bench, he said that the King

---

[5] *The Diary of Bulstrode Whitelocke*, ed. R. Spalding (British Academy Records of Social and Economic History, NS 13; Oxford, 1990), 153, and see also N. Fiennes in J. Rushworth, *Historical Collections*, III. i (1692), 105. *The Political Works of James I*, ed. C. H. McIlwain (Cambridge, Mass., 1918), 59. These, though edited as the *Works* of James I, are, of course, mostly the works of James VI. See below, n. 44.

[6] PRO SP 16/196/41 (*Sit potestas aliqua quae non est a deo? Neg.*). *Sermons or Homilies* (2 vols.; 1640), i. 75.

[7] *CJ* i. 166, 943.

'is God's lieutenant, and therefore must do no wrong'.[8] Sir John Eliot, writing in the Tower, where he had been sent for making a tumult in the House of Commons, said that kings were gods, because God 'foreseeing ... in respect of the infirmitie of their natures, men could not heare and live, he thus prepared a medium between them, a Moses, to be the keeper of the law, a deligate, a substitute, for the administration of the government'.[9] Anyone who has attended a Labour Party Conference should understand the significance of Eliot's decision to describe the King as God's delegate, and not as his representative: he was mandated. Yet, representative or delegate, it was still a doctrine of divine right. John Pym, in 1641, said that 'all sovereign princes have some characters of divinity imprinted on them; they are set up in their dominions to bee *optimi maximi*, that they should exercise a goodnesse proportionable to their greatnesse'. This speech too was not an exaltation of the King: it was introducing the articles of impeachment of Strafford, because 'there cannot be a greater lesion or diminution of majesty than to bereave a King of the glory of his goodness'.[10] In 1637 no less a figure than John Lilburne the later Leveller, on trial in the Star Chamber, said: 'if it were the meanest officer in the kingdom that took me, that were made an officer by the king's authority and power, I would submit unto him . . . for I know the King's authority is from God.' He further asserted that: 'I do hold it unlawful for any of God's people in their greatest oppression by the magistrate to rebel or to take up any temporal arms against them, whether the oppression be in spiritual or temporal things, but only to pray and to make use of God's two-edged sword.'[11] Lilburne was admittedly on trial, and facing a heavy sentence, but, if he had been tempering his views to secure acquittal, he would perhaps not have referred so plainly to the magistrate oppressing God's people.

These examples may serve to argue that belief in divine right was not a party creed. One reason why this was so is that the divine right of kings was not a doctrine in isolation: it was merely part of a larger doctrine, of what Tillyard called 'The Great Chain

---

[8] *The Lord Coke's Charge* (1607), sig. C. 4. *Commons Debates 1621*, ed. W. Notestein, F. H. Relf, and H. Simpson (7 vols.; New Haven, Conn., 1935), ii. 253.
[9] Sir J. Eliot, *The Monarchie of Man*, ed. A. B. Grosart (2 vols.; 1879), ii. 15.
[10] *Two Speeches Made by John Pym* (1641), 3.
[11] H. N. Brailsford, *The Levellers and the English Revolution* (1961), 84–5.

of Being'.[12] This was a doctrine of order and of harmony, in which each duly constituted authority had a divine right to be in its proper place in the hierarchy, and harmony was preserved by the acceptance by each authority that it had to remain within its station. Each divine right, then, had to run in formation, or else jostle, with all the other divine rights which made up an ordered universe, and all these divine rights were subject to the end, or purpose, for which God created them. We will find, then, that the divine right of kings had to share the field with the divine right of the law, the divine right of Parliaments, the divine right of prophets, the divine right of judges, Justices of the Peace, and inferior magistrates, the divine right of the nobility, and the divine right of husbands, fathers, and masters. Just as England was a patchwork quilt of competing jurisdictions, so it was a patchwork quilt of competing divine rights, and what determined people's views on the extent of the king's power was not whether they believed in his divine right, but their views, often shaded and obscure, on the relationship between his divine right and other divine rights. This is a method of classification which produces, not a division into two sides, but a spectrum which often shimmers according to the issue under discussion. For many, the crucial point was not the power of the king, but the power of God. Thomas Scott of Canterbury was not necessarily being controversial in referring to God 'whoe onely is an absolute sovereign': for many, God's sovereignty took up too much room to allow absolute sovereignty to anyone else.[13]

The central point about all these divine rights was that they were part of a doctrine of order, of which the order of the body politic was itself only a part. God was responsible for all this order: in the words of the *Homily of Obedience*:

in earth he hath assigned and appointed kings, princes with other governors under them, in all good and necessary order. The water above is kept and rayneth down in due time and season. The sun, moone, stars, rainbow, thunder, lightning, clouds and all birds of the ayre do keep their order. The earth, trees, seeds, plants, hearbes, corne, grasse and all manner of beasts keepe themselves in order: all the parts of the whole yeere, as winter, summer moneths, nights and dayes, continue in their order: all kinds of fishes in the sea, rivers and waters, with all fountaines, springs, yea the seas themselves, keepe their comely course and order: and man

---

[12] E. W. M. Tillyard, *The Elizabethan World Picture* (Cambridge, 1943), *passim*.

[13] Kent Archive Office, U 951/Z 10. I am grateful to Dr Richard Cust for this reference.

himselfe also hath all his parts both within and without, as soule, heart, minde, memory, understanding, reason, speech, with all and singular corporall members of his body in a profitable, necessary and pleasant order.

The conclusion followed that we ought to be obedient, not only to the king, but to 'his honourable Councell, and to all other noblemen, magistrates and officers, which by God's goodness be placed and ordered. For Almighty God is the only author and provider for this aforenamed state and order'.[14]

Thomas Scott was not necessarily controversial in holding that 'the Parliament, state and subordinate princes and magistrates, are no less Gods ordinance then the soveraigne magistrate', though he was highly controversial in adding on to this foundation a Calvinist doctrine of the right of inferior magistrates to resist: 'yf hee will not, they ought to do justice. Untill they did it, they alsoe were rebells, and accursed.'[15] This is an example of the building-up of God's sovereignty to the point where it allowed very little room for any other. Nicholas Fuller was perhaps slightly less controversial in claiming in the House of Commons that 'in this place, none between us and God',[16] and Cornelius Burges, preaching to the Long Parliament, was borrowing a standard point about judges when he told the Parliament that 'there is nothing makes you such faire images of God (in the relation you now stand) as due execution of justice and judgement'.[17] Not all of those who spoke of the divine right of Parliaments were even their partisans. Sir Francis Kynaston, Gentleman of the Privy Chamber, and shortly afterwards one of the very few people who believed a king could make law without a Parliament, told the Parliament of 1621 that 'this House is an idea of the celestial court of judgement'.[18]

Those who upheld the divine right of judges included James I himself. Addressing his first Parliament, he spoke to 'judges and magistrates in all sorts of places', and told them that, 'as Ezekias the good king of Juda said to their judges, remember that the thrones you sit on are God's, and neither yours nor mine; and that

---

[14] *Sermons or Homilies*, i. 70–1. Most of this is omitted in the extract printed in G. R. Elton, *The Tudor Constitution* (Cambridge, 1960), 15.

[15] Kent Archive Office, U 951/Z 10.

[16] *CJ* i. 1024.

[17] C. Burges, *The First Sermon* (1641), 71; see also p. 70.

[18] *Commons Debates 1621*, iii. 123; J. P. Sommerville, *Sir Robert Filmer, Patriarcha and Other Writings* (Cambridge, 1991), pp. xix–xx; PRO SP 16/233/52.

as you must be answerable to me, so must both you and I be answerable to God, for the due execution of your offices'.[19] In this speech, James conceded a vital point: an authority might enjoy divine right, even though its right to occupy its position was derived, not immediately from God, but mediately, from other human authority. James knew perfectly well that he, not God, appointed the judges, but this did not, in his opinion, prevent the judges from enjoying divine, and not merely human, right. Moreover, this doctrine was pleadable against the King, as Lord Chancellor Ellesmere very cleverly did, some six months later. James sent a messenger to the Lord Chancellor, requiring him, if consistent with justice and equity, to stay an injunction against a certain Mr Fourde. The Lord Chancellor nevertheless granted the injunction, whereat the disappointed Fourde petitioned the King, asking whether the command of the king or the order of the Chancellor should be obeyed, 'and such like words of injustice and shame'. Fourde then found himself in Star Chamber, on trial for sowing sedition between the King and his peers. He was sentenced to perpetual imprisonment, to lose his ears on the pillory, to riding with his face to the horse's tail with papers on his head, and to a fine of £1,000. He, as might be imagined, 'took the punishment grievously and impatiently', and Robert Cecil, giving judgment in the Lord Chancellor's absence, observed: 'let all men take heed how they complaine in wordes against any magistrate, for they are Gods.' The Lord Chancellor, on his knees, then induced the King to pardon Fourde, and the whole operation of putting the king in his place was concluded with a neatness subsequent Cabinets might well envy.[20]

In the little commonwealth of the family, divine right was an equally central part of the structure of authority. Daniel Rogers said that 'we know the man doth especially resemble the image of God, and in that respect is the wives head'. He was ordained by

---

[19] *CJ* i. 145. For judges, as for kings, such exaltation was double-edged. John Donne, in a passage quoted by the Fourth Earl of Bedford in his commonplace book, wrote:

> Judges are gods; he who made and said them so
> Meant not that men should be forced to them to go
> By means of angels.

(John Donne, Fifth Satire, ll. 57–9, *Complete English Poems*, ed. A. J. Smith (1971), 172: Bedford Estate Office, Bedford MSS XI, i. 51).

[20] J. Hawarde, *Les Reportes Del Cases in Camera Stellata*, ed. W. P. Baildon (1894), 176–7.

God, 'not as a reliefe of man fallen, but an addition of perfection to his creation, before ever sinne entered'.[21] Authority over children was equally by divine right, and much less limited: according to Dod and Cleaver, they were bound to obey even petty commands, 'for soe soone as the father hath commanded it, being a thing lawfull, God's stampe is set on it, and it carries the print of God's commandment, and hee, that thinkes himself too good to doe it, thinkes himself too good to obey God'. Similarly, servants were bound to obey masters, even if they were bad ones: 'for this in the naturall body we see, that if a man have a head subject to diseases, and full of infirmities, he will not abuse and contemne it: but he thinkes: this is my head, which God hath given me, and therefore I must not make it worse by il usage, but strive to make it better by all the meanes I can.'[22] Here, like James on the divine right of judges, Dod was conceding divine right to an authority acquired by human right. Men and women were not born servants: it was a relationship freely and contractually entered into—the master, in a valid sense, held an elective office. In a society which did not believe in slavery, the authority of master over servant must depend on an ascending theory of power, yet this power acquired by an ascending theory acquired a divine right like any hereditary monarch.

Perhaps the most crucial variable of all is the relationship between the divine right of the king and the divine right of the law. That both enjoyed divine right was commonplace: the question was of their comparative status and authority. To anyone with a formulated concept of legislative sovereignty, the essential point about law was that it had a human maker or makers. To such a person, the divine right of the law had to be a consequence, rather than a cause, of the divine right of those who made it. Yet there were two categories of people who might see the matter otherwise. Common lawyers, with an attachment to custom and to precedent, saw law as something which was not necessarily made; as Lord Scarman put it, it was like Topsy: it just growed. To such a person, it was possible, though not necessary, to see the law as something which conferred divine right on the king, rather than vice versa.

---

[21] D. Rogers, *Matrimoniall Honour*, 5–6. I would like to thank the Revd Dr Daniel Doriani for much help on matters to do with the godly household.

[22] J. Dod and R. Cleaver, *A Plaine and Familiar Exposition of the Ten Commandments* (1610), 192, 188.

The other category were the biblical supporters of the Mosaic law, who believed that law originated from God, and man merely amplified it. Sir Harbottle Grimston, giving the charge at Essex Quarter Sessions in 1638, said that 'man's laws . . . are but in the nature of expositions and commentaries upon that divine law, from whence as from a fountayne of justice, all humane ordinances have their derivation'.[23] Acts of Parliament, then, were not the *Decretum*: they were the *Glossa ordinaria*.

Others went rather farther in this direction than Harbottle Grimston. The Speaker, in his opening prayer in 1604, said 'no law can be good that is not agreeable to thy law, which containeth the fundamental equity of our laws'. Mr Strode, in the Parliament of 1621: 'moveth against swearing. Prohibited by the laws of God, on which ours depend. That our laws come short in this.'[24] He was arguing that there was a duty to make a law because the law of God so commanded. Peter Wentworth, in an image derived from the biblical King Hezekiah, was rather more explicit: 'it is necessarie for princes as well as for others, to doe those thinges that are pleasing and acceptable to God, and therefore when they shall sit upon the throne of their kingdomes they are commanded, to have the booke of God and to studye it, and not to departe therefrom either to the righte hand, or to the lefte.'[25] John White, Member for Southwark in the Long Parliament, was explicit in ranking the divine right of the law above the right of the king: 'in the first institution of kings God did set laws to limit them.'[26] This, no doubt, was a view with which James profoundly disagreed, but it was still a doctrine of divine right. This was a line which led back towards the resistance theorists Ponet and Goodman. Indeed, it almost directly echoed Goodman, that, 'when God appointed his people to have a king, he did with great circumspection as well appoynt them what manner of man they shulde chose, as the lawes by the which he shulde rule others', and Ponet, that 'before magistrates were, God's laws were'.[27]

---

[23] Herts. RO, Gorhambury MS IX A 9. I would like to thank Dr Julie Calnan for this reference.

[24] *CJ* i. 150, 537.

[25] BL Add. MS 24, 664, fo. 14ᵛ.

[26] *The Notebook of Sir John Northcote*, ed. A. H. A. Hamilton (1877), 9. For James's rejection of this view, see *Political Works*, 62.

[27] C. Goodman, *How Superior Powers Ought to Be Obeyed* (Geneva, 1558), 48; F. Raab, *The English Face of Machiavelli* (1964), 19.

Common lawyers were more cautious, and more divided, than the defenders of the Decalogue. Sir Edward Coke said that 'the law, whereof this summary is made, is of ancient usages warranted by Holy Scripture'. He said in Calvin's Case that 'The law of nature consists of the laws of: 1. Nature, the gift of God, which cannot be changed. 2. customs. 3. statutes. Nature writes the law of government in the heart of man for his preservation, by government and in obedience.'[28] Coke here does not make clear precisely which parts of the law are not subject to the will of a legislator, but the thrust of the argument tends to limit the powers of a human lawgiver.

These points may help to show why Professor Sommerville is crucially in error in his belief that 'of course, if kings held sovereign power, derived directly from God, it followed that all the rights and privileges of subjects depended on the royal will, and also that Parliament was wholly subordinate to the monarch'. For some people, no doubt, it did follow, and Sir Robert Filmer, whom Professor Sommerville is here discussing, is one of them.[29] However, it was not necessarily so, and whether it was so for any particular individual under discussion must be argued on an individual basis. The statement that the king's power was derived directly from God did not rule out the possibility of believing that other authorities, like that of fathers, were also derived directly from God. It did not even rule out the possibility of holding, with Ponet and Goodman, that the divine right of inferior magistrates was equally directly derived from God, and included the right of resisting kings. It did not rule out the possibility that the king's divine right, however directly it had come from God, might have come subject to terms and conditions imposed by God, and that the subject might oppose him if he broke those conditions. Nor, for a common lawyer, did it rule out the possibility that the common law was equally directly derived from God, and that the divine right of the king and the divine right of the common law, like Lords and Commons, had to learn to live with each other. The statement that the King's power was directly derived from God might be used either to limit his power or to increase it.

Coke's judicial rival, Lord Chancellor Ellesmere, in arguing that

---

[28] Sir E. Coke, *Ninth Report*, I, and in Hawarde, *Reportes*, 357–8.
[29] Sommerville, *Sir Robert Filmer*, p. xix.

the royal prerogative could not be delegated, suggested a very different emphasis.

For the King, in that he is the substitute of God ymediatelie; the father of his people and head of the commonwealth, hath by participation with God and with his subjectes, a discretion, judgement and feeling of love towardes those over whom he raigneth, onelie proper to himselfe and his place and person; whoe seeing he cannot into others infuse the wisdome, power and guifts which God, in respect of his place and charge hath enabled him with all, can neither subordinate any other judge to governe by that knowledge which the king can no otherwaies then by his knowne will participate unto him.

The judge must do 'what the law (which is the king's owne will) showeth unto him'.[30] This tends to exalt the divine right of the king over the divine right of the law, and Coke and Ellesmere enjoyed an equal claim to speak for 'the common law'.

It should perhaps have emerged already that one reason for the universal acceptability of divine right was that it provided a vocabulary and an imagery to limit royal power, as well as to exalt it. In this, too, it rested on a firm scriptural warrant, in this case Acts 5: 29, 'we ought to obey God rather than man'. This doctrine was repeated in the *Homily of Obedience*: 'yet let us beleeve undoubtedly (good Christian people) that we may not obey kings, magistrates or any other (though they be our owne fathers), if they would command us to doe any thing contrary to God's commandments. In such a case, we ought to say with the Apostle, wee must rather obey God then man.'[31] The *Homilies* spelt out that this doctrine justified failure to obey, but not rebellion. Yet telling a king publicly that his commands contradicted God's, even if not followed by rebellion, had a considerable critical force. This was

[30] L. A. Knafla, *Law and Politics in Jacobean England* (Cambridge, 1977), 198. Also E. Forset, *A Comparative Discourse of the Bodies Naturall and Politique* (1606), 16. For James VI and I's views on this subject, which are less simple than they are sometimes taken to be, see *Political Works*, 61–4, and Huntington Library, Ellesmere MS 1214, which is perhaps the best report of his opening speech to the Parliament of 1621. Tanner, *Constitutional Conflicts*, 5–6, read this as a claim to 'an independent legislative power for the Crown'. For another reading, see C. Russell, *The Causes of the English Civil War* (Oxford, 1990), 151. On both occasions, the context of James's argument was the claim that, both in Scotland and in England, kings had created Parliaments in general, and chose to summon them in particular. See also *Commons Debates 1621*, iv. 2–3, ii. 3–4. It was clearly James's intention to deny ancient constitution theory, and to deny to Parliaments any Melvillian power to act independently of the king. How much further he meant to take the point he was making is not clear. See below, n. 44.

[31] *Sermons or Homilies*, i. 74. For James's adherence to this doctrine, see *Political Works*, 61.

the doctrine invoked by John Burgess, accepting deprivation for refusing to subscribe to the canons of 1604: 'would God your Majestie would believe of us that the only feare of Gods displeasure hazardes us upon your majesties, whome if we did not feare less then God, neyther should we longe feare so much as we ought.'[32] Laud, for example, had no doubt what a serious charge it was to say the king's commands contradicted God's. When accused at his impeachment for imprisoning a man for a sermon saying we ought to obey God rather than man, he replied: 'no man doubts but it ought to be so, when the commands are opposite.'[33] For this very reason, he thought it a great offence to insinuate that the commands were opposite when they were not. Richard Hooker, quoting Bracton that the king was under God and the law, said the Royal Supremacy was subject to the same restriction: 'what man is there so brain-sick, as not to except in such speeches God himself, the king of all the kinges of the earth?' Professor Sommerville agrees that 'no Protestant believed that man should be obeyed rather than God'. I would qualify this statement only by reading 'Christian' instead of 'Protestant'. Though we agree on the point, I attach much more significance to its force as a check on royal authority than he does. Authority's regular fear of any statement that its commands contradicted God's suggests that it too saw a considerable danger in the practical application of this unchallenged theoretical principle.[34]

The same doctrine applied to divine right inside marriage. William Gouge insisted that wives 'may not be subject in any thing to their husbands, that cannot stand with their subjection to the Lord'.[35] It was a consequence of this doctrine that, in a religiously mixed marriage, a husband's divine right was perpetually under challenge. Even if the husband did not try to force his wife's conscience, husbands might react in a way which showed that they felt under threat. According to Daniel Rogers:

if they permit them not their religion with gibing and geering them openly, yet with a secret disdaine. If, (say they), our wives will needs be

[32] S. B. Babbage, *Puritanism and Richard Bancroft* (1962), 382. BL Add. MS 38, 492, fo. 94ʳ.
[33] *State Trials*, iv. 374.
[34] R. Hooker, *The Laws of Ecclesiastical Polity*, VII. ii. 3. J. P. Sommerville, 'The Royal Supremacy and Episcopacy *Jure Divino*, 1603–1640', *Journal of Ecclesiastical History*, 34 (1983), 557.
[35] Gouge, *Of Domesticall Duties*, 27.

precise, let them . . . You see, (say they), what our wives affect, they must have their wils, we must not crosse them, for then all were out of order, let them alone and run their course, as poore silly women may doe.

To all this Rogers replied: 'well, take heed, you wise fellows . . . lest God pull ye not downe from that pride and jollity.' 'What knowest thou, o man, whether God have appointed thy wife to occasion thy conversion? But as for following her steps to heavens, oh, it were too great an honour to the wife.'[36] The godly preachers, of course, took a quite different position when they were dealing with the popish wife of a godly husband: in that case the husband must 'stand upon his power', and not let his wife go to Mass.[37] The preachers, of course, were interested in true religion, rather than in the constitutional theory of marriage, and for them, as for many others, whether they reached for Rom. 13: 1 or for Acts 5: 29, depended, not on the authority involved, but on whether they believed the disputed doctrine to be true or false.

It was not only in matters of doctrine that Acts 5: 29 might apply. Daniel Rogers said that, 'if thou be pressed to any base thing, which conscience starts at, as to keepe loose company, to weare garish apparel, to traduce the godly, or what else soever indecent and impure; forfeit the pleasing of thy husband on earth, and please a better in heaven'.[38] William Gouge said a child must disobey his parent, not only if forbidden to go to the Protestants' churches, to hear a sermon, or to pray in a known tongue, but also to give just weight and measure, and to speak the truth when called as a witness.[39] Overall, then, Acts 5: 29 could be an all-purpose weapon to restrict authority.

Divine right could be used as a warning to sovereigns of what they could expect if they displeased their divine superior. Peter Wentworth told Queen Elizabeth: 'he that hath a good farme and hath none other holde thereof, but at his landlords pleasure, the best pollicie for him wee wolde thinke is to please his landlord. And this is the case (madame) betwixt you and God in respect of your kingdome.'[40] When James VI and I said that erring kings were

[36] Rogers, *Matrimoniall Honour*, 39–40.
[37] Gouge, *Of Domesticall Duties*, 380.
[38] Rogers, *Matrimoniall Honour*, 264.
[39] Gouge, *Of Domesticall Duties*, 474.
[40] BL Add. MS 24, 664, fo. 16^r.

remitted to God, 'the sorest and sharpest schoolemaster that can be devised for them', he spoke as one who hated and feared his schoolmaster, and the image was not an empty one.[41] Even the biblical source for the proposition that kings were Gods carried its own warning: as James said, 'in that same Psalm where God saith to kings, *vos dii estis*, he immediately thereafter concludes, but ye shall die like men'. That the warning shot had gone home can perhaps be deduced from the fact that James leaves out the second half of the verse: 'ye shall die like men, *and fall like one of the princes*.'[42] The text, though it gave honour to the king, was not usually used to confer very much power on him. When Roger Manwaring, a rare exception, tried to use it to claim for the king a sort of participation in God's omnipotency, Archbishop Abbot 'told him it is very blasphemy, and those words in the Psalms, *dii estis*, do warrant no such matter'.[43]

What, then, if anything, was controversial about James's views on divine right? There was nothing controversial about saying kings were gods, nor even about saying that they should not be resisted. Non-resistance was controversial in Scotland, for which *Basilikon Doron* and *The Trew Law of Free Monarchies* were written, but not so in England. It is important, as Dr Wormald has reminded us, to remember the Scottish context in which these works were written. The central thrust of James's work is always to claim that no authority can exist in the kingdom which is not derived from the king. He wrote to deny the Melvillian claims advanced for an independent power of legislation in the General Assembly, and, by extension, papal claims to an authority independent of the king's.[44] On the papacy, English Members of Parliament agreed with him, and, in attacking claims made on behalf of the General Assembly, he was attacking claims which had not been made in England since the death of Becket. In dealing with the Scottish Parliament, which was not one of the forces in Scotland which he

---

[41] *Political Works*, 69.

[42] Ibid. 309: Psalm 82: 7.

[43] R. Manwaring, *Religion and Allegiance* (2 vols.; 1627), ii. 23–6; *Proceedings in Parliament 1628*, ed. M. F. Keeler *et al.* (6 vols.; New Haven, Conn., 1983), v. 634.

[44] J. Wormald, 'James VI and I, *Basilikon Doron* and the *Trew Law of Free Monarchies*: The Scottish Context and the English Translation', in L. L. Peck (ed.), *The Mental World of the Jacobean Court* (Folger Shakespeare Library, 1991). I am grateful to Dr Wormald for allowing me to see this important article before publication. On James's moves towards royal supremacy in Scotland, see Russell, *The Causes of The English Civil War*, 37, 47–8.

found particularly hostile, James was mainly concerned to assert
that it could not make law without his assent. This left him with
a problem about how the Reformation Acts of 1560, which had
never been touched with the royal sceptre, had come to have the
force of law.[45] Similarly, the insistence of James and his partisans
that kings were not answerable to subjects provoked questions
about what had happened to his mother. In the margin of the
British Library copy of Dr David Owen's *Herod and Pilate Reconciled*,
its seventeenth-century owner has written: 'why was Mary of
Scotland beheaded in England?'[46]

Yet, even if James was not gunning for the English Parliament
in what he wrote as King of Scots, much of what he said about
the relationship between the king and the law was unacceptable to
many English lawyers. His statement that 'it followes of necessity,
that the kings were the authors and makers of the laws, and not
the lawes of the kings' is made about Scotland, but Coke would
have resisted its application to England, as he would James's
insistence that William had conquered England, as had many others
before him.[47]

There was a further potential for the growth of power when
James's ideas and those of his supporters were applied to the
doctrine, unknown in Scotland before the reign of James VI, of
the Royal Supremacy. To those who took literally the declaratory
preambles of the English Act of Supremacy and the Act in Restraint
of Appeals, the king was supreme head of the church by divine
law, whether any common or statute law recognized the fact or
not. The invocation of divine law might carry the conclusion that
he must be Supreme Head of the Church of Scotland, as well as
Supreme Head of the Church of England. To those who believed
that this created a separate sphere of ecclesiastical authority,
exercised by the king through his convocation, independent of
Parliament or common law, it was possible to argue that the king
had a divine right to govern the Church which the law did not
control. Lord Chancellor Ellesmere, giving the charge to the judges
in February 1604/5, replied to those who said the High Commission
had no warrant by law to do as they did that they did not need

---

[45] *Political Works*, 62. This passage has the effect, whether intended or not, of denying the
legitimacy of the Acts of the Parliament of 1560, which introduced the Scottish Reformation.

[46] D. Owen, *Herod and Pilate Reconciled* (1610), 57 (misprinted as '75').

[47] *Political Works*, 62–3. Sir E. Coke, *Ninth Report*, preface. See above, n. 30.

it, for their power was independent of the law. 'Whereas the King's matie, as it were inheritable and descended from God, hath absolutelye monarchicall power annexed inseparablye to his crowne and diademe, not by common law nor statute law, but more auncyente than eyther of them.'[48] Roger Manwaring developed this into the claim that 'the king is the sacred and supreme head of two bodies, the one spiritual, the other secular'.[49] In this view, his spiritual body might appear dangerously unchecked.

The other way in which James's views on divine right might appear to threaten law was his view on the inalienable right of hereditary succession. As Dr David Wootton has pointed out, James's succession was contrary to statute law, which upheld Henry VIII's will, leaving the succession to the Grey line, and possibly also contrary to common law, which asserted that an alien could not succeed, and so would have left the succession to Arabella Stuart, who happened to have been born in England. As Dr Wootton says, 'under these circumstances, to assert the supremacy of statute was to question James's title to the throne'.[50] The Jacobean Act of Recognition could not correct this statute, since it was only if James was already a lawful king that the statute could be passed by a lawful Parliament. The statute therefore refrained from including a normal enacting clause, making James king 'by authority of this Act'. Instead, the enacting clause said they had *recognized* James's title, 'beinge bounden thereunto bothe by the laws of God and man', and that he was king 'by inherent birthright' immediately on the Queen's death.[51] The effect of the enacting clause was to publish this opinion. In other words, James's divine right had overriden statute. This was welcome enough to the English Parliament at the time, since it was preferable to civil war, but there was a note of warning in Sir Edwin Sandys's remark that 'this House hath translated the crown from one line to another, which it could not do'. By 1621 Edward Alford appeared to have

---

[48] Hawarde, *Reportes*, 188. See also Owen, *Herod and Pilate Reconciled*, Epistle. On the relationship between the Royal Supremacy and the law, see C. Russell, *The Fall of the British Monarchies 1637–1642* (Oxford, 1991), 15–16, 34, 39–43, 158, 231–4, and other refs. under index.

[49] Manwaring, *Religion and Allegiance*, i. 5.

[50] D. Wootton, *Divine Right and Democracy* (1986), 30.

[51] *Statutes of the Realm*, I Jac. I cap. 1.

accepted this limitation: '*Parliamentum omnia potest* except altringe the right line of the crowne.'[52]

If an Act of Parliament could not determine the succession, here was a vital loophole in any Eltonian doctrine of the sovereignty and omnicompetence of statute. In Calvin's Case, Chief Baron Fleming appeared to be trying to drive a coach and horses through this loophole when he deduced from this doctrine that Calvin 'is a subjecte borne in respecte of the law of God, and not of the municipall lawes of this kingdome of Englaunde'.[53] If cases in court were to be judged on the law of God, even where it was in opposition to the law of England, the rule of law could indeed be held to be in danger. Fortunately, Coke, by developing a common-law doctrine of allegiance which made Calvin a subject, saved Fleming from himself, but the loophole remained a dangerous one. James himself was insistent that, 'at the very moment of the expiring of the king reigning, the nearest and lawful heire entreth in his place'.[54] Sir Edward Coke, in the Star Chamber, backed James up. He argued that

the king's matie, in his lawfull, juste and lineall title to the crowne of Englaunde, comes not by succession onelye, or by election, but from god onelye (so that there is no interregnum, as the ignoraunte dothe suppose, untill the ceremony of coronation) by reason of his lineall discente . . . and the very instant the breath was oute of her matie's bodye, Kinge James was the lawfull and rightfull kinge.[55]

Thus, the succession had come to be governed by divine right alone, and not by law. This does not mean that Henry VIII had not believed in his divine right: far from it. It meant that James brought with him, by the necessary circumstances of the case, a different doctrine of divine right from Henry's, and one which deprived his English Parliament of any say in the control of the succession. It was only out of courtesy that James thanked them for receiving him in the place 'which God had provided for me'. His doctrine of divine right, then, did in one way significantly diminish Parliamentary powers, for the power to determine the

[52] *CJ* i. 178, 951; *Commons Debates 1621*, v. 20.

[53] Hawarde, *Reportes*, 362.

[54] *Political Works*, 69.

[55] Hawarde, *Reportes*, 163–4. I would like to thank Dr Nicholas Tyacke for drawing my attention to this reference.

succession is a power in which all other powers may be included.[16]

We have, then, found a small spark of fire to go with this vast pall of smoke: we have found one issue on which the doctrine of divine right, as held by James, effectively exalted the king at the expense of parliament and of the law. It is, though, a spark of fire which showed no great signs of spreading: the succession, however great its theoretical significance might be, was in practice an enclosed issue, and showed little sign of producing fundamental change in thinking on other issues. Still less was it an issue of dispute between king and Parliament: the last thing James's first Parliament wanted was to go back to all the anxieties of an open succession. The Speaker, it is true, gave James an instant reminder that 'the ark of government of [this] kingdom hath ever been steered by the laws of the same',[17] but it was on the issue of the union, rather than that of the succession, that such anxieties were focused, and in the act for setting up Commissioners for the Union that official reassurance was administered. Nothing in James's doctrines restrained him from instigating the Act to limit the length of leases granted by bishops, in which an Act of Parliament was used to restrain the royal prerogative of dispensing, apparently at the king's request.[18]

The argument about whether the Commons' privileges were held by James's grant or of right, which was so dear to the Victorians, was one which was perfectly compatible with belief in divine right on both sides, and was in any case joined only on two brief occasions in 1604 and 1621. The dispute about the meaning of the Royal Supremacy, though capable of becoming a major theoretical dispute, was again compatible with belief in divine right on both sides. With the growing ecclesiastical harmony between James and his godly subjects, the issue was successfully buried until 1640. James's occasional argument that his power should not be 'disputed upon' was no more effective than such claims by rulers usually are, and there is no sign that James was ever utopian enough to expect otherwise. Whatever James's views on the relationship between him and the law may have been (and they

---

[16] *CJ* i. 145.
[17] Ibid. 146.
[18] *Statutes of the Realm*, I Jac. I caps. 2 and 3. On the issues raised by the union, see C. Russell, 'English Parliaments, 1593–1606', in N. Jones and D. Dean (eds.), *The Parliaments of Elizabethan England* (Oxford, 1990), 207–13.

were not simple, nor entirely designed for English use), anxiety about the issue faded with the disappearance of the Union issue after 1607. What seems to have been an effective final reassurance was administered by James's speech to Parliament in 1610, which was popular enough to be quoted against his son.

In the end, the system of beliefs associated with divine right survived unchallenged up to and beyond 1642 because it was a system of values equipped with an almost Hegelian capacity to produce its own antithesis. The exaltation of the king as God's deputy, as it exalted the king above men, equally stressed his subjection to God, and, crucially, it allowed his subjects to remind him of the fact, and to argue, with Sir Henry Finch, that 'the king's prerogative stretcheth not to the doing of any wrong'. In Finch's version, the courts were even allowed to give God's law precedence over the king's, and, for example, to treat Proclamations made on the Sabbath as void.[19] Such ideas meant that the king was subject to something more than his own individual interpretation of God's will: where the king's religion differed from the subject's, Acts 5: 29 actually imposed on the subject a *duty* of disobedience. Finally, if the king's God-given eminence appeared to be making him too lonely in his power, it was possible, in full reliance on the divine pattern, to quote Jethro's advice to Moses, 'in the multitude of counsellors there is safety', as asserting the divine right of conciliar government. With a system so versatile, it was no wonder that people found no need to look outside it: it did everything which could be asked of it, and, while it did that, there was no need to change it.

---

[19] Sir H. Finch, *Law, or a Discourse Thereof* (1627), 85, 7.

8

The Conflicting Loyalties of a 'vulger counselor': The Third Earl of Southampton, 1597–1624

NEIL CUDDY

In March 1619 James I almost died of 'stone, Gowte, spleene [and] a scowring vomit'. On what he and all observers thought would shortly be his death-bed, he advised his son Charles how to construct his new regime, and prepare for a Parliament which had now been effectively avoided for almost a decade. After his recovery, the King and 'the greate ones'—chiefly Buckingham, royal Bedchamber favourite—saw clearly in what 'ill estate for frends' such a new regime would have been. James, therefore, agreed to let those well disposed to Parliament 'speede better', and at the end of April, at the age of 45, Henry Wriothesley, Third Earl of Southampton, was at last made a Privy Councillor— by which the 26-year-old Buckingham reportedly 'strenthened himselfe'.[1] Southampton acknowledged no dependence, however. Not having sought the councillorship 'directly or indirectly by my self or any of my frendes', he felt all the more bound 'to serve [the king] honestly': otherwise he 'had much rather have continewed a spectator then become an actor'. And so he expected 'rather [to] performe the office of a counselor in keeping then givinge counsell', asking his 'good frendes' 'not to expect much from mee: you well know how thinges stand & pass with Us, & how little one vulger counselor is able to effect. All I can promise is to doe noe hurt.'[2]

What was Southampton's influence in Parliament, which made his 'friendship' attractive to Buckingham? Why did he feel a conflict

My thanks to Gerald Aylmer, John Bosher, C. S. L. Davies, Ian Gentles, Conrad Russell, David Starkey, Jenny Wormald, and the editors of this volume for their comments either on this chapter, or on earlier work underlying it. Responsibility for what appears here is, of course, mine alone.

[1] PRO SP 14/108/15, 16; SP 14/109/16.
[2] *The Letters of John Chamberlain*, ed. N. E. McClure (2 vols.; Philadelphia, Pa., 1939), ii. 234; PRO SP 14/108/86.

of loyalty—if no long crisis of conscience about it—in taking his Council oath? What counsel did he think it better to keep than give? To what was the higher loyalty directed, which meant that to serve the King 'honestly' would give him offence? What, in short, was a 'vulger counselor'? The answers will enable us to assess Southampton's (and his following's) political significance— and to raise questions of more than biographical importance.[3]

'Revisionism' over the past fifteen years has provided a refreshing antidote to Whig history, and a welcome return to scholarship in the sources, yielding detailed political narratives of often very short spans of time. But the consequence has been to break a formerly continuous political narrative into small pieces, and either to deny, or, by microscopic concentration, to evade, the connections between them. The periods of the early, and late, 1620s, the 1630s, and the wars after 1637 have each been described in very different terms, for very particular reasons. This prevents the Civil War imposing a misleading pattern on the half century preceding it. But it also tends to mask the coherence of the period as a whole in its own right—the extent to which issues recurred, principles divided politics, and the same men used similar tactics and adopted the same stances decade after decade. Southampton and his parliamentary following formed a continuous leadership in the Commons between 1604 and 1614; they maintained a 'popular' reputation that never lost credibility with the back-benches; they stuck to consistent, identifiable principles; and, while they were used as parliamentary managers by Robert Cecil and Robert Carr, their principles conflicted with a high-prerogative lobby in Council and Bedchamber with which James usually agreed— so causing much of the disruption in the neglected parliamentary history of these years. Though that period is the chief concern of this chapter, we can also look briefly beyond it, to suggest connections with the better-known politics of the 1620s: and, before it, to investigate Southampton's Elizabethan roots.[4]

[3] Biographies: C. Stopes, *The Life of Henry, Third Earl of Southampton, Shakespeare's Patron* (Cambridge, 1922); G. P. V. Akrigg, *Shakespeare and the Earl of Southampton* (1968); A. L. Rowse, *Shakespeare's Southampton: Patron of Virginia* (1965). L. Stone, *Family and Fortune: Studies in Aristocratic Finance* (Oxford, 1973), ch. 7, is important on the Earls' finances, 1530–1667. The work of Sue Griffin, under Dr Jenny Wormald's supervision, promises to provide a full account of the Earl and his politics.

[4] This interpretation varies from C. Russell, 'Parliamentary History in Perspective, 1604– 29', *History*, 61 (1976). C. Russell, *The Causes of the English Civil War* (Oxford, 1990), qualifies that earlier argument: but the admitted 'tunnel vision' (p. 29) caused by the imperative to explain the Civil War still compromises the coherence of earlier periods.

I

Southampton's political career began with the Second Earl of Essex and his faction. Comradeship in arms came first, against Spain on the Islands Voyage of 1597. The link was strengthened by ties of kinship, when in 1598 Southampton married Essex's cousin. In that year too, in Paris, came ideological initiation: there Southampton probably abandoned Catholicism for the Church of England, while Essex sent Henry Cuffe to read him Aristotle's *Politics*.⁵ It was in all a rapid introduction to what Essex stood for: anti-Spanish crusade; a following bound by kinship; a 'politique' religious stance; and, above all, noble leadership, both military and political. To justify the latter, Essex's circle drew on Calvinist writers like Hotman and du Plessis Mornay, urging the nobility to serve true religion; on classical aristocratic republicanism, in Tacitus and Aristotle; and medieval sources for the powers of the ancient nobility's inherited offices—indeed, taking the theory of female transmission of claims to titles and offices so far as to produce a self-perpetuating caste at the apex of the peerage, over which the Crown might have small influence. Thus Essex claimed not only his earldoms, but also the Constableship, combining supreme military command with a role brokering a disputed succession. Elizabeth made him Earl Marshal in 1597 probably because she hesitated wholly to deny him that inheritance.⁶

Essex's rivals claimed to be worried about where all this— particularly his military following—might lead. But we should beware of taking those worries at face value, and reading them too much in the light of the supposed 'outcome' of Essex's career— his 'rebellion' in 1601. Before the disasters of 1599–1601 Essex's stance is intelligible within Professor Collinson's 'monarchical republic'. The peculiar late-Tudor succession of a minor and two women removed one medieval (and early Tudor) focus of power— the entourage, perennial instrument of royal freedom of action—

---

⁵ Akrigg, *Shakespeare and Southampton*, 27, 34, 47, 130, 177–9.
⁶ M. James, 'At the Crossroads of the Political Culture: The Essex Revolt, 1601', in M. James, *Society Politics and Culture* (Cambridge, 1986); Folger MS G. b. 18, treatise of Dec. 1598, advancing this idea of nobility. R. McCoy, *The Rites of Knighthood* (Berkeley, Calif., 1989), ch. 4, and pp. 88–95. Essex's ruling on the Abergavenny case (Feb. 1599) used the Folger treatise's arguments, as did Shakespeare's *Henry V*, esp. Act I, sc. ii (1598): they underlay the English claim to France, and the Stuart claim to England; M. Axton, *The Queen's Two Bodies* (1977), ch. 7.

and concentrated power in the other focus, the Council, the nobility's usual forum. Yet, remarkably, Elizabeth ensured instead that her Privy Council was small, appointed 'by choyce . . . not by birth', directed by her plebeian creatures the Cecils, and attendant on her. Essex's stance tried to lever open this regime: it enabled him and his noble friends to demand a greater say, it undermined his rivals (particularly the Cecils, who could only ask 'what is gentility but ancient riches?'), and it attracted the ancient nobility as allies, and their cadet relations as followers—a Berkeley, a Neville, a Sandys, two Percies, a Manners, even a Howard. Northumberland told James that Essex harnessed noble discontent 'that places of honor [and] offices of trust are not laid in their handes to manage as thay were wont'.[7] Essex also took up 'commonwealth causes', securing clutches of Commons seats for his followers. But his purely political activities seem to have been limited, and, despite his agitation for patronage and offices, the Council was remarkably united in facing Parliaments. War imposed discipline: since Essex led the expeditions that fought it, and his following reaped the rewards, high wartime taxation (identified by Northumberland as the key 'popular' grievance of the 1590s) was something Essex could do only a little, as in 1593, to redress. Other 'popular' issues identified by Northumberland—monopolies and wardship—were raised and handled by the Cecils and their clients.[8]

So Essex and Southampton became increasingly isolated as leaders of a largely military following. Having failed to open the Council and conciliar patronage through political pressure, in 1599 Essex returned from Ireland with his second-in-command Southampton and tried a personal appeal to the Queen, storming the Bedchamber—the Court's inviolable inner sanctum. His disgrace and arrest followed, while Southampton, fighting in Ireland and the Low Countries, agitated for his restoration. In late 1600 Essex's sweet wines farm ended, breaking his lines of credit; and, as followers fell away, desperation led to plans to bypass the

---

[7] James, 'Crossroads', emphasizes the violent military tendencies of the faction; P. Collinson, 'The Monarchical Republic of Queen Elizabeth I', *Bulletin of the John Rylands Library*, 69 (1987), 394 ff., esp. pp. 423–4; *Correspondence of King James VI . . . with Sir Robert Cecil and Others*, ed. J. Bruce (Camden Soc., NS 78; 1861), 59.

[8] J. E. Neale, *Elizabeth I and her Parliaments, 1584–1601* (1957), 295, 306–12, 338, 353, 363; *Correspondence of King James VI*, 59.

Cecilian grip on the Council in a palace *coup*, with each Chamber to be captured by a faction member, and Essex and Southampton alone to enter the Privy Chamber and beyond. A pre-emptive summons on 7 February 1601 forced Essex's hand. But, from his house on the Strand next day, he turned away from Whitehall, to stage an incoherent demonstration in the City. Pathetic in effect, it was treated with deadly seriousness. Essex was tried for attempted usurpation; Southampton, Rutland, and Lord Sandys for conspiring to depose and slay Elizabeth. Southampton was also accused of fostering papist malcontents, and inciting Essex to rebel, both of which he strongly denied. Given his obvious involvement and the plans for storming Whitehall, his only defence was that he had throughout acted as a loyal friend and follower—not an initiator. It had the advantage of being broadly true. Ineffective for others, the plea got Southampton off with two years' in the Tower.[9]

II

Convicted of treason, Southampton lived thanks to Sir Robert Cecil.[10] On the face of it, this seems surprising: had there not been deadly rivalry between Cecil and Essex factions? In fact, after joining Essex in 1597, Southampton had written regularly to Cecil. He had still found Cecil 'kind and friendly' in 1600. And, at the trial in 1601, Southampton had even helped Cecil rebut Essex's counter-charges.[11] But as important as past sentiment and present gratitude were Cecil's calculations for the future. The Secretary remained in harness with the Howards, who had staked all on the Stuart claim. So, even as he tied himself to them, Cecil preserved as counterweight his links with what remained of the Essex faction—open supporters of James's right, who now looked to Southampton as leader. James VI also regarded 'poor Southamtone' with both sympathy and calculation. His release from the Tower (with his fellow conspirator Sir Henry Neville), arranged in advance

[9] James, 'Crossroads', *passim*; Stopes, *Life*, 190; Akrigg, *Shakespeare and Southampton*, 121–5.
[10] Akrigg *Shakespeare and Southampton*, 130; Rowse, *Shakespeare's Southampton*, 163–4; *Correspondence of King James VI*, 68.
[11] *Cal. SP Dom. 1595–7*, 448, 456, 464; HMC, *Salisbury*, ix. 341; x. 333; Akrigg, *Shakespeare and Southampton*, 152, 123–4. Cecil's links with Southampton suggest Essex–Cecil rivalry in the 1590s has been exaggerated.

and signed as one of James's first acts as King of England, was swiftly followed by the restoration of his lands and titles, and the grant of Essex's chief support, the sweet wines farm. These urgent gestures show the importance James and Cecil attached to the Essex faction's support at the accession.[12]

But, once established, James I thought again. The Council admitted more of 'the ancient nobilitie'—but not Southampton. Partly this was James's personal distrust. But it was also related to the general disappointment of the English in the accession settlement, as James set his own political agenda. Despite Cecil's attempts to ensure that no Scots held English office, Kinloss brought with Southampton's release his own appointment to the Council, and 'at once took possession, to the disgust of the Lords'. But the greatest change was the revival of an alternative focus of power to the Council: a politically important entourage, the first since Henry VIII, the last adult male to rule. The wholly Scottish Bedchamber was dominated by Sir George Home (later Earl of Dunbar), who had James's 'love, and knowledge of all his humours', and knew 'most of the others' secret thoughts'. This revived dual-centred politics threatened Cecil. Still important on the Council, he now had to make himself useful to the Bedchamber (and especially to Home). In James's first 'years that were as Christmas' he administered one of the great patronage bonanzas of English history, in which the Scots Bedchamber were chief beneficiaries. In the last resort, he had to co-operate to survive as chief English minister. These rival claims to his favour came just when he may have hoped to bring Southampton and his followers into the circle of power and patronage.[13]

Denied Council and Bedchamber, Southampton instead found a role in Parliament. His chance came as the new dual-centred politics created a division of counsels between the Council and Cecil on one hand, and James and his Bedchamber on the other. Each brought forward radical schemes in the first session of 1604. Cecil's priority was finance: James's was Union. And the two programmes clashed, as spokesmen associated with Southampton

[12] *The Letters of King James VI and I*, ed. G. P. V. Akrigg (1984), 189; *Correspondence of King James VI*, 51; BL, Cotton MS Titus BVII, fo. 443, 1 Apr. C66/1620.
[13] PRO SP 14/1/73; *Cal. SP Venetian*, x. 10; HMC, *Salisbury*, xvii. 87; N. Cuddy, 'The Revival of the Entourage: The Bedchamber of James I, 1603–25', in D. Starkey (ed.), *The English Court* (1987), 174–7, 195–202.

led the Commons to support the first, and oppose the second.

James put Union proposals to Parliament in 1604 despite Cecil's contrary advice: so the King personally dictated the bill (to change the name of his kingdoms to Britain, and set up a commission to frame measures for the next session), and entrusted its management to Ellesmere and Bacon. It ran straight into Commons opposition led by Southampton's followers. Sir Maurice Berkeley 'first turned the stream backward' by claiming the name-change would dishonour England; Sir Edwin Sandys next framed a legal objection to it as a threat to England's fundamental laws; Sir Herbert Croft moved to refer this to the lawyers; and Sir Henry Neville added the diplomatic perils of the change, as Sandys, Berkeley, and Croft prepared a team of speakers to put their case to the Lords and judges. Whereas James claimed the Union was complete in his person and merely needed recognition, this group maintained the accession of a private man who was also King of Scots had no effect on the public kingdom of England, or on James's public powers (limited by common law and Parliament) as its king. They thus made an implicit distinction between king and kingdom, and the king's private and public bodies. They won: the judges ruled the name-change would cause 'the utter extinction of all the laws now in force', and Cecil withdrew the proposal on James's behalf. The bill to set up a commission was then mauled by Sandys, Croft, and Ridgeway, for the same reasons: Cecil had to step in to strip it of references to any Union already established.[14]

These MPs had strong connections with Southampton. Sandys may have persuaded the earl to renounce Catholicism in 1598. He owed his seat to their mutual kinsman, the Essexian Lord Sandys; and he was named first to the committee for Southampton's Bill of Restitution. Croft, a former Essexian, got an early knighthood in 1603 by Southampton's means (through Cecil). Ridgeway served Essex in the Azores and in Ireland, and was probably closest now to Lord Deputy Mountjoy. Neville and Southampton had been fellow prisoners: in June 1604 they and Berkeley were arrested again. When Queen Anne's Court was established in late 1603, the ex-Essexian Sidney became her Lord Chamberlain, Cecil her High

---

[14] PRO PRO 31/3/37, 19/29 Feb., 11/21 Mar. PRO SP 14/7/75; *CJ* i. 176, 949–50; 179, 952; 186, 958; 188–9. PRO SP 14/7/85; *CJ* i. 180. Ibid. 218, 224–5, 228; 976–7, 979.

Steward, Southampton Master of her Game, and Sandys, Ridgeway, and Berkeley got places on her Council.[15]

Clearly, Southampton and his associates also had links to Cecil: the French ambassador saw them as 'closely bound' to him.[16] There is no sign that Cecil encouraged their opposition to Union—though equally there is no sign that he tried to stop it. But there is evidence of co-operation concerning Cecil's priority in 1604: finance. He began the session by floating the idea of a permanent tax to re-endow the Crown, in exchange for the abolition of the prerogative right of wardship. When Union left centre-stage, the wardship scheme was revived by Sandys, Berkeley, Ridgeway, and Neville. It looks like classic parliamentary management by 'men of business'—except that, even as they put forward Cecil's wardship plan, those 'men of business' were mangling James's Union proposals.[17]

The tension was wrecking the session: so something had to give. First, James's Bedchamber confidant Home, working with allies on the Council, tried to bypass Cecil's control of the Commons. The wardship scheme was ditched: Lords spokesmen told the Commons they were assaulting the prerogative by suggesting it, and should instead grant subsidies of gratitude that James's accession had secured their property—a high-prerogative line later characteristic of Henry Howard, Earl of Northampton. Over the next few days, Home (whose views were similar) used independent channels to 'sound out the disposition of the House' about a subsidy. Cecil apparently replied by setting up machinery to frame an 'Apology' for Commons proceedings, particularly on wardship (on Ridgeway's motion, supported by the Cecilian Speaker); drafted by Sandys and the wardship committee, it was twice read. But Home's soundings on the subsidy proved negative (on 12 June): and the Apology was overtaken by other events.[18]

---

[15] P. Peckard, *Memoirs of the Life of Mr. Nicholas Ferrar* (Cambridge, 1790), 102; P. Hasler, *The House of Commons, 1558–1603* (3 vols.; 1981), i. 172, and s.v. Sandys; *CJ* i. 941 (after the Councillors); Hasler, s.v. Croft; HMC, *Salisbury*, xv. 116; BL Add. MS 38139, fo. 104ᵛ.

[16] PRO PRO 31/3/37, 28 June/8 July. N. Tyacke, 'Sir Edwin Sandys and the Cecils: A Client–Patron Relationship', *Historical Research*, 64 (1991), 89–91, suggests direct links with Cecil; HMC, *Salisbury*, ix. 96; x. 31, 108; xi. 61, 413; xii. 498. Cecil got Neville an embassy in 1599. By 1603–4 the signs are that all looked first to Southampton, then to Cecil.

[17] *CJ* i. 207, 969; 211, 973; HMC, *Salisbury*, xxiii. 130–1; P. Croft, 'Wardship in the Parliament of 1604', *Parliamentary History*, 2 (1983), 40–1; cf. M. Graves, 'Managing Elizabethan Parliaments', in D. Dean and N. Jones (eds.), *The Parliaments of Elizabethan England* (Oxford, 1990), 57–61.

[18] HMC, *Portland*, ix. 11–13; HMC, *Salisbury*, xvi. 132–3; xxiii. 138–9, 140 ff. I am grateful to Conrad Russell for the point about Phelips.

Unable to bypass them, James, Home, and Northampton evidently next tried to isolate Cecil and destroy his contacts. About 9–13 June Home discussed Cecil with James, alone 'in his carowche'. Home reported the result: a 'secret cowrse' recognizing Cecil as 'meteste man to be counsellour in all matters of estett'—providing his 'love to [his] Ma[jes]ty exsedes aney perteculler respect thatt he can have eyther to hym selffe or his frendes'.[19] The 'frendes' who might have to be sacrificed were probably the Southampton group, for on 24 June Southampton, his fellow Essex conspirators Lord Danvers and Sir Henry Neville, Sir Maurice Berkeley, and some lesser followers were arrested. Interrogated next day by the Council, they faced charges of popish plotting (which have a distinct air of having been recycled from 1601—like the alleged aim of purging the Howards); and of conspiring 'to slay several Scots . . . about the person of the king', above all Home—both more original and more convincing, given the notoriety of the faction's views. Southampton reportedly had a 'mortal hatred' for the Bedchamber, and was questioned about talk 'against the Union, full of discontent . . . at his dinner table'. Set beside Neville's and Berkeley's key roles in the Commons against the name-change, the Southampton group look like the victims of an attempted purge. Southampton's friends believed the 'enemies' who invented the 'plot' were its supposed targets, Home and Northampton—Cecil's 'secret enemies' too, according to the French ambassador, while Southampton and company were his allies. It puzzled the ambassador how little Cecil seemed to feel a blow which apparently fell so close; but he was necessarily ignorant of the 'secret cowrse' which had squared him with James.[20]

But, again, Southampton survived. The charges would not stick, the suspects were released promptly 'to please the parliament', and the affair was hushed up completely enough to suggest the charges had been trumped up, and at high level. Southampton was apparently persuaded to drop the matter by Cecil, whose 'directions' he was promising to follow by 28 June, and who had probably

[19] Hatfield MS 108.115 (HMC, *Salisbury*, xvi. 254), Home to Cecil, my date 9–13 June 1604.
[20] Cecil actually helped try for a subsidy on 19 June: failure possibly triggered the arrests. Akrigg, *Shakespeare and Southampton*, 140–2; *Cal. SP Venetian*, x. 165, 168; PRO PRO 31/3/37, 28 June/8 July; 1/11 July. PRO SP 14/8/126; Hatfield MS 118.111, HMC, *Salisbury*, xviii. 378–9, *recte* soon after 25 June 1604.

managed to protect his friends after all.[21] Indeed, Southampton's survival massively strengthened the minister. The year 1604 demonstrated that Cecil's Commons spokesmen could defeat Union, and could be neither bypassed nor removed. James's choice was to entrust the management of Parliament wholeheartedly to Cecil and his contacts: or to do without Parliaments (and Cecil) altogether. So Cecil made the transition from Tudor to Stuart as an apparently indispensable parliamentary manager. And it was above all Southampton who gave him his following in the Commons.

But the Southampton group's support for Cecil came with conditions, as became clear in the Parliament's second (1605–6) and third (1606–7) sessions. Opposition to Union had already assumed a distinction between king and kingdom: in 1605–6 the distinction was applied to finance, to refuse anything more than token supply unless the funds were part of a public re-endowment of the Crown, so preserving them both from James (and his prerogative right to spend as he chose—prominently on his Scots Bedchamber); and from the Exchequer (which the Commons now saw as a sink of debt, thanks to his spending). In 1604 Cecil's wardship scheme had satisfied these criteria; in 1605 Cecil tried to meet them again. James and his Bedchamber were moved out of sight to Royston; the Council was put publicly in control of patronage, to convey an image of financial responsibility; and a re-endowment scheme involving the abolition of purveyance was framed. The result in February 1606 was two subsidies 'of love', proposed by Ridgeway and seconded by Berkeley (who Hoby thought were being used instead of Privy Councillors).[22] But Berkeley and Sandys then led the Commons to reject Cecil's scheme, on the grounds that purveyance was illegal, and buying it out was paying for justice. When Cecil tried instead to obtain a third subsidy, it emerged that his portrayal of fiscal responsibility had failed: Berkeley said 'when that money shalbe spent the king's wantes shall remaine', and called instead for 'some course . . . for supply [in] . . . perpetuity'. He was answered by Sandys's plan to endow the royal demesne with land drained at public expense from the fens. When Cecil forced a vote on an extra subsidy (to be

[21] Akrigg, *Shakespeare and Southampton*, 142; PRO PRO 31/3/37, 28 June/8 July; HMC, *Salisbury*, xvi. 263–4, *c.*28 June 1604.
[22] References in N. Cuddy, *Bedchamber, Parliaments and Politics under James I* (forthcoming), ch. 5; T. Birch, *The Court and Times of James I* (2 vols.; 1848), i. 60.

traded for redress of a petition of grievances), Sandys called again for re-endowment, and opposed a vote as divisive; the one-vote victory for the addition showed how right Sandys was, and how close to being able to turn the House against Cecil. The fen scheme was later revived by eleven 'undertakers': Sandys, Berkeley, Croft, Neville, Sir John Scot, Sir Thomas Smith (former Essexians), Henry Yelverton, and four others. James rejected it, amid euphoria at obtaining three subsidies in peacetime.[23]

The third session showed that even this limited support for Cecil's financial plans carried the price of freedom to oppose Union. As James denounced those who in 1606 separated 'the people's will, and the will of the king', the Southampton group systematically distinguished between the king's public and private bodies. Naturalization was the key. James wanted it most as a guarantee Union would last; back-benchers resisted it most fiercely, as a Scots passport to English patronage. Soon after the first session, James got the judges to rule that, by his accession and their common personal allegiance, Scots and English born after 1603 were naturalized in both kingdoms. In 1607 Parliament was asked to confirm this, and naturalize Scots born before 1603 (whose access to English offices James promised to restrict). Sandys's response (as in 1604 against the name-change) was to appeal against the King's proposals to the judges and the common law, with the Commons' case put by a team of speakers.[24] The grounds were familiar: allegiance was not to the king's private or natural body, but to his public or politic body, whose extent depended on parliamentary consent; so all Scots, whenever born, depended on parliamentary legislation for naturalization; and that— not James's promise—would stop *all* Scots holding office in England. This time, however, the judges found for James: allegiance went with the body natural. Berkeley refused to believe the laws, 'written with the blood of our ancestors . . . should admit such inconveniences as the participation under one personal subjection'. Even when Cecil offered to waive this and put patronage restrictions

---

[23] Cuddy, *Bedchamber, The Parliamentary Diary of Robert Bowyer, 1606–7*, ed. D. H. Willson (Minneapolis, Minn., 1931), 62, 70–2, 79, 81; *CJ* i. 284–5; PRO SP 14/21/13; *HMC, Salisbury*, xviii. 129, 131.

[24] B. Galloway, *The Union of England and Scotland, 1603–08* (Edinburgh, 1986), ch. 6. *CJ* i. 314, 339–40, 1019–20. Croft's friend Sir Roger Owen joined the team: among the lawyers on it, James, Crewe, and Brooke were associated with the Southampton group.

on Scots born after 1603, to get the Commons to pass legislation, Sandys refused even to talk unless the legal principle were fully surrendered. James, as before, then explored ways round Cecil and his contacts. He appealed to the Commons back-benches (31 March 1607), denouncing Sandys and company; then he 'showed his displeasure' in Council 'against great men, who were seducing the others to oppose his will', beginning with Southampton, proceeding to Pembroke, two ex-Essexians, and Cecil's brother. But the result was only Sandys's diversionary project for a 'perfect union', starting afresh and setting up a new commission to prepare more radical proposals for a future session. James—on advice from Dunbar—then dropped naturalization. The session ended with the remaining measure (repeal of hostile laws) mangled by Yelverton, working as in 1606 with the Southampton group.[25]

Cecil's failure to get his Commons contacts to compromise plunged him into a crisis of favour. During the session James told him he was indulging his friends at the expense of his loyalty: after it, he and Dunbar privately discussed Cecil's performance. The 'secret course' of 1604 was under review; and, as in 1604, James distrusted his links with the opponents of Union. James allegedly later told Cecil 'Yelverton is your kinsman', 'others . . . adverse to me depend upon you', and that Cecil 'might draw . . . them in if [you] list'.[26]

James's reaction to 1607 was comprehensive and deliberate. He asserted his spending prerogative, in gifts to his Scots, and the promotion of Dunbar's protégé Sir Robert Carr as a new Bedchamber favourite. Next he imposed discipline, in post-session vendettas against MPs—as Northampton advised. But there was an important ideological dimension to this: as well as the leaders of opposition, James also attacked their principles, which in his view implied a general assault on his prerogative. Lord Chancellor Ellesmere's campaign against common-law 'prohibitions' (which controlled 'prerogative' courts) caught Fuller and Croft, for using them against High Commission and the Council in the Marches

[25] Cuddy, *Bedchamber*; Galloway, *Union*, corrected (esp. pp. 111 ff.) by Bowyer, *Diary*, 224; *Cal. SP Venetian*, x. 494; *Ambassades de Monsieur de la Boderie en Angleterre* (5 vols.; Paris, 1750), ii. 199–200.
[26] HMC, *Salisbury*, xix. 30, 51, 20, 184–5; J. Cumming (ed.), 'Mr Henry Yelverton his Narrative of . . . being Restored to the King's Favour in 16[10]', *Archaeologia*, 15 (1806), 50–2.

respectively: both had also opposed Union by appeal to common law, and that seems to have been why James pursued them now, telling his judges that allowing prohibitions encouraged 'highheaded fellowes . . . such as Harbert Crafte' to 'oppose themselves against the government and state of kinges'.[27] Comprehensive denunciation came in Ellesmere's published judgment on Calvin's Case, confirming Scots born since 1603 as naturalized *de jure*. But it went further, describing the Commons' idea of the king's 'two bodies' as 'a dangerous distinction . . . between the king and the kingdom', taught only by 'traitors, as in . . . Ed[ward II's] time', 'treasonable papists' who believed in the popular basis of monarchical power, 'seditious sectaries and Puritans, as Buchannon . . . Penry, Knox', and those 'enemies, or at least mislikers of all monarchies', Plato and Aristotle—a summary of the sources for the ideas behind not only the Southampton group's Commons campaigns, but also Essex's aristocratic republicanism. Besides floating a possible treason accusation, Ellesmere proposed God ordained kings, from whom all laws came; king, kingdom, common law, and prerogative formed an indistinguishable unity; and some royal proclamations had the force of laws.[28] This campaign, especially the legal certainty provided by Calvin's Case, raised fears about the prerogative which charged parliamentary debate for the rest of the reign with an ideological content missing before.

James also explored rival counsels. Even as Cecil became Lord Treasurer in 1608, Northampton became Lord Privy Seal, and offered an alternative financial strategy. Rumours began after the 1604 session that 'many who know the king's mind . . . think [parliament] will not meet again'. In 1606 Northampton threatened 'if the king should work by his prerogative [alone] he should be as rich as Croesus'. The exploitation of Crown rights and prerogative powers by means of private enterprise—'projects' —was an attractive option in the practical present, especially to the influential Scots Bedchamber: as the debt mounted, they became exponents of the system. Northampton was also a cost-cutter, attacking 'corruption'

---

[27] Galloway, *Union*, 138; *Letters*, 296–7. L. Knafla, *Law and Politics in Jacobean England* (Cambridge, 1977), 115–16, ch. 6. Owen, and Sandys's brother, Sir Samuel, helped Croft lead a campaign to exempt the four shires from the Council in the Marches. R. Ham, *The County and the Kingdom: Sir Herbert Croft and the Elizabethan State* (Washington, DC, 1977), 230–1.

[28] Knafla, *Law and Politics*, 66–81, 128, 208, 244–9.

in several departments (which the uncharitable observed were all run by his enemies). The double strategy of pressing the prerogative and retrenchment would have a continuous subsequent history, into the 1630s, in the hands of Northampton's protégés, Cranfield and Sir Richard Weston. For the present it might make James less reliant on parliamentary supply—and on Cecil.[29]

Cecil protected his followers as best he could from Ellesmere. But he had more success against prerogative finance. In 1608 his decision to avoid 'projects', which rewarded private men at public expense, meant choosing what he saw as a lesser evil—prerogative impositions on trade. They might prove controversial: but they enabled him to bury 170 'projects' in a vetting subcommittee. Generally he pressed James to renounce prerogative finance 'because the courses to be held in parliament, and the use of that power (as it reacheth at the money . . . of your people) . . . make the worst passage to both'. He also aimed to stop the Scots Bedchamber dealing in these schemes, by putting them on a sort of 'civil list', making support of their estate public, clearing the way not only for parliamentary supply, but also possibly 'another step to the Union'. Cecil was as ever fighting on two fronts: against rival counsels, Councillors, and influences in the Bedchamber; and to preserve his support in the Commons. He never induced James wholly to switch his policy. But in 1610 Cecil did persuade him at least to try his alternative again: to appeal to Parliament to mend his finances by bargaining for re-endowment.[30] The Southampton group were central to this. In 1608 Bacon suspected Cecil of 'some furd[er] intent[ion] upw[ard] to wyn [the king] to the po[licy] of po[pu]l[arity?]'; remarked on 'the greatnes of some part[icular] subj[ects'] pop[ularity]'; and listed nearby '. . . Nev[ille], Yelv[erton], San[dy]s, Harb[ert] Cro[ft], Barkly'.[31]

In 1610 Cecil's proposals matched the terms of the Southampton group, who managed Commons negotiations for them. Sandys

[29] *Cal. SP Venetian*, x. 208; *CJ* i. 271. L. Peck, *Northampton* (1982), plays down his attachment to prerogative counsels; but cf. pp. 94 ff., 166, ch. 8.

[30] P. Croft (ed.), 'A Collection of Several Speeches and Treatises of the Late Lord Treasurer Cecil', *Camden Miscellany XXIX* (Camden Soc., 4th ser., 34; 1987), 298–312, May–Nov. 1608 (my date: cf. p. 311, and PRO SP 14/37/72); ibid. 293. Peck, *Northampton*, 95, elides Northampton's projects with Cecil's re-endowment schemes; but, as Dr Croft shows, Cecil repeatedly claimed they were antithetical.

[31] BL Add. MS 27278, fo. 23ʳ, and *The Letters and the Life of Francis Bacon*, ed. J. Spedding (7 vols.; 1861–74), iv. 73–4.

helped report Cecil's opening speech; his committee of grievances then set strategy, giving priority to 'support', a permanent tax to cover the annual deficit (£46,000 said Cecil), to be voted in exchange for the abolition of burdensome Crown rights, and appropriated to 'public' ends. Cecil also requested massive 'supply', to clear the debt and establish a deposit treasury. But James's spending on the Scots meant there was no enthusiasm for unsecured subsidies. So Sandys kept supply distinct (linked to grievances as in 1606); with Cecil's help, fended off calls by Caesar (in the Commons) and Ellesmere (in the Lords) that it come first; and with Berkeley, Croft, Owen (and others) drafted a message to James deferring it to the end of the session. On support, Cecil offered ten points (including aspects of wardship, and purveyance again) to be abolished for £200,000 p.a. Sandys and his committee of grievances had instead selected 'tenures and wardships' alone: purveyance was illegal. Cecil was probably aiming to arrive at a wardship deal, while avoiding any appearance that James was offering to bargain with the multitude (who had to be seen respectfully to ask). Indeed, weeks were spent requesting permission to deal.[32] At last James agreed; and, though his speech that followed (21 March), assuaging fears of the prerogative, ignored Commons bargaining and warned 'woe be to him that divides the weale of the king from the weale of the kingdom', the Commons set about doing just that. Berkeley outlined a timetable, and the Commons offered £100,000 p.a, 'tied to the crown' for wardship alone— which, assuming wardship was worth £40,000 p.a., would easily have covered the ordinary deficit.[33]

Faced with this offer, and probably encouraged by rival counsels (particularly in the Bedchamber), James changed his terms to £200,000 p.a. support, over and above what he lost in retribution; he was evidently 'more averse than he was afore' to the deal and Cecil's strategies. In late April, Sandys, Owen, Croft, and Berkeley drafted an answer, rejecting the new demand—but politely.[34]

[32] Cuddy, *Bedchamber*; A. G. R. Smith, 'Crown, Parliament and Finance: the Great Contract of 1610', in P. Clark, A. Smith, and N. Tyacke (eds.), *The Tudor Commonwealth, 1547–1640* (Leicester, 1979), esp. p. 118; *Proceedings in Parliament 1610*, ed. E. Foster (2 vols.; New Haven, Conn., 1966), i. 13 ff., 17; ii. 17, 30, 358–9, 32; *CJ* i. 401–3.

[33] *The Political Works of James I*, ed. C. McIlwain (Cambridge, Mass., 1918; repr. New York, 1965), 318; *CJ* i. 411, 414–15; HMC, *Downshire*, ii. 269.

[34] E. Lindquist, 'The Failure of the Great Contract', *Journal of Modern History*, 57 (1985), 625–31, argues James's (and Cecil's) terms were consistent from Feb. to Apr.; but cf. HMC, *Downshire*, ii. 271. Ibid. 279. *CJ* i. 423

Two months of deadlock followed. James (through Cecil) tried twice for subsidies, supposedly for defence, on 13 June offering appropriation for foreign emergencies. But the Southampton group blocked this with the grievance of impositions (so far avoided by Sandys's committee)—timetabling impositions debates after James raised his terms, starting a privilege dispute when he forbade discussion, finally organizing opposition to supply. When Ellesmere later alleged six speakers had used concerted tactics to defeat subsidies, he meant the Southampton group on 14 June, who deferred supply until grievances—especially impositions—had been answered. Stalemate caused James first to let the Commons debate impositions, then to lower his terms for the seemingly moribund support contract.[35] Cecil would have welcomed subsidies; but, by ruling them out, impositions obliged James to try his Contract again. It looked suspiciously—especially to Cecil's rivals—as though Cecil had used the leverage of the Southampton group in the Commons to move the King. In early July, with impositions having served their useful purpose, Cecil aimed for a compromise on them with Sandys and company: an act, recognizing present impositions and (tacitly) James's prerogative to them, but limiting him in future to imposing in Parliament. But it was not to be.[36]

The impositions debates helped rule out compromise. Bate's Case, the 1606 common-law ruling by Chief Baron Fleming on which they were based, argued that the King's private body dealt by prerogative with national issues like foreign policy, and so could regulate foreign trade by imposing on it; while his public body— king-in-Parliament—was subordinate, dealing only with the particular interests of individual subjects. The Southampton group consistently took an opposite view: as Whitelocke said in 1610, the king out of Parliament, 'sole and singular, guided merely by his own will', was inferior to, and controlled by, the king-in-Parliament 'assisted with the consent of the whole state'—which alone could tax. The debates ended in a petition calling for the abolition of existing impositions, and for an Act to ban impositions in future except by Parliament, thus denying James's prerogative. James's answer on 10 July (offering to pass a limiting Act of Recognition)

[35] *CJ* i. 421, 426–7, 439; *Proceedings in Parliament 1610*, i. 67, 279; ii 115–6, 123, 135 ff., 142–3, 148 and n.; Birch, *Court*, i. 115–16.

[36] *Parliamentary Debates in 1610*, ed. S. R. Gardiner (Camden Soc., os 81; 1861), 109; *Proceedings in Parliament 1610*, ii. 410 n.; *CJ* i. 445; Birch, *Court*, i. 122.

was thus unsatisfactory, so Cecil followed it with his own public arguments; and that night, the eve of another subsidy debate, he tried again in private, meeting 'Sir Henry Neville, Sir Maurice Berkeley, Sir Edwin Sandys, Sir Herbert Crofts, Sir John Scot, Sir Francis Goodwin, [Edward] Alford' (and another) about impositions at his house in Hyde Park. He failed; the next day yielded a single derisory subsidy, with a fifteenth lost to Sandys's opposition. Carleton was sure the problem was impositions. As with the name-change and naturalization, over impositions the Southampton group maintained their principled view of the king's relationship to Parliament and the common law—indeed White-locke drew an explicit parallel between those issues of 1604, 1607, and 1610. Again, the limits of the group's backing for Cecil were clear.[37]

Yet the group were Cecil's allies on support. Those at the Hyde Park meeting were suspected of being 'plotters of some new designs [in] . . . the great matter of the contract . . . which most of these did seek to advance'. As Commons attendances dropped, the Southampton group hurriedly assembled the Great Contract. They raised their second offer (now including purveyance); Cecil brought the divided Council 'to a perfect tune', got James to agree to £200,000 p.a. gross, and obtained a Commons majority for it. Sandys drew up the draft; Croft added to it the exemption of the four shires; Cecil clarified the support would be 'tied to the crown'. And a delegation of official spokesmen, led by Sandys and accompanied by Berkeley and Croft, delivered the Contract to the Lords.[38]

Had Cecil at last joined with the Southampton group, to replace prerogative with parliamentary finance, push aside his rivals on the Council, and curb his Scottish masters in the Bedchamber? The fifth session began in October 1610 with low attendances, and apprehension that James had turned against the scheme. He had; and it was probably Dunbar, and his allies on the Council, who had convinced him to do so. Officially, James's demands remained constant; in fact he put a demand for £500,000 supply back into the contract, reversing Cecil's and Sandys's separation of it from

[37] J. P. Sommerville, *Politics and Ideology in England, 1603–1640* (1986), 151 ff.; *Parliamentary Debates in 1610*, 103, 153–62; *Proceedings in Parliament 1610*, ii. 266–7; Birch, *Court*, i. 122–3; *CJ* i. 448.
    [38] Cuddy, *Bedchamber*; Birch, *Court*, i. 122–3; *CJ* i. 451–3; *Proceedings in Parliament 1610*, i. 158.

support. The Southampton group's opposition to supply would now extend to the entire Contract. Berkeley called for new answers to the grievances, especially impositions, which could now make or break the entire deal. But James insisted on a simple yes or no to his demands. Owen, Sandys, and Croft led the House to decline to proceed on James's new terms.[39]

Cecil had now lost the struggle to ensure James followed his counsels. His rivals came into their own; James as usual tried to bypass him; and, crucially, the Southampton group abandoned him. Ellesmere, Northampton, and Cecil jointly requested simple subsidies: Sir Samuel Sandys contemptuously said no; others insisted 'the wants of the king and the kingdom are two distinct things'; and Southampton virtually stopped attending the Lords. When James summoned thirty MPs—he called them the 'Thirty Doges'— to explain why they refused supply, the Southampton group dominated discussion. Neville attacked royal spending with 'a distinction'— 'where your Majesty's expense groweth by the Commonwealth we are bound to maintain it; otherwise not'. He was interrupted by Croft's account of the four shires; and that was followed by Sandys's justification of Commons' proceedings over impositions. But James refused further concessions on the latter.[40] Croft ended another raucous supply debate by moving to show James next day how the House was not satisfied; Cecil adjourned to prevent it; and another adjournment, to stop the reading of a list of Bedchamber debts assigned for payment, caused a crisis of distrust between James and Cecil.[41] An anonymous squib, sent to a Howard Bedchamber agent, suggested Cecil had arranged opposition to supply since his Contract failed, and planted anti-Scots speeches so James would curb his gifts to them. James pointedly told Cecil of his suspicion whether 'any . . . in the court should falsely father upon the people their own particularities'. Such charges were plausible in the light of Cecil's links in previous sessions: but by now the Southampton group actually seem to have

[39] Dunbar's role is argued in Cuddy, *Bedchamber. Proceedings in Parliament 1610*, ii. 303–5, 392–9, 314 ff., 320–2. Lindquist, 'Failure of the Great Contract', 640–2, argues James had not changed terms: cf. *Parliamentary Debates in 1610*, 131.

[40] *Lords Journals*, ii. 677–8; *Proceedings in Parliament 1610*, i. 169–73, 253–4; ii. 330 ff., 337–8 and nn., 400 ff.; *Parliamentary Debates in 1610*, 132–6.

[41] *Parliamentary Debates in 1610*, 142 ff.; HMC, *Salisbury*, xxi. 262–3; *Memorials of Affairs of State . . . Collected from the papers of Sir Ralph Winwood*, ed. E. Sawyer (3 vols.; 1725), iii. 235–6; *Cal. SP Dom. 1611–18*, 5.

been working against him. Dunbar and Carr urged James to order Cecil to reveal the Commons sources that had warned him to adjourn; but Carr, working with MPs who had dealt with Cecil 'very maliciously', had actually planted the rumours that triggered the adjournments. Given Croft's role in the first adjournment, the 'malicious' members probably included the Southampton group.[42]

Though James considered treason charges against MPs for making a difference between king and kingdom (as Ellesmere had earlier hinted), he dropped that with his investigation of Cecil's sources, as he dissolved Parliament.[43] That meant he dropped Cecil, too, whose claim to power depended on his ability to manage Parliament. The attempt of 1604 to deprive Cecil of his following failed; but in 1610, that following seems to have deserted him for another patron—Sir Robert Carr.

III

The Southampton group won a reputation as 'patriots' in 1604–10. James said some MPs 'had made themselfes as it were a confederacy . . . for the protection of all extravagant humours and conceipts among the people'; Caesar thought 'the present parliament men . . . held amongst the common people the best patriots . . . ever'; Sandys's friend wrote of 'sundry our trew patriotes', unhappiness with the dissolution; and Neville was described as one of 'those patriots . . . accounted of a contrary faction to the courtiers'.[44] Being unsullied by office helped: they were often linked with jobs Cecil might offer (as ambassadors, or in Ireland), but all the rumours came to nothing.[45] Croft preferred members of Cecil's household, but got only ineffective protection (against Ellesmere) after the 1607 session. Neville, also 'reconciled' then, was told by Cecil to offer a 'project', but was soon writing begging letters again. Whitelocke thought Cecil had been Neville's enemy, as much as

[42] HMC, *Salisbury*, xxi. 260–5; *Letters*, 316, 318–19.

[43] Sommerville, *Politics and Ideology*, 138 ff.; C. Russell, 'The Theory of Treason in the Trial of Strafford,' *EHR* 80 (1965), 30 ff.; cf. Russell, 'The Examination of Mr Mallory . . . 1621', *BIHR* 50 (1977), 131; PRO SP 14/58/35; HMC, *Salisbury*, xxi. 263.

[44] PRO SP 14/58/26; BL Add. MS 34324, fo. 61; PRO SP 14/62/44; HMC, *Buccleuch and Queensbury*, i. 102.

[45] HMC, *Downshire*, ii. 299; iii. 146, 180, 226; Birch, *Court*, i. 120; *Letters of Chamberlain*, i. 313, 321. *Cal. SP Venetian*, xi. 135.

Northampton, who openly 'hunted after' him.[46] In 1608, when impositions threatened Southampton's yield from sweet wines, Cecil (his 'only help') got him compensated; but in June 1611 it was Carr who got the farm safely converted to a £2,000 life pension. Most seriously, Cecil failed to get Southampton on to the Council. In September 1611 Pembroke got a seat, and Southampton 'retired himself into the countrie', while 'his spirit . . . walked very busilie about the court'.[47]

It was then that the Southampton group moved decisively to exploit their popularity and bypass Cecil. In October 1611 Neville proposed to 'undertake to deal with the Lower House, and then (so as my Lord Treasurer would not intermeddle) . . . better effects would come of the next session . . . than . . . of the former'; his link with James was through Sir Thomas Overbury to Sir Robert Carr. Now successor to Dunbar (who had died in January 1611) as the main power in the Bedchamber, Carr became in March 1611 the first Scot fully to join the English peerage, for the proclaimed reason 'that he was Gentleman of his Majesties Chamber'. This was James's defiantly Scottish role for him.[48] But on his own account Carr set out to win an English parliamentary following. His entourage was all-English, headed by Overbury, who had drawn MPs to follow him in 1610, and in 1611 had open contacts with Neville. Sir Robert Killigrew, Carr's second favourite, was Berkeley's brother-in-law and Neville's cousin; Southampton made him Captain of Pendennis Castle. Another favourite, Sir William Uvedale, was Southampton's neighbour and follower.[49] To these contacts Carr added financial responsibility and pro-English sentiment—refusing gifts from James, giving him back cash when he was penniless, and outlining his aims 'to preserve the nobility

[46] PRO SP 14/57/52; SP 14/43/22, *recte* Oct. 1607; O. Duncan, 'The Political Career of Sir Henry Neville . . .', Ph.D. thesis (Ohio State Univ., 1974), 212–15; HMC, *Salisbury*, xxi. 280; *Liber famelicus of James Whitelocke*, ed. J. Bruce (Camden Soc., os 70; 1858), 46–7.

[47] HMC, *Salisbury*, xx. 191, 193 (Hatfield MS 195.18); Cecil refused his offer to farm sweet wines impositions—an offer that shows how uncontroversial they seemed at first. PRO C66/1904; *Letters of John Holles*, ed. P. R. Seddon, i (Thoroton Soc., 31; 1975), 74; *Letters of Chamberlain*, i. 352, 27 May 1612.

[48] C. Roberts and O. Duncan, 'The Parliamentary Undertaking of 1614', *EHR* 93 (1978), 483; PRO SP 14/75/2.

[49] G. Goodman, *The Court of King James I* (2 vols.; 1839), i. 215; *Letters of Holles*, i. 73; HMC, *Mar and Kellie Supplement*, 52, *c.*Mar. 1613 (my date); HMC, *Buccleuch and Queensbury*, i. 101–2. *DNB* on Killigrew. Berkeley and Neville married, respectively, daughters of Sir William and Sir Henry Killigrew. Akrigg, *Shakespeare and Southampton*, 145.

heere', to be 'the courtier whose hand never took bribes', to 'preserve love betweene the king and his people', 'to ioyne his, and the publique good', and to promote 'worthy men'.[50] Cecil's death in May 1612 was thus liberation, not loss, for the Southampton group. Within days Southampton and his ally Sheffield were reported sure to be Councillors: 'no man is spoken of but ... Southampton' as Treasurer; and Neville was touted as Secretary, amid 'flocking of parlament men ... and meetings and consultation with Southampton and Sheffield at [Carr's] Chamber'.[51]

Neville now presented his 'undertaking' to James. Its meagre substance (left-overs from the Great Contract, seasoned with Neville's ideas to induce supply) matched its limited aim—token subsidies, to heal wounds, and to foster future meetings. To persuade James to call Parliament rather than resort to 'projects', it did minimize difficulties, again recommending James's 1610 compromise on impositions, and implying that spending on the Scots was no longer a problem. But Neville also made an implied assumption: that with Cecil gone, all would be well, and that he had been responsible for much of what went wrong in 1604–10. (He later said Cecil had misrepresented James to the Commons— not, of course, as others alleged, that Cecil was responsible for 'artificial animating of the negative' to James.) Neville had 'lived and conversed inwardly with the chief of them that were noted to be the most backward', and who led the Commons in the last Parliament; so he could now undertake they would do James service—and that those formerly intractable issues would not stand in the way of supply.[52] That summer, the group canvassed his programme. Neville visited his daughter, who had married a son of Sir Maurice Berkeley; the latter recruited his neighbours to 'treat ... with Sir H. N.' Neville also 'imparted' his undertaking to Sir Edwin Sandys, who was amazed impositions were omitted: according to Sandys, Neville replied 'it was of that difficulty as he could

---

[50] Birch, *Court*, i. 104, 7 Jan. *recte* 1611; PRO SP 14/71/6; *Letters of Chamberlain*, i. 444 (cf. 480).

[51] *Letters of Chamberlain*, i. 352, 358–9; HMC, *Downshire*, iii. 314–15; Winwood, *Memorials*, iii. 393.

[52] Roberts and Duncan, 'The Parliamentary Undertaking of 1614', 486–7; PRO SP 14/74/44, 46, and *Proceedings in Parliament 1614*, ed. M. Jansson (Philadelphia, Pa., 1988), 247 ff. Cf. Bacon's advice of July 1612 in *Letters and Life of Bacon*, iv. 365–6, 369–71 (my date), stressing the effect of Cecil's and Dunbar's deaths.

not tell how to include it'.[53] Possibly because of this, Neville thought again, and that autumn submitted (through Carr) a new compromise, proposing an Act implying James's prerogative right, but granting existing impositions for life only—avoiding universal principles.[54]

James was unconvinced. He left Cecil's offices unfilled and pushed Carr towards the Howards, the faction to which 'his Majestie inclynes most' in the struggle between them 'and the earl of Southampton'. In April 1613 Overbury went to the Tower for contempt; Killigrew, Neville, and Southampton tried to help him get out; but in mid-September he was poisoned to death by the Earl of Suffolk's daughter Frances and (probably) Northampton. Frances Howard's divorce from the Earl of Essex (heir to leadership of Southampton's faction) then led to her 'conjunction' with Carr. Northampton was behind most of this; he was also the political beneficiary of it; and, as before, there was an ideological dimension to James's turning to him. He was currently advising James against summoning Parliament, which would merely be to 'call his enemies together'; so, by October, 'projects' blossomed under his (and Ellesmere's) direction on the Treasury commission, and Carr was 'more in a Howards course' than before.[55]

But not wholly in a 'Howards course': by early 1614 Carr's 'greatness' appeared to have 'swallowed up the House with which he is matched'. 'Projects' failed; Northampton was ill; and Carr tried the parliamentary option again. In fact, a second undertaking took place in 1614. Suffolk and Pembroke put a version of Neville's proposals to the Council, and advised a summons. Carr probably floated a deal to cement their co-operation: rumour predicted Suffolk as Lord Treasurer, Pembroke Lord Chamberlain, and Carr Master of the Horse. Pembroke's motives are obscure, while Suffolk told Carr he was 'dissembling' in James's service. But Carr seems to have aimed to produce results. In addition to winning over these Councillors, he probably made a deal with Southampton, and certainly reached out to his followers. The Secretaryship finally

[53] *Letters of Chamberlain*, i. 374; Roberts and Duncan, 'The Parliamentary Undertaking of 1614', 488 n. 2; E. Farnham, 'The Somerset Election of 1614', *EHR* 46 (1931), 579–99 (esp. p. 581 n. 3). *Proceedings in Parliament 1614*, 244.
[54] Roberts and Duncan, 'The Parliamentary Undertaking of 1614', 481 n. 2; BL, Cotton MS Titus F IV, fos. 349–50, 346.
[55] Birch, *Court*, i. 248; *Letters of Chamberlain*, i. 450, 452, 480; Winwood, *Memorials*, iii. 462, 475; HMC, *Mar and Kellie Supplement*, 51–2, 55.

went to Carr's nominee, Sir Ralph Winwood, formerly Neville's aide. Neville's scheme formed the basis for the royal concessions that began the session. Sandys sat for Rochester by Carr's direct patronage, and in March got a patent for lands. Croft drafted arguments for exempting the four shires, for presentation, hinting he was not 'such a Common wealthes man' as to refuse reward for his service. Since he waited to deliver this to Carr, 'undertaking' continued during the session.'[16]

Sandys and Bacon both said there had been a real undertaking in 1614. It backfired, thought Bacon, because the new MPs on the back-benches believed, and were disturbed by, rumours that the leaders of 1604–10 were now 'undertakers'; and because a faction of 'Anti-Undertakers', based at court, spread those rumours as a deliberate strategy to destroy their credit. The evidence suggests that this was the case, and that Northampton was the instigator of it.[17] Winwood's subsidy debate went well until Sir Richard Weston (later alleged to have been working for Northampton) raised the matter of undertakers. The suspicions this aroused ruled out supply: Croft, Berkeley, Whitelocke, and Sandys instead moved for a committee to clear the rumours—and themselves. After three weeks' delay Hoskins (also probably working for Northampton) rejected their simple declaration, and called for a full investigation. The Southampton group (and their allies) countered that the charges arose from 'popery' (alluding to Northampton). But Northampton's mud stuck, since there *was* an undertaking. Neville created a diversion by owning up to (and being excused for) his now notorious advice of 1612. Weston, unimpressed, moved to carry on investigating, and Croft complained of an 'implicit concluding that there are still undertakers'. His worry is understandable: a week earlier he presented his four-shires paper to Carr, risking 'the scorne of that partie in parlament that . . . already brand me with

[16] HMC, *Portland*, ix. 28. P. Seddon, 'Robert Carr earl of Somerset', *Renaissance and Modern Studies*, 14 (1970), 61 ff.; HMC, *Downshire*, iv. 342. R. Kenny, 'The Parliamentary Influence of Charles Howard, Earl of Nottingham', *Journal of Modern History*, 39 (1977), 227; PRO SP 14/76/21. *Cal. SP Dom. 1611–18*, 226; PRO C66/1986. PRO SP 14/76/53, SP 14/77/15: Croft referred James to Lord Sheffield.

[17] *Proceedings in Parliament 1614*, 246; *Letters and Life of Bacon*, v. 179–83. Roberts and Duncan, 'The Parliamentary Undertaking of 1614', argue there was no undertaking in 1614, but pp. 490 and n. 3, 491, 493 n. 4, hint at it. Cuddy, *Bedchamber*, argues Northampton's role (cf. PRO SP 14/76/9; T. Moir, *The Addled Parliament of 1614* (Oxford, 1958), 28).

an over earnest desire' in James's service.[18] Northampton's rumours had in fact made real 'undertaking', and the alliance Carr had sought between moderate Councillors and the Southampton group, impossible.

Impositions finally 'addled' the Parliament, and it is probable that they did so because Northampton's attacks forced Southampton and his followers to break that alliance with Carr, Suffolk, and Pembroke ('to regain reputation . . . by . . . violent courses of popularity', said Bacon). An impositions bill, introduced just after the first subsidy debate, saw Berkeley, Croft, Brooke, Whitelocke, and Owen maintain their uncompromising stance of 1610. Later, James's appeal for subsidies was met by Sandys's report setting strategy for the Commons over impositions, citing the precedents of the name-change and naturalization in appointing a team of speakers to put the case against impositions to a conference with the Lords, appealing to the judges and common law against the prerogative—illustrating the continuous leadership, tactics, and principles in the opposition to James's views. Waiting for that conference, Sandys (and others) compensated further for rumours of a sell-out. To a claim that all kings by descent (like James) could impose, Sandys replied all kings 'howsoever they come in, settle their states by consent of their people'; foreign imposing Princes were tyrants; and (as one diarist heard it) 'impositions daily increase in England as it is come to be almost a tyrannical government'.[19] Southampton, equally courting popularity, led a party in the Lords (including Dorset, Chandos, Danvers, De La Warr, Knyvett, North, Rich, St John, Saye, Spencer, and Sheffield) to press for a meeting with Sandys's team. Ellesmere, backed by the Councillors—including Carr, Pembroke, and Suffolk—and all the bishops but one, opposed contact, delaying by ensuring the Lords first heard the judges. But Chief Justice Coke asked to hear the case argued by the King's counsel and the Lower House—playing to Southampton's hand, who used this to pronounce the legality of impositions still moot, claiming posterity would condemn them for refusing to hear 'the just complaintes of the people in a matter of right as they conceive'. Ellesmere won a Lords division to deny a

[18] Roberts and Duncan, 'The Parliamentary Undertaking of 1614', 492–3. *Proceedings in Parliament 1614*, 443; 238–9, 244–5. PRO SP 14/77/15.

[19] *Letters and Life of Bacon*, v. 179–83. *Proceedings in Parliament 1614*, 79, 93–4, 100 s.v. 5 May, 211 ff., 312, 316.

meeting, however; and James finally gave the Commons an ulti-
matum to supply or be dissolved. Sandys used the final debate to
echo his leader: European examples proved that admitting the
king's right to impose without consent would permanently change
the polity—'the main liberty of the people is engaged in this
question'—and future ages would be bound if they granted a
subsidy. Amid those ringing declarations, Parliament was dissolved.[60]

The team of speakers on impositions was called before the
Council next day to have its notes burnt. Sandys was ordered to
stay in London. Four MPs actually went to the Tower for seditious
speeches. And, as for the Lords, James was 'very angry with . . .
Southampton, Essex, Chandos, and divers others'.[61] Carr had failed
as dismally as Cecil as a parliamentary manager. When in July 1614
he left Pembroke out of an official share-out—Suffolk became
Lord Treasurer—the scene was set for another change at Court:
the advent of a new English Bedchamber favourite, George Villiers
(later Duke of Buckingham), candidate of Southampton, Pembroke,
and their agents; and the fall of Carr, on information provided by
Winwood about Overbury's murder.

IV

We have almost returned to our starting-point. To understand why
in 1619 Buckingham was canvassing the parliamentary support of
his former patron Southampton, one needs only to know that
James kept Southampton out of office and the Council, while Carr
fell, Villiers rose, and Pembroke became Lord Chamberlain in
1615; and that in 1616–17, the King successfully detached Buckingham from his former backers. So, still without office, the 'vulger
counselor' of 1619 took his seat on a predominantly hostile Council,
brandishing the popular reputation earned in 1604–14.

This account of that period suggests its politics were divided by
principles that were directly reflected in factional struggle, and not
only in the literature which Dr Sommerville has studied. It also

---

[60] HMC, *Hastings*, iv. 230–83, esp. pp. 256–7, 260–1. *Proceedings in Parliament 1614*, s.v. 6
June. Sandys, Berkeley, and Croft finally proposed token supply, conditional on a promise
of a future impositions conference; James refused.

[61] HMC, *Downshire*, iv. 426.

suggests that there was continuity in both those principles, and those factions. A sharp break between this world and that of late Elizabethan politics is immediately visible, at the obvious political boundary of James's accession. Opposing Union enabled Southampton and Sandys to convert Essex's somewhat rarified aristocratic republicanism into a potent, multi-purpose political weapon—a distinction between the 'king's two bodies'. Ellesmere was right that the idea had never been deployed as practical politics except by extremists and rebels—its currency in Elizabethan England was politically marginal. Yet in 1604–14 the distinction became the stuff of the parliamentary mainstream. We should not minimize the significance of a politics whose central feature for over a decade was a separation between king and kingdom.[62]

Neither should we write off the ideas generated by the issue of Union as anomalous—for those ideas were applied directly to supply. Appropriation and 'public' re-endowment have scarcely figured in work on early Stuart taxation, yet they were the central strategy of these years of peace. Already in 1606 the Southampton group were leading the Commons to reject obligation to grant subsidies for James's 'private' expenditures, especially on the Scots—or to pay debts arising from such spending. After 1608, opposition to James's prerogative income from impositions—modelled on the principles and tactics of opposition to Union—also prevented supply. Throughout 1604–14 the Southampton group ensured that any supply that was granted (two subsidies in 1606, one in 1610) was token—'for love', admitting no obligation. The exception was the extra subsidy of 1606, passed in return for redress of a petition of grievances—possibly suggested by Cecil's nephew, but, as the event proved, a strategic cul-de-sac. The Commons thus knew precisely the extent of James's wants, and refused on principle to supply them, unless strings—of appropriation—were attached.[63]

Because such real issues divided politics, Cecil and Carr (and

---

[62] Sommerville, *Politics and Ideology*, *passim*; Sommerville, 'Ideology, Property and the Constitution', in R. Cust and A. Hughes (eds.), *Conflict in Early Stuart England* (1989), 47 ff. Russell, *Causes of the English Civil War*, 23–4, 157–60: 'a very large proportion of the Parliamentary arguments in 1642 seem to have been drawn from the losing side in Calvin's case'.

[63] Cf. Galloway, *Union*, 166–9; works by G. L. Harriss and J. Alsop cited in Lindquist, 'Failure of the Great Contract', 621 n. 10; Russell, 'Parliamentary History in Perspective', 5–9, 13–14; Russell, *Causes of the English Civil War*, ch. 7.

Buckingham) had to use 'men of business' like the Southampton group to manage the lower House. Proposals capable of winning over the Commons could not be attributed directly to Councillors acceptable to the King; the Commons distrusted open links with James and his Council; and thus go-betweens, at one disavowable remove, were necessary. So, although Southampton and followers operated within a context of Court faction, aspired to office and reward, and took part in 'undertaking', we cannot therefore write off their activities (as 'revisionism' tries to) as the mere playing-out of Court faction in Parliament, with nothing more at stake than narrow self-interest, place, and profit. For the influence of their faction at Court depended throughout on their ability to lead the Commons' back-benches. Their appeal to the back-benches was based in turn on their consistent adherence to sophisticated and coherent principles—an appeal to common law against the pre-rogative, recognizing the centrality of Parliaments in politics. And their co-operation thus had to be on terms which preserved that 'popular' reputation. A counter-example may clarify this. Before the 1610 sessions James and Dunbar together made an independent attempt to win over 'opposition' by personally coming to terms with Henry Yelverton. It was a strategy of winning over Commons' leaders with place and favour which Bacon most vocally advocated. But when Yelverton reversed his earlier stance in the Commons, he was no longer 'thought so popular'. Carleton reported him 'so well canvassed' for his 'tyrannical positions' in support of impo-sitions 'that he hath scarce shewed his head . . . since'; Chamberlain later said he was made Solicitor-General for 'good service . . . in the parlement, and for the disgrace he seemed to sustain thereby'; and later one observer cited Yelverton to prove the Commons was unmanageable by such 'undertakers', who 'considering the factiousness of the time' might be able 'to do hurt in speaking against the king, but not . . . to do good' for him. Clearly, there was a divide: but Yelverton had crossed it, not bridged it. By contrast, the Southampton group (despite Northampton's rumour-mongering to the contrary) aimed to avoid Yelverton's fate in their 'undertakings', by bridging the divide while remaining true to their principles—using silences, delays, and the fudging of issues. In 1612 Neville tried to avoid the issue of impositions by tacitly recognizing those already in existence, and postponing resolution of the principle to the next reign. In 1614 Croft tried for compromise on the four shires by alleging (with a true politician's disingenuousness) that it made no difference whether (as James insisted) the prerogative Council in the Marches had jurisdiction there, or (as Croft wanted) the common-law courts at Westminster, since it was all equally the king's justice. And in each case it was James who rejected compromise: he spurned Neville's 'undertaking'; and his terse marginal comment that there was indeed 'a difference' in Croft's 'chaunge' effectively ended the four-shires issue. 'Revisionism' has ignored cases like Yelverton's, and used attempts at compromise like Neville's and Croft's to argue that there was no important conflict in the early Stuart period. In fact, both the delicacy of the attempts to find such compromise, and their failures, point clearly to the existence of significant and recurrent principled conflict between James and his opponents.[64]

In 1619 the Southampton group had a history of co-operation as parliamentary go-betweens, and were still well placed to reassume the role. The Earl had drawn closer to the party in the Lords he had led in 1614. Though Neville and Berkeley were dead, and Croft had fled abroad from his debts, in the Commons Sandys and Sir Edward Coke (Cecil's kinsman and Danvers's 'poor ally') would provide clear leadership. And, as Southampton's comments on appointment to the Council showed, he still saw a divide to be bridged between his counsels and those of the King.[65] But, in fact, Southampton maintained a more independent stance than ever in James's last Parliaments, which show further continuity with the principles he stood for in 1604–14—and 1619.

In 1621 the Southampton group stayed aloof from Buckingham, or any other influential conciliar faction. Foreign policy disagreement was probably one cause of this; but a key reason also seems to have been that after 1614 James began selling English titles—directly assaulting the Essexian view of a nobility of blood and leading to an unprecedented 'inflation of honours'—probably in deliberate response to aristocratic republicanism among the lay peers (for in 1614 only the bishops had given James a majority in

---

[64] Cumming (ed.), 'Yelverton his Narrative', *passim*; *Letters and Life of Bacon*, iv. 43, 365–7, 370; Birch, *Court*, i. 120–2; *Letters of Chamberlain*, i. 479, Oct. 1613; BL, Cotton MS Titus F IV, fos. 350, 351; PRO SP 14/76/53, fo. 1ᵛ; Russell, 'Parliamentary History in Perspective', 18–20, 22–4; C. Russell, *Parliaments and English Politics, 1621–29* (Oxford, 1979), 5–26.

[65] Hampshire RO, Wriothesley Deeds, 583, 16 Mar. 1617. HMC, *Salisbury*, xvii.332; S. White, *Sir Edward Coke and the Grievances of the Commonwealth* (Manchester, 1979), chs. 2–5, esp. pp. 45, 119 ff.

the Upper House). Buckingham promoted the sales; so Southampton used his party in the Lords to mount an attack on him (from which he narrowly escaped), and petition the King about the peerage. Coke and Sandys meanwhile responsibly prevented the revival of impositions, moved subsidies 'for love' at the start of the session—as had been originally intended in 1614—and managed an assault on the patents of prerogative finance, incidently destroying their enemy Bacon. Despite those positive signs, the failed attack on Buckingham proved costly, and Southampton was arrested (with Sandys) after the first session, accused of neglecting the Council (which he allegedly thought a board of 'boys and base fellows'), searching instead for 'supposed innate . . . liberties' to extend the power of the Lords, and consorting with those 'in the Upper and . . . Lower House which were the most stirring and active to cross . . . the present government'. Southampton, true to his protestations of 1619, had remained a 'vulger counselor'.[66]

His stance was vindicated in 1624. In 1622 Buckingham won Southampton as an ally, not (as sometimes alleged) by threatening to remove his pensions—the patents were for life—but by changing his own stance on foreign and domestic policy to match Southampton's, helping Prince Charles call Spain's diplomatic bluff and join a Protestant crusade. After the Madrid journey, the result in 1624 was an 'undertaking' that produced the only really successful Jacobean Parliament, thanks largely to the Southampton group. Sandys and Coke obtained subsidies to fight a war, appropriating them to avoid paying James's debt; their legislative programme enacted many of the reforms in the Great Contract, which were intended as before to make prerogative finance impossible; monopoly patents were outlawed; and even the man who stalled Southampton's pensions—Lord Treasurer Cranfield—fell to Sandys and company.[67] Prince Charles's and Buckingham's alliance with the 'patriot coalition' in 1624 meant that, for once, the really influential part of the Council and Bedchamber was allied with the Southampton group in Lords and Commons; James was

---

[66] R. Zaller, *The Parliament of 1621* (1971); Russell, *Parliaments and English Politics*, 10 ff., 14; *Commons Debates 1621*, ed. W. Notestein, F. H. Relf, and H. Simpson (7 vols.; New Haven, Conn., 1935), vii. 615–17; R. Lockyer, *Buckingham* (1980), ch. 4.

[67] Akrigg, *Shakespeare and Southampton*, 163; Cuddy, 'Revival of the Entourage', 221–2. T. Cogswell, *The Blessed Revolution: English Politics and the Coming of War, 1621–1624* (Cambridge, 1989), esp. ch. 2; R. Ruigh, *The Parliament of 1624* (Cambridge, Mass., 1971), esp. pp. 121–7; Russell, *Parliaments and English Politics*, ch. 3.

bypassed—and all went well. The comparison with the earlier catalogue of failure when those conditions were not fulfilled is some indication of the influence of Southampton and his following.

Southampton died in late 1624, on campaign for the Protestant cause, believing the counsels he had stood out for had at last prevailed. The next reign witnessed a reversal, as in 1625–6 Charles adopted the 'new counsels' described by Dr Cust.[68] But in fact much of the conflict that caused that reversal (particularly over tonnage and poundage) was rooted in issues (notably impositions) passed over in James's last years, and revived in the new reign; while Charles's 'new counsels' also bore many resemblances to James's old alternative of retrenchment, pressing prerogative revenues, and avoiding Parliaments if possible. Such continuities again suggest that it is more than accident, hindsight, or Whig history that makes so much of the seventeenth century fit Gerald Aylmer's description of it as a 'struggle for the constitution'.

[68] R. Cust, *The Forced Loan and English Politics, 1626–8* (Oxford, 1987).

9

The Public Conscience of Henry Sherfield

PAUL SLACK

I take it to be impossible to have true peace with God and
not wars with men ... For no man can have true peace with
God unless ... he shall profess to fear God and to make a
good conscience the rule of his actions ... If he be careful
therein, let him be sure he shall have wars with the drunkard,
with the profane swearer, with the maypole dancer, with
every loose man and swaggerer, nay almost (which is lam-
entable to speak) with all his neighbours. For all of them in
a manner will term him a Puritan, and perhaps the best of
them will tell him that he marreth all with his preciseness,
that he hath undone even the city or place where he liveth
by it.

Henry Sherfield, speech, c.1629

IN this speech, delivered to the sessions jury in Salisbury, perhaps
in 1629 (the manuscript notes are not dated), Henry Sherfield,
Recorder of the city, set out the demands of the Puritan conscience.[1]
He was reflecting on his own recent experience as one of those
engaged in sweeping away idleness, drunkenness, and beggary in
the town since 1623, the year of his election as Recorder. For
Sherfield and his colleagues, as for many godly magistrates, private
conscience and public duty had pointed satisfyingly in the same
direction in those years 'wherein the reformation hath been undertaken'; and they had produced the civic and civil dissension to
which Sherfield referred. The speech and the 'wars' which lay
behind it are classic instances of an essential feature of the 'Puritan
character' identified by Professor Collinson: the fact that it was 'in
contention'.[2]

The speech was also prophetic. In 1630 Sherfield engaged in

---

[1] Hants RO, Jervoise of Herriard collection, 44M69 L67, box 3, unsorted papers, notes
for speech on the text of John 14: 27. Later references prefaced by L are to the Sherfield
papers in this collection. I am greatly indebted to Mr J. T. L. Jervoise for permission to
consult and quote from them.

[2] P. Collinson, *The Puritan Character* (Clark Memorial Library, Los Angeles, Calif., 1989),
12.

one of the most famous acts of iconoclasm of the seventeenth century. He broke a painted window in St Edmund's Church, Salisbury, showing God creating the universe. He said it had 'troubled' his 'conscience by the space of twenty years, for that he could not come into the church, but he must see it, sitting right opposite to it'.[3] The act being without episcopal sanction, Sherfield was prosecuted in Star Chamber in 1633, fined, and effectively destroyed. The trial brought disgrace to the city and ruin to himself: he died, in debt to the tune of £6,000, in January 1634. For Sherfield, as for his stepson, Walter Long, and for William Prynne, both of whom wrote to him from the Tower in the early 1630s, the wars in which they had contended for a decade ended in defeat.[4]

These events have already been described in print, and need only be touched on briefly in what follows.[5] Since Sherfield first caught my interest, however, his private papers—correspondence, drafts of letters, notes for speeches and memoranda books—have become available in the Jervoise of Herriard collection deposited in the Hampshire Record Office, and they allow us to look more closely at the man himself.[6] This bulky archive tells us a great deal about the circumstances which nurtured what Gerald Aylmer terms 'the Puritan outlook', and about the sort of person to whom it appealed.

Voluminous though they are, Sherfield's papers have their limitations from this point of view. Aylmer defines Puritan characteristics as including 'an introspective temperament, a ready concern with guilt and anxiety, and . . . with salvation in the next world'.[7] Unfortunately, Sherfield left no diaries from which these characteristics might be measured, and apparently kept none. The memoranda books are essentially notes of his financial and legal dealings. It must be said also that the papers show little concern

[3] *State Trials* (3rd edn., London, 1742), i. 401.

[4] HMC, *Salisbury*, xxii. 277; L34/22–4; L39/88.

[5] P. Slack, 'Religious Protest and Urban Authority: The Case of Henry Sherfield, Iconoclast, 1633', in D. Baker (ed.), *Studies in Church History*, ix (Cambridge, 1972), 295–302; Slack, 'Poverty and Politics in Salisbury 1597–1666', in P. Clark and P. Slack (eds.), *Crisis and Order in English Towns, 1500–1700* (1972), 164–203. These articles were written while I was in Gerald Aylmer's department at York; it is a pleasure to be able to revisit Sherfield on this occasion.

[6] They have been used by Wilfrid Prest to illuminate his legal career in *The Rise of the Barristers* (Oxford, 1986).

[7] G. E. Aylmer, 'Collective Mentalities in Mid-Seventeenth-Century England: I. The Puritan Outlook', *TRHS*, 5th ser., 36 (1986), 9.

with the next world (though there are one or two prayers preserved amongst them),[8] and a good deal with this. They are the papers of a busy and successful man, a leading attorney in the Court of Wards, bencher of Lincoln's Inn, Recorder of Southampton as well as of Salisbury, Wiltshire JP, and MP in all the Parliaments from 1614 to 1629. There are few indications of introspection, therefore, though, as we shall see, those that there are are of some interest. The papers themselves, moreover—especially the letters, each carefully endorsed with date and name of sender—suggest a temperament unusually obsessed with the need to impose order on personal affairs. Above all, they reveal a man who was at every stage, and in almost every aspect of his life, impelled to justify himself, to measure his actions against his own sense of right and wrong, and to broadcast the result.

Sherfield was not particularly reflective about the workings of his conscience. Like many others in the early seventeenth century, he took it for granted that it was consistent with and sanctioned by the laws of God and man. He seems to have had no appreciation that the genuine moral convictions of an individual might conflict with properly constituted external authority; he was totally disoriented by that charge at his trial, and no doubt also by the different 'consciences' to which his judges—following his lead—felt it necessary to appeal.[9] It is not any conscious intellectual underpinning of his sense of moral duty which gives Sherfield his interest, for there was none, but rather the different sorts of circumstances in which he felt compelled to parade it.

Some of them were public, as in the Salisbury sessions, and it was on public occasions that the Puritan rhetoric of the magistrate, familiar from other studies, was most evident.[10] But the same embattled self-righteousness is exhibited in correspondence with friends and relations and in the rare but significant notes to himself. In private as well as public arenas, Sherfield drew on that intense personal assurance of the godly which fuelled—and flourished in—

---

[8] L66/3.

[9] *State Trials*, i. 399–418, *passim*. Cf. E. Leites (ed.), *Conscience and Casuistry in Early Modern Europe* (Cambridge, 1988), introduction. L36/5 shows Sherfield and Lawrence Hyde, another lawyer, referring to 'conscience' in discussing whether a sheep-stealer should be reprieved.

[10] See, e.g., R. Cust and P. G. Lake, 'Sir Richard Grosvenor and the Rhetoric of Magistracy', *BIHR*, 54 (1981), 40–53; V. M. Larminie, *The Godly Magistrate: The Private Philosophy and Public Life of Sir John Newdigate, 1571–1610* (Dugdale Soc., Occasional Paper No. 28; 1982).

wars: wars with sinners, with colleagues, with neighbours, and, not least, with kin.

I

Next to nothing is known of Sherfield's life before 1607, when, a year after being called to the bar, he married and his archive begins. He was already 35 years of age. He was born in 1572, the youngest of three sons of Richard Sherfield or Shervill, a corn-dealer and small farmer at Winterbourne Earls, near Salisbury.[11] When defending his respectability against a libel in 1608, he claimed to have been educated 'as well in the country schools as afterwards in the university', but there is no record of his being at either Oxford or Cambridge. He entered the significantly Puritan environment of Lincoln's Inn in 1598, at the relatively late age of 26, and he seems to have spent some time before then in Southampton.[12] Being a younger son, he was perhaps employed as a clerk or apprentice there; and it may be that he was patronized by Sir Thomas Fleming, a Lincoln's Inn man and Recorder of Winchester and then Southampton. Sherfield sat with Fleming's son as MP for Southampton when he first entered Parliament in 1614, and throughout his career many of his clients and the strongest of his connections lay in the triangle bounded by Salisbury, Southampton, and Winchester. The link with Fleming is supposition, however. What can be said is that Sherfield's origins were relatively obscure, and the legal training which set him up in a successful career came late.

Where so much is uncertain, the quality of Sherfield's early life has to be reconstructed from his later relations with his father and his brothers; and here the material is rich. His father's manuscript testament, drawn up in 1620, shows him to have been a man of idiosyncratic religious views and strong-minded, if not cantankerous, disposition. He describes himself as a 'recusant', but it is by no means clear precisely what kind of recusant he was. The general tone of the will is distinctly Protestant and some of his opinions suggest that by 1620, if not earlier, he may have had links

[11] Wilts. RO, Winterbourne Earls register; H. C. Johnson (ed.), *Minutes of Proceedings in Sessions, 1563 and 1574–1592* (Wilts. Rec. Soc., 4; 1949), 12.

[12] L64/1; L36/12.

with the Anabaptists or Brownists then active in Salisbury.[13] He
confessed his faith in Christ, for example, without reference to the
Virgin or the saints; and it was a Christ who had suffered 'for the
sins of the whole world', Christ who was 'both God and man' and
'God of His own bountiful goodness ... without any help of man',
a 'high mystery' spoken of at length, he says, in 'my last book'. (If
this was his own treatise, it does not, unfortunately, survive.) Yet
Richard was certainly no conventional Anabaptist, for his will also
leaves £5 to be divided among his grandchildren 'in the worship
of the blessed five wounds' of Christ, which introduces a jarringly
Catholic note. Here is a puzzling and intriguing mixture in an old
man in his eighties (he was married in 1560): a decidedly sectarian
interest in Christology on the one hand and some remnant of
Catholic devotion on the other. Perhaps the result of a prolonged
search for godliness, it is an instructively unstable background to
Henry's own (so far as we can tell) rigid and wholly conventional
Calvinism.

The testament's picture of relations between Richard and his
three sons is equally interesting. Henry—'Harry'—is clearly the
apple of his father's eye: 'a long time my dearest friend'. Roger,
the second son, who by 1620 lived some miles away at Middle
Wallop, Hampshire, receives no mention: he was the black sheep,
cutting himself off from the rest of the family from time to time.
Richard junior, the eldest son, had had the father's property at
Winterbourne settled on him, but he had failed to pay the agreed
maintenance to his father and mother, and, after many quarrels,
forced them out of his house. It was Harry who had picked up
the pieces and taken in the old man when he was left a widower.
It was Harry also who supported poor 'maids', his kinsfolk, in his
household, paid for the maintenance of Joan Chandler, another
kinswoman, for several years, and paid off the debts of Tristram
Sherfield, possibly a cousin, who died on a journey to New-
foundland.[14] By 1620 Sherfield had made himself, or been forced
to become, the mainstay of the Sherfield clan.

Not surprisingly, relations between the brothers were never easy.
The father was grieved at the 'many great fallings out between'
Richard and Henry, the former expecting 'reverence' from his

[13] L67, box 3, will of Richard Sherfield, 19 Jan. 1620; *VCH Wiltshire*, iii. 100–1; Wilts. RO,
Salisbury diocesan records, Subdean's Court, presentments, St Thomas Salisbury, 1621–3.
[14] L25/2, 3 *passim*; L67, box 2, notes on debts of Tristram Sherfield; L41/10.

younger brother, since he had been 'the foundation and builder
up of his great houses' and laid out 'many a pound' for him.[15]
Henry certainly borrowed from both his brothers early in his
career, and financial squabbles did not cease when the roles were
later reversed. But there were also clashes of temperament. Roger
often complained of illness and may have been unstable. Shortly
before his death, he confessed to 'a world of misdoing in my
youthful times . . . but as soon as I became well informed of my
God's ordinances, I became a new creature'; yet he constantly
'entertained troublesome conceits . . . most frequent when I should
rest', fretted about the poverty of his family, and contemplated
'man's mortality'. Richard was more sanguine, but also verbose
and volatile, complaining as often as Roger of 'affliction of mind and
pain of body', 'afflictions, and nothing but afflictions'. 'Sometimes I
compare myself unto Job,' he wrote with some accuracy in 1630.[16]

The surviving correspondence between the brothers is one-
sided: we have few drafts of Henry's letters back. But his brothers'
complaints that he was 'always grieved', 'impatient', 'discontented',
unwilling to 'take advice from your friends', are eloquent, as is a
draft letter from Henry to Roger of 1614 but 'never sent', angrily
justifying his failure to pay his debts and defending his 'reputation'.[17]
There is some indication here of the 'violent' character attributed
to the Recorder of Salisbury by his enemies at Court in the 1620s,[18]
and of its probable roots in sibling rivalry and the ambitions of a
youngest son to make space, and a career, for himself.

II

'Violent' may be an exaggerated epithet, but Sherfield certainly
shared his brothers' prickly, arrogant temper, while combining it
with a fixity of purpose which they conspicuously lacked. One of
the earliest documents in the archive is a bill submitted by Sherfield
to Star Chamber in 1608, complaining about libels on himself and
his wife allegedly distributed round the streets of Salisbury, where

[15] L67, box 2, Richard Sherfield sen. to Richard jun., n.d.
[16] L63/3, 10; L32/5, 22, 25, 27.
[17] L32/22, 27; L67, box 2, draft letter to Roger Sherfield, 1614.
[18] PRO SP 16/55/64; D. H. Willson, *The Privy Councillors in the House of Commons, 1604–29*
(Minneapolis, Minn., 1940), 188.

he had set up house.[19] The squib was written by a relation of his wife's first husband, George Bedford, a rich Salisbury clothier; and it appears to have cast aspersions on Sherfield's personal character, family background, and religious opinions—his 'integrity in the true worship of Almighty God'. It is not surprising that he should defend himself against public slander, but a draft letter of 1607 suggests a similar touchiness in private relations. Written to a close friend, Anthony Clifford (but again 'not sent'), it justified at length Sherfield's failure to entertain Clifford when he called shortly after the marriage and his wife 'would not suffer me to come down' (she was pregnant and afraid of some infection, perhaps smallpox). Even in a highly litigious age, when reputation was vitally important, Sherfield seems peculiarly sensitive to offences given and received, and unusually anxious to 'satisfy mine own conscience' in all his dealings.[20]

The same drive is evident in correspondence surrounding his search for a second wife after the first died in childbirth in 1613. When his brother Roger pressed him to remarry, partly in order to repay the debts owed to him, Henry retorted, 'I cannot term the selling of my body to be any other than a most base, vile and abominable thing.' He was equally high-minded in a letter, possibly to Sir James Ley, his patron, about the suggestion of marriage to a prosperous widow, Mistress Harding of Pewsey: 'I think it [the proposed match] sent of God or permitted by Him to try my disposition, and what manner of person I am ... to a man ... of no better worth than I am ... it is even an extraordinary temptation.' Yet at the same time he was hoping and plotting to marry Ley's daughter Mary, an aspiration prevented by other members of the Ley family who thought the match beneath her.[21] In the end, in 1616, Sherfield married Rebecca Long, widow of Henry Long of Whaddon, a minor Wiltshire gentleman and one of his clients.

The marriage—to outward appearances one of convenience, and

---

[19] L64/1.

[20] L41/11; L30/59. On the importance of reputation for men such as Sherfield, see A. J. Fletcher, 'Honour, Reputation and Local Officeholding in Elizabethan and Stuart England', in A. Fletcher and J. Stevenson (eds.), *Order and Disorder in Early Modern England* (Cambridge, 1985), 92–115; and for the contemporary concern about 'credit' more generally, M. Ingram, *Church Courts, Sex and Marriage in England, 1570–1640* (Cambridge, 1987), 292, 302–3, and S. D. Amussen, *An Ordered Society: Gender and Class in Early Modern England* (Oxford, 1988), 152–3.

[21] L67, box 2, draft letter to Roger Sherfield, 1614; L30/74; L40/19, 20.

a definite move up the social scale for Sherfield—must, by any standards, be accounted a success. Rebecca's letters to Sherfield, extending over fourteen years until her eyesight failed in 1630, are full of love and concern, remarkably touching testimony to the close bond between them. It was sustained in part by a shared Puritan piety, firm and useful in the face of adversity, but not obtrusive at other times. In December 1615 Rebecca hopes that their marriage will be to God's 'glory, the true comfort of us both and the good of ours'; and she thanks Henry in 1618 for 'good and godly admonitions and counsels' on her difficulties with her children.²² Counsels were often necessary. Mary Bedford, Sherfield's first wife, had brought him six children by her first husband, all still living in 1616; Rebecca had eight. Although Sherfield had only one child of his own, a daughter, Matilda, born to Mary, these fourteen Bedford and Long children also had to be educated, found positions, and married off; and he often counted the cost.²³

Two of the Long boys were particular thorns in his flesh. One was in the Fleet for debt. Another, who wished to sail with Ralegh, was in the end packed off to the Indies, having indulged for too long in an 'ungodly course of living'.²⁴ Sherfield also tried to prevent what he saw as unsuitable matches. He stopped Jane Bedford marrying one of the Nicholas boys (possibly Matthew, brother of the future Secretary of State)—though not without typically self-satisfied and self-deluding declarations that the choice must be hers:

I did leave Jane freely to do as she saw cause with many speeches that I would not be any breaker off of the business if her affection would draw her to go forwards with it. But I told her that it was indifferent to him [Nicholas] whether the match did go forward or not, which in truth he spake at his last being with me.²⁵

Nevertheless, Sherfield was far from being a rigid Puritan patriarch. He was able to tailor his tone to his audience, avoiding,

²² L31/14, 49.
²³ L43/11, 18; L34/15. His relationships with his stepchildren are fully described in R. Priestley, 'Marriage and Family Life in the Seventeenth Century: A Study of Gentry Families in England', Ph.D. thesis (Sydney Univ., 1988), which Alison Wall kindly drew to my attention.
²⁴ L31/2, 6, 9. A third, Walter Long, got one of Sherfield's servants pregnant: Wilts. RO, Subdean's Court, presentments, St Edmund Salisbury, 26 Oct. 1618.
²⁵ L25/3, 22 Aug. 1623.

for example, any excessive godliness in his letters to prospective parents-in-law;[26] and the letters of his children demonstrate that there was ample room for affection in the Puritan household. His relations with children—and, for that matter, with women—give the appearance of being much more relaxed than those with male contemporaries and elders, perhaps because he had no reason to doubt their respect. Yet his private notes show that he was not at ease with himself: he was aware that his ambitions (and perhaps affections) drove him to take on burdens he might have been wiser to avoid; and he was acutely anxious (though always after the event) about the consequences for his status in his own eyes and those of the world.

In 1612 and again in 1614, after Mary's death, he worked out the costs and benefits of his first marriage. Mary had brought him an estate worth a little over £3,000, part of which he had used to buy land; but he was bound by the marriage to provide a total of £1,250 in portions for the six Bedford children and a legacy of £1,000 or an annuity of £100 a year for his wife. He foresaw difficulties, and it was fortunate that Mary died first, though she did so leaving a further £700 to her children. Sherfield's conclusion was calculated, and wholly revealing: he intended to pay the various legacies

if I shall be able, but by good conscience I ought not to sell for it any part of my lands, for the mother bound me, being ignorant of her estate, to pay as much as she was worth if not more ... I do not forget that mine estate is held of much greater worth in the common reputation of the world. Yet is it only such as aforesaid. And for it I do with all possible thankfulness give the glory unto my God, who hath so wonderfully enabled me beyond mine own expectation. And I do with all humility beseech His Majesty to increase his goodness in me, and to endow me with patience and a thankful heart. Amen.[27]

When Sherfield repeated the financial and spiritual exercise in 1623, he was less optimistic. In a 'consideration of my gain or loss' by his second marriage to Rebecca Long, he calculated his profit over seven years at only £555. He had had to pay the Long children's debts 'to save my wife's life or at least her quiet'; and the main property, Whaddon, went to Walter Long on his marriage. Sherfield himself was now £2,000 in debt: 'I beseech God to help me out of it and make me to be thankful for all His blessings.'

[26] L42/15, 17; L47/12, 13.   [27] L26/3, 4. Cf. L30/31.

'Let it be accounted whether I have been such a gainer by my marriage as perhaps hath been received,' he complained:

I would have it observed that I have a virtuous and a religious wife who doth, I persuade myself, fear God, which I account my happiness. But if one should respect a worldly consideration only ... I well know that I might have reaped more worldly profit by my match if I had married a wife who had been single, without charge, without any portion at all.[28]

III

Although he might not have expressed it quite so starkly, even someone less self-absorbed than Sherfield would have been worried about the tensions between domestic obligations, private profit, and worldly reputation, if he had had so large an extended family—extended still further in Sherfield's case by the dozen nephews and nieces who at one time or another depended on him. There was less need for self-examination in the public world of business and the law, where obligation, profit, and reputation necessarily, and more easily, coalesced. There success depended on 'credit', in every sense, and hence on public esteem; but, because the boundaries of acceptable behaviour were relatively elastic, and the interests of self and family closely identified, Sherfield felt little call to search his conscience or restrain his ambition.

At the time of his death, his finances were tangled and hopelessly confused—probably deliberately, as his enemies alleged, in order to escape his creditors[29]—and his papers throw no clearer light on the propriety or otherwise of his dealings before then. Like many barristers, he seized his opportunities in handling the affairs of his clients, particularly in the Court of Wards, to advance his own interests. He lent them money, stood surety for their other loans, and from time to time acted as their banker. His memoranda books are full of notes of sureties, payments, and debts, and of the sums in cash he carried to and from London in his 'little black locked box';[30] but they provide nothing in the way of final balance sheets of his affairs.

[28] L26/10
[29] PRO SP 16/214/92; *The Earl of Strafford's Letters and Despatches*, ed. W. Knowler (2 vols.; 1739), i. 206; L67, box 2, certificate of LCJ Finch, Mich. 1635 (petition on dorse).
[30] L25/3, 9 Oct. 1624. Cf. Prest, *Rise of the Barristers*, 168–77.

His legal practice prospered under the patronage of Sir James Ley, Attorney of the Wards, 'the very strength of my existence', Sherfield said, and the support of 'my poor reputation which I tender as my essence'. It gradually brought him powerful clients. He acted in cases involving the Sackvilles, for example, and he was able to use Dorset as a support at the time of his trial.[31] He caught the eye of Robert Cecil, Master of the Wards, and in 1617 became steward of the Second Earl of Salisbury's west-country estates. He acted for the towns of Southampton and Salisbury in the Westminster courts and in Parliament. Sherfield built up a legal and political network of clients and patrons (and patrons who were also clients) which extended from Westminster down to Devon, and which would repay analysis. It always had a decidedly local focus, however—in Wiltshire and adjacent parts of Hampshire and Dorset.[32] It is noteworthy also how much of Sherfield's local influence rested on his extended family; he was striving to build a power base for his clan.

An early example is his taking on the wardship of the illegitimate son of Robert Wrottesley of Chippenham, a connection of the Longs of Whaddon and also of the Sherfields—the mother of the child was Sherfield's niece.[33] It involved regular payments to the mother and the charge of educating the boy; it fulfilled family obligation; and it gave access to ready cash. It also brought him further contact with Sir George Wrottesley of Britford, closer to Salisbury; and Sherfield's deep involvement in the finances of Sir George and of *his* ward and stepson, Sir Thomas Jervoise, occupies many of the papers (whose very survival is due to Jervoise's being Sherfield's chief creditor after his death).[34] Wrottesley and Jervoise became his firm allies, and their wives, on occasion at least, his trusting friends.[35]

There were other partnerships with closer kin, despite predictable

---

[31] Prest, *Rise of the Barristers*, 30–1; L40/3; L49/35; L60/25; L65/3, 5.

[32] Prest, *Rise of the Barristers*, 30–4. For Sherfield's earnings at the bar, see also W. R. Prest, 'Counsellors' Fees and Earnings in the Age of Sir Edward Coke', in J. H. Baker (ed.), *Legal Records and the Historian* (1978), 172–3, 184.

[33] L26/2, 3; L47/15, 28; G. Wrottesley, *The History of the Family of Wrottesley of Wrottesley, Co. Stafford* (Exeter, 1903), 391–2.

[34] Wrottesley, *History of the Family*, 394–5; F. H. J. Jervoise, 'The Jervoises of Herriard and Britford', *The Ancestor*, 3 (1902), 1–13; *Index to Administrations in the Prerogative Court of Canterbury*, vi. 1631–48 (Index Library, 100; 1986), 372; L67, box 2, cert. of LCJ Finch, Mich. 1635 (petition of Jervoise on dorse).

[35] L47/1–3; L67, box 2, Lady Lucy Jervoise to Sherfield, 29 Jan. 1631.

strains. Sherfield was involved with his brother Roger in the cultivation of woad, an enterprise perhaps learnt from the Bedford family of his first wife; and he invested in the projects of his stepson, George Bedford, a partner in a patent of monopoly for the cultivation of madder, which brought little profit before its collapse under attack from more powerful commercial interests.[36] A more spectacular and damaging failure was the appointment of his elder brother Richard as Sherfield's deputy in the stewardship of the Earl of Salisbury's western estates. Richard was dismissed by the Earl in 1624, having antagonized his tenants with 'strict penalties and law quirks' and drawn on himself 'the hate and ill opinion of that part of the country'. Henry rushed to defend his brother and the reputation of the family in terms scarcely calculated to appease Salisbury: 'My good Lord, you may perhaps now say and that justly too, that I am transported by passion, or else I would not write in this manner . . . Yet my Lord I beseech you be pleased to say it is but such a passion which worms discover when they are tread upon.'[37]

Worm or not, Sherfield was at the same time straining his relations with the Cecils by constructing an independent interest in the parliamentary borough of Old Sarum, where the Earls of Salisbury and Pembroke each sought control. Thanks to careful purchases of property, he and four of his 'brothers and kinsmen' were said by 1626 to have nearly half the votes in the pocket borough, and Sherfield was setting himself up as broker between the two grandees to determine whose pocket it should fall into.[38] There was good reason for the manœuvre: he needed Pembroke's support in the city of Salisbury, which he had always identified as his political base. As early as 1613 he tried to persuade Ley— another Wiltshire man—to lease College House, the grandest private house in the town, with the clear intent to occupy it himself. The plot failed, but, once safely elected Recorder in December 1623, he was having another Salisbury house redecorated and looking for political space. In 1625 he had enough influence to get

---

[36] L30/12; L63/5, 6; 144/2; 133 *passim*; *Cal. SP Dom. 1629–31*, 235; J. Thirsk, *Economic Policy and Projects* (Oxford, 1978), 171.

[37] HMC, *Salisbury*, xxii. 176, 195, 196; L. Stone, *Family and Fortune* (Oxford, 1973), 126–7; L2/15.

[38] HMC, *Salisbury*, xxii. 135–6, xxiv. 263–4; L Stone, 'The Electoral Influence of the Second Earl of Salisbury, 1614–68', *EHR*, 71 (1956), 394–8.

his stepson, Walter Long, chosen as MP for Salisbury alongside himself, not a sign of subservience, to Pembroke or anyone else.[39]

Sherfield seems to have been overreaching himself long before his fall. Yet there is nothing unusual in such ambitious use of legal opportunities, local position, clientage, and family to build up a powerful connection, even if few barristers were able to make it to the very top (and Sherfield was hampered by the mediocre political weight of his own patron, James Ley).[40] What is notable, however, is that there is little sign of Sherfield's conscience in all this. Still less is there any appreciation of inconsistency in the actions of a man whose parliamentary papers include a draft bill against patents of monopoly, and who criticized Buckingham for 'ingrossing' offices, lands, and pensions to 'himself, kindred and allies'.[41]

We have only one instance of self-examination in Sherfield's handling of his legal and business affairs. In one of his memoranda books in 1610 or soon after, he recorded in discreet law-French that he had been an intermediary in passing on to Ley a gilt cup worth £10 as a bribe. That seems of little moment. On 3 June 1626, however, sixteen years later, he adds, in English: 'For which I humbly ask forgiveness at God's hands, He having given me the grace never to offend in that regard since that evil act, I then detesting as abominable the same, with promise to God never to offend again in that manner, which He hath enabled me to do hitherunto ... *Sit Deo Laus*.'[42]

Here, one is tempted to say, towards the end of the Parliament which attacked Buckingham, Sherfield proved to his own satisfaction that he had kept his nose clean. Given the notoriety of Bacon's case, it is hardly an example of the most fastidious scruple; and Sherfield does not seem to have felt the need to examine his conscience so precisely in other business dealings.

---

[39] L40/4–7; L51/10–13; L34/31; Salisbury corporation archives, N101, letter to Pembroke, 16 Jan. 1626.

[40] Cf. Prest, *Rise of the Barristers*, 139–40, 180–2, 252–3.

[41] L21/1 (notes for speech on dorse), 2.

[42] L25/1, fo. 3 from end; Prest, *Rise of the Barristers*, 310. The self-congratulation was repeated a year later, in June 1627.

IV

For more frequent expression of the Puritan outlook we must turn elsewhere, from private affairs and personal and family aggrandisement, to the open political arena. We can find Sherfield's Puritanism given voice at the top, in Parliament, though in suitably studied and moderate form, since he was always able to adjust his language to the occasion. According to opinion in Salisbury, he had already won a parliamentary reputation in 1621, 'being of an acute wit and sound judgement, an eloquent orator, and of an undaunted spirit, and such a one that will not spare speech for his country's good'.[43] His parliamentary papers support the tribute, but they show, in the words of the same letter, a 'good commonwealthsman' rather than a godly zealot. They also show a man aspiring to be a leading Country spokesman.

In 1625 he was one of the first to oppose not only Buckingham, 'a cause of all our calamity', but also Montague and the Arminians, and he kept up both campaigns.[44] He spoke on the 'liberty of the subject' and against unfettered use of martial law, and, like other lawyers, collected materials on the history of parliamentary privilege.[45] He also had that Protestant awareness of the threat to English security and liberty from Catholicism, which was no less keen for being commonplace and not unreasonable in the circumstances of the 1620s. He drafted a bill for the Protestant education of the children of papists, and kept notes of a story that Buckingham consorted with Jesuits; and he got news about events at La Rochelle and in the Low Countries from his stepsons and sons-in-law, one of whom fought with the Dutch.[46]

Sherfield's notes for parliamentary speeches are usually unhelpfully brief 'heads', though they suggest the ordered approach of a lawyer turning more naturally to legal precedent than Scripture for support. A decisively Puritan note breaks through once, however, and it comes in a rounded indictment of the government in a

---

[43] L39/8.

[44] L21/1 (notes on dorse); L22/6; L39/67, 68; C. Russell, *Parliaments and English Politics, 1621–1629* (Oxford, 1979), 231, 345.

[45] R. C. Johnson *et al* (eds.), *Commons Debates 1628* (New Haven, Conn., 1977–83), ii. 188–9; L67, box 1, notes for speech on martial law; L39 *passim*.

[46] L67, box 1, draft bill for recusant children; L25/6, fo. 2; L42/24, 30, 32. Sherfield naturally had a copy of Ralegh's *History of the World*; he lent it to a Salisbury alderman: L25/5, back cover.

speech intended for 1625 (it is not clear whether it was actually delivered). Sherfield began with threats from abroad and the failure of English foreign policy, and went on to the failings of Buckingham as Admiral and then to his corruption at home. That led him to his peroration, an attack on the governors of the Church who favoured 'the pope and papistry' and 'the Arminians against the true orthodox Protestants', since he had no doubt that 'the radical cause of all these mischiefs hath been and is and will be the wrath of God drawn on us by our suffering of idolatry and superstition to lift up the[ir] head without controlment'.[47]

Behind this there was a coherent view of threats to the commonwealth from 'evils inward' as well as 'outward' which would have won widespread applause. Sherfield's closest allies in the Commons, including Sir Thomas Jervoise and Walter Long, would no doubt also have shared his sense of the hand of providence shaping affairs. But that vision would have struck a particular chord among his constituents in Salisbury. For it was there that Sherfield's Puritan rhetoric was practised, and probably there that it was learnt.

There are some hints of it in his dealings with Southampton, the other town which elected him Recorder, in 1618, five years before his triumph at Salisbury. His first speech there after his election discoursed on the nature of covenants, drawing on Old Testament examples, and underlined his own, albeit unworthy, role: 'Surely God hath sent me to you to serve you.' In practice, however, his service was distant and irregular, partly because his interests lay elsewhere, partly perhaps because he had few like-minded supporters in the town. In 1630 the mayor wished to 'procure reformation', but there is little sign of a response, either from other councillors or from their Recorder.[48]

Things were very different in Salisbury. His delight at his election—by a large majority—was anticipated by his wife, who sent him the news the day it occurred, desiring 'God to bless you in this your new office to His glory and your comfort', and adding, in the margin, 'Good night, Mr Recorder of Sarum'. His brother Richard saw it as a stepping-stone to bigger things: it would prove

---

[47] L67, box 1, notes for a speech on foreign affairs, 1625; there is no reference to its being delivered in *Proceedings in Parliament 1625*, ed. M. Jansson and W. B. Bidwell (New Haven, Conn., 1987). For a similar view to Sherfield's, see Cust and Lake, 'Sir Richard Grosvenor', 52–3.

[48] L36/12; L35/35 and cf. 3, 53–62.

'your strength in your country' which 'will be noted by the rank of great persons'.[49] Letters of congratulation also poured in from Salisbury citizens, giving their view of the event. He had trounced Lawrence Hyde and his friends in the Cathedral Close, and ensured victory for the municipal interest. But the town itself was riven by faction. Councillors who were pushing ahead with divisive schemes for the relief of the poor and the reformation of manners wrote assuming they had his support. Their opponents, including the mayor, hoped he would come and 'pacify' a 'distracted city'.[50]

Sherfield's letter of application for the post shows a studied restraint which was probably designed to appeal to both civic factions. Although he would say little about his qualifications, since 'we have all, by the badness of our natures, corrupt and blinded judgements of ourselves', he advised the council to elect someone who

preferreth the true religion and service of God before all other things, one who for his learning is able to advise you . . . no young man for in such passions and affections abound, no hasty nor rash man, for such a one will shame you all, no covetous person for such a one will rob you all, no heady or self-willed man, for such a one will weary you all . . . Choose no man because he is your neighbour, your friend, your brother, your son or your cousin . . .'[51]

Like many successful testimonials, it was eloquent and not wholly accurate.

There is no doubt, however, to which party Sherfield belonged: the Puritan advocates of reformation. He had long been a member of the vestry of St Edmund's Church, where they had their caucus. With their leader, John Ivie, he had been instrumental in getting a 'good minister of God's word', Peter Thatcher, appointed to the benefice earlier in 1623. Ivie was confident that the new Recorder would 'seek a Reformation of many long continued abuses': 'God have called you to it.'[52] Ivie is an extreme representative of Puritan social activism, but others in the faction shared his aspirations. 'I will not cease to pray for Sion,' said one; 'You are chosen by the Lord and His people to be our mouth,' wrote another when

---

[49] L31/26; L32/19.
[50] L30/65; L37/9–11. Cf. Slack, 'Poverty and Politics', 183–7.
[51] L37/15.
[52] L30/64, 67; L37/13.

Sherfield was elected MP in 1624.[13] There are suggestions that Sherfield—often away in London—was not always what his supporters wanted him to be. There seem to have been justified suspicions of his political manœuvring.[14] But he was successful in 1630 in getting a new charter, confirming the town's independence of the bishop and the Close,[15] and locally he was a determined and consistent advocate of civic and social reformation.

He could also use the rhetoric of his allies when occasion demanded, and the chief occasion came with the plague of 1627, when sickness and the flight of the richer citizens left the city desolate. In the middle of the epidemic Thatcher wrote to Sherfield, who was safely ensconced in Lincoln's Inn, giving him his cue. God's punishment showed the urgent need for the sort of reforms men were 'in conscience bound' to promote.[16] On his return to Salisbury, in a remarkable speech at the first sessions after the plague, Sherfield took up the challenge. Echoing the pre-sessions sermon (perhaps by Thatcher) he called for 'a Reformation, a true and real reformation of this city'. Drunkenness and profane-swearing should be rooted out: 'Let us use severity now and not lenity, for the wrath of God is gone out against us.' Magistrates should make a 'covenant' together to 'use all the good ways and means which God shall discover unto us to bring to pass even what God hath determined to do'. Another speech in 1628 against 'fleshly concerns' and that quoted at the beginning of this essay, possibly of 1629, maintain the same tone.[17]

It is difficult to tell how much of this was the calculated playing of a popular tune, and how much a personal response to the judgements of providence. It cannot have been wholly calculation, however. While Sherfield may not have been as overwhelmed by the evidence of 'God's wrath' in the plague as his allies in Salisbury, he had described its heavy hand in the nation's affairs to the Parliament of 1625; and that vision can only have been intensified by political developments since then. If religious perceptions and expectations in Salisbury sprang from local contentions and afflic-

---

[13] L37/41; L30/78.
[14] L37/38, 39.
[15] L37/23, 25, 27; Slack, 'Religious Protest', 297–8.
[16] Slack, 'Poverty and Politics', 184–5.
[17] L38/54; L67, box 1, Thomas Abbott to Sherfield, 16 June 1628 (notes on dorse). For a perceptive analysis of later expressions of the same attitude, see B. Worden, 'Providence and Politics in Cromwellian England', *P & P*, 109 (1985), 55–99.

tions, they had meaning for the Recorder because they were wholly consistent with his view of his own role and of the play of events in the wider world.

V

Against this background, Sherfield's act of iconoclasm in October 1630 can occasion no surprise. It may well have had little importance for the man himself at the time. The vestry had authorized him to take down the offending window; there was a precedent—though admittedly decades before and with ecclesiastical approval—in another Salisbury parish. If he knew that there was an episcopal injunction against the demolition, and though this could not be proved at his trial it is likely that he did, he thought he could square Bishop Davenant, with whom he often did business.[58] The act was of a piece with his whole career and fitted his perception of himself. The Puritan magistrate must cleanse his parish from idolatry and superstition, and demonstrate the town's independence of the Cathedral Close. Political and personal clouds might be looming—his stepson Long was in the Tower because of his opposition to the Crown, and his debts were mounting—but that was all the more reason for him to assert his local authority. This 'man all in black', muttering to himself, witnesses alleged, as he attacked the window with his black staff, had no option.[59] It looks in retrospect like an act of hubris; but family, character, his career in Lincoln's Inn, Parliament, and Salisbury all dictated it.

More interesting than the act itself for our purposes are its consequences. It brought Sherfield's world crashing about his ears, and forced him back, once and for all, on to his conscience. As his political enemies gathered against him, as the King himself supervised arrangements for his trial in Star Chamber, as the Church faction in Salisbury moved to challenge the new charter, Sherfield sought the only refuge and defence he could. Petitioning the King, he declared himself 'guiltless of any offence, he not being then convinced in his own conscience that he had committed any'.[60] His imperative need to 'preserve a good conscience' echoed

[58] Slack, 'Religious Protest', 295, 298; L38/34.
[59] *State Trials*, i. 402.
[60] L65/6, 8.

throughout his defence at his trial, and in the remarks of those among his judges who took his part. 'Tenderness of conscience' cut little ice, however, with Attorney-General Noy, another old associate. One can almost hear the sarcasm as he cleverly pinpointed Sherfield's shift of position and its implications: 'It was done for Reformation; his conscience could not bear it. If it should be lawful for private men to do thus, what will they do next?'[61] It was a question Sherfield could not have answered to his own satisfaction. Circumstances had turned an act of locally acknowledged public duty into one that had to be defended on the shifting sands of private morality.

Sherfield was happier on the more familiar ground of his reputation. Although his judges in Star Chamber declined (by a majority) to deprive him of his place as Recorder, the King was adamant that he should not perform the duties of his office. In a painful meeting Noy pressed him to resign, but Sherfield refused: 'I hold my reputation much dearer to me than my life.'[62] In reality, he well knew that his reputation was gone, and with it his credit and that of his allies and relations. He had been insulted in open court at Dorchester Assizes, arrested for the debts of his brother Richard, and badgered by children and in-laws fearful of ruin.[63] Wrottesley and Jervoise were both in desperate financial straits, and only Lady Lucy Jervoise could write to him with anything like personal affection and encouragement: 'These are latter days and dangerous times; yet God is the same He was and will not forsake those are His.'[64]

It must have been difficult to persuade himself of that in 1633, the year of his trial, when the city of Salisbury called him to account for keeping 'much of the City money in his hands'; fire destroyed his house at Winterbourne; and he had to humiliate himself by public submission to the bishop, confessing that his act in St Edmund's had been 'under pretence of godly zeal'.[65] Yet divine providence was the only remaining prop for Sherfield's conscience, once authority and reputation left him. He had never

[61] *State Trials*, i. 401, 407.
[62] L41/5; Prest, *Rise of the Barristers*, 261, 414–16.
[63] L25/5, 29 Jan. 1631, 2 Mar. 1632; L43/23. Cf. L41/7, 8; L42/10; L46/19.
[64] L67, box 2, Thomas and Lucy Jervoise to Sherfield, 29 Jan. 1631; Jervoise to Sherfield, 20 July 1633.
[65] L38/42; *Cal. SP Dom. 1631–3*, 588; PRO SP 16/233/88; SP 16/236/75.

needed it so desperately. Hence in 1631 he was defiant in his affirmation of God's justice and favour, and particularly when defending himself in the forum where his character was formed and where we began: in his relations with his brothers.

There was a fraternal conference as debts accumulated and creditors threatened. It turned into pointed bickering. 'You told me I did torture, rack and torment you,' writes Roger: 'I say you have not . . . as much as troubled my mind . . . You threaten me with the curse of God . . . I tell you that I . . . have made as great conscience of all my ways as any one of your new purchased acquaintance.' Richard was also full of admonition, against Henry's obstinacy, his refusal to submit to the King, and his rejection of all advice, 'a fault in you which hath put off many hearty speeches intended for your own good'. Like his father before him, Richard had had 'such fears for you as knoweth God have been my companions even from my youth'.[66]

As might be expected, Henry's replies were unyielding. He brushed aside Roger's gibes against Puritan consciences: 'The hand of God is heavy upon me, and I have nought of comfort, but those wordly comforts upon which I most rely (whereof you were not the least) do seem to make haste to fly from me. But when all are gone, I have a God in whom I trust that He will never forsake me.' As for Richard's raking up of the past, that could only 'increase our vexation':

What you do in that respect I know not, but I do verily believe that all mine afflictions and crosses come to me even from and by the immediate hand of God. Which being so were it not madness, if not worse, to suffer oneself to be too much transported by impatience? For what is it so to do, but to spurn and kick against God himself? . . . Afflictions should bring us nearer to God, and not put as further from Him . . . You may think I have met with my share, and cannot but meditate of much sharper, and I confess, did not God support me, I should have let go my hold long ere this.[67]

There is no profound religious reflection here, not even a hint that Sherfield thought his own sins might have brought his afflictions upon him. Familiar as it is by now, however, it is hard not to have some admiration for his stubborn self-righteousness,

[66] L63/9; L32/29.
[67] L67, box 2, draft letter to Roger Sherfield, 21 Mar. 1631; L32/39.

on the eve of the disasters of 1633 which finally dislodged him: he was buried in St Edmund's churchyard on 28 January 1634. It is difficult also to find a better instance of the ways in which belief in an ordered and active providence lent support to contenders—and particularly losing contenders—in the countless wars of the early seventeenth century. So self-conscious and ambitious an operator as Henry Sherfield could scarcely have given shape to his life, justified his success, or reconciled himself to failure, without it.

10

William Dowsing, the Bureaucratic Puritan

JOHN MORRILL

You shall make you no idols nor graven image neither rear
you up a graven image, neither shall you set up any image
of stone in your land, to bow down unto it, for I am the
Lord your God. And if you will not be reformed by me in
these things ... I will destroy your high places and cut down
your images and cast your carcases upon the carcases of your
idols.

(Lev. 26: 2, 23, 30)

Then shall it come to pass, that those that ye let remain of
them shall be pricks in your eyes, and thorns in your sides,
and shall vex you in the land wherein ye dwell.

(Num. 33: 55)[1]

WILLIAM DOWSING is one of those second-ranking Englishmen
whom historians and others half-know. He is important enough
to rate an entry in the *Dictionary of National Biography*; the journals
he kept of his official visits in 1643–4 to the churches of Cambridgeshire and Suffolk with authority to remove from them all the
monuments of idolatry and superstition have been frequently
reprinted[2] and much discussed; and he has been held up as the

---

I wish to thank John Blatchly, Frank Bremer, Patrick Collinson, Arnold Hunt, David Smith,
Paul Slack, and (above all) Tim Wales for their most helpful comments on an early draft
of this essay.

[1] Two of the five mottoes referred to at the head of William Dowsing's journal describing
his iconoclasm in Cambridge in December 1643, according to an early eighteenth-century
transcript. See below, n. 2.

[2] The editions most often cited are, for Cambridge and Cambridgeshire, J. G. Cheshire
(ed.), 'William Dowsing's Destructions', *Trans. of the Cambs. and Hunts. Archaeol. Soc.*, 3 (1914),
77–91, and, for Suffolk, *The Journal of William Dowsing*, ed. E. H. Evelyn White (Ipswich,
1885). My own reading is based, for Suffolk, upon the latter, and for Cambridge upon the
collated edition of texts by A. C. Moule, 'The Cambridge Journal of William Dowsing,
1643', *The History Teachers' Miscellany* (1926), 1–16.

model of puritan vandalism in the Civil War era.[3] Yet he is a
shadowy figure and there is more to be gleaned from a study of
his journal than the usual recitation of extracts which turn him
into the grim reaper of wooden angels on roof-beams, stone saints,
and stained-glass cherubs. This chapter will seek both to find new
ways of analysing his journal and to reconstruct something of the
social milieu and mental world of a stolid fanatic.

I

William Dowsing (1596–1668) is a man whom we see from time
to time throughout his life as he scuttles out of the shadows
through a well-lit room and then back into the shadows.[4] He has
proved an elusive quarry, especially as he is hard to find in the tax
records.[5] He was born in Laxfield in north-east Suffolk, the younger
son of Wolfran Dowsing, a prosperous yeoman-farmer,[6] and he
moved to Coddenham about fifteen miles to the south and west,

---

[3] As by M. Aston, *England's Iconoclasts* (Oxford, 1988), 74–84; J. R. Phillips, *The Reformation of Images* (Berkeley, Calif., 1973), 185–8; A. Kingston, *East Anglia and the Great Civil War* (1897), 330–3; A. L. Rowse, *Reflections on the Puritan Revolution* (1986), 45–9.

[4] The earliest transcriber reported that the Suffolk Journal had been 'found in the library of Mr Samuel Dowsing, of Stratford, being written by his Father, William Dowsing' (Iveagh MSS 435, printed in *Journal of William Dowsing*, p. 237). The library is that discussed below, sect. II. The man here identified as the iconoclast was the William Dowsing of Stratford, whose 1668 will refers to lands near Laxfield and in Coddenham and Stratford and to his eldest son, Samuel, to whom he bequeathed all his books and papers. Two genealogies confirm the picture (that of Matthias Candler, vicar of Coddenham, in 1655 (BL MS Harl. 6071, fo. 358 (copy in Bodl. MS Tanner 257, fo. 186), and a later one (BL Add. MS 19127, fos. 126ᵛ–127ʳ)). Many other William Dowsings have been pursued through the records on my behalf by Tim Wales, and this William fits all the known facts, and no other William Dowsing fits any of them!

[5] He is probably but not certainly the William Dausonne of Stratford St Mary in the *Ship Money Returns for the County of Suffolk, 1639–40*, ed. V. B. Redstone (Ipswich, 1904), 209 (the transcript says Dansonne, but the original (BL MS Harl. 7542, fo. 99) is better rendered Dausonne). However, I cannot find him in the Suffolk subsidy rolls at any point in the reign of Charles I. He can be found in Stratford in the tax records for the 1660s (e.g. PRO E179/257/7, Free and Voluntary Gift, 1661).

[6] It was John Blatchly who pointed out that the William Dowsing of Laxfield (1596–1678), usually said to be the iconoclast, could not be the man, and who drew my attention to the will of William Dowsing of Stratford (d. 1668). This is clearly the will of the iconoclast, as a comparison of the hands in the various documents used below demonstrates. The following biography owes much to the perseverance, skill, and determination of Tim Wales, who scoured the PRO, the British Library, and the House of Lords Record Office in search of Dowsing, armed initially with little more than the will. He made several crucial discoveries, especially Dowsing's name in an Essex petition of 1642 and he took the Dedham link further than I would have done and taught me its significance.

in the very heart of Suffolk, no later than the early 1620s, the date of his marriage to Thamar Lea, daughter of a minor Puritan gentleman who resided in Coddenham.[7] He acquired copyhold land there, presumably from his father-in-law. By 1637 eight of his ten children by Thamar had had their births recorded in the Codden- ham parish register,[8] and he appears under that parish in a militia list for the autumn of 1638.[9] He and his family then disappear from the parish, and the births of two remaining children, and the death of Thamar in the spring of 1640, are not recorded.[10] In 1642 we find him signing a petition of the godly in Essex and by 1643[11] he is almost certainly resident in Stratford St Mary[12] on the Suffolk side of the River Stour, just across from Dedham, whose lecturer, Matthew Newcomen, we will find was just one of many friends there. It would seem that he remained in Stratford until his death in 1668.[13] But he could have gadded across the border to append his name to those of his friends in Dedham,[14] just as he may well have gadded to sermons there throughout the period.[15]

Although some contemporary documents, such as his letter of appointment as the Earl of Manchester's visitor, describe him as a gentleman,[16] he looks much more like a typical yeoman. His will tells us that he possessed freehold and copyhold lands in Brundish and Wilby parishes (contiguous with his birthplace-parish, Laxfield),

[7] The 'William Dowe' who appears in the Coddenham subsidy for 1621 (PRO E179/182/476) may be our William Dowsing.
[8] Suffolk RO, FB 37/D1/1–2.
[9] PRO SP 16/411/307.
[10] For her death, see below, p. 187 and n. 17. His move appears to coincide with the decision of Thomas Waterhouse, minister and schoolmaster at Coddenham, to emigrate to New England (N. C. P. Tyack, 'Migration from East Anglia to New England before 1660', (Ph.D. thesis (London Univ., 1951), appendix II, xi.
[11] HLRO, Petitions Box 1641–2, Essex petition to House of Commons presented 20 Jan 1642. See below, n. 23.
[12] Irritatingly, the Stratford parish registers are missing for the crucial years 1637–53.
[13] The Dedham records are unusually complete, and, had he lived on that side of the border, he would surely be found amongst them (Essex RO (Colchester Branch Office), D/P/26/1/2 (parish registers); D/P/26/5/1 (churchwardens' accounts); D/Q/23/5/1, fo. 47 and D/Q/23/15/1 (Dedham Free School Records)).
[14] HLRO, Petitions Box 1641–2.
[15] When he arrived in Stratford he would have found that the lord of the manor (Sir Edward Sulyerd) was a recusant (PRO SP 23/211/201); and that the vicar, Dr Samuel Lindsell, was a Laudian and ceremonialist (C. Holmes (ed.) *Case Books of the Suffolk Committees for Scandalous Ministers, 1644–6* (Suffolk Record Soc., 55; 1970), 37–8). The depositions against Lindsell were taken in early April 1644 while Dowsing was away from Stratford, so his name does not appear amongst the accusers.
[16] *Journal of William Dowsing*, 6–7.

in Coddenham, and in Stratford. By his will, the Coddenham lands were to be sold for an estimated capital sum of £300 (suggesting an income to Dowsing of c.£15–20), which was to be divided between four of his daughters. The Brundish and Wilby lands were to provide annuities worth £11.50 a year for the children of his second marriage and to be the main inheritance of his only surviving son by his first wife. His Stratford lands were to provide for his wife during her lifetime and then for the son of his second marriage.[17] His house in Stratford had five hearths, according to an assessment made in 1674.[18] It would be surprising in view of all this if his income was below £50 p.a.; or if it was much more than £80 p.a.

There are hints of a godly background. His grandfather's will of 1614 contains a classic 'puritan' preamble.[19] He married into a family which used Old Testament names for the children, his wife Thamar bearing the most distinctive and striking.[20] Despite his knowledge of both Latin and Greek,[21] he does not appear to have been to university himself (although his nephew and his namesake (godson?), with whom he has usually been conflated, and later his own eldest son, Samuel, were sent to Emmanuel, academy of the godly).[22] More important is his signature on an Essex petition to the House of Commons presented on 20 January 1642. The petitioners thanked the House for its 'great care and extraordinarie endeavour to settle our religion and peace', but apprehended 'a great stopp of reformation in matter of religion' and a threat from 'papists and other ill-affected persons ... ready to act out the parts of those savage bloodsuckers from Ireland.' It called for the exclusion of the bishops from the House of Lords and other

---

[17] Suffolk RO (Ipswich), Archdeaconry of Suffolk Wills, IC/AAI/98/149.

[18] S. H. A. Hervey (ed.), 'Suffolk in 1674: Being the Hearth Tax Returns', *Suffolk Green Books*, xi, no. 1 (1905), 231. This assumes his widow had not moved to another house in Stratford following her husband's death. No earlier return for Stratford survives.

[19] PRO PROB 11/125, fos. 68ʳ–69ᵛ.

[20] There are three Tamars in the Old Testament: the unfortunate wife of Onan who seduced Judah; the daughter of David, sister of Absalom, victim of an incestuous rape; the daughter of Absalom, much admired for her beauty.

[21] The annotations in his library include quotations in both. In relations to those annotations, Arnold Hunt of Trinity College, Cambridge, has commented to me that 'it is clear from his style of annotation that he copied references out of the books themselves and not from a commonplace book, suggesting autodidactism rather than a university-trained habit of mind'.

[22] J. Venn and J. A. Venn, *Alumni cantabrigiensis*, pt. I, *to 1751* (5 vols.; 1922–7), ii. 63.

effectual measures of reformation. William Dowsing's distinctive holograph is to be found about two-thirds through the accompanying list of more than five thousand signatories, in close proximity to those of Matthew Newcomen, of three inhabitants of Dedham who were to appear in Dowsing's will, and of many other inhabitants of that town.[23]

In the almost complete absence of personal correspondence, details of his private life have largely to be derived from his long but formal will. This contains hints of tensions between the children of his two marriages, and precautions about his wife short-changing her stepchildren. But once again the evidence merely tantalizes. The will also contains no religious preamble and no bequests to charitable uses. But he willed small sums to a group of men and women in Dedham who can be identified with leading supporters of reformation there in the 1640s and probable members of a semi-separatist congregation there in the 1660s, and to the deprived minister who served them.[24] The most important of this group was probably Bezaliel Angier,[25] a prominent clothier. Bezaliel, the brother of the prominent Lancashire Dissenter John Angier, had been born in Stratford but spent all his adult life in Dedham. His godliness is confirmed by Oliver Heywood in his exemplary life of John Angier.[26] His name appears in close proximity to those of Dowsing and Matthew Newcomen, the Dedham lecturer, in the Essex Puritan petition of 20 January 1642;[27] he was an elder for Dedham in the classis set up in 1646, and a long-standing governor of Dedham School;[28] he was left ten shillings by Dowsing in his will and was asked to see the will fully performed. In his own will,

---

[23] HLRO, Petitions Box 1641–2; the Dedham identifications are based on my transcriptions from the Dedham sources listed above, n.13.

[24] Robert Astie, for whom see *DNB*, and A. G. Matthews, *Calamy Revised* (1934), 18, and sources there cited.

[25] In the Old Testament, Bezaliel was the son Uri, son of Hur, and (ironically enough) was a skilled craftsman in metal, stone, and wood, who was appointed by Oholiab to make the furniture of the tabernacle (Exod. 31: 1 ff., 35: 30 ff.).

[26] E. Axon (ed.), *Oliver Heywood's Life of John Angier of Denton* (Chetham Soc., NS 97; 1937), 32, 47–8, 96, 134, 136, 163 n. Bezaliel was the perfect Puritan name—even in the shortened form he preferred to use, Beza Angier!

[27] HLRO, Petitions Box 1641–2.

[28] Essex RO (Colchester), D/Q/23/5/1, fo. 47, and D/Q/23/15/1 (Dedham Free School Records); W. A. Shaw, *A History of the English Church during the Civil Wars and under the Commonwealth* (2 vols.; 1900), ii.388 (the elders were John Alefounder, Henry Fenn, Robert Salmon, Robert Webb, Clement Fenn, Bezaliel Angier—three of whom are referred to in Dowsing's will).

made in October 1678, he left £5 for distribution amongst 'some faithfull ministers of the Gospell or the widdows of deceased ministers that are lowe in their estate', and ten nobles for the poor of Dedham, 'which is all I give because I had twentie nobles taken from me and given to the poore in my liftyme', a reference to fines under the Conventicle Act.[29]

It can be speculated that Dowsing's decision to move to the Stour Valley in 1638 or 1639 is related to his desire to place himself in an area where, over successive generations from the 1550s, there had been steadfast witness to a hotter sort of Protestantism.[30] His personal links with godly ministers can be seen in his only surviving letter, which he wrote to Matthew Newcomen in 1643 with messages for Harbottle Grimston MP and for his 'interest in parliament men'.[31] We will see how this 'interest' probably extended to the Earls of Warwick and Manchester.[32]

Dowsing's will also contains references to his library (a collection of several dozen works in English and with a strong evangelical Protestant bias) to which we will return.

All the straws are blowing in the same direction; and they come together to produce that historiographical straw man—the godly middling-sort Puritan: a man of comfortable means, uncertain social status (younger son, connected to minor gentry), educated, well read, with indirect and third-hand contacts with powerful and influential leaders of the godly coalition in the 1640s.

II

William Dowsing was a yeoman-farmer with a substantial library; and it is unusual for the historian to be able to find out as much about such a man's reading habits as we can about Dowsing's. He bequeathed his library to his eldest son, and that son, thirty-five years later, sold it to a London bookseller, Mr Huse.[33] He in due

---

[29] *Statutes at Large* (1829), v. 513–14 (16 Car. II, cap. 1); v. 648–51 (22 Car. II, cap. 1).

[30] The networking of the godly in this area is currently being explored by Tom Webster in a Cambridge Ph.D. due to be submitted in the course of 1992.

[31] From a letter drafted on the back of a sermon, see below, pp. 187–8. The letter is drafted on to the imprimatur granted by Henry Elsynge, clerk to the Parliament, for the publication of Jeremiah Whitaker's *Christ the Settlement in Unsettled Times* (Ipswich Town Library (now in Ipswich School), Parliamentary Sermons, vol. 6, no. 3). See below, n. 55.

[32] See below, p. 188.

[33] *Journal of William Dowsing*, 4.

course sold it piecemeal. Fortunately Dowsing was an inveterate and meticulous annotator. Thus he wrote his name on the title-page of everything he owned. He even had volumes stamped with his own monogram.[34] I have been able to recover twenty-three of his books in ten libraries in Britain and the United States. In addition, his annotations contain cross-references to other works in his collection, and these add a further twenty-five titles to the list.[35]

His taste was eclectic. It contained some works of biblical exegesis, usually from a safe Calvinist stable. Thus he possessed Gervase Babington's *Comfortable Notes upon the Five Books of Moses*[36] and Joseph Caryll's multi-volume commentary on the Book of Job.[37] The library contained far more controversial theology, and here he did not confine himself to works he approved of. Thus he owned Pocklington's Laudian contribution to the altar controversy[38] and an unnamed work of Bishop Bilson's.[39] He possessed a work he refers to as *Laws of Church Policy,* perhaps Parker's *De politeia ecclesiastica.*[40] But he owned much more Puritan and anti-Catholic polemic, including Tyndale's *Obedience of a Christian Man,*[41] Heinrich Bullinger's *A Most Sure and Strong Defence of the Baptisme of Infants,*[42] Thomas Clarke's *The Pope's Deadly Wound,*[43] George Wal-

---

[34] The nicest example is Dr Williams's Library, London (3029.D.24), a copy of George Walker, *The Manifold Wisedome of God, in the Divers Dispensations of Grace by Iesus Christ* (1641), which is still in its contemporary sheep. William Dowsing's initials are stamped in gilt in the centre of each board, with a floral ornamentation. (I am deeply grateful to Mr Arnold Hunt for drawing this volume to my attention.) The six volumes of parliamentary sermons were thus stamped until clumsily rebound in the early twentieth century.

[35] Pressure on space has prevented me giving a full account of his library. I hope to pursue this topic and to publish a list of his books and where they can be found in a separate article.

[36] Marginalia in his copy of *Eikon Alethine* (1649), 75. See below, n. 51.

[37] Suffolk RO (Ipswich), Archdeaconry of Suffolk Wills, IC/AAI/98/149. This reveals that he gave all his books to his eldest son, except for this commentary, which he left to his wife to comfort her in her distress! For some interesting comments on Caryll's *Commentary,* see J. S. McGee, *The Godly Man in Stuart England* (1976), 235–6.

[38] Marginalia on a sermon in Parliamentary Sermons, vol. 3, no. 8 (Cornelius Burges, *The Vanity and Mischief of the Thoughts of a Heart Unwashed,* preached 30 Apr. 1645), title-page. See below, n. 55.

[39] Ibid.

[40] See below, pp. 187 and n. 89.

[41] Copy in Cambridge University Library, Syn. 8.54.172.

[42] Bodl. MS Tanner 942 (2). Dowsing acquired the English translation by J. Veron, published in 1551.

[43] The title-page only is in the Ames collection of title-pages in the British Library. I am grateful to Arnold Hunt of Trinity College, Cambridge, and David Pearson of the British Library for assistance with this collection.

ker's *The Manifold Wisedome of God, in the Divers Dispensations of Grace by Iesus Christ,*[44] John Robinson's *The People's Plea for Exercise of Prophesie,* and two works by the puritan exile, Thomas Dighton.[45] One striking volume in this part of the collection is a copy he acquired in 1638 of John Bale's parodic edition of Princess Elizabeth's translation of Margaret of Angoulême, *A Godly Medytacyon of the Christen Sowle.*[46] A third major part of the collection consisted of works on classical and modern history (Plutarch,[47] Livy,[48] and Josephus;[49] Ralegh's *History of the World,*[50] Bacon's *History of Henry VII,*[51] and Hayward's *History of Edward VI*[52]). He also owned three different editions of Foxe's *Acts and Monuments.*[53] A fourth part consisted of works of political theory: most notably an edition of Polybius which he acquired in 1651,[54] and one of the major republican answers to the *Eikon Basilike*[55] (which he purchased alongside a copy of *A Narration of the Title, Government and Causes of the Execution of Charles Stuart, King of England).*[56] His annotation

[44] Dr Williams's Library, London (3029.D.24).

[45] Dowsing's copies of Robinson and Dighton are bound together with two other of his pamphlets in Dr Williams's Library (564.B.30). The title-pages with their characteristic comments are printed in R. Harris and S. K. Jones, *The Pilgrim Press: A Bibliography and Historical Memorial of Books Printed at Leyden by the Pilgrim Fathers* (Cambridge, 1922), plates 11–13.

[46] Copy in the British Library (C.12.d.1). This had been published in 1548 and Dowsing acquired it in 1638. I am grateful to Patrick Collinson and Arnold Hunt for drawing it to my attention.

[47] Parliamentary Sermons, vol. 3, no. 5 (William Goode, *The Discovery of a Publique Spirit,* preached 26 Mar. 1645), 8. See below, n. 59.

[48] Marginalia in his edition of Polybius, now in the Houghton Library at Harvard.

[49] Marginalia in his edition of *A Diamond Most Precious* (Folger Library), at p. 43. The work he calls *The Destruction of Troy* (Parliamentary Sermons, vol. 3, no. 8, p. 25) is almost certainly Sir Thomas Wroth's translation of Book II of the *Aeneid* (1620).

[50] Marginalia in his edition of *The History of Polybius the Megalopolitan* (1634), now in the Houghton Library at Harvard. See also Parliamentary Sermons, vol. 2, no. 9 (Stephen Marshall, *The Song of Moses,* preached 15 June 1643), 38.

[51] Marginalia in his copy of *Eikon Alethine* (1649), as transcribed by C. Deedes, 'Further Portraiture of William Dowsing', *East Anglian Notes and Queries,* 2nd ser., 11 (1905–6), 33–5.

[52] Ibid.

[53] Ibid. His marginalia show he owned editions printed in 1610 and 1641. For reference to a third edition, that of 1576, see Dowsing's marginalia on Lazarus Seaman, *Solomon's Choice* (Parliamentary Sermons, vol. 5, no. 21), at p. 41.

[54] *The History of Polybius the Megalopolitan* (1634). I am grateful to Paul Hopkins for transcribing the marginalia for me when the book was on sale at Sotheby's in 1988. (The title-page and a memorial on the annotations can be found in the Sotheby catalogue for the sale of books on English literature and history, 21–2 July 1988, at lot 10.) The translation is by Edward Grimston, nephew of Harbottle, for whom see below, n. 90.

[55] Discussed in C. Deedes, 'Further Portraiture', 33–5.

[56] Ibid.

of these books is especially detailed and agitated, suggesting deep concern about recent political events. Finally, there are a number of works which are more difficult to classify. In 1640 he bought a copy of *A Diamond Most Precious*, a guide for masters and servants published in 1577.[57] He spent 25 December 1643 in Cambridge, having just begun his work as an iconoclast. His reading that day was Francis Quarles's *Divine Fancies: Digested into Epigrammes, Meditations and Observations*, a book he annotated in a way that showed that he had very mixed feelings about it.[58]

The largest single cluster of works in his collection, however, is the collection of 171 sermons preached to the Long Parliament (1640–6) which he had bound together into six fat volumes.[59] He received most (but not all) within fourteen days of their publication,[60] and he read them as they arrived, although he was occasionally in such a hurry that he had to add a written reminder to himself to return to it later for a fuller study.[61] The collection consists of almost all of the sermons preached at the monthly Fasts before the House of Commons up to the middle of 1646;[62] of all the much smaller number of the published sermons preached before the Lords at their monthly Fasts in the same period;[63] and twenty-eight sermons preached before one or both Houses on other special occasions (the death of Pym, the signing of the

[57] Now in the Folger Shakespeare Library in Washington, DC. Dowsing noted: 'I r[ead] this booke 6, 7 June 1640, a month want 2 day after my wives death. I have cause to eat my bread with ashes.' He clearly now needed to learn how to direct the servants!

[58] See the discussion by C. Deedes, 'A Portraiture of William Dowsing, the Parliamentary Visitor, 1643/4', *East Anglian Notes and Queries*, 2nd ser., 7 (1897–8), 17–19.

[59] These six volumes are now in the Old Town Library of Ipswich, which is kept in the Headmaster's study of Ipswich School. For its arrival there in 1725, see J.Blatchly, *The Old Town Library of Ipswich* (Woodbridge, 1989), p. 49. (There is a catalogue of the 171 sermons, alphabetical by author, in ibid. 138–47.) I owe an enormous debt of gratitude to Dr John Blatchly, Headmaster of the School, for telling me about this collection and for making the sermons available to me in the Cambridge University Library in 1987 and again in 1991.

[60] Based on a comparison with the dates of receipt recorded by George Thomason on the copies that came into his London bookshop (in the Cornmarket Press edition: R. Jeffs (ed.), *Fast Sermons to Parliament, November 1640–April 1653* (facsimile edn., 1970–1)).

[61] e.g. Parliamentary Sermons, vol. 1, no. 4 (Thomas Hill, *The Right Separation Encouraged*, preached 17 Nov. 1644); vol. 3, no. 22 (Joseph Caryl, *Heaven and Earth Embracing*, preached 28 Jan. 1646).

[62] One sermon is missing from 31 Mar. 1642, together with nine of the ten published for the second half of 1642. My comparison of the remainder is against the list printed in J. F. Wilson, *Pulpit in Parliament* (1969), 239–46.

[63] A total of twenty-five sermons before the Lords, mainly for the period Oct. 1644–May 1646, and mainly bound together as vol. 1.

Covenant, the victories at Marston Moor and Naseby, etc.).[64] It is not clear whether he was on a subscription list so that the missing sermons are ones he received which have subsequently been lost; or whether he bought them as and when he could and missed out from time to time. What is clear is that he annotated and argued with the texts of these sermons more than with almost any of the books in his collection which I have seen.

All his books are carefully annotated. He began by writing his name on the title-page, followed by the date of purchase and the date on which it was read. He then (with the precision of the business man on Southern Region working his way through a crossword puzzle in his daily newspaper) went through the text completing or providing the biblical references. He either knew the Bible by heart (including the chapter and verse of every saying) or he went through everything he read with a concordance at his elbow. In a sample of ten sermons, I counted the addition of 194 references to twenty-six books of the Bible. Sometimes this would lead him into a fierce exegetical riposte to the preacher: when Samuel Rutherford used Acts to argue against the magistrate granting liberty of conscience, Dowsing wrote in the margin: 'Whereas you say they preach not against sins of 2 Table, what did Christ, Acts 24: 26 ... and if you had well minded vers 23 of the same chapter you might have found he had there spake against brib[e]s.'[65] Beyond this compulsion to add biblical references (and an almost equal compulsion to add cross-references to Foxe's *Acts and Monuments*),[66] Dowsing's annotation followed a common pattern. Frequently, he added to the title-pages of books and sermons an index of items that were of particular interest to him;[67] frequently he scored the margin with

[64] Mainly bound together in vol. 2.

[65] Parliamentary Sermons, vol. 1, no. 11 (Samuel Rutherford, *A Sermon*, preached 25 June 1645), 34.

[66] Often these references are tangential, a thought association triggered by the author. A general discussion in a tract of the biblical terms for ministers of the gospel leads to the aside 'see Latimer's Judgment in dislike of the ye priest for a minister, *Acts and Monu*' (Dr Williams's Library, 564.B.30 (5), *True Modest and Iust Defence of the Petition for Reformation* (1618)). Down to 1641, Dowsing always give page references to an edition of 1610; thereafter to an edition of 1641.

[67] To take a random example: on the front cover of a sermon by Francis Cheynell, *Sion's Memento* (preached to the Commons on 31 May 1643 (Parliamentary Sermons, vol. 3, no. 9)) Dowsing wrote: 'nothing from Babylon to build Zion with', p. 32; 'scandalous & ignorant to be kept from the Lord's Supper', p. 39, 31. On the clerk's imprimatur to the previous sermon, which he clearly had also at his side (and this too was his usual practice) he had seventeen index entries, including 'Pope Joane a whore'; 'separation before reformation';

varying degrees of emphasis;[68] and less usually he summarized a passage in the margin or engaged in argument with the author.

His habits of reading suggest an obsessively tidy mind; a man sufficiently meticulous to go through a text manually making corrections included in an erratum slip on which he then scrawls 'mended'.[69] His method of reading was calm, methodical, purposeful; but it belied, as we shall see, an intensity of feeling that lay behind that calm manner.

Dowsing's marginalia and adversaria tell us much about his convictions and obsessions. We have evidence of his purchases from 1620 until 1651, and we can trace his commitment to godly reformation through the 1620s and 1630s to a high point in the early 1640s before something of a collapse of self-confidence becomes evident around the mid-1640s.

In 1620 Dowsing acquired and read a series of tracts published in Leyden on behalf of English exiles there. Two of them, by William Euring and John Robinson, were lightly annotated, although they show evidence that Dowsing knew the works of Cartwright. However, he took much more interest in two works by Thomas Dighton—*Certain Reasons of a Private Christian against conformitie to kneelinge in the very act of receiving the Lord's Supper*, and *The Second Part of a Plain Discourse of an Unlettered Christian*. The marginalia are persistent but monotonous: 'all persons that desire life ar tied to the Worde & not to carnall Reason'; 'what is not waranted & grounded on God's Word is sin'; 'all that conforme without warrant from the word are not of the truth'; 'every ceremony is evill'; 'antichrist the ordeyner of cermonies that belong to God'; 'faith founded only on scripture'.[70] In the other tract purchased in 1620—*A True Modest and Iust Defence of the Petition for Reformation*—Dowsing was less in an endorsing than in a confrontational mood, meeting the conformist arguments head on: on ceremonies in the Church of England—'the popish use of practice & government that are still retayned I would also be removed'; he denied one familiar argument—'the office of

'episcopacy *iure humano*'; 'Ambrose put Theodosius fro the sacrament'; 'Romish and English liturgy'; 'graven images to be burnt'; and 'Brownisme'.

[68] Single or double lines; words of emphasis ('observe', 'consider', 'mark well') and a drawing of a hand with pointed finger (i.e. a pilcrow) at a key passage.

[69] Dr Williams's Library, London (3029.D.24).

[70] Dr William's Library, London (564.B.30 (3)), 1, 10, 17, 70, 73; (564.B.30 (4)) 9.

B[ishop] & presbiter ar one by the word of God'; he rejected an argument against popular participation in worship—'this is but a popish distinction taken from *John* 7. 48, 49 that the common people were cursed. See Cowper on *Romans* 8. 9';[71] 'your argument have no ground from scripture therefore your conclusion is false.'[72] This was a man with fire in his belly. He was not content with the Church as it was, and he yearned to purify it. He was willing to listen to and endorse the protests about the corruptions of the Church he found in the writings of radical separatists, if not to join them in their howling wilderness. By 1640, however, he had moved to the Stour Valley, into the heartland of passive disobedience to Laudianism, into an area that was a terminal for the New England Ferry. His reading, and, it would seem, his contact with SMECTYMNUUS,[73] were designed to keep his hunger for reformation very keen.

In the early 1640s Dowsing had no doubts of what *had* to be done: '11 evils to be reformed', he noted at the head of his copy of a sermon by Obadiah Sedgwick that he read in February 1642, and he took note of 'the publike plots of fallow ground which need a further breaking up'.[74] The priorities were unambiguous: episcopacy was 'Babylon's love token';[75] 'the Lord's Supper polluted', he noted, as Marshall thundered against 'the promiscuous multitude everywhere, not only allowed, but even compelled to the receiving of it . . . multitudes wallowing in all prophaneness and licentiousness'.[76] When, in addition to a welter of such highlightings, we add his preoccupation with idolatry throughout the Church, the pressure on this meticulous man to take upon himself a key role in the battle with popery becomes easy to understand. 'The walls of Jerusalem were 70 years in finishing', the advocacy of

[71] W. Cowper [Bishop of Galloway], *Three Heavenly Treatises upon the Eighth Chapter of the Romanes* (1609, and many subsequent edns.).

[72] Dr Williams's Library, London (564.B.30 (5)), 54, 190, 162, 153.

[73] An acrostic of the initials of Stephen Marshall, Edmund Calamy, Thomas Young, Matthew Newcomen, Uuilliam Spurstowe, five ministers who attacked the institution of episcopacy in 1641.

[74] Parliamentary Sermons, vol. 4, no. 18 (O. Sedgwick, *England's Preservation*, preached 25 May 1642), at pp. 24–6. There were four such plots: idolatry, superstition, ignorance, and 'idoll' [*sic*] ministry.

[75] Parliamentary Sermons, vol. 5, no. 1 (Samuel Rutherford, *A Sermon*, preached 31 Jan. 1644), title-page.

[76] Parliamentary Sermons, vol. 4, no. 9 (S. Marshall, *A Sermon*, preached 17 Nov. 1640), title-page and p. 35; and cf. his comments in Parliamentary Sermons, vol. 6, no. 8 (J. Ley, *The Fury of War*, preached 26 Apr. 1643), title-page and pp. 41, 43.

ceremonies was a 'wicked policy', and the country was 'wallowing in blood ... [on] the onely account that could be given of it, a Bishop's Rochet, a Surplice or a Cross'.[77] Shortly after noting these words, Dowsing was, as we will see, drafting what amounted to an application for the post of Iconoclast General in east Anglia.[78]

But from 1643 on, and especially from 1645, dark clouds were forming. He began to lose confidence in the two Houses and their determination to carry through the great work of Reformation. He approved Calamy's denunciation of the 'oppression, the injustice in the Parliament's committees in the Counties'.[79] 'Committees of Parliament put in and restore corrupt priests into the ministry,' he wrote twelve months later.[80] He distrusted the Scots, saying of part of one of Gillespie's sermons that it was 'rather Scottish devinity or no sence'.[81] The sermons marking the signing of the Covenant in the autumn of 1643 were the only ones of the 171 he did not bother to annotate.[82]

More disturbing to him, however, was liberty turning to licence. 'Corrupt books crept in,' he noted of a list which included *The Bloody Tenant of Persecution* and *The Compassionate Samaritan* anathomized by Lazarus Seaman in September 1644;[83] and Mortalism, Divorce, Antinomianism, and a denial of the divine inspiration of Scripture were amongst those he gloomily noted as 'blasphemous errors' after reading a sermon in February 1645.[84]

Two things preoccupied him throughout 1645–6: the role of the civil magistrate in religion and the extent to which liberty should be extended to tender consciences. Nothing throughout the recoverable parts of his library was so intensively annotated as those sermons which addressed those issues. Initially he seems torn,

[77] Parliamentary Sermons, vol. 2, no. 2 (Jeremiah Burroughs, *Zion's Joy*, preached Sept. 1641), title-page and pp. 27, 39.

[78] See below, pp. 187–8.

[79] Parliamentary Sermons, vol. 1, no. 5 (Edmund Calamy, *An Indictment against England*, preached 25 Dec. 1644), title-page and pp. 11–12.

[80] Parliamentary Sermons, vol. 3, no. 11 (Richard Byfield, *Zion's Answers to the Nation's Ambassadors*, preached 25 June 1645), title-page and p. 34.

[81] Parliamentary Sermons, vol. 1, no. 1 (George Gillespie, *A Sermon*, preached 27 Aug. 1645), at p. 15.

[82] Parliamentary Sermons, vol. 2, nos. 10–11 (T. Coleman, *The Heart's Engagement*; J. Caryll, *The Nature, Solemnity, Growth, Property, and Benefit of a Sacred Covenant*).

[83] Parliamentary Sermons, vol. 5, no. 21 (Lazarus Seaman, *Solomon's Choice*, preached 25 Sept. 1644), title-page and at p. 41.

[84] Parliamentary Sermons, vol. 3, no. 2 (John Whincup, *God's Call to Weeping and Mourning*, preached 29 Jan. 1646), title-page.

annotating and indexing alternative points of view.[85] But gradually he seems to have come to a point of repose: he indicated his approval of preachers who call upon the civil magistrate to involve themselves in the work of reformation, to set the limits to freedom, and to police those limits.[86] And, after showing sympathy for those who found classical presbyterianism too rigid, and after approving Hugh Peter's plea that 'those who held errors' be counselled rather than punished,[87] he came down firmly against Independency and separatism. In perhaps the most heavily scored and annotated of all the sermons, Thomas Coleman's *Hope Deferred and Dashed* (which he read on 13 November 1645), Dowsing emphatically endorsed the following passionate outbursts:

We are to have Classical and Presbyteriall meetings; let them be to us as it were little universities; let our employments in them be opening of scripture, diving into the sense of difficult places; handling heads of divinity; searching into the grounds and redressing of erroneous opinions; resolving cases of conscience, communicating the experiences of the ministry, discovering Satan's depths and such like . . . For these particular men ['Independents', Dowsing adds] I doe here professe I reverence their persons . . . [yet] under this notion of Independencie weavers and taylors may become pastors . . . so that one may binde his sonne prentice to a cobler and at seven yeares end he may goe at free a minister . . . A christian magistrate as a christian magistrate, is a Governour of the Church; all Magistrates, it is true, are not christians, but that is their fault; all should be, and when they are they are to manage their office under and for Christ. Christ hath placed Government in His Church.[88]

Given what was to happen in the years that followed, this classic defence of non-separating Congregationalism on the New England model cannot have afforded him much comfort. Shortly after this he recedes into the mist. In 1649 and 1651 he was reading about

[85] Parliamentary Sermons, vol. 1, no. 1 (G. Gillespie, *A Sermon*, preached 27 Aug. 1645); vol. 3, no. 17 (Francis Taylor, *God's Covenant, the Church's Plea*, preached 29 Oct. 1645); vol. 3, no. 26 (Francis Cheynell, *A Plot for the Good of Posterity*, preached 25 Mar. 1646).

[86] Parliamentary Sermons, vol. 3, no. 14 (John Lightfoot [untitled sermon], preached 23 Aug. 1645), at p. 30.

[87] Parliamentary Sermons, vol. 2, no. 28 (Hugh Peters, *God's Doings and Man's Duty*, preached Apr. 1646), title-page. See also his approval of John Maynard's analogy that, 'if a man is constrained to cut off a limbe desperately infected with a gangrene, must he therefore part with a usefull member for every little inflammation and distemper'. Dowsing notes 'Liberty of conscience granted to ye godly hinder not restraint of other' (Parliamentary Sermons, vol. 3, no. 4 (J. Maynard, *A Sermon*, preached 26 Feb. 1645), title-page and at pp. 27–8).

[88] Parliamentary Sermons, vol. 3, no. 13 (Thomas Coleman, *Hope Deferred and Dashed*, preached 30 July 1645), at pp. 26–7.

the rights and wrongs of the Regicide and pondering Polybius' prescriptions for political stability. In the 1660s a new crisis of conscience seems to have driven him, at the very least into semi-separatism. In truth, we lose sight of him. What we can say is that, when he was called to his only public duty in the winter of 1643/4, his private conscience was fully formed. His belief that God would build a New Jerusalem if only the godly would clear the site was at its height. In December 1643 his sun was at its zenith.

III

On 6 March 1643 Dowsing took a printed copy of Jeremiah Whitaker's *Christ the Settlement in Unsettled Times*, a Fast sermon preached before the House of Commons on the previous 25 January, and he drafted a letter to Matthew Newcomen on to the back of it. The opening must have made the Dedham lecturer wince:

Syr my kind respect to you. This is let you understand I canot but take it ille that in 2 yeeres space you returne not my booke I lent you of Church Policy.[89] I have desired you to write to Mr Grimston[90] for it & tell him it was not your owne. You told mee you would writ I heare not of it yet. I pray with out more delay, write to him & let me begett the parties absolute answ[er] betwene this and march 25 & then if god permit me with life & helth I will come or send to you for it. I had rather losse 10 s[hillings] by farr that that very book, because there are divers notes in it[91] & divers bookes cite that booke & that edit[io]n, though I feare my booke is pulled apeces by the printer that since printed it in a quarto edit[ion], for it is printed by some Parliament mens action.

The letter continues with some choice biblical reproofs. Dowsing then changes tack completely and a thoroughly shaken Matthew Newcomen was given an opportunity to make amends.

Sir, if you have anie interest in parliament men, now we have an army at Cambridge it might be a fitt tyme to write to the Vice Chancellor of

[89] Just possibly a reference to Hooker's *Laws of Ecclesiastical Polity*, but more likely a reference to T. Parker's *De politeia ecclesiastica* [1620]. I am grateful to Patrick Collinson for the suggestion.

[90] Presumably Harbottle Grimston jun., MP and Recorder of Colchester (where Matthew Newcomen had been born, and where his brother Thomas was a controversial Laudian minister). See *DNB*.

[91] For a discussion of the way Dowsing annotated his own books, see above, pp. 182–3 .

Cambridge & Mayor to pull down all ther blasphemous crucifixes, all superstitious pictures and reliques of popery according to the ordinances o' parliament. I only reffere you to that famous story in Ed[ward VI's reign] how the English got the victory against the Scots in Museleborough field the same day & hower the reformation was wrought in London and images burnt—*A[cts] & M[onuments]*[92] edit[ion] last.[93]

We will never know whether this was a letter of application. It seems to have been treated as such. Within a few weeks, as the Earl of Manchester took over as commander of the Eastern Association, Dowsing was appointed as provost-marshall of the army of that association. Between August and December his accounts show him attending Manchester at the siege of King's Lynn, making arrangements for prisoners of war, and equipping troops who were being sent into Essex.[94] He resigned his commission on 18 December 1643, the day before his appointment as the Earl of Manchester's commissioner for removing the monuments of idolatry and superstition from the churches of Cambridgeshire and Suffolk. It is pure speculation, but not wildly implausible, to imagine that Newcomen shared Dowsing's letter with Grimston, who shared it with his friend and mentor the Earl of Warwick, who had a word in the ear of his son-in-law, the Earl of Manchester. How else might this stolid yeoman have got the job?

IV

Dowsing was commissioned by Manchester under a parliamentary Ordinance of 26 August 1643. This, according to the Houses, rooted itself 'upon their serious considerations how well pleasing it is to God, and conduceable to the blessed reformation of His worship . . . that all monuments of idolatry and superstition should be removed and abolished'. It required the removal and/or destruction of all fixed altars, rails, chancel steps, and of 'all

---

[92] i.e. John Foxe's *Acts and Monuments* (or *Book of Martyrs*). The edition in question is that of 1610, and Dowsing's previous sentence is a close paraphrase of Foxe.

[93] *Parliamentary Sermons*, vol. 6, no. 3 (Jeremiah Whitaker, *Christ the Settlement in Unsettled Times*, preached 25 Jan. 1643), verso of imprimatur.

[94] PRO SP 28/13, pt. II, fo. 210ʳ. I am grateful to Dr Gordon Blackwood for this reference. See also the probable reference to him in the accounts of Samuel Moody, Suffolk County Treasurer, for the year 1643: PRO SP 28/176, pt. I, p. 31.

crucifixes, crosses, and all images and pictures of any one or more persons of the Trinity, or of the Virgin Mary and all other images and pictures of Saints or superstitious inscriptions in or upon all and every Church'. The task was laid upon all churchwardens, who could levy a parish rate for removal and making good. In the event of their failure to act, JPs were ordered to act upon complaint from any party and to make defaulting churchwardens bear the cost themselves.[95]

His commission from Manchester, dated 19 December 1643, summarized the Ordinance of 28 August, and empowered Dowsing to put it into effect in 'the several associated counties'. It was without limit of time.[96]

Dowsing's commission seems to have been unique. No similar commission for any other county or association has survived, and there is no evidence of any other person or group of persons undertaking a similar task. Richard Culmer seems to have had some commission for his smashing of windows in the face of a hostile crowd at Canterbury Cathedral, but his writ seems to have been specific to that cathedral.[97] If Dowsing's journal had not survived, we would still know something of him, both from hostile accounts in Royalist propaganda[98] and from many churchwardens' accounts.[99]

But Dowsing did keep a journal in which he kept a record of his travels and activities as iconoclast. The journal itself has long been lost, but two separate transcripts from it were made in the early eighteenth century, and these have been frequently republished since. Because those interested in printing it have always been local antiquarians interested in either Cambridgeshire or Suffolk, it has

[95] C. H. Firth and R. S. Rait, *Acts and Ordinances of the Interregnum 1642–1660* (3 vols.; 1911), i. 265. The Ordinance specifically excluded 'any image, picture or coat of arms in glass, stone or otherwise . . . set up or graven onely for a monument of any King, Prince or nobleman, or other person which hath been commonly reputed or taken for a saint'.

[96] The commission is printed in *Journal of William Dowsing*, 6–7.

[97] The best discussion of Culmer is in Aston, *England's Iconoclasts*, 84–95. He also tried to remove glass and other images from his own parish church, but as incumbent rather than as commissioner.

[98] e.g. [J. Barwick], *Querela cantabrigiensis* (Oxford, 1646), 17–18, with its famous evocation of Dowsing as one 'who goes about the country like a Bedlam breaking glasse windows . . . [and] compelled us by armed souldiers to pay forty shillings a colledge for not mending waht he had spoyled and defaced'.

[99] e.g. Cambs. RO, P20/05/01 (Cambridge, All Saints); P22/05/03 (Cambridge, Holy Trinity); P26/05/01 (Cambridge, St Botolph).

always been published in two halves. But it is possible to reconstruct it as a single journal covering the sixteen Cambridge colleges, the twelve parish churches in the city and the eighty-four in the county of Cambridge and the 146 parishes in the county of Suffolk.[100]

We do not have a portrait of him, only a verbal caricature. The vicar of Kesgrave, which he visited on 27 January, described him as a grim person clad in the sombre garb of the Puritans 'with a tall hat'.[101] We know that he was at least sometimes accompanied by a deputy[102] and by soldiers.[103] His first task in each church was to make an inventory of all objects of idolatry and superstition; his second was to destroy what he conveniently could and to leave orders for the destruction of the rest. In the early weeks he tried to see everything done by himself and his party, including the levelling of chancels and the removal of crosses from spires and church gables. But he soon realized how such a policy would slow him down. Henceforth he almost always left instructions that chancels were to be levelled and crosses on roofs removed by named persons within a specified period (usually fourteen or twenty-eight days). On the other hand, he and his party continued to take responsibility for all offensive inscriptions, for altars and for most other accessible depictions in stone, wood, and glass. In Suffolk he tells us that he completed all such tasks in 113 churches, but that he left some of the work to others in twelve churches and all of the work to others in fifteen churches. Most of these last fifteen can be explained by his being in a hurry. For example, on 5 February he was journeying from home to Cambridge and he visited just three

---

[100] There is an outside chance that he might also have been active in Norfolk. Despite Mr Ketton-Kremer's assertion that 'broadly speaking it may be said that the same measure of destruction took place in Norfolk and Suffolk alike', the evidence he himself adduces shows that the very things Dowsing targeted (see below, pp. 197–9 have a far higher survival rate in Norfolk (R. W. Ketton-Kremer, *Norfolk in the Civil War* (1969), 253–7). My sampling of twelve sets of churchwardens' accounts also shows no sign of any visitations during the periods between his periods of activity in Cambs. and Suffolk.

[101] Cited in S. P. Andrews, 'The Tour of William Dowsing', *Suffolk Fair* (Oct. 1978), 19.

[102] e.g. *Journal of William Dowsing*, 23–4.

[103] e.g. Suffolk RO (Ipswich), FC198/A2/1, Blythburgh Churchwardens' Accounts: 'paid to Mr Dowson that came with the troopers to our church about the taking down of images and brasses off the stone.' The Blythburgh records also yield another warning. Dowsing has frequently been accused of having his troopers damage the angel roof by shooting at it. But, John Blatchly tells me, 'in 1974, in the course of restoration work, the lead shot with which the roof angels were peppered was shown conclusively to be of a type not used before the eighteenth century. The churchwardens' book for 1761 records: "to powder and shott to shoot jackdaws of the church and steeple"'!

churches on his forty-mile journey—two in Bury St Edmunds and one in Kentford (presumably the two places where he stopped for refreshment).[104] In each case he made a quick inspection and left instructions but undertook none of the work himself. As we will see, he also became less demanding with time.

On a handful of occasions he records that some of the work had been done before he came (and it is clear that most of the altar rails and vestments had been taken down and got rid of in 1641/2); on a few more occasions he says or implies that he met with a warm and eager response, that is with a party eager to cleanse its church but waiting for external authority to arrive so that the work could be undertaken. Equally, on a few occasions he met with sullen or passive non-co-operation (keys lost, ladders missing).[105] But the number of such instances is too small for generalization. Perhaps more striking is the variety of officers he commissioned to undertake work after he went. In Cambridgeshire he laid the responsibility on fourteen pairs of churchwardens, seven ministers, one overseer, one sequestrator (of the living of Shingay), 'Lord North's man' (at Kirtling), the squire's widow (at Hinxton), and a 'widow Rolfe' (at Ickleton).[106]

William Dowsing was the bureaucratic Puritan. If something was in the Ordinance, it was removed or ordered to be removed. If it was not in the Ordinance, it was left behind, as the quantity of stained glass containing coats of arms or royal insignia which remains even today bears testimony. He only began to remove angels, organs, and holy water stoups after they were mentioned by name in a subsidiary Ordinance of May 1644.[107] This was no blind fanaticism, but resolute enforcement of what the Bible and parliamentary injunction had ordered. He followed both literally and unswervingly.

His journal is a record of visits to 250 churches and chapels in Cambridgeshire and Suffolk. Is it a complete record? It seems not. It is possible, on the basis of close attention to his itinerary, to suggest that he almost certainly visited more Cambridgeshire churches and may have visited more elsewhere. Table 10.1 is a record of his progress. Laid out like this, it becomes obvious that there

---

[104] Bury was twelve and Kentford twenty-five miles into his journey.
[105] *Journal of William Dowsing*, 21–2.
[106] Moule, 'Cambridge Journal', nos. 39, 76, 65, 57.
[107] Firth and Rait, *Acts and Ordinances*, i. 425–6.

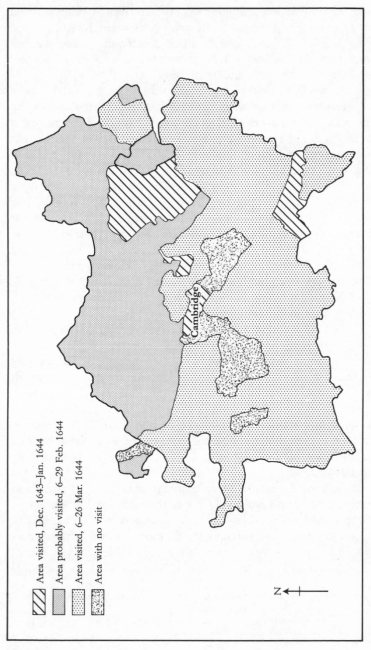

Area visited, Dec. 1643–Jan. 1644

Area probably visited, 6–29 Feb. 1644

Area visited, 6–26 Mar. 1644

Area with no visit

Map 10.1 Dowsing's visits to Cambridgeshire, December 1643–March 1644

Table 10.1. Dowsing's itinerary, December 1643–September 1644

Date (1643–4)	Itinerary
21 Dec.–5 Jan.	visits Cambridge colleges and city churches
6 Jan.–9 Jan.	visits churches *en route* from Cambridge to home
9 Jan.–19 Jan.	at home in Stratford St Mary
19 Jan.–5 Feb.	tours within Suffolk
6 Feb.	leaves Suffolk, visits a parish near Cambridge
6 Feb.–20 Feb.	no evidence (but see below)
20 Feb.–23 Feb.	visits Brinkley (Cambs.) and Suffolk churches and arrives home.
26 Feb.–6 Mar.	visits Suffolk churches
6 Mar.–26 Mar.	visits most Cambs. parishes in three sweeps from Cambridge
3 Apr.–15 Apr.	visits Suffolk churches
15 Apr.–17 July	no evidence
17 July–30 Aug.	visits Suffolk churches
1 Sept.–16 Sept.	no evidence
26 Sept.–28 Sept.	visits Suffolk churches

is at least one hole in the record: what was he doing beween his arrival in Cambridgeshire on 6 February and his departure on 20 February? Map 10.1 provides a possible answer. Dowsing systematically searched Cambridge city during his first visit and the south of the county in four separate sweeps. On 6 February he entered Cambridgeshire and arrived at Chesterton on the outskirts of Cambridge On the 20th he left the county through Brinkley. Is it not plausible to assume that in the period in question he was sweeping through all the northern parishes, leaving via Bottisham on his way to Brinkley, which he records visiting?

What makes this more likely is that the survival rate of those monuments and inscriptions proscribed by the Ordinances was equally low in the Cambridgeshire parishes he is known to have visited and the rest. By comparison, the survival rate in the parishes of the Isle of Ely is much higher. I base this statement on a study of the meticulously recorded visits of an eighteenth-century antiquary in search of monumental inscriptions,[108] on two modern

---

[108] William Cole's inventory drawn up between the 1730s and the 1760s (printed in W. M. Palmer, *Monumental Inscriptions and Coats of Arms from Cambridgeshire* (1932)).

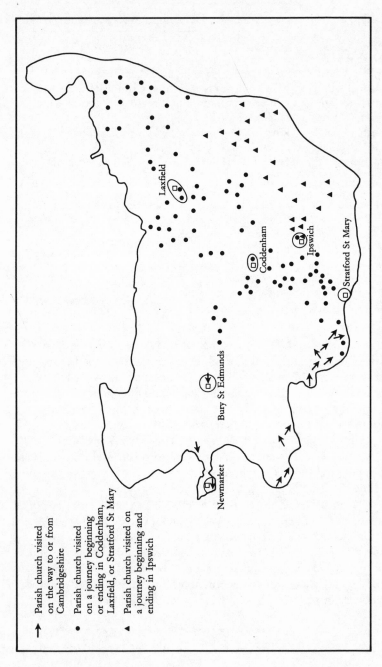

Parish church visited
on the way to or from
Cambridgeshire

Parish church visited
on a journey beginning
or ending in Coddenham,
Laxfield, or Stratford St Mary

Parish church visited on
a journey beginning and
ending in Ipswich

Laxfield

Coddenham

Ipswich

Stratford St Mary

Bury St Edmunds

Newmarket

Map 10.2   Dowsing's journeys in Suffolk, January–September 1644

inventories of churches, and on personal visits to more than half the churches in the county and in the Isle.[109] Proscribed images and inscriptions survive in six of the ninety-six Cambridgeshire parishes he visited, and two of the thirty-six not mentioned in his journal; but in eight of the twenty-five in the Isle. Furthermore, survivals in the shire are items easily overlooked in a crowded itinerary—such as a single bench-end of St Michael weighing souls on one of the poppy head bench-ends at Ickleton,[110] or an alabaster saint in a niche in a side chapel at Little Shelford.[111] One of the two parishes in north Cambridgeshire, Isleham, is remote and adjacent to the Isle, is cut off by floods for much of the winter, and is so full of surviving images it is tempting to think that it is one he did pass by.[112] There is no church in the shire which can still boast of such rich woodcarvings as survive at Wisbech St Mary, stone dragons such as on the font at Witcham, stained glass as at Wisbech or Rampton, or a reredos such as the one at Coveney illustrating the Passion.[113] It would seem that either a couple of pages of his journal became detached, or he never got round to writing up the north Cambridgeshire part of his journey.

In Suffolk, his work takes a different form. Map 10.2 indicates the area he covered in his recorded visits. The scattered parishes to the west indicate places he alighted in as he journeyed to and from Cambridgeshire. Otherwise there is a concentration in the south and east, but no hundred or deanery was completely unvisited. The question which naturally arises in relation to Suffolk is what Dowsing was doing between 15 April and 17 July, and between 1 and 26 September. Might he have been visiting the many parts of Suffolk, that 70 per cent of the parishes, not recorded in his diary? It is harder to establish this than it is for Cambridgeshire. First of all, we know that in Suffolk he had a team of deputies, some of whom seem to have accompanied him (as on a journey through central Suffolk in late February), but some of whom seem to have worked independently of him. On reaching Elmsett on 22 August,

[109] Four volumes of the inventory drawn up by the Royal Commission on Historical Monuments for the City of Cambridge (2 vols.; 1959), west Cambridgeshire (1968), and north-east Cambridgeshire (1972); N. Pevsner, *The Buildings of England: Cambridgeshire* (2nd edn., 1970); personal visits to seventy-two parish churches.

[110] Pevsner, *Cambridgeshire*, 412.

[111] Ibid. 503, 504, 430, 451.

[112] Ibid. 419; Palmer, *Monumental Inscriptions*, 143–4.

[113] Pevsner, *Cambridgeshire*, 496.

Dowsing recorded that 'Crow, a deputy, had done before we come.'[114] When he appointed his six deputies, he seems, in at least two cases, to have nominated the hundreds for which they were to have responsibility.[115] Parish records reveal that at least one of these was making his own visitation of parts of the county. According to the rector of Lowestoft, 'there came one Jissope with a commission ... to take away from gravestones all inscriptios one which he found orate pro anima ... He tooke in our churche so many brasses as hee sould to Mr Josiah Wild for five shillings.'[116] Secondly, my inspection of thirty churches Dowsing did visit and of thirty others is less informative than for Cambridgeshire, since Dowsing clearly got less exacting with time and left more untouched. From March 1644 onwards he took far less trouble to complete the work himself and was increasingly likely to leave it to local officials to carry out his orders. Thus there is no real evidence, as there is for Cambridgeshire, that he spent the intervals in his diary on the stump through Suffolk. I find one other fact revealed by plotting his itinerary on the map very suggestive. His work in Suffolk consisted less of the kind of week-long sweeps of twenty or so parishes he favoured in Cambridge; rather he tended to make far more short expeditions. It is, in fact, possible to divide his Suffolk work into twenty-one separate expeditions. Only twice, in separate sweeps of the Suffolk coastal parishes in 23–30 January and 27–30 July, is there anything to match his long excursions through Cambridgeshire. A plotting of his routes reveals that at least fourteen of the twenty-one expeditions began or ended near to one of three hub villages: Laxfield (where he was born), Coddenham (where he had lived c.1620–40), and Stratford St Mary (where he was living).[117] The fact that he was still operating from

[114] *Journal of William Dowsing*, 30. For a probable identification of Crow see 'Receipt at Risby', *East Anglian Notes and Queries*, 2nd ser. 1 (1885–6), 172. If he did come from Risby (near Bury St Edmunds), but was working at Elmsett, near Ipswich, he was clearly not a 'local deputy'.

[115] J. Browne, *History of Congregationalism and Memorials of the Counties of Norfolk and Suffolk* (Ipswich, n.d.), 154.

[116] Quoted in A. P. Andrews, 'The Tour of William Dowsing', *Suffolk Fair* (Oct. 1978), 16–19. Unfortunately, the very detailed account of Jessup's visit to Gorleston which is the centrepiece of many discussions of Civil War iconoclasm, as in Aston, *England's Iconoclasts*, 78–80, was many years ago shown to be a nineteenth-century forgery (M. R. James, 'A Dowsing–Jessop Forgery', *Notes and Queries* (2 June 1906), 421–2). The forger seems to have been Evelyn White (*Journal of William Dowsing*, 11).

[117] His earliest trips were Stratford-based; his later ones Laxfield- or Coddenham-based, or moving between the two.

Table 10.2. *Patterns of iconoclasm* (figures by percentage of parishes visited)

Iconoclasm	Cambs* (96 parishes visited)	Suffolk (147 parishes visited)
Images destroyed in	95	92
Chancels to be levelled in	50	39
Altar rails removed in	11	2
Inscriptions removed in	32	41
Crosses to be removed in	46	21
Holy water stoops destroyed in	1	8
Other iconoclasm occurred/ordered in (angel roofs/wall-paintings/organs)	5	6

* Includes *parish* churches in city of Cambridge and throughout the county, but not Cambridge college chapels.

his home bases in August and September makes it likely that he had been preoccupied with other things—his farm?—in the intervening period. The three-week gap in September, coinciding with harvest, is particularly suggestive.

V

What else does Dowsing's journal tell us about Civil War iconoclasm? I would suggest that it tells us first about the earlier iconoclasms; that it tells us something of his priorities; and that it affords hints about the popularity of the godly reformation in its supposed heartland.

Dowsing records some things in more detail than others. His journal entries allow us to know in considerable detail how many inscriptions on tombs he destroyed and in most cases exactly what the offending words were. It also tells us precisely where he reordered the east end (by the removal of rails and the levelling of chancels); it tells us about orders for the removal of crosses on spires and in chancel arches; and, much less precisely, it records the removal of 'popish' or 'superstitious' images in glass, wood, and stone. In only one-quarter of the entries is it possible to differentiate these 'images' by location and material. Within those constraints, Table 10.2 tabulates his visitations.

His diary clearly indicates what the first Reformation had most effectively concentrated on and already destroyed. There is a splendid and moving passage in J. J. Scarisbrick's *The English People and the English Reformation* which makes this point:

The Reformation simplified everything. It effected a shift from a religion of symbol and allegory, ceremony and formal gesture to one that was plain and direct: a shift from the visual to the aural, from ritual to literal exposition, from the numinous and mysterious to the everyday. It moved from . . . a religion that sought out all the senses, to one that concentrated on the word and innerliness . . . The late medieval parish church had consisted of a 'mysterious succession' of semi-independent spaces cut off from nave and chancel by parclose screens of stone and wood . . . Here again the Reformation simplified. As the side altars and screens of guilds and chantries came down, nave and chancel were turned into a single, open auditorium in which the faithful could assemble to hear the minister proclaim the word of God, plain and unadorned.[118]

Margaret Aston's analysis of the iconoclasm of 1530–70 is as perceptive as it is detailed. Examining the statutes and injunctions of the period, she admirably captures the ambiguity of official approaches. There was a tension between a literal interpretation of the second commandment—'they wanted to erase not simply the idols defiling God's churches, but also the idols infecting people's thoughts'[119]—and a willingness to distinguish between images which had been worshipped and those which could retain value as aids to prayerfulness—a distinction another recent historian summarized as that between abused and non-abused images.[120] I would like to suggest that those responsible for the iconoclasm of 1530–70 took this in practice to mean the difference between those images which were part of the 'devotional apparatus'[121] of late medieval Catholicism, and those which were essentially instructional and ornamental.

The first Reformation was firmly directed against the doctrine of the communion of saints, the doctrine that bound together the

---

[118] J. J. Scarisbrick, *The English People and the English Reformation* (Oxford, 1983), 163–4.
[119] Aston, *England's Iconoclasts*, 7.
[120] Phillips, *Reformation of Images*, 82–3, 89.
[121] The phrase is Margaret Aston's (*England's Iconoclasts*, 20 ff.).

living and the dead as a community of believers helping one another in preparation for the Day of Judgement. The living prayed constantly for those members of their family and local community who had gone before them, and even enlisted them into their fraternities. They also benefited from the chantries others had founded. They looked to the saints and the host of heaven to watch over and protect the living and to intercede for them with the Father. Every *active* manifestation of that communion of the living and the dead was destroyed in the first generation of the Reformation: the side altars, the chantries, the reliquaries, the shrines, the Doom and the paintings that illuminated that theme. What was left behind for Dowsing were passive reminders of that discredited theology: the stained glass, the invocations on tombs (and more rarely in glass);[122] images in stained glass; and (as a result of early Stuart changes) the communion table presented as an *altar*, a place of sacrifice.[123] Most of the images in stone and wood which had survived were ornamental (bench-ends, roof adornments) rather than instructional. And that is what marked out Dowsing's priorities: he was first and foremost concerned with using his chisel to obliterate or lever off the invocations to prayer on the tombs of the long-dead; and he carefully itemizes them: '[St] Mary's at the Tower [Ipswich] JAN the 29th. We took up 6 Brass Inscriptions, with *ora pro nobis*, and *ora pro animabus*, and *cujus animae propitietur Deus*; and *pray for the soul* in English.'[124] Second in importance was

---

[122] For examples in glass, see Moule, 'Cambridge Journal', no. 12 (Toft), 53 (Whittlesford), 78 (Shepden). At Toft he also removed an inscription from a bell (*ora pro anima S[anc]tae Catharinae*).

[123] Patrick Collinson has pointed out to me an awkward exception to this principle: the relentless Elizabethan vendetta against crosses and crucifixes. I am not yet in a position to account for this.

[124] *Journal of William Dowsing*, 19. It has been maintained that Dowsing took great care to remove only the offensive words of invocation, leaving the commemorative plate itself. J. Blatchly, 'The Lost and Mutilated Memorials of the Baile and Wingfield Families at Letheringham', *Proc. Suffolk Institute of Archaeology*, 33/2 (1974), 168–94, which shows that Dowsing removed just one square foot in different sections out of a total of fourteen square feet of brass, is a splendid case-study. But, while that may have been Dowsing's intention, it often proved difficult not to pull off the whole inscription while trying to remove part. When William Cole made his tour of Cambridgeshire churches in the early eighteenth century, he found some inscriptions in parish chests where they had been cast, broken in half, in 1644. At Girton and Swaffham Bulbeck, for example, the whole plate had been removed (Palmer, *Monument Inscriptions*, 66, 160). See also the comment on the removal of '19 superstitious inscriptions that weighed 65 pounds' at Wetherden (White, *Journal*, 21). For an instructive example of a man troubled about 'popery' in the church but who was willing to consider such inscriptions for members of his own family, see S. P. Salt, 'The

the levelling of the chancels. It seems that most chancel screens
had survived down to the 1580s and 1590s and had then been
mostly removed in a little remarked flurry of activity.[125] The opening
up of the east end had led to a polarization of opinion about how
best to conduct the holy communion service, and had led to the
'Laudian' altar policy of the 1630s, with the railing of altars in
perhaps 90 per cent of all parish churches and the placing of
'altars' on raised daises at the east end in most churches. Dowsing's
records strongly suggest that most altar rails had vanished even
more quickly than they had appeared—only seven needed his
attention in the 250 parishes he visited.[126] But almost half still had
chancel steps. In the early weeks he and his companions dug them
up themselves, but, from 1 January 1644 onwards, only six chancels
were levelled in the course of his visitation; in the other 101 cases
it was left to (often named) individuals. At Covehithe[127] in north-
east Suffolk, he recorded that 'there was 4 Steps, with a vault
underneath, but the first two might be levelled, which we gave
orders to the churchwardens to do'.[128] Here his severely practical
approach to iconoclasm comes through. When it came to the
hundreds of images he destroyed in stone, glass, and wood, my
itinerary, in the company of modern inventories, leaves me in little
doubt that his principal targets were those pictures and images
which would be a distraction to the worshipper. No complete
window has survived for a church he visited; no reredos or wall-
painting except for those uncovered in recent times from behind
their sixteenth- or seventeenth-century lime washes. What is striking
is that, as time wore on and Dowsing became more hardened and
resigned to the limits of the possible, he stopped bothering so
much about purely ornamental (bench-ends, angel roofs) and the
largely out of sight (stone angels on fonts). Thus, only two such
font-carvings survive for the Cambridgeshire villages he visited,
while almost half the thirty Suffolk churches visited by Dowsing

Origins of Sir Edward Dering's Attack on the Ecclesiastical Hierarchy, 1625–40', *Historical Journal*, 30 (1987), 34 n.

[125] I am grateful to Dr Diarmaid MacCulloch for pointing this out to me.

[126] J. Morrill, 'The Church of England, 1642–9', in J. Morrill (ed.), *Reactions to the English Civil War* (1982), 109–10.

[127] *Journal of William Dowsing*, 26, has Cochie. Study of his itinerary suggests that between Benacre and Rushmere he would have passed through Covehithe. John Blatchly has suggested to me that what the original said was not Cochie but Co'ehi'e.

[128] *Journal of William Dowsing*, 26.

in 1644 and the current writer in 1991 had fonts with 'banned' images. The only damaged fonts were those he had visited before March.

VI

Dowsing was, as his library indicates, a sincere and godly man. He undertook the work of state iconoclast because he believed that the Reformation was impeded by images that distracted the mass of the people from paying attention to the word of God; because many of the images perpetuated a false and discredited theology of Grace; and because he believed it was the duty of the Christian magistrate to enforce the second commandment, and that God might well withhold victory over the King until his graven images were destroyed. Perhaps like Samuel Ward, the Ipswich town preacher who systematically obliterated the word 'pope' from the books in his library as though it represented a kind of ectoplasm that menaced his peace of mind as he sat writing his sermons,[129] Dowsing simply felt in the presence of evil when he saw a carving of the persons of the Trinity or of the host of Heaven. He was no mindless vandal, but a man driven by personal conviction. He is very much of a piece with others whose private worlds have been opened up for us by scholars in recent years. Like the town clerk of Northampton, Robert Woodford, or the Warwick schoolmaster, Thomas Dugard, whose diaries have been dissected by John Fielding[130] and Ann Hughes,[131] we sense the build-up of tension, or internalized anger, amongst the godly in the years before 1642—what I would call the coiled-spring effect. Unless we grasp the bitterness of those years, and the sense that the Protestant cause and therefore God were being betrayed, then the release of pent-up energy in the early 1640s cannot be understood.

Many puzzles remain. Why should this new fervour against images have welled up in the breasts of Henry Sherfield, Richard Culmer, and William Dowsing at this point? For decades, parish churches taken over by godly cliques had remained much as the

---

[129] I am grateful to John Blatchly for this information.

[130] J. Fielding, 'Puritan Opposition to Charles I: The diary of Robert Woodford, 1637–1641', *Historical Journal*, 31 (1988), 769–88.

[131] A. Hughes, 'Thomas Dugard and his Circle: A puritan–Parliamentarian Connection', *Historical Journal*, 29 (1986), 771–94.

first reformers had left them. In most parishes there was enough anger against the ecclesiastical authoritarianism of the 1630s to see altars and rails as expensively destroyed in 1641–2 as they had been expensively fitted a few years earlier. But, in Samuel Ward's Ipswich, in godly Cawston, and in precise Aylsham, stained glass and statuary which had marked the devotion of the pre-Reformation devout looked down untroubled at parishioners who, scrupulous over word and gesture, impassively ignored them. In part, this new fervour of *some* of the godly is to be seen as a response to Laudian idolatry, which released new passions and caused some to look to the survival of distracting images as the reason for so many men and women failing to respond to the word of God.

But each of the godly had to make his or her stand on his or her own issues. Just as ministers in Essex had to decide whether to choose between exile and an uneasy struggle to sustain duty to a flock with the strains on conscience involved in a partial conformity, so men like Dowsing had to work out how, in their particular and humble circumstances, they could best serve the Lord. Determined and disciplined pollution control was just one of the options. But it was the one chosen by William Dowsing.

He was just a small farmer who emerged briefly from obscurity. But he reminds us—as we seem constantly to need reminding—that religious conviction was the motor that drove to arms those men who made the Civil War happen. His is a telling example of a life rooted in a quite remarkable biblicism. He reminds us that men of humble status were able to make independent political choices in the 1640s. Dowsing was very much a plain russet-coated captain that knew what he fought for and loved what he knew. He demonstrates that iconoclasm was an important part of a wider programme of godly reformation. It was not just part of an ecclesiastical reordering, but was seen as part of the reordering of the world to make it fit for the return of Christ. We see in him the central dilemmas of Puritanism in the 1640s: certainty about what to destroy, and uncertainty about what God would have in its place; a controlled self-righteousness that channelled a toxic mixture of anger and hope into a destruction of the past (ancient constitutionalism, stained-glass windows), and a febrile search for a new land of Canaan.

But ultimately he is the bureaucratic Puritan. This was no blind fanatic, but a grim and determined man taking a pride in obeying

God and the letter of the law. See him, with an Ordinance in his pocket and an escort of soldiers at his back, confronting the Fellows of Pembroke College, Cambridge, and engaging in quickfire exchanges of biblical texts: Mr Weedon and Mr Boldero denied the right of the laity to interfere in ecclesiastical affairs; Dowsing cited the popular election of apostles in Acts 1, and the work of King Josiah in taking down images.[132] Others pointed out that the book of Exodus called on the Israelites to make images of cherubim; Dowsing pointed out that Deuteronomy required them to destroy all such images. The dispute ranged over the right of Parliament to legislate in the absence of the king, and the meaning of Queen Elizabeth's Injunctions and of the Homily against Idolatry. But Dowsing had the last word:

Weedon said, reading St Paul's sermons was better than preaching then now we used, because it was not scripture. I told them God saved by foolishness of preaching & not reading and alleged I Cor. i, 21;[133] I told them, if reading was preaching, my child preaches as well as they, and they stared one at another without answere.[134]

In March 1643 Dowsing told Newcomen that God had given the armies of Edward VI victory over the Scots at Musselburgh the day the destruction of images was wrought in London, and because that destruction was wrought. He would have believed that in some measure Fairfax was given victory on 25 January 1644 at Nantwich over the troops returned from Ireland because on that day he, William Dowsing, wrought destruction of images at Orford, Snape, and Saxmundham. Herein lies the strength and the agony of the Puritan Revolution.

[132] For the popularity of Josiah as a type for the Edwardian iconoclasts, see Aston, *England's Iconoclasts*, 246–50.

[133] 'For after that in the wisdom of God the world by wisdom knew not God, it pleased God by the foolishness of preaching to save them that believe.'

[134] Moule, 'Cambridge Journal', 5.

11

A Man of Conscience in
Seventeenth-Century Urban Politics:
Alderman Hoyle of York

CLAIRE CROSS

IN his *Eboracum* published in 1736 Francis Drake related that in 1650, 'upon the same day of the month of January, and as near as possible at the same hour of the day on which the royal martyr suffered the year before', Thomas Hoyle, alderman of York and one of the city's representatives in the Long Parliament, hanged himself in his lodgings at Westminster. In 1669 Mrs Alice Thornton described how 'after that horrid murder' the tormented man cried out that ' "He saw the king follow him without a head", and said he had no hand in his blood', and at other times proclaimed 'I am damned for the blood of the king'. Her source seems to have been a propaganda tract, *The Rebell's Warning-Piece*, of February 1650, purporting to contain a confession in which the former Parliamentarian declared:

I no sooner slumbered, but I saw pass by my bed the late king, attended with the Earl of Strafford, the Bishop of Canterbury, the Lord Capel, and numbers before and behind him, bearing palms in their hands, singing this anthem, 'He that is faithful to the end, and overcometh, shall inherit all things, and I will be his God, and he shall be my son'.

Without doubt Hoyle 'grew excessively melancholy' in his last months, yet equally indisputably all through his life by his words and actions he demonstrated his commitment to the 'godly' cause. Whether his inability to reconcile his loyalty to his religion with his allegiance to the Crown, however, constituted the sole or even the major reason for his suicide seems somewhat less incon-

I should like to thank David Scott for his very helpful advice and comments. Apart from book titles, all seventeenth-century spelling has been modernized.

trovertible three centuries after the event than his Royalist adversaries at the time chose to believe.[1]

Like so many of York's leading citizens, Thomas Hoyle was not a native of the city. Born about 1587 in Slaithwaite in the West Riding, the son of Thomas Hoyle, esquire, early in the seventeenth century he learnt his trade with Matthew Topham, a merchant of St Martin's, Micklegate. As Topham's servant, he may have travelled extensively upon his master's business in England and abroad, as two other young merchants in the parish certainly did. By 1611 Hoyle had completed his apprenticeship and in that year set up as a merchant in his own right. In 1611 he married Elizabeth Maskewe, the daughter of a wealthy York innkeeper and member of the Twenty-Four, so binding himself yet further to the mercantile élite. Somewhat belatedly he took out his freedom of the city in January 1612, and so began his ascent of the ladder of civic preferment.[2]

The ethos of the upper ranks of York society to which Hoyle had now gained admission differed very greatly from that of a generation earlier, when a minority still sympathized with Catholicism. By 1600 the civic governors had enthusiastically adopted an active form of Protestantism propagated by the first notable city lecturer, Richard Harwood, who had taken up his post in 1585. Hoyle experienced this godly civic Protestantism during his apprenticeship with Topham, who on his death endowed three annual sermons at his birthplace of Coverham. Increasingly, aldermen and councillors were expecting regular preaching, not only from their civic lecturer but also from their parochial ministers, even though the twenty-five poorly endowed parishes of York did not possess the resources to attract university-educated Protestants. Hoyle himself encountered at first hand the problem of obtaining and keeping well-qualified clergy in 1613 on becoming churchwarden of St Martin's, Micklegate, at the age of 26.[3]

[1] F. Drake, *Eboracum* (1736), 172; *Autobiography of Mrs Alice Thornton*, ed. C. Jackson (Surtees Soc., 62; 1875), 212; *The Rebell's Warning-Piece* (endorsed 19 Feb. 1649[/50]), BL Thomason Tract E. 593 (13); *Yorkshire Diaries and Autobiographies in the Seventeenth and Eighteenth Centuries*, ed. H. J. Morehouse (Surtees Soc., 65; 1877), 145–6.

[2] York City Library, R. H. Skaife, 'Civic Officials Of York', MS ii. 395–7; York Borthwick Institute, Prob. Reg. 42, fos. 694ᵛ–695ᵛ; CP H 1978; 'Paver's Marriage Licenses', *Yorkshire Archaeological Journal*, 12 (1893), 158; M. F. Keeler, *The Long Parliament, 1640–1641: A Biographical Study of its Members* (Philadelphia, Pa., 1954), 224–5.

[3] Cross, 'Priests into Ministers: The Establishment of Protestant Practice in the City of York, 1530–1630', in P. N. Brooks (ed.), *Reformation Principle and Practice: Essays in Honour of A. G. Dickens* (1980), 222–5; Borthwick Prob. Reg., 42, fos. 694ᵛ–695ᵛ; PRY/MG 19, fos. 152–5.

In Hoyle's first year of office the rector of St Martin's recorded the baptism of Hoyle's first son, William. The child lived for only a month, and his death marked the beginning of a threnody lasting all the rest of Hoyle's public life. The year 1614 saw the birth of Jane Hoyle, who survived until she was two; after the burial in 1616 of a second, unnamed daughter, a son, Thomas, died in 1617, aged less than a week. Faced by one family tragedy after another, Hoyle and his wife turned to the Church for consolation, forging the first of their intimate links with a York incumbent on 30 April 1616, when Elizabeth Hoyle, 'sister unto Mr Thomas Hoyle', married the parish minister, Mr Philip Nesbitt.[4]

Already a merchant of substance exporting cloths valued in excess of £5,500 through the port of Hull, at this juncture Hoyle widened his horizons and sought office outside his parish. On 15 January 1614, with Richard Bayne, he was sworn one of the two city chamberlains, and from this year onwards came to be employed more and more on corporation business, in 1615 being placed on a council committee to view the Knavesmire, in 1616 being appointed one of the auditors of the city's accounts, in 1617 being named among the four from Micklegate ward deputed to confer with councillors over raising money to pay for the recent royal visit, for setting the poor on work, and for augmenting the stipend of the city preacher. In January 1619 the corporation formally recognized his status by electing him, at the age of 32, a member of the common council. Again he took part in discussions over accumulating a stock to provide employment for the poor and in the following year in plans for building a workhouse.[5]

Between 1618 and 1622 Hoyle and his wife had four more children: Elizabeth and Rebecca, born in 1618 and 1621, who both lived beyond infancy, a second Thomas, buried, aged one month, in June 1620, and Susanna, who died, less than six months old, in 1622. The deaths of these children 'very young and tender' seem to have further deepened the piety of Thomas and Elizabeth Hoyle. Together on the Sabbath day they led their household in public and private worship, in catechizing, and in repeating sermons; 'then', their chaplain related, 'the whole family, the church, the word of God and all was commended unto the Lord's blessing,

[4] Borthwick PRY/MG 1, pp. 75, 76, 77, 79, 80.
[5] B. M. Wilson, 'The Corporation of York, 1580–1660', M.Phil. thesis (York Univ., 1967), 314; York City Archives, Housebook 34, fos. 25ᵛ, 26ʳ, 63ʳ, 129ʳ, 159ᵛ, 163ᵛ, 191ᵛ.

and we were fitted and prepared for to take our rest'.[6]

Very much in the manner of Ignatius Jourdain in Exeter, from his godly household Hoyle strove to spread godliness in the city, at first by example but increasingly from 1621 through civic office. Having been chosen sheriffs for the coming year, he and John Vaux set a precedent on St Matthew's Day, 1621, by curtailing the feasts customarily provided by the sheriffs for the aldermen and Twenty-Four, giving in lieu no less than £50 each to city charities and particularly to that designed to create work for the poor. At the end of their year the two sheriffs automatically became members of the Twenty-Four. From 1622 onwards until the calling of the Long Parliament Hoyle invariably attended at the very least half the council meetings annually, and in most years many more. In 1623 he helped audit the city's accounts, with Sir Arthur Ingram drew up a composition between York and Hull merchants, and formulated new regulations concerning the better observation of the Sabbath and the attendance of the lord mayor, aldermen, and the Twenty-Four at the Minster.[7]

The accession of Charles I stirred the council into fresh action. In 1625 Hoyle and other councillors drafted a programme for the city's representatives in the first Parliament of the reign, and took further steps to relieve the poor, devised precautions against the plague, and reduced the number of alehouses. The following year he supported a resolution forbidding 'two companies of players to play in the city', and yet again assisted in preparing a remit for the city's MPs. Later in the year the corporation, considering York to have been unjustly burdened in the matter of ship money, nominated Hoyle 'to ride to London to solicit the lords of his majesty's most honourable Privy Council concerning the release, or at least the mitigation, of the charge of the ship'. His assiduity in the city's business soon received its reward. On 26 October 1626 he was elected an alderman in the place of William Robinson, deceased, and appointed one of the wardens for Micklegate ward. Again in 1627 he went down to London to continue the negotiations over the ship-money payments. Yet, just when his public career seemed

[6] Borthwick PRY/MG 1, pp. 84, 86, 87, 88, 90, 93; J. Birchall, *The Non-Pareil* (York, 1644), 15, 17.

[7] F. B. Troup, 'An Exeter Worthy and his Biographer', *Trans. of the Devonshire Association for the Advancement of Science, Literature and Art,* 29 (1897), 350–77; York City Archives, Housebook 34, fos. 29ᵛ, 241ᵛ, 257ʳ, 260ʳ, 261ʳ, 270ʳ, 277ʳ.

crowned with success, he suffered a fresh series of private sorrows. His 5-year-old daughter, Rebecca, died in June 1627; his fourth son, Thomas III, born in August 1627, lived for only a year, while Samuel was buried on 9 December 1628, a scant eleven days after his baptism. As their chaplain observed, though the Hoyles 'had much experience in matter of prosperity, yet [they] had also great experience in matter of adversity'.[8]

Hoyle's public career, nevertheless, continued to advance. Together with Sir Arthur Ingram, he stood as one of the two candidates for the city at the parliamentary elections in the spring of 1628, only to have his hopes disappointed by a partial sheriff, who, refusing a poll, declared for an outsider, Sir Thomas Savile. On appeal, however, the Commons overturned the verdict, and by June 1628 Hoyle had taken his seat. Very soon after, he found himself being nominated to committees considering petitions from the Goldsmiths and the Exchangers and enquiring into the Greenland patent. He seems to have been present in the House for the discussions on the Petition of Right, as he certainly was in the early months of 1629 which saw the attack upon Arminianism, but once again confined his committee work to hearing petitions from the Turkey merchants and to deliberations on an Act for the increase of trade.[9]

Soon after the dissolution of Parliament and his return from Westminster, Hoyle was elected by the Merchant Adventurers' Company as their governor. In March 1630 he joined with three other leading traders in drawing up a list of grievances suffered by York merchants at the hands of Dunkirk privateers. In 1630, also, the city chamberlains determined to follow the lead set by Hoyle and Vaux, and asked the council's permission to give a donation to the poor as an alternative to their traditional celebrations, both because of the excessive charges incurred and because the festive days, Easter Eve, Whitsun Eve, and Christmas Eve, ought more properly to be observed as fasts than feasts. The council's increasing moral censoriousness manifested itself in even so apparently trivial a matter as the sale of fruit when it commissioned Hoyle to find room for apple-sellers in the Thursday market and thus deprive

[8] York City Archives, Housebook 34, fos. 313^v, 316^r, 325^r; Housebook 35, fos. 2^r, 5^v, 17^v, 24^v, 33^v, 34^r; Borthwick PRY/MG 1, pp. 98, 99, 100; Birchall, *The Non-Pareil*, 23.
[9] *CJ* i. 879, 890–1, 915, 919, 926.

them of any excuse for vending their produce on the Sabbath day.[10]

At about this time Hoyle gained a mentor and friend in the person of William Hart, a one-time merchant and pastor of the English church at Emden. After his employment on the Continent, Hart had retired to York, where, on an even more generous scale than that of godly merchants in Gloucester, he had given to the corporation two separate benefactions of £100 to be lent biannually to thirty poor traders of the city. In his old age he went to live with the Hoyles and may, in fact, have acted as their personal chaplain, reinforcing their belief in the corporation's duty to ameliorate the lives of the city's less fortunate inhabitants.[11]

The many aldermen who shared Hoyle's philosophy regarded virtually all aspects of the corporation's undertakings in a moral light, and this was particularly the case in their defence of the city's privileges. When in 1631 Hoyle reported the intention of Sir Henry Slingsby, one of the deputy-lieutenants, to claim precedence over the lord mayor at the musters, the corporation asserted the lord mayor's superiority in no uncertain terms. The negotiations for the confirmation of the charter proved even more vital for the city, which dispatched Hoyle to London as its spokesman in the summer of 1631. He found the 'business very tedious' and warned that it would 'be also very chargeable'.[12]

Scarcely had Hoyle returned from London when plague threatened the city in August 1631. At Wentworth's prompting the council sat in emergency session almost every other day for the remainder of the year, and Hoyle, again like Jourdain in Exeter, never wavered in his duty, in the first weeks overseeing the watch at the gates and posterns to prevent the entry of potential carriers; then, when this precaution failed, supervising the isolation of the sick and providing for their food and medical care. On 19 September, at the council's request, Hoyle and his old master, Matthew Topham, went 'to move my lord president and the masters of the church that there may be a general fast'. He and his fellow

[10] M. Sellers (ed.), *The York Mercers and Merchant Adventurers, 1356–1917* (Surtees Soc., 129; 1918), 234; York City Archives, Housebook 35, fos. 79ʳ, 80ʳ, 87ᵛ, 88ᵛ.

[11] P. Clark, '"The Ramoth-Gilead of the Good": Urban Change and Political Radicalism at Gloucester 1540–1640', in P. Clark, A. G. R. Smith, and N. Tyacke (eds.), *The English Commonwealth 1547–1640* (Leicester, 1979), 167–87; York City Archives, Housebook 35, fos. 99ʳ, 100ᵛ.

[12] York City Archives, Housebook 35, fos. 101ᵛ, 106ʳ, 167ʳ.

councillors raised allowances for those confined to their houses
for fear of spreading the infection, and dispatched others to lodges
built specially outside the walls. Day after day he played his part
in enforcing the council's tight control over the city. Very gradually
the sickness abated; by December the corporation felt able to lift
most of the quarantine regulations and the number of council
meetings reverted to normal. Yet even after these quite exceptional
exertions Hoyle gained no respite from his labours. Once again he
obeyed the call of duty and, being the alderman next in seniority,
on St Blaize's Day, 3 February 1632, accepted the office of lord
mayor.[13]

Hoyle's election day began auspiciously with the news that his
friend, William Hart, had decided to give a third £100 to the city
to be lent to poor traders on the same terms as before, and the
year culminated in the grant of the new charter on 19 July 1632.
As the health of the inhabitants continued to improve, in July the
corporation ordained 'a general thanksgiving to God in preserving
us from the sickness called the plague'. With the disputed election
of 1628 in mind, the council resolved in September that in future
none but citizens should represent York in Parliament. Under
Hoyle's leadership, though not on quite the same ambitious scale
as in early Stuart Salisbury, the city made yet further efforts to set
the poor to work, decreeing that even the inmates of the city's
hospitals should play their part, carding or spinning yarn for the
looms in the workhouse. Still extremely sensitive to any real
or imagined slights to their corporate authority, the councillors
announced, in response to the prebendaries' attempt to restrain
walking in the Minster, that 'they intend hereafter to stay one for
another in their closet in the body of the church and come in
orderly together into the choir'.[14]

The new charter, received with such general acclamation, proved
something of a mixed blessing, since the transfer to the city of
certain localities previously under the jurisdiction of the dean and
chapter served only to intensify the tension between the corporation

---

[13] W. T. MacCaffrey, *Exeter, 1540–1640* (Cambridge, Mass., 1958), 234, 273; York City
Archives, Housebook 35, fos. 112ᵛ–154ᵛ; P. Slack, *The Impact of Plague in Tudor and Stuart
England* (1985), 220, 318–19.

[14] P. Slack. 'Poverty and Politics in Salisbury 1597–1666', in P. Clark and P. Slack (eds.),
Crisis and Order in English Towns 1500–1700 (1972), 164–203; York City Archives, Housebook
35, fos. 154ᵛ, 173ᵛ, 176ᵛ, 179ᵛ, 186ᵛ.

and the Minster. When Charles I visited York in May 1633, Laud seized the opportunity of encouraging the prebendaries to assert their rights over the laity, which led to Dr Wickham attempting to occupy a seat in the Minster choir above that of the lord mayor. At this affront to civic pride the council voted by a majority not to attend the Minster at all until a satisfactory solution could be found. Eventually in December Lord Justice Hutton succeeded in proving that the mayor held his seat by ancient custom and Wickham had no alternative but to forgo to his claim. Having established their right, the councillors dispatched Hoyle and Vaux to Goldsborough to thank Hutton for his pains.[15]

Memorable as the year may have been in the annals of the city on account of the royal visit, to Hoyle's household it brought only further anguish. In April John Hoyle died, aged 3, to be followed to the grave in August by his year-old sister, Anna; Hoyle and his wife had now only one surviving child, their teenage daughter, Elizabeth. The family also lost its spiritual guide, William Hart, buried in St Martin's choir on 25 May 1633. In his will the old man left gilded pots to his 'godly and dearest friend, Mr Alderman Hoyle, and to my lady, his wife, for some remembrance of my thankfulness for their great love and constant kindness towards me'.[16]

Just when these afflictions descended upon him, Hoyle fell victim to the petty harassment of the Laudian ecclesiastics now in power in York. Very soon after his elevation to the archbishopric, Richard Neile had taken steps to uncover Protestant irregularities throughout the diocese, and early in 1634 his officials dispatched to the churchwardens of St Martin's, Micklegate, a detailed list of interrogatories, which included questions asking whether they had seen 'Thomas Hoyle and Matthew Topham sit with their hats on their heads in time of divine service' and whether there had been divers parishioners 'who neglected to kneel at the general confession and to stand up at the saying of the creed, and which have not done due and lowly reverence at the name of our Lord Jesus when it was mentioned in time of divine service'. One churchwarden maintained that he had spent much of his year of office abroad on business, and did not know what had been happening, the

[15] York City Archives, Housebook 35, fos. 208ʳ, 211ʳ, 221ʳ, 223ᵛ, 230ʳ.
[16] Borthwick PRY/MG 1, pp. 102, 105, 108; Prob. Reg. 42, fos. 215ʳ–216ᵛ.

other that he had been suffering from an eye ailment and had not been able to see what worshippers had been doing in church, but it seems clear that the former lord mayor, together with some of the most influential men of the parish, had indeed indulged in these minor gestures of nonconformity.[17]

Pressure from the Church courts served only to confirm Hoyle's adherence to 'godly' Protestantism. He had brought a young minister, John Birchall, to York early in 1633, and the new incumbent, inducted to St Martin's in April, soon filled the vacuum created by Hart's death. To the annoyance of Neile's lieutenants, the rector did not live, as would have been proper, in his parsonage, but in Hoyle's household, where he disseminated his form of Calvinism, doubtless expressing there, as he certainly did in the pulpit, 'contrary to his majesty's declaration in that behalf', his belief concerning the impossibility of the elect falling from grace. Within a year of his arrival in the city, Birchall made his first appearance in court to explain his defiance of this royal prohibition. In 1635 Neile's officials brought a further accusation against him, of holding illegal conventicles. In the autumn of that year, they claimed, Birchall had joined an expedition arranged by Alderman Hoyle for his wife, his daughter, Elizabeth, and other relations and friends to inspect his newly acquired manor house at Colton in the parish of Bolton Percy, not far from York. The party had taken horse at about eleven o'clock and reached Colton an hour later. 'And a little after they had put off and laid away their riding clothes, some of the company desired to walk into the grounds and take the air', but 'Mr Alderman Hoyle said, "Nay, I pray you, Let us go to prayers first". And thereupon they kneeled down in the parlour of the said Mr Alderman's house there, and the said Mr Birchall prayed for the space of three parts of a quarter of an hour.' Birchall, while admitting its extempore nature, claimed that the prayer he then offered could in no way be regarded as seditious but

was to this purpose that he confessed sin, and begged favour and grace for Christ's sake, praying also God to bless our king, queen and whole state, giving thanks also to God for his mercies spiritual and temporal, and for the temporal means here and elsewhere given to Alderman Hoyle

[17] A. Foster, 'The Function of a Bishop: The Career of Richard Neile, 1562–1640', in R. O'Day and F. Heal (eds.), *Continuity and Change: Personnel and Administration of the Church in England 1500–1642* (Leicester, 1976), 33–54; Borthwick CP H 1978.

and his, together with a desire that we might rightly use them; and that He would bless them to us and our posterity.[18]

Quite apart from his own treatment and that of his chaplain, Hoyle had other reasons for disliking the churchmen favoured by the King. Together with Sir William Belt and Sir William Allanson, at the corporation's request he had gone to London in April 1636 to attend upon Charles, 'according to his majesty's reference upon a petition exhibited by the dean and chapter touching the difference between the city and them'. There he had again encountered Laud, who refused to allow York's legal adviser to speak at the Council board, and gave great offence to the corporation's representatives by pointedly asking 'Are not the clergy fitter for government than the city?' These bullying tactics worked in the short term and for the remainder of the decade the archbishop more or less contrived to impose his will. In June 1637 a cowed mayor and corporation complied with a royal proclamation and agreed no longer to process in the Minster with the civic sword erect.[19]

Yet, despite these external vexations, within his own family the mid-1630s constituted for Hoyle perhaps the most tranquil period in his adult career. In February 1635 Mrs Hoyle bore her last child, a fourth Thomas, who appeared to be surmounting the hazards of early childhood, while their only daughter, Elizabeth, was now approaching maturity. Looking back to this period, Birchall admiringly recalled the mother's concern for her daughter: 'Oh, her care over her! oh, her prayers for her and with her!' In February 1636 the marriage took place between the 17-year-old Elizabeth and another member of York's civic élite, Thomas, son of Alderman Christopher Dickinson of the parish of All Saints, Pavement. A freeman of the city by birth, Dickinson had already attained considerable substance as a merchant, in 1634–5 alone exporting cloths worth more than £3,700 through the port of Hull. Equally significantly, he soon also embarked upon a career in urban government, on 21 September 1638 being elected one of the sheriffs for the following year. In March 1639 Elizabeth and Thomas Dickinson's son was born, and named after his maternal grandfather and father. Briefly it seemed that, after the tribulations

[18] R. A. Marchant, *The Puritans and the Church Courts in the Diocese of York, 1560–1642* (1960), 76, 229; Drake, *Eboracum*, 273; Borthwick CP H 2010; CP H 2123.

[19] York City Archives, Housebook 35, fos. 302ᵛ, 336ᵛ; HMC, *House of Lords*, NS xi, Addenda (1962), 400.

of their earlier life together, Thomas and Elizabeth Hoyle might now be entering into a serene middle age.[20]

Throughout this time Hoyle never lost sight of the needs of the church in the city, and in particular in his own parish. By taking Birchall into his household, and so freeing him from all domestic expenses, he had effectively enhanced the value of the benefice, but this drew upon the minister the displeasure of the ecclesiastical authorities, who objected to the dilapidated state of the rectory, which Birchall claimed remained uninhabitable, despite the sums he had spent on it. While continuing to support Birchall, Hoyle also concerned himself with improving the financial prospects of his successors in the living. To this end he purchased the advowson of St Martin's and additional land in Drax, which, in conscious imitation of the practice of the London feoffees for impropriations, in January 1638 he conferred upon a trust in perpetuity. Those whom he chose to administer the property included his equally committed fellow alderman, John Vaux, regarded by Archbishop Neile as the leader of York's 'puritan party', John Penrose, the father of the young merchant Henry Penrose, who had learnt his trade with Hoyle and married one of his maids, the London minister William Gouge, DD, one of the London feoffees before their dissolution by Laud in 1633, and Walter Price, the London feoffees' principal agent. From 1638 the patronage of St Martin's belonged officially to its leading inhabitants, and the parish for the first time possessed a living sufficient to attract and retain a learned incumbent.[21]

Hoyle must have been aware that at St Martin's he and his fellow aldermen were acting in defiance of the Laudians, who indeed also desired to augment inadequately endowed parochial cures, but not at the cost of the increase of lay influence within the Church. In May 1639 a council meeting determined that Henry Ayscough, a mildly nonconformist preacher in Birchall's mould, should still be paid his full stipend as city lecturer though now

[20] Birchall, *The Non-Pareil,* 17; Borthwick PRY/MG 1, pp. 114, 115, 121; CP 2123; York City Library, R. H. Skaife, 'Civic Officials of York', i. 315; York City Archives, Housebook 36, fo. 14ᵛ; Wilson, 'The Corporation of York, 1580–1660', 265, 323, 325.
[21] Borthwick Chancery AB. 28, fo. 54ʳ; PRY/MG 1, p.103; Bp. C & P III/6; Marchant, *The Puritans and the Church Courts,* 75, 277; I. M. Calder, *Activities of the Puritan Faction of the Church of England 1625–33* (1957), pp. xi–xxiv; G. Lawton, *Collectio rerum ecclesiasticum* (1842), 26; *Yorkshire Diaries and Autobiographies,* 129; York City Library, R. H. Skaife, 'Civic Officials of York', ii. 564–5.

inhibited from preaching on Sunday afternoons. Yet these York councillors do not seem to have seen their opposition to the local High-Churchmen in any sense as opposition to the Crown. Hoyle played an active role in the preparations for the King's second visit in March 1639, when he stayed in York for a month before travelling north to meet the Scots. Later in the same year he joined in representations to the King against plans to remove the local trained bands, and participated in the apparently unending negotiations with the Minister prebendaries over the conflicting jurisdictions of the dean and chapter and the city.[22]

Then in the autumn of 1639 there occurred a fresh succession of catastrophes which must have overshadowed Hoyle's civic and national duties and from which he may never have totally recovered. In mid-November his baby grandson, Thomas Dickinson, died, and Thomas, his 4-year-old son, fell gravely ill. So habituated was his mother to inclining her will to the will of God that she confessed to her chaplain 'I could never yet get my heart enlarged in praying for his life, because . . . the Lord had a purpose to take him unto Himself'. Her fears proved to be only too well founded, and the Hoyles buried their 'dear and only son' in St Martin's a week after their grandson. Then a fortnight later there took place a further calamity, for which Hoyle was totally unprepared. On 9 December, although apparently in her usual health, Elizabeth Hoyle remarked at dinner, 'Husband, you are not like to enjoy me long.' That evening in her parlour, as she closed 'with her God in prayer', she suffered a stroke, and in a very short space her soul departed 'unto the Lord Jesus'. By the end of 1639 Thomas Hoyle had lost his wife, his grandson, and all of his thirteen children except for his daughter Elizabeth.[23]

At the very time he stood most in need of spiritual consolation, his minister, John Birchall, again came under the censure of the ecclesiastical courts, initially for residing with Hoyle and not in his parsonage, then much more seriously for his nonconformity. The case proceeded against him in the High Commission throughout January, February, March, and April 1640, the court finally dismissing him in early May on his promise of 'due conformity hereafter to the laws, canons and constitutions of the Church of

[22] York City Archives, Housebook 36, fos. 21ʳ, 22ʳ, 23ᵛ, 24ᵛ, 27ᵛ, 31ᵛ.
[23] Borthwick PRY/MG 1, p. 123; Birchall, *The Non-Pareil*, 14, 18, 31.

England'. Already a sick man, Birchall seems to have been broken by this constant surveillance; he died in his turn in the autumn and was buried in the chancel of his parish church on 1 November.[24]

The demoralization of the godly in St Martin's in 1640 mirrored that of their co-religionists in the city at large, where the Church courts had silenced the city preacher and forced other ministers into conformity. At first the corporation felt it politic to adopt a submissive stance, and on the death of the Lord Keeper in late February offered the stewardship of York to the Earl of Strafford. York's representation in the Short Parliament further demonstrated Wentworth's hold upon the city. Despite the resolution passed during Hoyle's mayoralty, the lord president of the Council in the North succeeded in gaining one of the borough's seats for his deputy, Sir Edward Osborne, while the other went to a conservative alderman, Sir Roger Jacques. Yet, at this nadir in its fortunes, the corporation still retained some vestiges of its former independence, deliberating in August whether or not Charles should be offered a gift on his third visit to the city. In September the King moved his Court to York, and held his great Council of peers in the deanery, but not even the monarch's presence could eradicate the desire for redress of grievances among a section of the governing élite. In late October the council began looking ahead to the forthcoming Parliament and to the changes it might achieve. This time, ignoring Strafford's intervention, the corporation retained its representation firmly in its own hands, choosing as burgesses for the city Sir William Allanson and Thomas Hoyle.[25]

While he could scarcely have anticipated this in November 1640, the calling of the Long Parliament marked a watershed in Hoyle's public career, as it seems to have done in the life of a like-minded fellow merchant, John Blakiston, one of the representatives of Newcastle upon Tyne. Although Hoyle had made regular visits to London and further afield on his own and the city's business, until 1641 York had always remained his base; from 1641 the demands of national politics forced him to live almost permanently in Westminster. In the Long Parliament his financial expertise once again came to the fore, and between November 1640 and April 1641 the House placed him on committees to look into monopolies

[24] Borthwick HC AB. 19, fos. 97ʳ, 98ʳ, 101ᵛ–102ʳ, 103ᵛ, 105ʳ, 109ʳ, 111ᵛ, 115ʳ, 118ʳ, 119ᵛ, 122ʳ, 126ʳ; Marchant, *Puritans and the Church Courts*, 229.
[25] York City Archives, Housebook 36, fos, 39ᵛ, 46ʳ, 49ᵛ; *Ca. SP Dom. 1640–1*, 158.

and a petition concerning trade, and to prepare bills to remedy the
complaints of inland ports and to reform the system of customs
farming. When Parliament discussed the raising of funds at the
beginning of March, Hoyle and Allanson each promised personal
loans of £500 in ready money. Very occasionally at first, the
Commons applied Hoyle's talents in other directions—to investigate the parliamentary representation of Tewkesbury and the
enfranchisement of the county palatine of Durham—but at this
stage the committees to which he was assigned gave him little
opportunity for expressing his religious concern. He must, however,
soon have heard that his own council had determined on 10
February 1641 to draw up a petition 'against the bishops and the
ecclesiastical courts': on 3 May he revealed his own sympathies by
signing the Commons' protestation to defend the true, reformed
Protestant religion. Already in York in the early summer the tables
had been turned upon the Arminian church officials, and, as articles
of impeachment were being prepared in London against Cosin and
Laud, in York Thomas Dickinson was serving with Alderman Vaux
on a parliamentary commission to take statements from two of
Neile's erstwhile supporters, the prebendaries Phineas Hodson and
Henry Wickham.[26]

While Charles was keeping his Court in York from January 1642
until the following August, Hoyle was at Westminster, and so
avoided the direct conflict of allegiance to Crown and Parliament
confronting his colleagues on the city council. Nevertheless, perhaps
imperceptibly, he found himself aligned with the Parliamentary
side. In January 1642 the Commons placed him on a committee
to confer with officers from the navy over the number of ships
to be put to sea to secure the defence of the kingdom. By the
time the Civil War actually began in August he had made a
conscious decision to support Parliament and had further assisted
the cause financially by venturing £450 in Irish land. On 25
October, in the only one of his speeches recorded in the *Commons'
Journals*, he 'declared himself to assist the Earl of Essex according
to the vote in the House, with his life and fortune'. Subsequently
in December his organizing talents were being employed in making

[26] R. Howell, *Newcastle upon Tyne and the Puritan Revolution* (Oxford, 1967), 174; *CJ* ii. 30,
43, 49, 61, 64; York City Archives, Housebook 36, fo. 58'; *The Journal of Sir Simonds D'Ewes
from the Beginning of the Long Parliament to the Opening of the Trial of the Earl of Strafford*, ed W.
Notestein (New Haven, Conn., 1923), 439 n.; HMC *House of Lords*, NS xi. 255.

provision for the Parliamentary army in Yorkshire, and in the same month he became a member of the standing committee charged with raising money for northern occasions.[27]

During the Royalist occupation of York in 1643 and 1644 Hoyle remained in Westminster and never appeared at meetings of the corporation; he, therefore, had no opportunity to voice with his fellow councillors his opposition to the breach of the city's charter when, at the King's command, the military governor ordered Sir Edmund Cowper to continue as lord mayor two years beyond his term. In February 1643 Hoyle was nominated to the committee for sequestering the estates of persons at war against the Parliament; later in the year he joined one committee set up to investigate licences granted by the King to the Eastland Company, another to consider a petition from the Merchant Adventurers over the export of wool, and a third to administer the financing of the Parliamentary forces. In April 1643 he was among those deputed to procure funds to succour Lord Fairfax, in September to intervene with the commissioners of the customs to supply naval provisions, and, in the absence of Sir Henry Vane, he chaired the committee for the navy. Very occasionally the *Commons' Journals* afford a glimpse of Hoyle's religious sympathies. On 6 June 1643 he took 'the New Oath and Covenant'; on 11 October Parliament thought fit to add him to the committee 'for abolishing idolatry'. Probably, however, his most important public service went on in the Gold-smith's Hall on the committee for compounding, of which he became a member on 23 December 1643.[28]

Throughout the first half of 1644, when for three months Parliament's forces were besieging York, Hoyle devoted himself to Parliamentary affairs in Westminster, deliberating on means of rating the northern counties, attempting to raise arms and munitions for the forces in the north, and making plans to relieve 'the distressed British regiments in Ulster'. At this time, too, he found increasing opportunities for exercising his religious interests, sitting on one committee charged with extending the taking of the

---

[27] P. Wenham, *The Great and Close Siege of York 1644* (Kineton, 1970), pp. xvii–xviii; *CJ* ii. 378, 822, 888, 891; *Calendar of State Papers Ireland, Adventurers 1642–59*, 295.

[28] *CJ* ii. 957, iii. 17, 44, 56, 118, 239, 243, 253, 273; *Calendar of Proceedings of the Committee for Compounding*, i. 2; J. W. Clay (ed.), *Yorkshire Royalist Composition Papers*, i (Yorks. Archaeological Soc., Record Ser., 15; 1893), 200; ii (YAS Record Ser., 18; 1895), 98; iii (YAS Record Ser., 20; 1896), 108.

Covenant, on another overseeing the sequestration of ill-affected ministers, while in March he gave evidence for the prosecution at the trial of Laud. Belatedly, the House of Commons seems to have come to a realization of the economic burden constant attendance upon the House placed upon merchants in particular and devised a form of recompense for some of its more active members. After he had been removed from his trading base in York for three and a half years, in August 1644 the Commons approved an 'ordinance for putting Thomas Hoyle, esquire . . . into the office of King's Treasurer's Remembrancer in the Exchequer . . . to continue in it during the pleasure of both Houses'. The post may have brought him as much as £1,200 a year until his death.[29]

The victory of the Parliamentary forces at Marston Moor led directly on 16 July 1644 to the surrender of York to Fairfax, who at once faced the problem of restoring civilian government to the city after nearly four years of military rule. On 19 August the Commons received a petition from John Geldert, Stephen Watson, Robert Knight, and Percival Levitt, citizens of York, asking that preaching ministers be sent down and that Mr Hoyle be installed as their mayor. The House responded by instructing the committee for Yorkshire to prepare an Ordinance 'for disenabling of Sir Edmund Cowper, now the reputed lord mayor from continuing any longer in executing the office of lord mayor . . . and to enable and appoint Mr Alderman Hoyle to execute the place and office of lord mayor of York until the election day'. Always a zealous upholder of the city's privileges, Hoyle went out of his way in September 1644 to observe constitutional proprieties. Although all those in the council chamber on 30 September submitted 'very cheerfully and readily' to Parliament's Ordinance which they were 'very desirous to perform to the uttermost', they still went through all the customary ceremonies to elect Hoyle lord mayor until the next St Blaize's day. Once in office, he set to work to re-establish the council's authority, inspecting St Maurice's Church and its surrounding area damaged by fire and, a portent for the future, at the end of October overseeing the taking of the National Covenant in All Saints, Pavement, by the aldermen, privy council, and common council, and other of the 'best' citizens. Many reminders

---

[29] *CJ* iii. 404, 408, 422, 507, 574, 577–8; HMC, *House of Lords*, NS xi, Addenda (1962), 400; Keeler, *Members of the Long Parliament*, 224–5; R. Davies (ed.), *The Life of Marmaduke Rawdon* (Camden Soc., 85; 1863), 127.

persisted of former military engagements: public areas of the city required cleansing and some buildings needed to be repaired. Wounded soldiers were being accommodated in St Anthony's Hall, and at the corporation's behest Hoyle sought Fairfax's assistance in preventing Royalist prisoners begging in the streets. Furthermore, the lord mayor and the aldermen had to consult frequently over the heavy financial assessments now being imposed on the city. To complete the remodelling in December the Long Parliament, in response to a letter from Fairfax, Hoyle, and the local committee of the Northern Association, disfranchised as delinquents Sir Roger Jacques, Sir Robert Belt, Sir Edmund Cowper, William Scott, Robert Hemsworth, and John Myers. To fill their places in January 1645, the corporation elected six new aldermen from those who had taken the National Covenant, including among their number Hoyle's son-in-law, Thomas Dickinson. Consequently, when the lord mayor delivered the seals of office to his successor on 3 February 1645, he could leave York in the assurance that the government of the city now lay in politically reliable hands.[30]

Back in Westminster by May, Hoyle resumed his service on committees for raising money and troops in the south-west, for placing 'able and godly ministers', and, particularly appropriately in the light of his recent experience in York, for disfranchising several aldermen and common council men of Bristol and for settling the government of that city. On 1 January 1646 the Commons voted him on to the committee for the Ordinance, but subsequently in late March licensed him to go into the country. Some five years previously Hoyle had married again and had two sons by his second wife, John and his younger brother Timothy, baptized at St Margaret's, Westminster, on 5 February 1644. Thomas and Susanna Hoyle's short visit to York saw the burial of Timothy alongside his twelve half-brothers and sisters in St Martin's, Micklegate, and his parents cannot have entertained great hopes for John's survival. Hoyle could still, however, take comfort in his daughter, Elizabeth, who in February 1647 found herself at the summit of York's social hierarchy when her husband succeeded Geldert as lord mayor.[31]

While his son-in-law was taking steps to strengthen the Par-

[30] *CJ* iii. 597, 613, 719; iv. 5; York City Archives, Housebook 36, fos. 106ᵛ, 110ʳ, 110ᵛ, 111ʳ, 112ᵛ, 113ʳ, 114ʳ, 116ᵛ, 117ʳ, 119ʳ, 123ᵛ.

[31] *CJ* iv. 153, 211, 319, 394, 489; A. M. Burke (ed.), *Memorials of St Margaret's Church, Westminster* (1914), 188; Borthwick PRY/MG 1, p. 136.

liamentary cause in York as Edward Elvins was doing in Worcester, Hoyle turned all his attention to Westminster. Early in 1647 he reported back to Parliament from the committee of the Northern Association and seems to have given most of his time to compounding with delinquents; though he was absent from the House for several months in the autumn, he returned to the Commons in November to sit on a committee to raise money for the militia in Tower Hamlets and acted as a teller in the House in February 1648 and again in the following July. Then in August came the blow which may have induced the deep depression which afflicted him for the rest of his days. Aged only 30, Elizabeth, 'late wife unto the worshipful Alderman Dickinson', died in York. Although the Commons placed him on several committees that autumn, he seems to have lost his commitment to his work and in November received leave to go into the country.[32]

Hoyle did not withdraw from Parliament after Pride's Purge. That he participated in the King's trial, however, and so shared the responsibility for the spilling of his blood, was a subsequent invention of embittered Royalists like Mrs Thornton, who bore a personal grudge against him and his family. In the first half of 1649 his name did not appear on any Commons' committees and he may well have determined to retire from public life. In July his adversaries put about a rumour 'that Alderman Hoyle ... hath cut his own throat, which without doubt proceedeth from the inward distemper of his soul occasioned by the murther of the king'. The equally hostile author of *The Rebell's Warning-Piece* asserted that he twice attempted to kill himself in the latter half of the year, and that the House and the army had dispatched Mr Peters, Mr Dell, and other ministers to try to rouse him from his melancholy. Then, after not being mentioned in the *Journals* for nine months, in late October Hoyle once more began to be appointed to Commons' committees. On 22 January 1650 the lord mayor of York and some of his brethren wrote asking Allanson and Hoyle to use their influence to obtain some of the former fabric lands for the upkeep of the Minster. On 29 January the Commons read for the first time an Act for the preaching of the gospel in Wales and consigned it to a committee of which he was a member. If, by trying to

[32] P. Styles, *Studies in Seventeenth Century West Midlands History* (Kineton, 1978), 241–2; *CJ* v. 53–4, 62, 78, 329, 348, 363, 473, 635; *CJ* vi. 27, 47, 53, 67; Borthwick PRY/MG 1, pp. 136, 143.

involve him in parliamentary business, his friends hoped to divert him from his sorrows, their stratagem signally failed. On 30 January Hoyle hanged himself at his house in Westminster, leaving a widow and a son, John.[33]

Despite all the odds, John Hoyle, who can only have been 7 or 8 in 1649, lived to manhood. Educated first at Emmanuel College, Cambridge, and then from 1660 at Gray's Inn, he subsequently practised as a lawyer in London. All his life he seems to have been haunted by the shame of his father's death, which his political enemies never allowed him to forget. By all accounts he was a very clever man, and a bibliophile, who squandered his talents at taverns, theatres, and bawdyhouses. On several occasions he showed his open contempt for the Restoration establishment; yet in all other respects he totally rejected the religious and moral values of the Parliamentarians of the previous generation. As the lover of Aphra Behn he has gained posthumous fame in the late twentieth century, but in his own age men like Bulstrode Whitelocke recoiled from him as 'an atheist, a sodomite professed, a corrupter of youth and a blasphemer of Christ'. He died in a drunken brawl in Fleet Street in 1692.[34]

Since no personal papers of any kind have survived and information on his suicide comes only from hostile sources, whether public or private griefs drove Thomas Hoyle to take his life can never be conclusively determined. A year before Hoyle killed himself, Ralph Josselin had set out in his diary how, in February 1649, he himself had been 'much troubled with the black providence of putting the king to death', though even in his grief he could still hope 'the Lord ... in mercy do us good by the same', and reproach 'the weaker sort of Christians' for becoming 'passionate' in regard to the execution. The loss of his first wife and fourteen of his children would have been more than sufficient to have caused Hoyle's profound depression. Perhaps the execution of the King made his life finally unendurable. Hoyle's closest colleagues, spared the succession of family calamities he had suffered, reacted

---

[33] D. Brunton and D. H. Pennington, *Members of the Long Parliament* (1954), 63; D. Underdown, *Pride's Purge: Politics in the Puritan Revolution* (Oxford, 1971), 138, 217; *Mercurius pragmaticus*, part 2, no. 14 (17–24 July 1649); Drake, *Eboracum*, 534; *CJ* vi. 313, 317, 321, 325, 327, 336, 352.

[34] J. Venn and J. A. Venn, *Alumni cantabrigienses*, pt. I, vol. ii (Cambridge, 1922), 422; A. Goreau, *Reconstructing Aphra: A Social Biography of Aphra Behn* (Oxford, 1980) 189–206; M. Duffy, *The Passionate Shepherdess: Aphra Behn 1640–89*, (1977), 132–9, 254–5, 286, 289.

very differently to the King's death. Sir William Allanson accepted the constitutional changes and remained a loyal adherent of the Commonwealth for the rest of his life. In York Thomas Dickinson, knighted by Cromwell during his second term as lord mayor in 1657, continued his father-in-law's tradition of local and national service, representing the city in Parliament in 1654 and 1658. Disfranchised at the Restoration, he retreated to his country house at Kirkby Hall.[35]

In 1650 the London coroner charitably determined that Hoyle had not been of sound mind at the time of his suicide, thus allowing his estate to descend to his widow and son. Reflecting on the tragedy after more than a decade, the former York minister, John Shaw, whose daughter had received part of her education in the alderman's household, declared that Hoyle 'was generally accounted a very good man'. In their final verdict his friends dwelt upon his life, and not upon his death, and all his life he had striven to live according to his principles. Intending to ridicule Hoyle as 'that man of conscience', Denzil Holles in his *Memoirs* perhaps spoke more truthfully than he knew.[36]

[35] *The Diary of Ralph Josselin 1616–83*, ed. A. Macfarlane (British Academy, Records of Social and Economic History, NS 3; 1976), 155; Keeler, *The Long Parliament*, 224–5; Wilson, 'The Corporation of York 1580–1660', 265, 299; York City Library, Skaife, 'Civic Officials', i. 315.

[36] The coroner's verdict on Hoyle's death supports the thesis that a more lenient attitude towards suicide emerged over the course of the seventeenth century which is set out in M. MacDonald and T. R. Murphy, *Sleepless Souls: Suicide in Early Modern England* (Oxford, 1990); *Yorkshire Diaries and Autobiographies*, 145–6; 'Memoirs of Denzil, Lord Hollis', in *Select Tracts Relating to The Civil Wars in England in the Reign of King Charles the First* (1815), i. 268.

12

The King's Servants:
Conscience, Principle, and Sacrifice
in Armed Royalism

P. R. NEWMAN

IN November 1986 Gerald Aylmer, in a Presidential address to
the Royal Historical Society, subsequently published,[1] dealt with
the problem of Royalist attitudes. It was, perhaps, the most
difficult of a series of addresses on 'Collective Mentalities in
Mid-Seventeenth-Century England'. In a shrewd and wide-ranging
survey of evidence, Dr Aylmer sought to establish precisely what
it was for which the Royalists fought. His conclusion that 'the
strength and fighting spirit of [the King's] supporters may well
have owed more to the concepts of honour and loyalty than to
the force and validity of [argument]' recognized that Royalism was
essentially emotive. Yet it was also a conclusion that may be felt
to mirror that which Dr Aylmer had earlier arrived at in his
consideration of Puritanism: that it was 'temperament more than
it was a doctrine'.[2] The difference lay in the fact that, whereas, for
a study of Puritan attitudes, there exists a wealth of primary source
materials, for a similar study of Royalist attitudes, there is virtually
nothing. Dr Aylmer's study of Royalist belief was based upon the
polemical writings of more-or-less professional communicators,
engaged in a long, repetitive, and sometimes sterile war of words
with the King's opponents. Dr Aylmer's conclusion concerning
the basis of committed Royalism, therefore, was in reality a
conclusion forced upon him by the lack of clear, reasoned state-

This paper was prepared in York Minster Library. I am grateful to my colleagues Bernard
Barr and Nancy Wilson for facilitating my work. Most of the individuals mentioned in the
text will be found in P. R. Newman, *Royalist Officers in England and Wales, 1642–1660* (New
York, 1981). Only where specific references are drawn from that work, however, is the
book cited in the notes.

[1] G. E. Aylmer, 'Collective Mentalities in Mid-Seventeenth-Century England, ii. Royalist
Attitudes', *TRHS* 5th ser., 37 (1987), 1–30.
[2] Aylmer, 'Collective Mentalities in Mid-Seventeenth-Century England, i. The Puritan
Outlook', *TRHS* 5th ser., 36 (1986), 1–25.

ments of belief by the armed supporters of the King.

Royalism was, as John Kenyon put it,[3] a matter of 'gut loyalty to the King, either as a person or as an institution'. It is arguable that, in that fundamental, emotive response to the gathering political crises of 1641 and 1642, lay the roots of that Royalist party, the creation of which struck John Morrill as 'remarkable'.[4] That gut loyalty, according to Kenyon, could 'often override religious doubts', and he went on to quote the contemporary observation of Sir Edmund Verney to Edward Hyde which has been utilized so often by historians:

My conscience is only concerned in honour and gratitude to follow my master. I have eaten his bread and served him near thirty years, and will not do so base a thing as to forsake him, and choose rather to lose my life, which I am sure to do, to preserve and defend those things which are against my conscience to defend.[5]

By which Verney meant, probably, episcopacy.

Sir Edmund Verney sealed his commitment to the King in battle, killed in the first major engagement of the Civil Wars at Edgehill. His attitude, as I shall demonstrate, was not by any means unique. Principle, wherever we find evidence of the attitudes of individual Royalists, did dominate conscience if it was not in itself an expression of conscience. Sacrifice, personal and material, was for many a logical consequence of adhesion to principle, something towards which many Royalists were inexorably moving; something, even, which some of them embraced as their cause suffered eclipse. 'I escaped one great danger at Wigan', the Earl of Derby wrote to his wife in 1651,[6] 'but I met with a greater at Worcester; I was not so fortunate to meet with any that would kill me.' Derby's death on the scaffold was days away when he wrote. He was not so 'fortunate' as Sir Bevil Grenville, who died of wounds sustained in battle in July 1643. Of Grenville, his servant and friend Anthony Payne observed, 'He fell, as he did often tell us he wished to die, in the great Stewart cause, for his country and his King.'[7]

---

[3] J. Kenyon, *The Civil Wars of England* (1988), 39.

[4] J. Morrill, *The Revolt of the Provinces: Conservatives and Radicals in the English Civil War, 1630–1650* (1976), 31.

[5] Ibid.

[6] *The Stanley Papers*, ed. F. R. Raines, iii (Chetham Soc., 66; 1867), p. cc.

[7] Quoted in J. Stucley, *Sir Bevil Grenville and his Times* (Chichester, 1983), 148. The words ascribed to Payne may be fictitious. The sentiment, however, is precise.

For the fighting men who espoused the King's cause, it is apparent, from what evidence there is, that principle guided their conduct. Principle, firmly grounded in 'concepts of loyalty and honour', expressed itself in the idea of service. Those Royalists who left behind them any record of their thinking clearly demonstrated that they regarded themselves as servants of their royal master, and, under such an obligation as customarily falls upon a servant, to address themselves firstly and primarily to the interests of their master. Sir Edmund Verney had 'served [the King] near thirty years' and would 'follow my master' in consequence of that. The sacrifice of life and property in such a service was inherent, since for many Royalists life and property were clearly at the King's disposal. The enemy, the Parliamentarians or 'Parlimenteers', recognized this Royalist attitude of mind. In April 1651 Charles Rosecarrock of Trevena in Cornwall, who had fought as a cavalry officer for Charles I, was reported to London as 'one ready for new action' who had been 'formerly in the old service all along'.[8] The 'old service' may be felt clearly to represent for committed Royalists what the more familiar 'good old cause' came to represent for die-hard Republicans. To view committed Royalism as an expression of honourable and principled service is to draw closer to what underlay the sacrifice of Verney, Grenville, Derby, and many others.

The equation of service with Royalism was neatly expressed by Clarendon: 'they who were looked upon as servants to the King being then called "Cavaliers".'[9] This was a truer definition than that of Joshua Sprigge writing in 1647, who observed of events in 1642:

As divers Souldiers and other loose people flocked to Court; so, many well-affected Citizens and others testified their affection, in a voluntary way, to the Parliament, the preservation of their persons and priviledges. These called the other Cavaliers, and they termed these Round-heads; whence arose those two Names, whereby in common talk the two parties in this War were by way of nick-name distinguished.[10]

[8] Newman, *Royalist Officers*, 318.

[9] *The History of the Rebellion and Civil Wars in England ... by Edward Earl of Clarendon*, ed. W. Macray (6 vols., Oxford, 1888), i. 456. By 'servants' Clarendon does not here mean those holding offices of profit under the Crown, but those perceived to be attached to the King and the Court by association.

[10] J. Sprigge, *Anglia rediviva* (1647), 3.

Sprigge's use of the word 'voluntary' in connection with the actions of the Parliament's supporters, further offers a contrast to the principle of obligation which underlies such of the statements of principle by Royalists that we have. By the same token, his equation of Cavaliers with a threat to 'priviledges' of the Citizens, demonstrates that he, and others, regarded the Royalists as instruments of the arbitrary royal will—the servants who, like bailiffs, would seize upon the persons, goods, and freedoms of the recalcitrant.

The clearest and lengthiest expression of principle from a committed Royalist is not necessarily the most representative, but is couched in terms that all thinking Royalists would have understood. Like Verney, Sir Henry Slingsby permitted principle to override conscience:

I could never be of y^t opinion y^t ye government of ye Church, as it is now establish'd by Bishops and ArchBishops to be of absolute necessity so y^t ye taking of y^m away should quite overturn ye state and essence of ye cristian church; but I am of opinion y^t ye taking of y^m out of ye church as ye government is now establist and so long continu'd, may be of dangerous consequence to ye peace of ye Church; for admitting y^t government of Bishops be not of divine right, nor in every point, as it is now exercis'd, of Apostolical right, yet we find some foundations thereof in ye wrighting of ye Apostles, y^t there was not intended a [parity] amongst all ye presbiters, but some in dignity above ye rest . . . The comon people judges not wth things, as they are wth reason or against, but long usage wth y^m is instead of all, so y^t they would think y^mselves loose and absolv'd from all government w^n they should see y^t wch they so much venerat'd so easily subvert'd.[11]

Slingsby could see and appreciate the need for reform, but there were more important considerations, not least social and governmental stability. But these political matters aside, he was quite sure that 'Civill Justice, wch as it abhors Neutrality, so it will not admitt a man should falsify y^t trust wch he hath given',[12] provided a greater imperative, for him at least. In Slingsby's case—and he was to emerge as a die-hard Royalist and made the ultimate sacrifice for his principles in 1658—the matter of principle developed in him. In 'A Father's Legacy', written to instruct his sons, he observed:

My high obligations confirmed by Oath, and bound in, I must confess,

[11] D. Parsons (ed.), *The Diary of Sir Henry Slingsby* (1836), 67–8.
[12] Ibid. 120.

with an inviolable tie of Religious Love, had so inseparably united my thoughts to the devotion of allegiance; as the serious and constant Observance of it begun to have that influence over me, as in the end it Resolv'd to a case of Conscience.[13]

Slingsby entered the Civil War as a King's man guided by principle in much the same way as Sir Edmund Verney: he shelved considerations of conscience. Surviving the battles and the sieges, unlike Verney, he came to find that the principle became for him the matter of conscience, which enabled him to face with equanimity his death on the scaffold. The total eclipse of the 'Stewart cause' for which Bevil Grenville had died did not lessen Slingsby's obligation of loyalty. It is apparent that the attitudes of men such as Slingsby, Grenville, and Verney may not have been universally shared by all Royalists, but the similarity of attitude amongst those who did, privately or publicly, articulate their beliefs, argues for a collective mentality.

Lord Capel's attitude to his own impending execution in 1649 is markedly similar. 'In this last act of my life ... dying in and for so good a cause as this is,' Capel admonished his son,

I would not have you neglect any honourable and just occasion to serve the King and the Country, with the hazzard of your life and fortune ... I would have you engage yourself—as I thanks be to God for it have done ... out of a conscience of your duty only.[14]

Capel's injunction compares well with the motives attributed to William Cavendish, Earl of Newcastle, who spent the years from 1644 to 1660 in exile. His second wife, Margaret, the sister of the Royalist cavalry general Sir Charles Lucas who was shot out of hand at Colchester in 1648,[15] wrote in her memoir of her husband:

he thought it his duty rather to hazard all, than to neglect the commands of his Sovereign; and resolved to show his fidelity, by nobly setting all at stake, as he did, though he well knew how to have secured himself, as too many others did, either by neutrality or adhering to the rebellious party ...[16]

---

[13] Ibid. 207.

[14] HMC, *12th Report*, Appendix Part IX (1891), Beaufort MSS, 36–7.

[15] Lucas and his fellow officer Sir George Lisle were subjected to summary execution. The case is discussed by J. H. Round, 'The Case of Lucas and Lisle', *TRHS* NS 8 (1894), 157–80.

[16] C. H. Firth (ed.), *The Life of William Cavendish Duke of Newcastle* (1886), 19.

Like Capel, who would have had his son do as he had done, we are told that Newcastle

had two sons that were young ... with him in the wars ... Sir Charles Lucas desired my Lord to send his sons away when the [battle of Marston Moor] was fought, yet he would not, saying, his sons should show their loyalty and duty to his Majesty, in venturing their lives ...[17]

The principle of honourable obligation we find in Slingsby, Verney, Capel, Newcastle, and others was present, too, in Henry, Third Lord Spencer of Wormleighton, who was killed in battle at Newbury in 1643. In September 1642 Spencer expressed his reluctance about the war in a private letter, but again, despite his misgivings, he was driven by an attitude of mind that transcended all else.

How much I am unsatisfied with the proceedings here, I have at large expressed ... neither is there wanting daily handsome occasion to retire, were it not for gaining honour; for, let occasion be never so handsome, unless a man were resolved to fight on the Parliament side, (which for my part I had rather be hanged) it will be said, without doubt, that a man is afraid to fight. If there could be an expedient found to salve the punctilio of honour, I would not continue here an hour.[18]

Lord Spencer may have preferred to opt out; he presumably, like Newcastle, 'well knew how to secure himself', had he chosen to do so; but the principle of honour—expressed in this letter in personal terms—was crucial. He would not serve the Parliament, nor would he be thought of as a coward; thus he remained with the King's armies and perished in the King's cause, perhaps with less resolution than others may have shown or pretended to, but that is not evidenced. He might, like Slingsby, have discovered that the matter of principle became a matter of conscience. He was certainly not lacking in a sense of his obligations towards his king.

The elements of loyalty and sacrifice were, in the view of Edward Walsingham, exemplified in the life and death of Sir John Digby, the epitome, it would seem, of Roman Catholic commitment to the King's cause. Digby died slowly, from wounds sustained in action at Taunton, and he died painfully:

his unstayned Loyalty towards his King, whose cause hee espoused and

---

[17] Ibid. 172–3.
[18] Eliot Warburton, *Memoirs of Prince Rupert and the Cavaliers*, 3 vols. (1849), i. 337–8.

courageously mayntayned in so many bloody battailes wherein hee runne eminent hazard of his Life which at last hee most willingly sacrificed in defence of his Soveraigne King Charles, and sealed the Writ of his Allegiance with his owne blood.[19]

We do not need to be impressed by Walsingham's hyperbole to recognize that Digby, like Capel, Newcastle, and others, regarded the hazarding of his life as a true token of his principle of loyalty to the King. For Walsingham, Digby was one of a number of 'hon^ble Lords, valiant knights and gentlemen with many resolute and brave souldiers' who 'writ in bloody characters the Authenticall Copie of their faithfull Allegiance'.[20]

The working of the principle of loyalty, of service, is widely evidenced in the middle part of 1642. The future Parliamentarian Lady Brilliana Harley observed in a letter: 'Sr William Pelham rwites [*sic*] me word he has given up his liftenatcy and his gooing to Yorke, to the king; being his saruant, as he rwites me word, and so bound by his oth.'[21] Joshua Moone, the biographer of John Belasyse, wrote of his master being 'fully satisfied in that he adhered unto, wherein religion, honour and loyalty he conceived were sufficient arguments to him'.[22] The Countess of Denbigh, writing to her Parliamentarian son, taxed him with matters of principle:

I can not refrone frome righting to you and with all to beg of you to have a care of your selfe and of your honner . . . as you have ever professed to me and all your friends that you would not be against the person of the King . . . go to the King to gane the reputation you have loust.[23]

It was reported of Sir Edmund Verney that he 'sath if the kainge commands he must goo', and 'your father lyke a good sarvant i belive is much for his master'.[24] Sir Edmund's sons were to be split in their choice of sides, and the Royalist Edmund wrote to Parliamentarian Ralph:

your being against the king: give me leave to tell you in my opinion tis most unhandsomely done, and it greaves my hearte to think that my

[19] G. Bernard (ed.), 'Edward Walsingham's Life of Sir John Digby 1605–1645', *Camden Miscellany*, vol. XII (Camden Soc., 3rd ser., 18, 1910), 118–19.

[20] Ibid. 89.

[21] T. T. Lewis (ed.), *Letters of the Lady Brilliana Harley* (Camden Soc., OS 58; 1853), 161.

[22] HMC, *Ormonde*, NS ii. 378.

[23] HMC, *4th Report*, Part I (1874), Denbigh MSS, 259.

[24] F. P. Verney, *Memoirs of the Verney Family during the Civil War* (2 vols.; 1892), ii. 87, 88.

father allready and I, who soe dearly love and esteeme you, should be bound in consequence (because in duty to our king) to be your enemy.[25]

Sir Lewis Dyve, incarcerated in the Tower of London in 1646, wrote:

Though loyalty is now reputed for the greatest crime, and noe man subject to so much hazard as he that professith it, yet whilst I have a being in this world noe terror of death or torments, shall by God's assistance ever divert me from that duty and servis I owe you as my soveraigne.[26]

It is nevertheless still the case that the most evocative statement of principle by a Royalist pre-dates the Civil War by three years. In April 1639 Sir Bevil Grenville wrote to his friend Sir John Trelawney:

I cannot contain myself within my doors when the King of England's standard waves in the field upon so just occasion, the cause being such as must make all those that die in it little inferior to martyrs. And for mine own part I desire to acquire an honest name or an honourable grave.[27]

Given Grenville's enthusiasm when faced with war against the 'barbarous and implacable' Scots, it is justifiable to suppose that he did indeed court death in the 'Stewart cause', as was subsequently said of him, in 1643. This single-minded sense of duty, in Grenville's case more clear-cut than that of Verney, troubled by conscience as he was, was progressively embraced by Sir Henry Slingsby and, it would seem, all the while carried by Digby, Capel, and others.

There is no indication that, for these Royalists at least, loyalty and obligation towards the King were in any way conditional. Even Lord Spencer, claiming to be in despair at the course of events, did not qualify his loyalty, though he clearly would have been somewhere else if his reputation could have survived it. It was the loss of reputation that the Countess of Denbigh urged upon her rebellious son. It would be hard to expect the enthusiasm of Sir Bevil Grenville to be limited by conditional concepts of loyalty, but likewise the quiet, undemonstrative Slingsby gives no hint that his resolute principle of loyalty was dependent in any way upon

[25] Ibid. 136.
[26] H. G. Tibbutt (ed.), 'The Tower of London Letter Book of Sir Lewis Dyve', *Bedfordshire Historical Record Soc.*, 38 (1957), 55.
[27] Stucley, *Grenville and his Times*, 78.

the actions and words of the King. It is this attitude, which cannot be called unthinking or simply conservative, which may be felt to form the backbone of that Royalist party which had emerged by mid-1642 as a formidable guarantee of the King's determination to wage war against the Parliament. There is evidence that for Sir Edmund Verney, for example, the elevation of principle over conscience involved considerable mental disquiet: that it was not mere emotive response for him.

The urgency of loyalty and the principle of obedience may well be understood in the context of what was seen by Royalists, not least the King himself, as a straightforward contrast of loyalty with only too apparent treason. The King was, for these Royalists, confronted by straightforward rebellion, and recently J. S. A. Adamson has laid stress upon the way in which this rebellion was, initially anyway, personified by Parliament's chief general, the Earl of Essex.[28] Adamson's contention seems to be that the Civil War was, in both a broad and specific sense, a re-enactment of the great baronial rebellions of the late Middle Ages, in which the opponents of the king sought to use force to remove evil counsellors. Basing his argument upon extensive familiarity with contemporary views of medieval history, Adamson pushes the figure of the Earl of Essex to the forefront of resistance to the policies of the King. If his view is accepted, then the only matter of principle where participants and onlookers were concerned lay in a power struggle between the Crown and elements of the nobility. If that were the case, then so clear-cut a perception of what was at stake might well explain the unqualified loyalism of men like Verney, Grenville, and Slingsby. For them it would have been a matter of resisting rebellion, and they could, to follow Adamson's view, dissociate that rebellion from the workings of the Parliament, recognizing in their loyalty no conflict of interests. If that was so, then it was a simplistic view, but not for that reason necessarily dubious. We are obliged, after all, to seek to see events as the participants saw them, if we are to understand the fundamentals of allegiance, and Adamson's case offers insight into Royalist attitudes.

In this context, it is possible to assess the reasoning of side-

---

[28] J. S. A. Adamson, 'The Baronial Context of the English Civil War', *TRHS* 5th ser., 40 (1990), 93–120.

changers such as Sir Hugh Cholmeley, Parliament's active governor of Scarborough, who in 1643 went over to the King. For Cholmeley, 'the othes of alleagiance and protestacion, both obliging protection to the King's person' played upon his conscience. He came to perceive that which others had seen from the start, that the proceedings of Parliament and of its armies were directed against the Crown itself and not against evil counsellors: 'Sir Hugh began to consider how ill the Parliament prosecuted those grounds and pretences they made when hee was first embarqued in there imployment . . ."[29] Historians have spoken of Cholmeley as returning to his allegiance, which may be seen as an act of principle, whereas abandonment of the Parliament itself might be felt to lack something where personal honour was concerned. Cholmeley's decision indicates he had always been a Royalist, but that his perception of what the war was about was, in his own view, long clouded by the moral imperative under which Parliament masqueraded. Cholmeley did what the Countess of Denbigh's son did not do, and rescued his reputation in the eyes of loyalists: he suffered for that personal imperative, but no more so than did men who were outright Royalists from the summer of 1642.

Quite how far Royalists were able to distinguish the institution of Parliament from the rebellion of the Earl of Essex is unclear. We might suppose that they believed, although they could not for long have deluded themselves in this, that they were fighting for king and Parliament. This was, after all, the vehicle for the actions which most Parliamentarians took in the war against the Cavalier party. Those Royalists who expressed their loyalty in words, or such statements as have survived the turmoil of the 1640s, did not venture into the territory of nice constitutional or, indeed, political argument. Sir Henry Slingsby's animadversion upon the role of episcopacy was, after all, fairly pedestrian, although it gets us closer to what the average Royalist thought than do the writings of the polemicists such as Filmer and Digges.

In a search for the events and developments which led to the outbreak of Civil War, insufficient attention has been paid to an incident that occurred in Yorkshire on or around 30 April 1642. The King, his Court established at York, which city was to be his

[29] C. H. Firth (ed.), 'Sir Hugh Cholmeley's Narrative of the Siege of Scarborough, 1644–5', *EHR* 32 (1917), 570.

headquarters in the build-up to Civil War, had sought to seize upon the arsenal lodged in Hull. Parliament's governor of Hull, Sir John Hotham, declined to admit the King into the port. For Royalists, Hotham's action was a direct challenge to the King's authority, and one of them responded accordingly. The news of this incident spread across the country like wildfire. On 3 May a London correspondent of Sir Richard Leveson informed him that Sir Francis Wortley had drawn his sword 'sayinge I am for the Kinge . . . it was onely affirmed by one that but heard it from another'.[30] Two days later Lady Harley at Brampton Bryan in Herefordshire wrote: 'And now we heare that S⁰ Francis Wortly drwe his sword and asked whoo was for the King, and so 18 foolowed him.'[31] The story was disseminated in the Verney family as well: 'I am sory to hear my brother wortly hath cariede himsefe so folishly. Ane unfortunate man he is every way ...'[32] As late as 23 June, the incident was still current in London, John Turbervill writing to John Willoughby:

All men now that are for the Parliament, are no more termed Roundheads, but Hothamites, from Sir John Hotham; and all those that are for the King, are called Wortheleshites [*sic*], from Sir George Wortheley, that drew his sword in defence of the King at Hull, against Sir John Hotham; and 'tis thought if he could have come nigh him, he would have quickly despatched him.[33]

The significance of Wortley's action lies in its polarizing implications, and the rumour of it was so strong and widespread that Wortley himself felt obliged to issue a tract justifying himself. 'A Declaration from York' published in London in June 1642 was intended by Wortley not only to exculpate himself from the furious reaction of Parliament to his action, but to set it in a context that men like Grenville would have understood. Wortley wrote:

I was willing to doe my Prince and Countrey that good service (as I conceived it) and being amongst others of my quality, the first in order of ranke, and his Majesties servant, I must acknowledge that I was well

[30] HMC, *5th Report*, Part I (1876), Sutherland MSS, 147.
[31] Lewis, *Letters of Brilliana Harley*, 158.
[32] Verney, *Memoirs*, ii. 85.
[33] W. C. and C. E. Trevelyan (eds.), *Trevelyan Papers*, iii (Camden Soc., OS 105; 1872), 222–3.

pleased with the service, my heart and conscience, excusing me from all malignant thoughts of contradiction or opposition.[34]

Wortley[35] was no young Royalist desperado by any means. He was almost 50, and had been a knight since 1610 and a baronet since 1611. He was seated at Wortley Hall, in Yorkshire, and was a leading gentry figure in his county. That is what made his action so significant, causing the House of Commons to denounce him as a 'prime and pernicious Royalist' and the House of Lords to consider impeaching him of high treason. Disparaging remarks about him in the Verney papers aside, it is evident that Wortley perceived in April 1642 the precise nature of the challenge which Parliament, through Hotham in Hull, was making to the person of the King. In his 'Declaration' Wortley grounded his action in drawing his sword in the dictates of his 'heart and conscience' which sentiments later formed the basis of other Royalist declarations, if somewhat less public in their expression. For Wortley, the actions of Sir John Hotham at Hull were those of a rebel, and the response of the drawn sword was a gesture of defiance towards a rebel. Turbervill's letter from London shows how the impression of the deed filtered rapidly through into the awareness of the masses, making Wortley a household name (whether derisively or not), to counter-balance the fame attaching to Sir John Hotham. In propaganda terms, however people shrank from what Wortley had done—for his action expressed vividly the impending split within society—Wortley's action gave a fillip to the sentiments of proto-Royalists. Turbervill's account of popular nicknames circulating in London demonstrates also that the division between the friends of Parliament and the friends of the King was already profound, and that Wortley personified at last that existing division.

Sir Francis seems to have been drained of much of his energy by his performance in April 1642. Although he commanded for the King in his native county under the Earl of Newcastle, he never again enjoyed the eminence he had known in the spring and summer of that year. But the memory of the Parliament was long, and in 1644 Wortley was transported as a prisoner to London and gaoled in the Tower, where, despite petitions, some endorsed by Sir Thomas Fairfax, he died in 1652. Wortley, therefore, like

<hr />

[34] BL Thomason Tract E. 153 (1).
[35] Newman, *Royalist Officers*, 422.

Grenville, Capel, Slingsby, and others, came to sacrifice from the starting-point of principle. We do not know if his resolution was as strong in 1652 as Slingsby's was in 1658, but his death in prison was the consequence of his stand on principle, and, though less dramatic than Slingsby's death, was akin to that of the many Royalists who, driven into exile, perished as exiles in the countries of western Europe in the 1650s. Parliament forced the ultimate sacrifice upon those it would not pardon, soldiers of the 'old service'.

Sacrifice was both physical and material. Wortley and the exiles lost everything, and died in reduced circumstances, brought to that pass by their committed resistance to rebellion against their king. Some who made the material sacrifice in time recovered part or all of what they had lost, either by coming to terms with the Parliament and the regimes of the 1650s, or by surviving to enjoy the Restoration of the monarchy in 1660. An interesting and important figure is that of Edward Somerset, Lord Herbert of Raglan, from 1645 Earl of Glamorgan and from 1646, the year of his father's death, Second Marquess of Worcester. Somerset's career and politics remain to be thoroughly studied, and the readily accessible documentary evidence relating to his actions during the Civil War merely serves to emphasize this lack of detailed study. He was a Roman Catholic, heir to one of the greatest fortunes enjoyed by any landed family in the kingdom, and he committed all of his resources to the King without hesitation. His claims as to how much he expended in the 'Stewart cause' are partly verifiable from other evidence, and there is no reason to doubt that the material sacrifices he and his family made were staggering. Yet, on the other hand, from his own account[36] he recognized that there was a point at which personal honour recoiled from certain actions committed in the King's name and cause. He recognized a duality of reputation, that expressed in devotion to the Crown, and that expressed in the deportment of a great landed peer towards his inferiors.

Parliament's hostility towards Edward Somerset recognized the crucial role his money played in militarizing south Wales for the King in 1642/3. That hostility increased markedly as a result of Somerset's involvement with negotiations with the Irish Catholic

---

[36] HMC, *12th Report*, Beaufort MSS, 56–63, for this and all ensuing quotations. See also Newman, *Royalist Officers*, 350–2.

Confederacy in 1645 on behalf of the King. When he finally handed himself over to the government in 1652, he was gaoled, and in 1655 granted a pension of £3 a week by Cromwell. It is implied that this was only forthcoming because of the intercession of Somerset's son, who had conformed to the new order and abandoned the family's Catholicism. The degree of material sacrifice involved in Somerset's Royalist principles may be gauged from setting the 1655 pension against the total expenditure of the Somerset family, which, in 1667, Somerset told the House of Lords, had amounted to £918,000. Nor was this a round figure, for Somerset itemized his expenditure in a long peroration that dwelt upon his services to King Charles I, and the way in which promises made in return had been dishonoured since the Restoration in 1660.

The importance of personal honour to Somerset is everywhere apparent in his speech of 1667, leading to a telling account of a confrontation between him and another Royalist general that seems to have taken place in 1643. Having just remarked that he paid over £6,000 'down upon the naile' to a force of 4,800 men he raised for operations around Gloucester, he went on:

I kept a table for [my Life Guards] not only at Glocester sidge, but all the way to the west, without soe much as making use of free quarter, but all upon the penny, for General Ruven complained of me to the Kinge, who graciously and smilingly reprehending me publickly, I desire to know my accuser, and called my Lord General Ruven, afterwards made Earle of Branford, before his Majesty, who objecting that it was of ill example and made them to be thought the more burdensome, my humble replye was that I yielded to his Excellencie to be a better soldier, but still to be a soldier of fortune, here today and God knows where tomorrow, and therefore needed not care for the love of the people, but though I were killed myselfe I should leave my posteritie behind me, towards whom I would not leave a grudge in the people, but whilst I could serve his Majestie upon my own purse and creditt I would readdyly do it, and afterward leave it to such as his Lordship.

For Somerset the principle of loyalty to the king is not in itself conditional, but, if his observations are to be accepted, then the manner in which that loyalty might be expressed would be determined by his material circumstances. That would, of course, be true of any fighting Royalist: enemy occupation of rent-producing lands would effectively curtail the infusion of personal finance into the forces raised by country gentry; but it is interesting to see the point so explicitly stated by Somerset, given that we have only his account of this exchange to go on. The effective ousting of landed army commanders by professionals or promotions from the ranks in the Royalist armies is sufficiently well attested now to be a historical fact. Ruthven, of course, was there from the beginning in 1642, but he was, as a Scottish professional, recruited by the King and paid a salary—a type of Royalist towards whom Somerset evidently entertained misliking. Yet Somerset himself had introduced such men into the Royalist armies, as he admitted. He had, he said, in the spring of 1642,

took order for a table to be kept for several experienced officers who by this meanes were kept from takeing armes for the Parliament, and were reddy for the King's service, and the defrayinge of their debts heare, their jorney into Yorke, and theire table there, which none of them but two knew it came from other hand than the Kinge's privie purse ...

Somerset recognized what published studies of the Royalist armies have yet clearly to delineate, the distinction to be drawn between men such as himself, Slingsby, Grenville, Verney, and their kind— Royalists by attitude—and those drawn into that allegiance initially by money and rank. A distinction between principled Royalism and Royalism by association, perhaps.

Somerset expressed the sentiment that he would have been willing to 'have suffered tenn tymes more for soe good a cause, and for soe gracious and oblidgeinge a master as the late King'. His principles of loyalty were inculcated in his childhood, a point which Somerset needed to emphasize in view of the religious recusancy of his family:

Amongst Almighty God's infinite mercies to me in this world I account it one of the greatest that His divine goodnesse vouchsafed me parents as well carefull as able to give me virtuous education ... by which meanes, had it not been my owne faulte, I ought to have become better able and more capable to serve Almightie God, my King, and contry, which obligatory ends of theirs have I allwayse had in myne eyes as drawinge and suckinge them thence ...

His implicit insistence that there could be no conflict of interest between Roman Catholicism and loyalty to the Crown, at least in his case, ought to alert scholars to a solution to what Dr Aylmer in his paper on Royalist attitudes[37] described as the 'profoundly puzzling' commitment of Catholics to the royal cause. A striking distinction between the leadership and polemics of the opposing parties in the Civil War must be the obsessive anti-Catholicism of the Parliamentarians. Infused as the King's enemies were with nightmares of popish conspiracy, it was essential for them to tarnish the principles of Royalists by association with the alleged Romish conspiracy. That this propaganda took little effect amongst the Protestants of the Royalist army, whatever some of them said to exculpate themselves when they were beaten, may be attributed to the fact that Royalists were more concerned with overt and practical demonstrations of loyalty to the Crown in time of crisis than they were with the religious differences which for generations had been played upon to create an otherwise non-existent conflict of interests within society. The commitment of Catholics such as Somerset, and Sir John Digby, cited earlier, ceases to be puzzling if we accept that the touchstone for Royalists was that of honourable loyalty to the Crown. It should not, therefore, occasion surprise that Catholic gentry reared in everything other than religious doctrine like their Protestant counterparts, shared that concept of principle, reputation, and commitment which marked men such as Slingsby, Verney, and Grenville. Catholics who suffered under recusancy legislation, and Protestants who suffered from the imposition of ship money, might find the burdens onerous, but by virtue of their concept of kingship, accepted the right of the Crown to enforce measures that might not be liked. For the Royalists, Catholic or Protestant, it is evident that, once the Crown seemed to be threatened by rebellion, niggling discontents over taxation and imposition would fall away. This residual, powerful, and sustained sense of loyalty to the Crown is what created a Royalist party during 1641 and 1642, and, if those within Parliament moving towards a limitation of the royal prerogative failed to take account of that, then clearly they had lost touch with a reality that the King himself had not. The King did not need to create a Royalist party, for it arose itself in opposition to the spectre of rebellion.

Dr Aylmer's address to the Royal Historical Society on the subject of Royalist attitudes was the first significant reappraisal of a difficult issue for a long time. The nature of the evidence was

---

[37] Aylmer, 'Royalist Attitudes', 11.

such that he was obliged to resort to the published works of gifted writers. His conclusion that the 'concepts of honour and loyalty' underlay commitment to the King was unavoidable. Royalism was based upon a principle of obedience and duty which, for those who sided with the Parliament, had become redundant to a greater or lesser extent. Those few written texts and letters which remain to us from the active Royalists of the Civil Wars serve to underline Dr Aylmer's conclusion. It may well be a pointless exercise to take the subject of Royalism and to seek to define it in terms of ideology: for Royalism was an expression of an ancient and widely shared set of values, and it may well have been the case that those values were not confined to the articulate and largely literate gentry.

The raising of armed rebellion against the King, as Royalists saw the developments of 1642, by elements of the House of Lords and the House of Commons, revitalized archaic but deeply felt principles of loyalty. Those principles sustained a massive Royalist war effort from 1642 to 1646, and underlay the insurrection of 1648 and the renewed war of 1650/1. They enabled Sir Henry Slingsby, when it might have seemed that all hope of a restored monarchy was gone, to die with equanimity on a scaffold and to partake in a lesser measure, of the martyrdom—as Royalists saw it—of the King he had served. The murders (Lucas and Lisle at Colchester, for example, and Kemys at Chepstow) and the executions (Capel, Derby, Slingsby, and others), and the deaths in battle (Grenville, Verney, Digby, and many more) marked with sacrifice the end of the journey which principles of loyalty had obliged them to undertake. Historians of the Civil War require to be aware that, for those who espoused it, the 'old service' rested on as much principle as 'the good old cause', and a more ancient and accepted principle. The monarchy, after all, did come back, in the lifetimes of many thousands who had seen it overthrown.

13

Conscience, Constancy, and Ambition in the Career and Writings of James Howell

DANIEL WOOLF

THE English Civil War divided far more than the three kingdoms through which it raged. It also divided men and women, brothers and sisters, fathers and sons, from each other and, in some cases from themselves. The years between 1640 and 1660 offer numerous instances of men forced by circumstance to change sides, sometimes without realizing they had done so, and generally to the outrage of former allies. Throughout the conflicts and long afterwards accusations of violated oaths and perjured consciences flew back and forth. Some who changed sides, such as Henry Rich, Earl of Holland, or the John Hothams, paid for their perceived perfidy with their lives. Others, such as the Royalist-turned-Republican pamphleteer Marchamont Nedham, survived the Restoration to die in their beds. And then there were those, like Clarendon, forced to bob up and down on a sea of seemingly implacable extremes, all the while struggling to remain anchored to their convictions.[1]

Even those who avoided open changes of allegiance were frequently forced to equivocate, to dissemble, and, sometimes, to swallow their principles in the face of an unstable political and religious situation, for the sake of self, property, and family. This chapter concerns the vicissitudes experienced by one neglected figure, the poet, letter-writer, and would-be royal servant, James

Gerald Aylmer first introduced me to Howell many years ago in our discussions of seventeenth-century historical writing; I am very happy to have this opportunity to push the discussion further.

[1] B. Donagan, 'A Courtier's Progress: Greed and Consistency in the Life of the Earl of Holland', *Historical Journal*, 19 (1976), 317–53; B. H. G. Wormald, *Clarendon: Politics, History and Religion, 1640–1660* (2nd edn., Cambridge, 1964); R. Ollard, *Clarendon and his Friends* (New York, 1988). Numbers following titles refer to D. G. Wing, *Short-Title Catalogue of Books Printed in England, Scotland, Ireland, Wales, and British America and of English Books Printed in Other Countries, 1641–1700* (3 vols.; New York, 1945; 2nd edn., 3 vols.; 1972–88). In certain cases reference will also be made to E. Arber, *A Transcript of the Registers of the Company of Stationers of London, 1640–1708* (3 vols.; 1913–14), hereafter cited as 'Arber'.

Howell (*c*.1594–1666).² Howell's thought reflects a recurring concern with the problem of conscience: not just when to obey it, but when to subordinate it to the requirements of peace and public order; when, in other words, to give over one's convictions and engage rationally with one's enemies in what Howell would call 'Down-right Dealing'.³

HOWELL'S EARLY LIFE

The fourth son of a minor Welsh family with pretensions to an ancient pedigree, Howell grew up in the shadow of his brother Thomas (bishop of Bristol, 164, 4–6) to whom he owed little.⁴ Although he spent the greater part of his life in London, throughout his career he played upon his origins, which provided both a mark of distinction and a partial explanation for repeated disappointments. As he remarked from prison in the 1640s, his whole

---

² J. Howell, *Epistolae Ho-Elianae: The Familiar Letters of James Howell*, ed. J. Jacobs (1890), hereafter abbreviated as *FL*. Howell lacks a biographer; for his life and various aspects of his works see the following: G. Coleridge, 'The Letters of James Howell', *Contemporary Review*, 172 (1947), 368–71; S. Lee, 'Howell, James', *DNB*; J. Reilly, 'A Jacobean Chatterbox', in Reilly, *Of Books and Men* (New York, 1942), 237–44. Most recently, see M. Nutkiewicz, 'A Rapporteur of the English Civil War: The Courtly Politics of James Howell (1594?–1666)', *Canadian Journal of History*, 25 (1990), 21–40. The genuineness of Howell's letters has been much discussed, for example in V. M. Hirst, 'The Authenticity of James Howell's *Familiar Letters*', *Modern Language Review*, 54 (1959), 558–61. A few absolutely genuine letters of Howell do survive, many of which are printed by Jacobs in an appendix or 'supplement' to his edition of *FL*; these will be cited as *FL*, suppl.

³ On the problem of conscience as dealt with by English and European casuistry, see T. Wood, *English Casuistical Divinity during the Seventeenth Century* (1952), 67–102; K. T. Kelly, *Conscience: Dictator or Guide? A Study in Seventeenth-Century English Protestant Moral Theology* (1967), 79–118; C. W. Slights, *The Casuistical Tradition in Shakespeare, Donne, Herbert, and Milton* (Princeton, NJ, 1981), pp. 3–34; E. Leites (ed.), *Conscience and Casuistry in Early Modern Europe*, (Cambridge, 1988), of which M. Sampson, 'Laxity and Liberty in Seventeenth-Century English Political Thought' (pp. 72–118) and J. P. Sommerville, 'The "New Art of Lying": Equivocation, Mental Reservation, and Casuistry' (pp. 159–84) are particularly helpful in the present context.

⁴ BL MS Harl. 4181, fo. 258; on the greater value of friendship over fraternity, see *FL* 557 and Epictetus, 'Of Friendship', *Discourses of Epictetus*, II. xxii (trans. G. Long, New York, n.d.), 180–2. Howell may have been aware that Thomas had been obliged to apologize on behalf of his over-eager younger brother to Sir Francis Windebank for James's having 'lately broken in upon you, soe farre beyond the bounds of common modesty' (*Cal. SP Dom. 1635–6*, 204, 2 Feb. 1636; *FL*, suppl. 655). In a letter dated 26 Mar. 1643, Howell would distinguish between the love which he owed to his friends, especially those who had supported him 'in this my long affliction', and the natural affection due to his brothers and sisters, which they might simply bequeath to their own children (*FL* 422, 434).

life had been 'nothing else but a continued succession of crosses'.[5] Howell's writings present their author as interested in but not preoccupied with personal advancement and therefore capable of dispassionate observation of events. After taking his BA at Oxford in 1613, Howell initially found employment as steward of a glass factory. In 1616 the owners decided to send him abroad in search of materials and workmen, and he began the first of a series of travels that would shape his thought and his writings. The first part of his widely read *Familiar Letters* (a series of epistolary volumes assembled and mainly written while Howell was imprisoned in the Fleet during the 1640s) offers a retrospective itinerary of his peregrinations, together with his impressions of foreign countries.

On his return to England in 1622 Howell first fulfilled a series of tutorial posts, before undertaking, later that year, a mission to Spain and Sardinia to negotiate the release of an impounded English vessel.[6] Howell remained in Madrid during the negotiations over the Spanish match, and it was on this expedition that Howell initiated a connection with John Digby, Earl of Bristol, and his family which would endure for forty years. In particular, he became friendly with Sir Kenelm Digby, who arrived in Madrid in 1623.[7] They shared an interest in natural philosophy and medicine, and Digby later claimed Howell as one of the first beneficiaries of his 'sympathetic powder', which Digby applied to a wound Howell had received on his hand while intervening in a duel—not the last time that Howell would thrust himself in as an unwelcome peacemaker.[8]

Howell made no secret of his distrust for and dislike of the 'many-headed monster', the 'mechanick' sort of people, and he was always an admirer of aristocracy, both for its place in the

---

[5] Howell, *The Preheminence and Pedigree of Parlement* (1644), H3106, repr. and appended to Δενδρολογια *Dodona's Grove, or the Vocall Forest* (pt. one, 4th edn., 1649), 17; *FL* 358–9. See below, n. 48.

[6] G. F. Warner, 'Two Letters of James Howell', *EHR* 9 (1894), 127–30; Warner, review of Jacobs' edition of the *Familiar Letters*, *EHR* 8 (1893), 156–61.

[7] *FL* 276, 280, 340.

[8] K. Digby, *A Late Discourse Made in a Solemn Assembly of Nobles and Learned Men at Montpellier in France* (1658), 6–10; R. T. Petersson, *Sir Kenelm Digby* (Cambridge, Mass., 1956), 54; BL MS 5947, fo. 155 (Howell to Earl of Bristol, 23 Apr. 1630); I owe this last reference to the kindness of my colleague, Cynthia Neville. His friendship with the Digbys apparently made Howell unacceptable to the Duke of Buckingham, to whom he applied for employment on his return from Spain—Howell believed the Duke had been told he was 'too much *Digbyfied*' (*FL* 239).

social hierarchy and its potential to govern the realm in counsel with the monarch. Throughout his life he cultivated connections with families such as the Sidneys and the Herberts, and numbered several of Charles I's courtiers among his friends, including Edward Sackville, Earl of Dorset, the Caroline diplomat and later moderate Royalist.[9] The *Familiar Letters* consequently create an impression of a 'true cosmopolite' with excellent connections among his social superiors, while at the same time projecting a distaste for urbanity and novelty. Howell thought of himself as a simple man, fond of quiet contemplation and devotion, yet no country fellow. As he remarked to a friend, Howell felt he could not be called a rustic so long as he lived in a noble household. Accordingly, the late 1620s saw Howell attached to a series of noble masters. As secretary to Emmanuel, Lord Scrope, later Earl of Sunderland, who was president of the Council of the North, Howell was elected to the Parliament of 1628 as Member for Richmond, Yorkshire. Howell remained with Scrope after his replacement by Sir Thomas Wentworth, who promised him the reversion of the next attorney's place at York, which Howell, who despised provincial life, chose to sell.[10]

Sunderland died in 1630, and two years later Howell accompanied Robert Sidney, Second Earl of Leicester, on an embassy to Denmark for which he arranged the travel plans.[11] On his return to London with Leicester in March 1633 Howell spent his time pursuing royal employment and writing newsletters to Francis Windebank and to Wentworth, whom he visited in Dublin in 1639, just before the lord deputy's return to England as Earl of Strafford. It was probably through Strafford that Howell received a reversion to a clerkship of the Council.[12] As Civil War loomed, Howell

[9] D. C. Smith, 'The Fourth Earl of Dorset and the Personal Rule of Charles I', *Journal of British Studies*, 30 (1991), 257–87.

[10] *FL* 106, 373, 443.

[11] *FL*, suppl. 650 (to Wentworth, 5 May 1629); Bodl. MS Rawl, C.354, fos. 1–43; *Cal. SP Dom. 1631–3*, 382, 390, 409, 412. Howell was already known to the Court as a useful informer (PRO SP 16/19/100, Howell to Edward Conway, Jan. 1626). The connection with Leicester may have been a critical one from the point of view of Howell's development of a neo-Stoic outlook: Leicester was the nephew of Sir Philip Sidney, whose life provided a model for Jacobean neo-Stoics such as Fulke Greville, and he was father of the later classical republican, Algernon Sidney.

[12] PRO SP 16/245/33; *FL*, suppl. 656–7 (to Wentworth, 28 Nov. 1635). It was probably in the 1630s that Howell proposed the establishment of an office for the central registration of foreigners living in England, to be reported by parish churchwardens to a 'consul'. The undated proposals for this were clearly intended to create a position for Howell himself: Bodl. MS Bankes 6, fos. 57–8, 65–6.

seemed, briefly, very close to the type of appointment he had sought for twenty years. On being sworn in to the clerkship at Nottingham in 1642, however, he discovered that the place vacated by Sir Edward Nicholas had been filled by Sir John Jacob. Howell was offered the next vacancy, but this promise would never be fulfilled.[13] It is this first in a series of dashed hopes which would produce, in combination with a long period of imprisonment during the war, the distinctive flavour of his reflections on matters of loyalty and conscience.

NEO-STOICISM AND HOWELL'S MORAL OUTLOOK

Before tackling Howell's career during and after the Civil War, it would be best to lay out the contours of his thought on matters of politics, religion, and personal duty, and explore some of its principal sources. Howell was not a systematic, much less an original thinker. As far as political thought is concerned, he drew widely, and sometimes indiscriminately, from authors as various as Aristotle and Suarez, Machiavelli and Giovanni Botero.[14] His debts to many of these were acquired at second-hand, mainly through conversation or casual reading, and he rarely acknowledged his sources. In some ways, he was the typical late Renaissance intellectual: a learned *bricoleur* who, by his own admission, borrowed more books than he bought and frequently devoured them too hastily; one should read, he remarked, not to acquire deep knowledge for its own sake but to make 'useful application of it in common discourse'.[15] But, while he cannot be described as adhering exclusively to any particular philosophical school, a great deal of what Howell says concerning human nature and politics derives from an outlook first formulated by the later Roman Stoics (especially Epictetus, Seneca, and Marcus Aurelius) and adapted to post-tridentine Christianity by the great Flemish scholar Justus

---

[13] *FL*, suppl. 657, 667.

[14] *FL* 421.

[15] *FL* 413, 526. Howell's stated reading habits closely resemble those of an earlier 'professional' writer, Gabriel Harvey, as described in A. Grafton and L. Jardine, ' "Studied for Action": How Gabriel Harvey Read his Livy', *P&P* 129 (1990), 30–78. For two wide-ranging studies of the late Renaissance continental context, see D. Wootton, *Paolo Sarpi: Between Renaissance and Enlightenment* (Cambridge, 1983), and W. McCuaig, *Carlo Sigonio: The Changing World of the Late Renaissance* (Princeton, NJ, 1989).

Lipsius amidst the religious warfare of the later sixteenth century. Lipsius, perhaps the most influential European author of the time, changed countries, religions and allegiances several times, all the while preaching a doctrine of 'constancy', borrowed from the ancient Stoics, particularly Seneca. Lipsius defined constancy as 'an immovable strength of minde neither lifted up, nor pressed down with external accidents'. He contrasted constancy with obstinacy, a rigid inflexibility 'proceedinge from pride', while urging submission of religious conviction to secular authority for the sake of order.[16] Elsewhere, in the Tacitean-influenced *Sixe Bookes of Politickes*, he also defended the notion that a degree of dissimulation, of disguising one's true beliefs behind a veil of outward conformity, is both permissible to the rational man and even desirable.[17]

Lipsius' works, translated into English in the 1590s, were there augmented by English versions of two other important neo-Stoic works, Pierre Charron's *Of Wisedome* and Guillaume du Vair's exposition of *The Moral Philosophie of the Stoicks,* and by the very influential writings of Montaigne, whose position on issues such as religious controversy in many ways approximated that of Lipsius.[18] In the first forty years of the seventeenth century neo-Stoic views, and the distinctively Lipsian 'attic' prose style, found a number of celebrated exponents in England, including Francis Bacon, Sir Walter Ralegh, Ben Jonson, Fulke Greville, and Bishop

---

[16] J. Lipsius, *Two Bookes of Constancie*, trans. R. Stradling (1595), I. iv. 8; J. L. Saunders, *Justus Lipsius: The Philosophy of Renaissance Stoicism* (New York, 1955); A. Grafton, 'Justus Lipsius', *American Scholar*, 56 (1986–7), 382–90; Q. Skinner, *Foundations of Modern Political Thought* (2 vols.; Cambridge, 1978), ii. 281–3; G. Oestreich, *Neostoicism and the Early Modern State*, ed. B. Oestreich and H. G. Koenigsberger, trans. D. McLintock (Cambridge, 1982), 13–75. Oestreich's work has been criticized for its conflation of neo-Stoicism with another late Renaissance movement, Tacitism, with which it has similarities and connections but also some crucial differences (B. Worden, 'Constancy', *London Review of Books*, 5 (20 Jan. 1983); see also J. H. M. Salmon, 'Stoicism and Roman Example: Seneca and Tacitus in Jacobean England', *Journal of the History of Ideas*, 50 (1989), 199–225; K. C. Schellhase, *Tacitus in Renaissance Political Thought* (Chicago and London, 1976), 133–40.

[17] J. Lipsius, *Sixe Bookes of Politickes or Civil Doctrine*, trans. W. Jones (1594), IV. xiv. 117; P. Zagorin, *Ways of Lying: Dissimulation, Persecution, and Conformity in Early Modern Europe* (London and Cambridge, Mass., 1990).

[18] P. Charron, *Of Wisedom, Three Bookes*, trans. Samson Lennard (1608); Guillaume du Vair, *The Moral Philosophie of the Stoicks*, trans. T. James (1598), ed. R. Kirk (New Brunswick, NJ, 1951); M. de Montaigne, *The Essayes or Morall, Politike and Millitarie Discourses*, trans. J. Florio (1603). Lipsian views were also available in England in the form of his commentaries and glosses on Seneca in *The Workes of Lucius Annaeus Seneca*, trans. Thomas Lodge (1614), to which edition I refer throughout.

Joseph Hall.[19] Although he was given on occasion to euphuistic repetition and bombast, much of Howell's writing belongs within this broad tradition. His style is epigrammatic and terse, although more accessible than that of Jacobean neo-Stoics such as Greville. He does not cite Lipsius or Charron (or numerous other contemporary authors from whom he is known to have borrowed material). He does, however, make frequent reference to Cicero—often associated with the Stoics despite Lipsius' antagonism to Ciceronian prose style—Seneca, and Marcus Aurelius. Images of each of these (together with that perennial symbol of *imperium*, Julius Caesar) adorn the frontispiece to the *Familiar Letters*, and Howell singled them out as models of letter-writing.[20] He also admired the imperial administrator and miscellanist Aulus Gellius, whose *Noctes Atticae* he had read and whose career offered some parallels with his own.[21] Among ancient Stoics, Seneca's teachings placed a particular emphasis on the conscience, in the sense of knowing the difference between right and wrong, and it is thence that Howell's recurring theme that a good conscience is its own reward appears to be derived.[22] As with Gellius, there are interesting

---

[19] The influence of neo-Stoicism on English politics has not been adequately addressed: J. P. Sommerville's excellent book on early Stuart political thought, *Politics and Ideology in England, 1603–1640* (1986), for instance, has nothing to say on the subject. In the meantime, see A. McCrea, 'Neostoicism in England: The impact of Justus Lipsius' Neostoic Synthesis on English Political Thinking, 1586–1650', Ph.D. thesis (Queen's University (Canada), 1991). I am indebted to Dr McCrea both for having allowed me to read and cite her thesis, and for her helpful comments on an earlier version of this chapter. If she is correct, Lipsian neo-Stoicism, heavily laced with Tacitean strains which further reinforced the need for dissimulation in public life, had become so familiar by 1640 that direct acquaintance with the original Lipsian texts was no longer essential for a person to hold neo-Stoic views. Some neo-Stoics, notably Bishop Joseph Hall, maintained such opinions despite explicitly rejecting the Lipsian formulation of them. Howell's circle of friends included several individuals who can be considered English neo-Stoics, such as Digby and Ben Jonson. Howell was acquainted with Jonson and wrote verses for the memorial volume which appeared after the great poet's death in 1637 (BL Add. MS 5947, fo. 200 (Howell to Sir Thomas Hawkins, 5 Apr. 1636); *FL* 276, 332; B. Duppa (ed.), *Jonsonus Virbius, or, the Memorie of Ben. Johnson revived* (1638), 32).

[20] *FL* 14–15, 496; for the influence of Cicero on humanist thought, see Skinner, *Foundations*, i. 84–9.

[21] *FL* 210.

[22] *FL* 375; on Seneca, see F. H. Sandbach, *The Stoics* (1975), 160. For the importance of Seneca to the Christian humanist tradition, and the place given Senecan treatises like *De clementia*, along with Cicero's *De officiis*, in the university curriculum, see M. Todd, 'Seneca and the Protestant Mind: The Influence of Stoicism on Puritan Ethics', *Archiv für Reformationsgeschichte*, 74 (1983), 182–99, and Todd, *Christian Humanism and the Puritan Social Order* (Cambridge, 1987), 28–9.

parallels between the two men's lives, since both endured periods
of powerlessness during which they were obliged to resort to
dissimulation and flattery—which Howell denounced in others
though he was well acquainted with the art—in order to survive
stormy political times.[23]

In the carefully fashioned self of the *Familiar Letters*, and
elsewhere, Howell adopts a stance of Christian resignation towards
his own fate and towards the apparent madness that besets the
world, and especially England. This is an attitude, expounded by
Lipsius, which recognizes the obligation on the virtuous citizen
to provide counsel and to act in accordance with duty, while
acknowledging the overarching control of providence.[24] 'You know
better than I', Howell remarked to Kenelm Digby, 'that all events,
good or bad, come from the all-disposing high Deity of Heaven.'
It is God who commands the winds and weather which drive the
'great Vessel of the world' and who invariably sends a calm after
every storm; we will all experience better times if we simply live
long enough. The virtuous man will therefore neither withdraw
from the world nor rail at its torments. It is the 'school of affliction'
which has brought Howell, Job-like, to 'such a habit of patience,
it hath caus'd in me such symptoms of mortification, that I can
value this world as it is'. The content individual recognizes his lot
and endures, and 'he is the happy man who can square his mind
to his means and fit his fancy to his fortune'. At the same time,
however, he has a duty to self-preservation which to Howell meant
not mere survival but the taking of opportunities where they
presented themselves, 'it being one of the essential properties of
a wise man, to provide for the main chance'.[25]

The clearest statement of this position comes in a letter dated
early in 1644, which specifically takes up two Senecan dicta: *Nihil
est infelicius eo cui nil unquam contigit adversi* (the unhappiest man is he
who has felt no adversity) and *Nullum est majus malum, quam non
posse ferre malum* (which Howell christianizes as 'There is no greater
cross, than not to be able to bear a cross'):

[23] *FL* 19.

[24] Lipsius, *Sixe Bookes of Politickes*, III. v. 47.

[25] *FL* 218, 509, 519, 626; M. Aurelius, *Meditations*, IV. iii; VIII. xiv; IX. xlii; Epictetus, 'Of
Contentment', *Discourses of Epictetus*, I. xii; du Vair, *The Moral Philosophie of the Stoicks*, intro.
31–7, text 76–81; M.-S. Røstvig, *The Happy Man: Studies in the Metamorphoses of a Classical Ideal*
(2 vols.; Oslo and Oxford, 1954–8), I, *passim*.

Touching the first, I am not capable of that kind of unhappiness, for I have had my share of adversity: I have been hammer'd and dilated upon the anvil . . . Touching the second, I am also free of that cross; for, I thank God for it, I have that portion of Grace, and so much philosophy, as to be able to endure, and confront any misery. 'Tis not so tedious to me as to others, to be thus *immur'd*, because I have been *inur'd* and habituated to troubles.[26]

This same quality of resignation carries with it a duty, stressed by Seneca and by some neo-Stoics, to guard against intemperate outbursts of emotion. Because man is rational, he is capable of living a life of *ataraxia* or inward tranquillity, free from the influence of the passions.[27] Much of Howell's rambling thought on human behaviour is contained in his *Familiar Letters*, and in *The Vision*, a short dialogue between 'Soul' and 'Body', probably written in the late 1640s and published in the winter of 1651/2. In both the lesson is the same: the task of the virtuous citizen is to harness, rather than utterly to purge, the passions which arise from bodily humours and turn them to good use; they are to be made servants not slaves. 'As long as there are men, there must be malignant humours, there must be vices, and vicissitudes of things,' he commented in one letter. 'As long as the world wheels round, there must be tossings and tumblings, distractions and troubles, and bad times must be recompens'd with better.'[28]

The soul is the divine spark of immortality in man; the body is 'but a socket of clay that holds it',[29] and *The Vision* considers their relationship in the specific context of the upheavals of the 1640s and 1650s. Body begins the dialogue by lamenting that Soul makes man 'a self-tormentor, a persecutor and crucifier of himself', puzzling his brain with 'sturdie doubts'. In response, Soul complains

[26] *FL* 358–9, emphasis in original. The metaphor of a 'cross' for personal burdens occurs in Lodge's Seneca, 'Of the Constancy of a Wise Man', *Workes*, 664, which includes introductory comments by Lipsius; cf. Epictetus, 'Of Constancy', *Discourses of Epictetus*, I. xxix.

[27] Seneca, 'Of Anger', III. xxi, in *Workes*, trans. Lodge, 510–81; Du Vair, *Moral Philosophie of the Stoickes*, 61ff., 82–91.

[28] Howell, *The Vision: Or a Dialog between the Soul and the Bodie* (1651), H3127; Arber, ii. 387; *FL* 354, 598–9. In the dedication of a late work, *The Parly of Beasts* (1660), H3119, Howell approvingly cites the 'principle among the philosophers, that as the conduct of the passions (which arise from the humors) is the greatest prudence, so the conquest of them is the gretest prowesse, when they grow rebellious' (A3ʳ). On the Stoic and neo-Stoic doctrine of the passions, see C. B. Schmitt and Q. Skinner (eds.), *The Cambridge History of Renaissance Philosophy* (Cambridge, 1988), 360–74.

[29] *FL* 598–9.

that the passions which course through Body make its life unnecessarily turbulent. 'The passions are as so many pleaders wrangling at a bar, and Reson, my chiefest facultie, should be their chancelor.' Body indeed concedes that, although the stars can be held responsible to some degree for his irrational acts, these must mainly be laid at the doorstep of the will, as ruled by 'interior passions' which have 'too great a dominion in me'.[30]

With age comes maturity; survival past the climacteric year of 63 gives a man a freedom from his baser instincts.[31] Although an admirer of antiquity and its authority, Howell was not inclined to accept the notion of the inevitable decay of the world. He subscribed to the paradoxical commonplace that the old age of the world was the present, not the remote past, and that the true 'ancients' were his contemporaries.[32] But, if mankind had now attained this degree of maturity, why did the passions still so clearly rule both individuals and commonwealths? Here a mere metaphysical conceit becomes a commentary on the present, since, in Howell's view (which duplicates that of Lipsius in *Of Constancy*), the worst passion that besets the world is religious dissent over externals and ceremonials. 'And the worst is, that Peeple fall out about meer nicities, and extern indifferent forms; for though they agree in the fundamentals and doctrin, yet they come to exercise mortal hatred one to the other.'[33] Although much of his wartime writing had been concerned with political issues such as the proper relation of king to Parliament, Howell was no secularist, and he saw the Civil War as fundamentally a confessional conflict which had generated secondary political and constitutional issues, rather than the other way around: sectaries and Presbyterians, rather than lawyers, were the principal victims of his pen. Writing to the moderate churchman Daniel Featley in 1644, he expressed the view that 'These times (more's the pity) labour with the same disease that France did during the League.' This made it all the worse for England, since, in Howell's view, strife over religion was at once

---

[30] *The Vision*, 4, 28, 36.
[31] Ibid. 63.
[32] 'Antiquity is venerable, therefore the older the author is, the more to be valued, it being a maxim that may bear sway in divinity as well as in heraldry, *Tutius est cum patribus quam cum fratribus errare*' (ibid. 96); Howell, *Londinopolis; An Historicall Discourse or Perlustration of the City of London* (1657), H3090, preface.
[33] *The Vision*, 65.

the most foolish and the most terrible form of human conflict. As he wrote to a friend near the end of the war:

Good Lord, what fiery clashings we have had lately for a cap and a surplice! What an ocean of human blood was spilt for ceremonies only, and outward formalities, for the bare position of a table! But as we find the ruffling winds to be commonly in cemeteries, and about churches, so the eagerest and most sanguinary wars are about religion.[34]

Outward conformity could be reconciled with private conviction, as Howell suggested in his own account of his private spiritual devotions, because the rubrics of religion provide a starting-point for piety, not a rigid limitation upon it. ''Tis true, tho' there be rules and rubricks in our Liturgy sufficient to guide every one in the performance of all holy duties,' he wrote to another acquaintance, 'yet I believe every one hath some mode and model or formulary of his own, specially for his private cubicular devotions'. At the same time, he admitted that, while he always tried to apply 'every tittle of the service to my own conscience and occasions', he also acknowledged spiritual authority and the constitutions of the Church, 'and I hold this obedience to be an acceptable sacrifice to God'.[35]

   This attitude might at first seem to contradict the stalwart Royalism and fierce anti-Puritanism of some of Howell's writings of the late 1640s, which had blamed the War in large measure on the Presbyterians and their Scottish allies. But the contradiction is apparent rather than real: like Lipsius, Howell believed in the necessity of religious uniformity, not because one and only one faith was true, but precisely because the rightness of any one form of observance was ultimately unknowable and was of no consequence to salvation. The greatest evil wrought by Puritan zealots is their meddling with details, their incessant search for grounds of division though 'true love is nothing else but an appetit of Union'.[36] Howell's version of toleration entailed neither an impossible universal agreement among men, nor an absolute

---

[34] *FL* 442, 607; cf. *FL* 486, 506–8, and 551 for similar statements of revulsion against the attack on the Established Church, and Howell's belief that the number of witches and 'monstrous things' abroad in England could be attributed to this.

[35] *FL* 333–7.

[36] *The Vision*, 73. For this aspect of Lipsius' thought, see the important article by R. Tuck, 'Scepticism and Toleration in the Seventeenth Century', in S. Mendus (ed.), *Justifying Toleration: Conceptual and Historical Perspectives* (Cambridge, 1988), 21–35.

freedom of practice; instead, it demanded respect for differences of opinion on insignificant matters and subordination of personal conviction to the public order preserved by the State. The alternative was hatred and bloodshed. As Howell put it in one of his letters:

Difference in opinion, no more than a differing complexion, can be cause enough for me to hate any. A differing fancy is no more to me than a differing face. . . . If I have a fair opinion, tho' another have a hard-favour'd one, yet it shall not break that common league of humanity which should be betwixt rational creatures, provided he corresponds with me in the general offices of morality and civil uprightness.[37]

Given man's passionate nature, how are differences of opinion to be reconciled? It is here that the *conscience* plays a critical role by keeping the balance between emotion and reason. As Soul remarks to Body in *The Vision*, 'I like it very well, that you make the conscience your guide, and that you use to listen to his counsell,' since this is the 'chiefest part of a wise Christian'.[38] This begs a further question: what, on these terms, is conscience? Is it a mere conviction that one knows what is best? And how is one to resolve potential conflicts between one's conscience and the call of duty? Howell attempts to resolve these questions largely by equating *genuine* conscience with duty or obedience, and by arguing that conscience must be informed by tradition, law, and a sense of public good; it must not be autonomous and particularist but take guidance from social authority.[39]

Since man is now in his old age, he ought to be turning away alike from the pursuit of office and from the chimerical pursuit of absolute truths towards the quiet contemplation of accepted theological verities. The worst trap of all is to succumb to extreme scepticism—to Howell virtually the obverse of extreme conviction—and reject tradition purely out of some false inner compulsion which passes as conscience but which is truthfully

---

[37] *FL* 553. Compare a similar remark of 1635 in *FL* 337, wherein Howell confesses to a strong aversion to 'those schismaticks that puzzle the sweet peace of our Church, so that I could be content to see an Anabaptist go to Hell on a Brownist's back'.

[38] *The Vision*, 78.

[39] Todd, *Christian Humanism*, 176–9, 191–2; Slights, *The Casuistical Tradition*, 10–23.

spiritual pride: Lipsius' 'obstinacy'.[40] One can meditate on truth without disputing it, claiming a monopoly of it, or, worst of all, inflicting one's views on others. 'It is enough to be soberly wise, to be contented to be of Gods court, not of his councel, specially of his cabinet councel. Nor in adiaphorous things must you be to violent, strict and insolent, or hating any to destruction.'[41] In one of his later poems (edited, appropriately enough, by the Royalist deserter and Cromwellian panegyrist, Payne Fisher), Howell offered some further considerations on the limitations of knowledge, while again calling for the mastery of passion and for the subordination of personal conviction to circumstance in the interest of the public good.[42] In 'A Contemplation upon the Shortness and Shallowness of Human Knowledg' he offers numerous examples of human

[40] *The Vision*, 154. It is tempting, but misleading, to try to find a source for Howell's rejection of theological and liturgical disputation in the thought of his friend and correspondent Edward, Lord Herbert of Cherbury, for whose *The Life and Raigne of King Henry the Eighth* (1649) Howell wrote commendatory verses: see Herbert's *De veritate* (Paris, 1624). Although there are some similarities in tone, Howell does not come close to Herbert's protodeistic position that all religions share 'common notions' which make ceremonies superfluous, and he deals with difference of opinion largely negatively, with little of Herbert's ecumenism.

[41] *The Vision*, 80–1. Howell here echoes the moderate Protestant position, adopted, for instance, by Melanchthon and Hooker, that matters of ceremony are *soteriologically* indifferent and suitable to be left to the State; this is overlaid by the broader Stoic and neo-Stoic notion that the vast majority of things, being neither absolutely good nor absolutely evil, were therefore also *morally* indifferent (Epictetus, 'On what is Meant by Indifferent Things', *Discourses of Epictetus*, II. vi; M. Aurelius, *Meditations*, esp. VI. xxxii; Saunders, *Justus Lipsius*, 104; Sandbach, *The Stoics*, 29, 30). Cf. the views on 'points indifferent' of Howell's younger contemporary Sir Thomas Browne, who also shared Howell's Stoic disavowal of hatred as well as his distrust of the 'hydra' of the irrational multitude (Browne, *Religio medici* (1642), in *Works of Sir Thomas Browne*, edn. G. Keynes (2nd edn., 4 vols.; 1964), i. 14, 54, 70–80).

[42] 'The Progress of the Human Soul, or the whole history of man', *Poems upon Divers Emergent Occasions*, ed. P. Fisher (1664), H3104. The portrait of Howell facing the title-page has a new motto, *Sub mole resurgo* (from under troubles I rise anew), which in his later years supplemented his earlier motto *Senesco non segnesco*. The career of Payne Fisher (1616–1693), or Fitz-Pagani Piscatoris as he termed himself in his Latin verse, mirrored that of Howell, though Fisher was both more successful (at least initially) and a more blatant opportunist. A professional soldier turned poet, he abandoned the Royalist army after Marston Moor (the Parliamentary victory which he would celebrate in verse in 1650) to become a writer in London. A skilful panegyrist, much in demand, he ultimately became poet laureate to Cromwell. After the Restoration, he tried unsuccessfully to ingratiate himself with the monarchy by writing anti-Cromwellian literature, but spent most of the rest of his life in and out of the Fleet—a further parallel with Howell's career (*DNB*, s.v. 'Fisher, Payne'; Payne Fisher, *Marston Moor* (1650); *Inauguratio Oliveriana* (1654); *Oratio anniversaria in diem inaugurationis serenissimi nostri principis Olivari* (1655); (with Marchamont Nedham) *The Speeches of Oliver Cromwell, Henry Ireton, and John Bradshaw, Intended to have been Spoken at their Execution at Tyburne 30 June 1660* (1660). What Howell thought of his editor, given Fisher's association with Nedham, we can only guess.

ignorance. If man is unable to divine the secrets of the natural world—why, for instance, the lodestone attracts metal, and why sympathetic powders can heal—how, then, can he presume to pronounce on the correctness of details of religion? Better far to trust to tradition and avoid the acrimony created by so-called 'tenderness of conscience'.[43]

LOYALTY AND EQUIVOCATION

Considerations of conscience cut close to home with Howell. Although priding himself on loyalty to friends and allies, he was dogged throughout the second half of his life by accusations of time-serving and lukewarmness which produced frequent apologies and defences: a letter to the King dated 3 September 1644 expresses Howell's concern that 'among divers things which go abroad under my name reflecting upon the times there are some which are not so well taken; your Majesty being inform'd that they discover a spirit of indifferency, and lukewarmness in the author'.[44]

The charge of faint loyalty was all the more upsetting since in Howell's own eyes he was a 'martyr' to the Royalist cause. On a visit to London early in 1643 Howell was arrested in his chambers, his books were seized, and he was imprisoned in the Fleet. There he remained for eight years, on his account purely for his allegiance to the King, but more likely because of the insolvency to which he confesses in the *Familiar Letters*. He hoped to 'o'ercome all these pressures, survive my debts, and surmount my enemies', but, despite modest literary success, his failure to obtain the clerkship and the fall of former allies like Windebank and Strafford had left Howell close to ruin.

> Here lies intomb'd a Walking Thing,
> Whom Fortune, with the State did fling
> Between these Walls. Why? Ask not that;
> They both being blind, know not for what.[45]

It was this period of confinement that turned Howell with even greater zeal to writing; not for the last time in literary history,

[43] *Poems upon Divers Emergent Occasions*, 4–5.
[44] *FL* 488–9.
[45] *FL* 355, 367, 369, 374; Howell, 'Upon Himself, having bin Buried Alive for Many Years in the Prison of the Fleet, by the State or Long Parliament for his Loyalty', in *Poems upon Divers Emergent Occasions*, 62; *Cal. SP Dom. 1660–1*, 12.

penury hastened the pen. The works which he published over the next seven years, and in particular the early editions of the *Familiar Letters*, were calculated to earn some income, but they were also part of his deliberate construction of a public image, a persona through which Howell could explain his political wavering as the only course open to a reasonable man.

Almost immediately after his imprisonment, Howell was forced into a defence of parliamentary privilege in order to deflect William Prynne's charge that he was 'no friend to Parliaments, but a malignant'. Prynne based his objections on a few mildly anti-parliamentary remarks Howell had made in his first substantial work, *Dodona's Grove*, published in 1640.[46] Like many of Howell's writings, this was a political allegory which cloaked his real thoughts in parables and imagined dialogues, effectively allowing their author to distance himself from his own text if called to account: parables, he would remark in his reply to Prynne, 'though pressed never so hard, prove nothing'. Howell's tale is set in a forest called 'Druina', in which all the personalities of English and European politics were represented as trees or other types of plant: the king, for instance, as a 'Royal Oak'.[47]

It is genuinely difficult to discern Howell's true views of Parliament within the foliage of *Dodona's Grove*, and in defending that work Howell would continue to equivocate so as to offend neither side. In 1644 he issued from the Fleet a series of tracts intended

---

[46] W. Prynne, *The Popish Royall Favourite* (1643), 42, and *A Moderate Apology against a Pretended Calumny* (1644). Howell, *Dodona's Grove, or the Vocall Forest* (two parts, 1640, 1650): 'Dodona' was the site of an ancient Greek oracle, the focus of which was an oak tree. All references to part one will be to the fourth edition (1649), H3061. This was a popular work which acquired readers on both sides of the conflict: Captain Adam Eyre 'red the later end of the Vocall Forest' to pass the time on 24 Sept. 1647 (A. Eyre, *A Dyurnall or Catalogue*, in *Yorkshire Diaries and Autobiographies in the Seventeenth and Eighteenth Centuries*, ed. H. J. Morehouse (Surtees Soc., 65; 1877), 63).

[47] The choice of an oak to represent the king is more than a mere allusion to its 'royal' qualities. The oak was equated with Christian virtues such as fortitude, and the prophetic reference in Isa. 6: 13 was associated with the Virgin (J. Douglas Stewart, '"Death Moved not his Generous Mind": Allusions and Ideas, Mostly Classical, in Van Dyck's Work and Life', in A. K. Wheelock, jun., S. J. Barnes, and J. S. Held (eds.), *Anthony Van Dyck* (Washington, DC, 1990), 72; I am indebted to Professor Stewart for a copy of his valuable essay and a helpful discussion of neo-Stoic iconography). Neo-Stoics also equated the oak with constancy, a virtue that Charles I's defenders, Howell included, repeatedly claimed on his behalf (see Howell, *His Majesties Royal Declaration or Manifesto to all Forrein Princes and States, Touching his Constancy in the Protestant Religion*, in Howell's *Twelve Severall Treatises, of the Late Revolutions in these Three Kingdomes; Deducing the Causes thereof from their Originals* (1661), H3123).

to present a carefully worded, moderate position, and at the same time to urge a general return to reason. *England's Teares* consists of a series of 'laments' from England to the City of London, in which are elaborated the very themes of conscience and constancy which he would work out more abstractly in *The Vision* a few years later.[48] According to England, all her present woes are due to passion and in particular to jealousy, and she expresses the hope that 'my king and great counsell will take a course to bring them to their old English temper again, to cure me of this vertigo, and preserve me from ruine'. This is hardly an encouragement to Cavalier Royalism but rather a plea for flexibility on both sides: Howell wished to persuade the King that his own prerogative would be enhanced by taking the advice of this 'Great Council', and subjects that they ought to defer to the king's judgement.

I desire my gracious soveraign to think that it was never held inglorious or derogatory for a king to be guided and steer his course by the compasse of his great councell, and to make his understanding descend and condescend to their advice; nor was it ever held dishonourable for subjects to yield and bow to their king (to be willows, not okes) . . . Let them consider well they are but outward church-rites and ceremonies they fight for, as the rigidst sort of reformers confesse.[49]

Parliament must 'consider that the royal prerogative is like the sea, which as navigators observe, what it loseth at one time or in one place, gets always in some other'. The King, in turn, must realize that 'the privilege of parliament, the laws and liberties of the

[48] Howell, *England's Teares for the Present Wars* (1644), H3070, trans. into Latin as *Angliae suspiria, & lachrymae* (1646), H3055; Howell, *The Preheminence and Pedigree of Parlement* (1644), H3106. Under the slightly different title *The Pre-eminence and Pedigree of Parlement*, this work is also appended to the second (Oxford, 1644, H3059) and subsequent editions of the first part of *Dodona's Grove*. This text may have been issued without the permission of either Howell or his usual printer, Richard Heron, who acquired rights to both on 4 Nov. 1645 (Arber, i. 201). Both *England's Teares* and *The Pre-eminence and Pedigree of Parlement* were printed by Heron separately in 1644 and republished together later that year in a 'second' edition (really only a reprint with minor corrections, despite Howell's claim to have revised each tract) entitled *Two Discourses, Lately Reviewed and Enrich'd by the Author*. Both the single editions and the *Two Discourses* were printed by Heron, who claimed in a note at the beginning of the latter that he was presenting the works together for the convenience of the reader and because they had been earlier 'surreptitiously printed in Oxford, and els where, but mistaken in divers places'. In citing these works I have used the texts of each appended to the fourth (1649) edition of the first part of *Dodona's Grove*, H3061. *Dodona's Grove* occupies pp. 1–168 of this and is followed by *England's Teares* at 169–91; the *Pre-eminence* follows, separately paginated, 1–23.

[49] *England's Teares*, 163, 174, 184.

subject, is the firmest support of his crown, that his great councel is the truest glass wherein he may discern his peoples love, and his own happiness'. The Queen, now abroad, ought to return to play the peacemaker, to intercede between her husband and his Great Council; this, in turn, will recall Parliament to its proper function as a law-making body proferring advice to the Crown, and will wrest it from the hands of 'polemicall committees'. The true Parliamentarian's duty in all this is to lay aside individual zeal —what is, again, being mistaken for conscience—and 'regulate all exorbitant fancies of novelists, in the exercise of holy religion'. Without obedience and the subordination to law of the 'changeable humours and extravagancies of men, there can be no peace or piety'; the chaos will continue and England will likely fall victim to decay of trade and foreign invasion.[50]

The obverse of this tract balancing the duties of king, nobles, and Parliament to each other and to the country can be found in Howell's praise of Parliament itself in *The Pre-eminence and Pedigree of Parlement*, a tract which in substance and style hearkens back to earlier works on parliamentary privilege by John Selden and Sir Robert Cotton, both of whose works Howell would eventually edit.[51] In this tract Howell assumes the perspective of the Parliamentarian, and ascribes most of what is good in English law, including Magna Carta, to its influence. It is the great strength of England and its monarchy that it maintains such an institution, in contrast to other realms; it is parliament which makes the king rule over free men, not slaves, and through which he may remedy their grievances. No one who loves England can be antagonistic to Parliament's role as a legislature. 'Therfore whosoever is avers or disaffected to this soveraign law making court, cannot have his heart well planted within him: he can be neither good subject, nor

[50] Ibid. 185, 186–7, 188.

[51] In an undated manuscript letter to John Selden, Howell sent several of his works to the great lawyer, praising the latter's 'universality of knowledge' (BL MS Harl. 7003, fo. 374). Howell's defence of parliamentary and especially aristocratic privilege was influenced by Selden's *Priviledges of the Baronage of England* (1642), and he would later publish an English edition of Selden's *Mare clausum*. Howell's debt to Cotton was, if anything, even stronger (K. Sharpe, *Sir Robert Cotton 1586–1631: History and Politics in Early Modern England* (Oxford, 1979), 223–47; R. Cotton, *Cottoni posthuma: Divers Choice Pieces of that Renowned Antiquary Sir Robert Cotton*, ed. J. Howell (1651); this was dedicated by Howell in Apr. 1651 to the Parliamentarian officer Sir Robert Pye; in his preface Howell remarks that all Cotton's efforts in Parliament 'were to assert the publick liberty, and that prerogative and priviledge might run in their due channels').

good patriot; and therfore unworthy to breathe English air, or have any benefit, advantage, or protection from the laws.'[52]

In the second part of the tract, Howell extended this rule to himself, in order to deny both that he was in any way a 'malignant', and that he was hostile to Parliament, 'that great Senate, that high Synedrion, wherein the wisdom of the whole state is epitomised'. He held the Long Parliament to be of 'the wholsomest constitution (and done by the highest and happiest reach of policy that ever was established in this island, to perpetuate the happiness thereof)'. Above all, Howell expressed the wish that his reader might know his innocence by peering into his heart. 'I could wish there were a crystal window in my brest,' he wrote, 'through which the world might espie the inward motions and palpitations of my heart, then would he be certified of the sincerity of this protestation.'[53]

Any malignity on his part, Howell insists, springs from his humours, not his mind, and he goes to bed at night without harbouring grudges or evil thoughts. Yet, he admits, all men are unbalanced in some capacity or other; according to 'Stoick' principle, the world unfolds as it does because of 'this innate, mutual strife'.[54] Explaining the controverted passages of *Dodona's Grove*, Howell admitted that these did indeed criticize the behaviour of *particular* MPs in the Short Parliament. But, he added, he had never intended in it to offend Parliament *as an institution*, having once been a Member and hoping some day to be so again. In any case, whatever he wrote of State affairs in 1639–40 was not necessarily applicable in the changed circumstances of 1643. Events and situations change, and men must respond accordingly, without being taken to task for apparent inconsistencies. 'Not one amongst twenty is the same man to day as he was four yeers ago, in point of judgement, which turns and alters according to the circumstances

[52] Howell, *The Pre-eminence and Pedigree of Parlement*, 13.

[53] Ibid. 14. This remark, a classical commonplace, was also made by James I in his speeches to Parliament in 1605 and 1610 (*The Political Works of James I*, ed. C. H. McIlwain (Cambridge, Mass., 1918; repr. New York, 1965), 285, 306). Protesting his sincerity would prove a major impetus behind the several volumes of the *Familiar Letters*, letters being for Howell the 'keys of the mind', which 'open all the boxes of one's breast, all the cells of the brain, and truly set forth the inward man' (*FL* 495). In electing to follow the Ciceronian and Senecan epistolary model, rather than the inward monologue made public of essayists such as Montaigne or Bacon, Howell further emphasized his own apparent lack of artifice, without necessarily closing off the possibility that what is said in such writings may be dissimulation.

[54] *The Pre-eminence and Pedigree of Parlement*, 15; *FL* 559; Howell, *The Parly of Beasts*, sig. b; Saunders, *Justus Lipsius*, 191, 196, 205.

and successe of things.' A decision to act one way at one time in no way binds a man to similar actions in the future. Even beliefs may change, in accordance with the principle that experience is the best tutor. 'It hath been always my practice,' Howell declared, 'in the search and eventilation of natural verities, to keep to myself a philosophical freedom, and not to make any one's opinion so magisterial and binding, but that I might be at liberty to recede from it upon more pregnant and powerful reasons.'[55] If this seems to a modern reader very much like cynical special-pleading, it is also an espousal of constancy and, by implication, of the need to dissemble. Constancy combined with dissimulation allows the politic man to trim his sails in the face of changes in the wind which, over a long voyage, will matter not; they permit both the adjustment of principle to circumstance and, where necessary, its disguise.

While he acknowledged the necessity of flexibility, Howell paradoxically regarded personal ties such as those of *amicitia*, the 'religion of friendship', as inviolable.[56] Repaying loyalty in kind was particularly important, and Howell never forgot the principal blemish on his royal oak, Charles I's surrender of Strafford's life in 1641. This was an issue which apparently gave Howell some difficulty because of the clear conflict it presented between conscience and duty, and his position here is not altogether consistent with his views elsewhere. When, in 1650, he extended the allegory of *Dodona's Grove* into the 1640s, he attempted a half-hearted casuistical explanation of the king's apparent betrayal of 'Rhodophil' (Strafford) to his enemies.[57] Should Charles have assented to the execution of his trusted servant, having already defiantly proclaimed in the 'Senate' that he would not? In Howell's version of events, a way out is offered by the primate of Lurana, who argues that 'his Majesty had two consciences, one personall the other politicall, and though the first resisted, he might do it by the second'.[58] The

---

[55] *The Pre-eminence and Pedigree of Parlement*, 22; *FL* 533; cf. M. Aurelius, *Meditations*, VIII. xvi: 'To change your mind and defer to correction is not to sacrifice your independence.'

[56] *FL* 74, 194, 442.

[57] *Dodona's Grove, or the Vocall Forest*, pt. two (1650); *FL* 600–2.

[58] *Dodona's Grove*, pt. two, 79. Howell's allegory or his memory has slipped here: the primate of Lurana (Ireland) was of course Ussher. But it was the archbishop of York, John Williams, who had in fact counselled Charles (against the advice of Bishop Juxon that the king could not assent to a Bill which condemned a man whom he knew to be innocent) of his public versus private consciences (S. R. Gardiner, *History of England from the Accession of James I to the Outbreak of the Civil War, 1603–1642* (10 vols.; 1883–4), ix. 365).

king's assent, however personally repugnant, may have been the correct decision at the time, made under extreme pressure during a highly inflammatory political situation. But, as it turned out, Rhodophil's sacrifice, and the king's subordination of personal conviction to national need, had quite the opposite effect: while briefly silencing the noise of the 'Poplar' assembly (the pun is Howell's) for a moment, it lowers the upper house of the Elms (nobles) in public esteem to such a degree that a huge gap between king and people is opened up. Unlike James Harrington, who would look further back, Howell placed the decline of aristocratic influence in England squarely in Charles I's hands. Other attacks follow, first against the 'prime Yew' (Archbishop Laud), who was 'cried up to be the source of all the present calamities', then several of the judges—accused of allowing arbitrary power—and finally the courts themselves. The floodgates of innovation are opened wide, the worst thing which can happen to a balanced commonwealth:

Innovations are of dangerous consequence in all things, specially in a setled and well temper'd state, therfore ther should be great heed taken before any ancient court of judicature erected time out of mind as a pillar to support common justice by the wisdom of our progenitors, be quite put down; for it may shake the whole frame of government.[19]

If the King could be faulted for ignoring his own conscience, the fault on the other side was not lack of conviction but too much faith in it, especially among the Presbyterians, for whom 'Spirituall pride went under the name of tendernes of conscience'. Though MPs have a duty to assert liberties and make wholesome laws, they bear some of the responsibility for the recent calamities, for failing collectively to exercise *moderation* in their demands, 'that golden rule wherby all great counsells should square their deliberations'. In a two-part dialogue entitled *Casuall Discourses, and Interlocutions betwixt Patricius and Peregrin*, largely concerned with events in 1641– 2,[60] Peregrine, a traveller, asks Patricius, a nobleman, to explain

---

[19] *Dodona's Grove*, pt. two, 88–90, 117; J. Harrington, *The Commonwealth of Oceana* (1656), in *The Political Works of James Harrington*, ed. J. G. A. Pocock (Cambridge, 1977), 190–8; B. Manning, 'The Aristocracy and the Downfall of Charles I', in B. Manning (ed.), *Politics, Religion and the English Civil War* (1973), 36–80. Howell believed that many of the problems which had led to the Civil War had origins in the earlier seventeenth century, but did not go so far in this regard as Arthur Wilson, whose *History of Great Britain* (1653), on which see *FL* 613, blames the Civil War largely on the government of James I.

[60] *Dodona's Grove*, pt. two, 157, 167; Howell, *Casuall Discourses, and Interlocutions betwixt Patricius and Peregrin* (1643?). A complete version of this tract, revised by Howell in the late

the causes of current distempers. Patricius replies that, just as there appear from time to time storm clouds to disrupt the weather, and monsters to violate nature, so even within the most well-balanced kingdom there are those with rotten hearts, in this case 'a pack of perverse people (composed for the most part of the scummie and basest sort) multiplied in England, who by a kind of natural inclination, are opposit so point blank to monarchy in state, and hierarchy in church, that I doubt if they were in Heven . . . they would go near to repine at the monarchical power of God Almighty himself'. This number embraces the English Presbyterians who stirred up the London populace, and the barbarous Irish rebels.[61] It also includes the preachers who incited rebellion in Scotland where 'the woman [sic] and baser sort of mechaniks threw stooles and stones at the bishops heads' on reading of the liturgy: dislike of the Scots as quixotic trouble-makers is a recurring theme of Howell's work.[62] But the most blameworthy are several of the

---

1650s, would not appear until 1661, when it was reprinted complete with a 1642 imprint, in *Twelve Severall Treatises*. As Patricius notes at p. 119 in a moment of authorial intrusion, the very discourse in which they are engaged 'was stopp'd in the press by the tyranny of the times, and not suffer'd to see open light till now'. On 21 July 1643 George Thomason purchased a book by Howell, not listed by Wing, entitled *A Discourse Continued between Patricius and Peregrine Touching the Civill Wars of England and Ireland* (G. K. Fortescue, *Catalogue of the Pamphlets, Books, Newspapers, and Manuscripts Relating to the Civil War, the Commonwealth, and Restoration, Collected by George Thomason, 1640–1661* (2 vols.; Kraus repr., Nendeln, Liechtenstein, 1969), i. 275). Howell's *The True Informer, who Discovers to the World the First Grounds of this Ugly Rebellion and Popular Tumults in England, Scotland, and Ireland. Deducing the Causes therof in an Historicall Discours from their Originall. Written in the Prison of the Fleet, anno 1642*, two editions of which appeared with an Oxford imprint (possibly spurious) in 1643 (H3121, H3122), would seem to be the edition acquired by Thomason, sometimes listed bibliographically as *Discourses between Patricius and Peregrine* or as *The Historicall Passages of England since the Beginning of this Miserable Blood-shed and Breach of all Good Lawes by Rebells, from October 1642 to this Present July, 1643*. Neither of these last two titles occurs in Wing, but they are mentioned respectively in W. T. Lowndes, *The Bibliographers' Manual of English Literature*, ed. H. G. Bohn (6 vols.; 1869), ii. 1129–30, and in *National Union Catalogue: Pre-1956 Imprints*, (723 vols.; Chicago, 1968–81), vol. 257, 176.

[61] *Casuall Discourses*, 11; Howell, *Of the Land of Ire*, in *Twelve Severall Treatises*, 201–7, dedicated to Mr E. P. (Endymion Porter), from the Fleet in Apr. 1643; the latter book was first published under the pseudonym Philerenus as *Mercurius Hibernicus* (Bristol, 1644), H3093.

[62] *Casuall Discourses*, 16; *FL* 345; cf. Howell, *Bella Scot-Anglica. A Brief of all the Battells, and Martiall Encounters which have Happened 'twixt England and Scotland* (1648), repr. in *Some of Mr Howell's Minor Works* (1654), H3115, the thesis of which may be summed up in Howell's statements that 'Scotland hath been alwayes apt and forward to apprehend any occasion to invade and visit her neighbour England', and that 'the Scots have been alwayes farre inferiour to the English (except in these latter unlucky invasions) in poynt of true prowesse, and national power' (p. 17). Howell repeats an image from one of the critical Tacitean texts of the early 1600s, Traiano Boccalini's *The New-Found Politicke*, trans. John Florio *et al.* (1626),

King's servants, such as Strafford's enemy, the older Sir Henry Vane, opportunistic nobles like the Duke of Hamilton and Earl of Holland, and the Members of both Houses who stirred up the mob during the trial and attainder of Strafford. The hounding of the 'Straffordians' was for Howell a good example of the violation of true parliamentary liberty, of the principles of Magna Carta and the Petition of Right. 'I thought that freedom of opinion and speech, were one of the prime priviledges of that great nationall Senat.' Worse, it is another instance of the persecution of men 'because against the dictamen of their consciences they would not vote the earl of Strafford to death'.[63]

In flinging about such charges of disloyalty, Howell may have been displacing perceptions of his own behaviour on to others. This sort of projection is perhaps most evident in a 'letter' allegedly written in 1644, and first published four years later, to his remote kinsman Philip, Earl of Pembroke, in which Howell chided the former Lord Chamberlain for putting personal conviction ahead of his oaths to the king.[64] From the early days of James I, through the Protestation, the Solemn League and Covenant and the Engagement, to the Glorious Revolution, oaths were a frequent topic of discussion, especially in casuistical literature. Howell's treatment of this subject in his letter to Pembroke casts further light on the reciprocal duty between subjects and sovereign and adds a further dimension to his peculiar doctrine of conscience.

The oath, to Howell, is the most sacred of all ties which bind one person to another, and the grave consequences which ensue from its breaking provide another recurrent theme of his writings.[65] The

---

116–17, wherein the shade of Lorenzo de Medici, placing England in the balance of Europe, finds it weighs less with Scotland attached.

[63] *Casuall Discourses*, 32.

[64] Howell, *A Letter to the Earle of Pembrooke* (1647), H3085, repr. in *Twelve Severall Treatises*, 122–41, as *A Sober and Seasonable Memorandum Sent to the Right Honourable Philip Late Earl of Pembrock, and Montgomery, &c. To Mind him of the Particular Sacred Ties (besides the Common Oath of Allegiance and Supremacy) wereby he was bound to Adhere to the King his Liege Lord and Master. Presented to him in the Hottest Brunt of the Late Civill Wars*, to which edition I refer. The tract is dated at p. 141 'From the Prison of the Fleet 3 Septembris 1644. J.H.'

[65] Howell's various treatises on foreign governments discuss the important ceremonial role of oaths, and the solemnity involved in taking them; e.g. *A Discours of the Empire, and of the Election of a King of the Romans, the Greatest Business of Christendom now in Agitation* (1658), H3065, 101–5. Dated from Howell's residence in Holborn, 1 Jan. 1659, this book thus appeared six months after the successful imperial election of Leopold I, and, perhaps more significantly, three months after the death of Cromwell renewed questions about the establishment of the Protectorate on a hereditary principle.

motto *Juramentum ligamen conscientiae maximum* which appears on the title-page indicates the theme of this missive: Pembroke has violated rather than honoured his conscience by breaking the sacred oaths he had sworn to his royal master. 'Now, the strongest tye, the solemnest engagement and stipulation that can be betwixt the soul and her Creator, is an oath,' by which Howell means not swearing but 'serious and legall oaths, taken with a calm prepared spirit, either for the asserting of truth, and conviction of falshood, or for fidelitie in the execution of some office or binding to civill obedience and loyaltie, which is one of the essentiall parts of a Christian'.[66] To break an oath, as Pembroke and others have done, is not to follow one's conscience but to dishonour it, since any oath must have been taken on reflection and with sincerity in order to have effect. Once taken, it is not retractable *even if it conflicts* with one's conscience—though, here again, Howell's notion of conscience is one dictated not by personal sensitivity but by an awareness of tradition and duty. To repudiate a legal oath is thus to succumb to passion, not conscience. Conversely, to force another to take an oath is to destroy the proper relationship between the spoken statement of fealty and the inner voice which attests to its rightness; doubtless with the Solemn League and Covenant in mind, Howell chides those who 'of late yeares have fram'd such formidable coercive generall oaths to serve them for engins of state to lay battery to the consciences and soules of poor men, and those without the assent of their soveraign, and opposit point blank to former oaths they themselves had taken'.[67]

'DOWN-RIGHT DEALING'

By the time Howell's letter to Pembroke appeared in print, the first War had been fought and the country was settling in for two tense years of tortuous negotiation and diplomacy between king, army, Parliament, and the Scots. Howell had once cited approvingly the proverb that 'the spectator oft-times sees more than the gamester'; a prisoner still, he played upon his non-involvement in

---

[66] Howell, *A Sober and Seasonable Memorandum*, in *Twelve Severall Treatises*, 123, 124. For similar language in another neo-Stoic, see Bishop Hall's disquisition on oaths, *Certaine Irrefragable Propositions Worthy of Serious Consideration* (1639), 1–7; F. L. Huntley, *Bishop Joseph Hall 1574–1656, a Biographical and Critical Study* (Cambridge, 1979).

[67] Howell, *A Sober and Seasonable Memorandum*, in *Twelve Severall Treatises*, 125.

the war in order to encourage all parties to come to terms. In a short pamphlet tract entitled *Down-right Dealing, or the Despised Protestant Speaking Plain English*, he continued to present himself as 'an impartiall observer of the present transactions of the court, city, and camp', devoted only to the public peace.[68] The central theme of this tract is that the War has done little to resolve the tensions of 1642. As Lipsius had once put it, the pursuit of armed victory with the attendant risk of defeat is less desirable a way to end a civil war than the achievement of a negotiated settlement.[69] Howell's intent is not to nurture further faction or discontent 'but rather to quench it', and he begins by appealing to King Charles to come to terms with his enemies: 'Now forasmuch as what is past recall, is also past cure, since what might have been commanded, cannot now be entreated, since power cannot, policy must, since rage cannot prevaile, let reason reconcile, make necessity a vertue, and rather conquer by courtesie, then compell by soveraignty.'[70]

Howell was now, be it noted, urging a degree of flexibility far beyond that which he had put to the King in his earlier writings: even tradition might now have to be jettisoned for the sake of peace. The King ought at least be prepared to put his own duty as monarch ahead of thoughts of prerogative and religious convention in the face of overwhelming opposition to them; to precisely what sort of settlement he would have Charles agree remains unclear, though some form of presbytery is implied. 'Can it consist with Wisdome', Howell asks, 'to esteem any thing to [*sic*] great or good to be parted withall, for the reconcilement of so bloody a difference, for the making up so large a breach?' Is there any point of principle so great that it cannot be let slip to stem the 'deluge of crimson confusions, as have already and do dayly again threaten to break in upon your kingdomes?' Ultimately, this is nothing less than a call for the King to do exactly what Williams had counselled in the case of Strafford: subordinate his private conscience to public duty. Not, as Parliament might have it, by taking some false oath such as the Solemn League and Covenant,

---

[68] *Down-right Dealing, or the Despised Protestant Speaking Plain English to the Kings Most Excellent Majesty, the Honourable Houses of Parliament. The City of London. The Army. And all other Peace-Desiring Commons of this Divided and Self-Destroying Kingdome* (1647), H3069 (copy in the Thomas Fisher Rare Book Library of the University of Toronto). For similar sentiments, see *FL* 538 (10 Dec. 1647).

[69] Lipsius, *Sixe Bookes of Politickes*, VI. vii. 106; Tuck, 'Scepticism and Toleration', 22.

[70] Howell, *Down-right Dealing*, 3, 5.

but merely through allowing reason and common sense to prevail in negotiations. 'Now is the time', Howell concludes, 'to manifest your self herein, and by some self-denying testimony effectually act for the re-establishing the poor Commons of England in their ancient birth-rights . . .'[71]

But such pragmatism must run both ways. As for the 'Grave Senators' of Parliament, to whom Howell next turned, he wonders aloud if it can 'consist with the peace and wellfare of the kingdome, especially considering the state and temper of the people, and the present exigences of the State', that they should be themselves divided into multiple factions and interests. Howell asks that they put aside all differences and 'unanimously joyn and act for the securing of the kingdome'. A similar appeal is made to the citizens of London, who, even more than Parliament, have allowed faction to rule faith. Again, too great a sensitivity to private conscience has paradoxically led to the decay of genuine Christian piety.

Hath your earnest pursuit of Religion, forst Religion to a squat; truely you have strove so much for Religion in the Church that it is to be feared you have lost it in your hearts; these are the fruits of division, your presbytery, and independency, your outward formes and formall circumstances; what have you strove so long for the shaddow that you have lost the substance.[72]

As for the 'gentlemen' of the army (by which it is clear that Howell meant the senior officers), who are 'swaid by passion not reason', they, too, must be prepared to lay aside 'particular interests' in the name of peace. All sides must co-operate to exorcise the 'spirit of fury' that grips the land. 'Let soveraigns seek the good of their subjects, and subjects the honour and peace of their soveraigns. Let parliaments be faithful, and people peaceable. . . . Let king, parliament, city, army, and people unite and joyn in the bonds of love, and leave judging, suspecting and reviling one another.'[73]

---

[71] Ibid. 6, 7; for Williams's advice, see above, n. 58.
[72] Ibid. 7, 8, 9.
[73] Ibid. 13, 16.

ESTABLISHING AN ENGLISH VENICE

Such pacificism was, of course, unsuccessful, and it is evident from works first published anonymously in 1648 and 1649, and later reprinted by Howell, that he regarded the imprisonment, trial, and execution of the King as acts of an arbitrary and tyrannical government, driven by a base mob:

> So fell great Britains Oke by a wild crew
> Of mongrel shrubs which underneath him grew;
> So fell the lyon by a pack of curs,
> So the rose wither'd twixt a knot of burs
> So fell the Eagle by a swarm of gnats,
> So the whale perished 'twixt a shoal of sprats.[74]

But the conscience, Howell remarked in one of his letters, is 'apt to follow the conqueror', and he apparently found ways to keep his own clear while taking steps to gain favour with the new regime and improve his circumstances. As he himself had once ironically written about Sir Walter Ralegh, 'What will not one in Captivity promise, to regain his Freedom?'[75] Although no evidence survives that he actively sought employment by the commonwealth regimes, neither did he refuse it: he participated, likely as an interpreter, in a case against the Spanish ambassador brought to the Council of State in 1649, and two years later he translated, at the Council's instance, the Spanish account of the trial of the assassins of the republic's ambassador Anthony Ascham.[76] For all his protests against forced oaths, it is likely that Howell took the Engagement (the prerequisite for any state employment); at any event he reiterated his loyalty to the Long Parliament in the second part of *Dodona's Grove*, wherein he declared himself bound to submit to

[74] Howell, 'A Sudden Rupture upon the Horrid Murthering of his Late Majesty' (n.d.), *Poems upon Divers Emergent Occasions*, 96. Cf. comments on the 'black tragedy' of 1649 in *FL* 552 (20 Mar. 1649), and Howell's sentiments in the following works: *A Glance upon the Ile of Wight*, item 11 in *Twelve Severall Treatises* (also in *Some of Mr Howell's Minor Works*, 373–93); *An Inquisition after Blood* (1649), H3080; *A Winter Dreame* (1649), H3129 (*Some of Mr Howell's Minor Works*, 1–20). On seventeenth-century attitudes to the mob, whose passions were contrasted by Stoics and neo-Stoics with the rationality of the nobleman, see C. Hill, 'The Many-Headed Monster', in *Change and Continuity in Seventeenth-Century England* (1974), 181–204.

[75] *FL* 23.

[76] *Cal. SP Dom. 1649–50*, 178 (9 June 1649); A. de Hierro, *The Process and Pleadings in the Court of Spain, upon the Death of Anthony Ascham*, trans. J. Howell and printed by W. Dugard, printer to the Council of State (1651).

anything done by its authority in Church or State.[77]

Released on bail from the Fleet some time in 1650, and adjusting to the prospect of life in a republic, Howell dedicated to the Rump his 1651 survey of the history and government of Venice, *S.PQ.V.* Ostensibly a plea to all Christian nations to come to Venice's aid in its hour of need, it is difficult to see this as anything other than an attempt to impress the 'most noble senators' of England, the Rump MPs, by drawing parallels between the two republics. 'England hath reson to affect Venice more than any other, for in point of security ther is much resemblance between them, being both seated in the sea, who is their best protector.'[78] The book casts further light on his belief in constancy in political life, and on his related conviction that a reassertion of aristocratic influence would be necessary in the new commonwealth if its descent into the humorous anarchy of a popular state was to be arrested: a position which, somewhat strangely, anticipates in reverse that to be taken by Milton a few years later in citing Venice as one possible model against the return of monarchy.[79]

As early as 1642, in his *Instructions for Forreine Travel*, Howell had praised Venice above all European states. To a degree, Howell shared the general distrust of things Italian so common in Renaissance English thought: he warned his reader that 'she is able to turn a saint into a devil, and deprave the best natures'. Though Italy was 'the nurse of policy', it encouraged vice as much virtue— elsewhere he would quote the familiar saying, *'Inglese italianato è diavolo incarnato'*. Genoa he especially disliked, subscribing to the epithet that Genoa had women without shame and men without conscience.[80] Rome, or Petropolis as he called it allegorically in a number of works, he treated with the same caution as a city ruled

[77] Howell, *Dodona's Grove*, pt. two, 168–79; J. M. Wallace, *Destiny his Choice: The Loyalism of Andrew Marvell* (Cambridge, 1968), 43–68; Q. Skinner, 'Conquest and Consent: Thomas Hobbes and the Engagement Controversy', in G. E. Aylmer (ed.), *The Interregnum: The Quest for Settlement, 1646–1660* (1972), 79–98.

[78] Howell, *S.PQ.V. A Survay of the Signorie of Venice, of her Admired Policy and Method of Government* (1651), sig. B1ʳ (entered at the Stationer's Register, 7 Jan. 1651: Arber, i. 358); Z. S. Fink, *The Classical Republicans* (2nd edn.; Evanston, Ill., 1962), 42–4, 48–9.

[79] J. Milton, *The Readie & Easie Way to Establish a Free Commonwealth* (two edns., 1660), in *Complete Prose Works of John Milton*, ed., D. M. Wolfe (8 vols.; New Haven, Conn., 1953–82), rev. vol. viii. 371, 436.

[80] Howell, *Instructions for Forreine Travel* (1642), ed. E. Arber (English Reprints, 16; 1869), 41; J. Lipsius, *A Direction for Travailers*, trans. J. Stradling (1592); Boccalini, *The New-Found Politicke*, 172–5.

by the papacy; Florence he regarded as an unstable republic that had only recently learnt the virtue of monarchy; Naples was a thorn in the side of the Spanish monarchy, its people temperamentally given to revolt. But Venice he adored, 'a rich magnificent city seated in the very jaws of Neptune'. Both in the *Instructions* and in many later writings, particularly *S.PQ.V.*, Howell presented Venice as the very essence of a balanced state, apparently untroubled by its lack of a real monarchy, though, equivocating once again, he protested against the 'shallowest and silliest sort' of Cavaliers who spoke as if Howell 'had chang'd his principles, and were affected to republiques'.[81]

Howell had certainly read Guicciardini, and it is reasonably likely that he was familiar with Gasparo Contarini's classic praise of Venice.[82] In discussing Venetian institutions, Howell adopted the panegyrical tone of Contarini's well-known text, stressing the predominance of the aristocracy as the source of Venetian stability. Never one to give up a clever turn of phrase or metaphor, Howell repeatedly plays in his works on the long-standing sexual image of 'fair Adriana' as a virgin, a maritime power, and virtually an island (hence providing a good analogy with England), surviving a thousand years constant in its Christian faith and ever able to maintain a front against perfidious Italian allies, Spanish and French incursions, and the ever-looming threat of the Turk. In the face of all these assaults from without, 'she hath continued a Virgin ever since, nere upon twelve long ages, under the same forme and face of government, without any visible change or symptome of decay, or the least wrinkle of old age'. Its military and commercial prowess derived from its control of the Adriatic, and Howell intended his readers to draw the obvious parallel with England's position in the Channel. This was not, in fact, the only analogy he wished to make, drawing attention to a famous hexagram on Venice by Sannazaro, for which that poet had reputedly received £300 per line.[83] Despite this broad hint, no such remuneration from the Rump was forthcoming. Undaunted, he would write to the Council of State, at some point after the start of the first Dutch War in 1652, proposing that, in view of the devolution of

[81] *FL* 602, 640.

[82] G. Contarini, *The Commonwealth and Government of Venice*, trans. L. Lewkenor (1599); Fink, *The Classical Republicans*, 28–51; J. G. A. Pocock, *The Machiavellian Moment: Florentine Political Thought and the Atlantic Republican Tradition* (Princeton, NJ, 1975), 197, 272–330.

[83] *S.PQ.V*, sig. B2ʳ; *FL* 80.

goverment from monarchy to republic, he should update Selden's 1635 treatise *Mare clausum*, in order to sustain the claims Selden had advanced for England's dominion over the near seas.[84]

Much of Venice's success he ascribed to a collective political wisdom or 'prudence' embodied in the Consiglio dei Pregadi or Senate, rather than in the doge, a mere figure-head. Unlike the fickle Florentines and Milanese, or the unruly Neapolitans, who have endured twenty-eight revolutions in three centuries (including, most recently, Massaniello's), Venice has remained constant to itself, an enemy to change, but prepared to confront it when necessary.

Always more given to peace than war, it has nevertheless kept 'the potentst Princes in a counterpoise; wherby she hath often adapted her designes, and accommodated her self to the condition of the times, and frequently changd thoughts, wills, frends and enemies'.[85] Venetian strength thus derives from its citizens' practice of another virtue praised by neo-Stoics, the maintenance of a peaceful, contemplative, and inward-looking life. Its citizens, 'the truest patriots and most public souls that I have known remaining among men', are commercially prosperous and politically active, in moderation, but the city is also less territorially ambitious than other states. Howell did not accept the commonplace that peace leads inevitably to effeminacy, corruption, faction, and eventually war; a lasting peace should be the supreme good of *imperium*. Nor,

---

[84] BL Add. MS 32093, fo. 370 (Howell to Council of State, n.d., printed in *FL*, supp. 661). A note in the BL catalogue ascribes this letter to '*c*.1657', but 1651–2 makes more sense; in that year there appeared an English translation of Selden by Marchamont Nedham under the title *Of the Dominion, or Ownership of the Sea, Two Books*. This was published by William Dugard by appointment of the Council of State, suggesting Howell had simply put his bid in too late. Not to be outdone, Howell would reissue Nedham's translation in 1663 under the title *Mare clausum; the Right and Dominion of the Sea, in Two Books*. Having been robbed of this opportunity by a man whom he probably regarded as the lowest form of turncoat, Howell had the satisfaction of replacing Nedham's anti-Stuart preface with Selden's original dedication to Charles I, along with an 'advertisement' by himself denouncing Nedham as 'one no way affected to our ancient and happy government of monarchy, who was also an immediate servant to our usurping states', while defending the faithfulness of the Nedham translation on the grounds that in 1652 Selden had still been alive and they would not have had the nerve to 'abuse his writings to his face'.

[85] *S.PQ.V.*, 180; *FL* 78. In 1650 Howell had published his translation of Alessandro Giraffi's *An Exact Historie of the Late Revolutions in Naples*, and compiled a continuation entitled *The Second Part of Massaniello* (1650), H3112A, which would be republished twice, in 1652 and 1663.

apparently, did he share Machiavelli's position, later adopted by
Harrington, that a republic ought to consider sacrificing the stability
of a mixed government for the expansionism possible in a state
dominated by armed citizens.[86]

It is, then, its practice of a particularly *conservative* variety of
prudence or policy that has kept Venice great and which is so
clearly lacking in other Italian and European states. Venetian
conservatism Howell attributes primarily to the dominance of the
nobles who make up the Senate and major councils. Howell
conceded the mixed nature of the Venetian regime: a grain of
monarchy, a dose of democracy, an ounce of optimacy. But it was
the 'ounce' that he expanded upon, in his discussion of the various
noble councils which really ran the city. In drawing some rather
forced analogies between Venetian public officials and classic
Roman officers such as the quaestors (*Camarlinghi*, or treasury
officials), censors *(savi del consiglio)*, and aediles (the various *pro-
vveditori, all'acque, al sal, alle biave,* and other such officers of public
works), Howell was at the same time making a further analogy
with England, through the familiar humanist topos of *similitudo
temporum*, as he had once put it, all human events 'have their
parallels from times past'.[87] His especial praise of the *Consiglio dei
dieci*, here classicized as a more successful and extended version of
the ancient Roman 'Decemvirate', is thus a barely concealed attempt
to provide classical underpinnings for the peculiar position of the
Council of State in relation to the Rump. Although every Venetian
office has a Roman analogue, it is the endurance of the Ten and
the sovereignty of the Senate that attest to Venice's greater
longevity.[88] The 'damage-control' aspect of this message is unmis-
takable: England, having abandoned monarchy, should at least

---

[86] Howell, *Parly of Beasts*, 95; Howell, *A Discourse of Dunkirk* (1664), H3063, *passim*; Fink,
The Classical Republicans, 52–89. It is also part of Venetian character to recognize the difference
between policy (which includes the legitimate practice of secrecy and dissimulation) and
craft: these are similar in end but not in means. Policy, here defined in Lipsian terms, is
honourable, while craft on the other hand 'cares not what oaths she swallows and breaks
afterwards, she cares not what lies, fears, and jealousies she creates to amuse the silly vulgar,
and therby to incite them to arms and rebellion' (ibid. 95); and, unlike policy, craft also
makes religion the cloak for all her sins.

[87] *FL* 508.

[88] The endurance of Venice twice as long as its Roman model (which 'hardly continued
a republic 700 years', p. 206), is also contrasted by Howell with other regimes, e.g. in
Howell, *A Discours of the Empire*, 106–9.

choose to emulate the Venetian version of a republican constitution.

Most of Howell's writing following his release from prison in 1650 or 1651 was literary rather than political: over the next few years his publications included *Londinopolis* (an account of the city's history and major sites of interest), various books on grammar, orthography, and proverbs, numerous translations from French and Italian, and his *Lexicon tetraglotton,* a dictionary in four languages, the publication of which was supported by Bulstrode Whitelocke, a frequent correspondent and reader of Howell's works from 1654 until the Restoration.[89] But the dispersal of the Rump and the advent of the Protectorate required both further comment and still another reversal of direction on Howell's part, this time towards a limited hereditary monarchy. In 1654 he completed a partial edition of the notebooks of Sir John Finet, Charles I's master of the ceremonies, a book which he would publish two years later as further encouragement to Cromwell in the establishment of a quasi-monarchical court.[90] He also reprinted several tracts previously issued anonymously in 1648–9, including *The Instruments of a King,* dealing with the nature of royal sovereignty.[91] A year later, in 1655, Howell dedicated to Cromwell *Som Sober Inspections Made into the Cariage and Consults of the Late Long Parlement,* a devastating

---

[89] Howell, *Lexicon tetraglotton* (1660), H3087; *The Diary of Bulstrode Whitelocke,* ed. R. Spalding (British Academy, Records of Social and Economic History, NS 13; Oxford 1990), 508, and also 393, 413, 485, 492.

[90] J. Finet, *Finetti Philoxenis: Som Choice Observations of Sir John Finett Touching the Reception and Treatment of Forren Ambassadors in England,* ed. J. Howell (1656), F947; *Ceremonies of Charles I: The Note Books of John Finet 1628–1641,* ed. A. J. Loomie (New York, 1987), 13. Howell's edition of Finet covers mainly ceremonies of James I's reign, thereby avoiding mention of his unfortunate successor. Entered in the Stationer's Register on 27 Nov. 1654, this work was published only in April 1656 (Fortescue, *Catalogue,* ii. 145; Arber, i. 460; ii. 56).

[91] The 1654 compilation of *Some of Mr Howell's Minor Works* also includes reprints of Howell's *Letter to the Earl of Pembroke, A Trance or Newes from Hell,* and *Bella Scot-Anglica.* Some of these tracts could be read, in the new circumstances of 1654, not as a plea for the restoration of the Stuarts but as a statement of the need for some sort of monarchical authority in the absence of an effective peerage. Late in the same year there appeared a work which advised the Protector and his council to settle the government by inviting the King back, under certain conditions, following Cromwell's death (J.H., *An Admonition to my Lord Protector and his Councill of their Present Danger* (1654), H1316, dated by Thomason 2 Oct. 1654). This is unlikely to be by Howell, and the second edition of Wing attributes it to James Heath. In style it does not closely resemble any of Howell's known later writings; though its message is broadly similar to that in one of Howell's known later works, *A Brief Admonition of Some of the Inconveniences of all the Three Most Famous Governments Known to the World* (1659), it takes far more critical a view of Cromwell's own behaviour than Howell was prepared to espouse in 1654.

attack on the regime that he had so warmly applauded three years earlier, and on its failure to contain the thirst for novelty rampant among the 'mechanick' populace.[92] Despite Cromwell's prominent role in the execution of the King, Howell flatters Oliver, in tones which echo Marvell's panegyric of the protector published the previous January, as a champion of liberty and property and an opponent of the tyranny of a perpetual Parliament; 'Hercules-like', the Protector has 'quell'd a monster with many heads'.[93]

Given Howell's stated opposition to the Regicide and his instinctive Royalism, this was a masterpiece of dissimulation, recognized as such by at least one Royalist: Sir William Dugdale gleefully recommended that a friend read Howell's newly published work, 'wherein, cogging up [the] protector (for to him he dedicates it) with some superlative language for destroying that monster (as he calls it) [he] hath taken the boldness to speak more truth, barefaced, than any man that hath wrote since they sate; nor doth he spare the Scot and Presbyterian'[94]. But it also suggests that Howell had lost his earlier faith in the aristocracy's ability to provide a principle of balance within a republican government. The political silence or exile of all but a few peers since 1649, and the apparent domination of the Rump regime by the worst sorts of sectaries, impelled Howell to shift the weight of his argument back towards the more straightforwardly monarchical opinions he had espoused in the early 1640s. This loss of confidence in the peerage is conveyed in verses, published in 1654, which Howell penned to commemorate the death of his friend the Earl of Dorset, who had died two years previously:

[92] *Som Sober Inspections Made into the Cariage and Consults of the Late Long Parlement, whereby Occasion is Taken to Speak of Parlements in Former Times, &c.* (1655), H3116. Unless otherwise noted, all references are to the fourth edition, which appeared under the title *Philanglus* (1660), H3102. This is possibly the unspecified work which on 4 Sept. 1655 Howell sent to Whitelocke (a man of similarly moderate views), 'for his judgement of it, before its printing' (Whitelocke, *Diary*, 413). Entered for publication on 4 July, it would appear in print on 24 Sept. (Arber, ii. 1; Fortescue, *Catalogue*, ii. 128).

[93] A. Marvell, 'The First Anniversary of the Government under O.C.', in *Poems and Letters of Andrew Marvell*, ed. H. M. Margoliouth (3rd edn., 2 vols; Oxford, 1971), 108–19; Wallace, *Destiny his Choice*, 107.

[94] 'Read it through, I pray you, upon my recommendation, though in some things he do commit little mistakes, and in others doth blunder a little' (Dugdale to J. Langley, 9 Oct. 1655, HMC, *5th Report*, 176).

Lords have bin long declining, (we well know)
And making their last Testaments, but now
They are defunct, they are extinguish'd all,
And never like to rise by this Lords Fall.[91]

The death of Oliver on 3 September 1658, and the return of
the Rump the following May, did not make the Restoration of the
monarchy inevitable. But it provided a further reminder of the lack
of constitutional stability, and many minds were already running
towards the old regime. In 1659 Howell issued still another political
plea, entitled *A Brief Admonition of Some of the Inconveniences of all the
Three Most Famous Governments Known to the World: With their Comparisons Together*. Once more, Howell presented himself as a moderate appealing for good sense and charity rather than partisanship,
though he acknowledged the difficulty of doing so. 'I know that
many of you will read this pamphlet with prejudicate opinions: but
I think myself as free from that in writing of it, as I am from
any design, but the recalling passionate men to a temper, leading
to a settlement of our countrey.' Again, too, he denied any wish
either to enumerate past wrongs or speculate philosophically on
the abstract advantages of monarchy, aristocracy, and democracy.
Such words 'so charm us with their sounds, that we loose in our
passions the consideration of the things themselves.... I am not
so capable of mending faults in government as of finding of them;
I shall leave that for the wise, but think it a task only for a
truly free parliament, without comptrollers.' Although explicitly
disclaiming strong feelings for or against any of the Aristotelian
forms of government, the tract leans discernibly in the direction
of monarchy on the grounds of national security.[96]

CONSCIENCE AS ITS OWN REWARD

With the return of the King, Howell, now in his mid-sixties, tried
again to achieve the elusive rewards of office. One by one he made
a series of proposals for his employment, each of which was in

[91] Howell, *Ah, Ha; Tumulus, Thalamus: Two Counter-Poems* (1653), H3054; Thomason dated
his copy 12 May 1654 (Fortescue, *Catalogue of the Pamphlets...*, ii. 65, E 228 (1)).

[96] Cf. Howell's letter to Sir Edward Walker of 23 Mar. 1660 concerning fear of Anabaptist
revolt and the decay of trade, and on the likelihood of the King returning (*FL*, supp. 664;
R. Hutton, *The Restoration: A Political and Religious History of England and Wales, 1658–1667*
(Oxford, 1985), 21–123).

turn denied: that he assume the long-promised clerkship of the
Council; that he be appointed secretary to the Commission for the
Regulation of Trade; and that he become tutor, by virtue of his
linguistic skills, to Catherine of Braganza.[97] Howell was not the
only former Royalist to find the rising Stuart sun less warm than
anticipated. Within a year of the Restoration, many of Charles II's
most faithful adherents were to be bitterly disappointed by their
failure to achieve the rewards of loyalty. Many had lost estates and
other personal property, suffered exile or imprisonment, and now
sought recompense if not advancement. Against this, they saw
former Roundheads being favoured, an indemnity being offered to
virtually every subject other than regicides and certain other
excepted persons, and former grandees like Monck, belated con-
verts to Royalism, growing fat with titles and offices. Howell, who
for nearly twenty years had been playing a game of dissimulation,
equivocation, and compromise, now produced a broadside which
offers a final statement of the principles according to which he
had precariously balanced the rival demands of conscience and
ambition. *A Cordial for the Cavaliers* was published by Henry Marsh
in the summer of 1661.[98] Addressed to the 'worthy and deserving
gentlemen' who felt themselves aggrieved by their lack of royal
reward, Howell began by reminding them that 'he who dischargeth
a good conscience, hath enough of his own wherewith to reward
himself, though he receive no compensation from anywhere else'.
Rewards may come from king, country, and God, and in Howell's
view the preservation of the kingdom, and of the status of the
gentry and aristocracy atop it, should be reward enough, at least
for a time; the King would happily reward all his supporters were
he not in great poverty from debts created from twenty years of
struggles with 'that accursed usurping commonwealth'. In the
meantime, he urges the Cavaliers to be patient, citing his own case
as an example of loyalism which has made its own reward.

In the confus'd medley of mundane affairs, the proverb often is verified,
Some have the happ, but some stick still in the gapp. Some have the fortune of
preferment, some not, and twill be so to the worlds end. The author
hereof though during the many yeers that he was in prison for his loyaltie,

[97] *Cal. SP Dom. 1660–1*, 12, 288; *Cal. SP Dom. 1661–2*, 37.
[98] Howell, *A Cordial for the Cavaliers* (1661), H56A and H3058A. The dedication is dated
20 July 1661, only a few days after Howell's futile application to Clarendon (11 July) for
the position of tutor to the Queen (*Cal. SP Dom. 1661–2*, 37).

had sworn over his head in an office of credit that hee shold have had *de jure*, yet it nothing discomposeth him, being more then in hope of a compensation some other way.[99]

Coming from as lukewarm a Royalist as Howell, this must have been too much, and one among the Cavaliers, Roger L'Estrange, was quick to respond, accusing Howell of collaboration first with the Rump and then with Oliver. Like Howell, who was two decades his senior, L'Estrange had spent several years in prison during the first Civil War. Unlike Howell, he had gone abroad in the early 1650s to join the Court in exile, and he cannot have been the only ex-Cavalier to find the *Cordial*'s self-righteous preaching of patience too bitter a pill to swallow. 'The Cordial (Sir) of a good conscience, we carry in our bosomes, for we have not stood out a twenty years persecution, to blood, beggery, and bondage, we knew not why.' Howell must surely have been cut by L'Estrange's sharp rebuke: '*We* never hackny'd out our selves for wages, or reward.'[100] As he had done nearly two decades earlier with Prynne, but from an ironically opposite perspective, Howell was once more obliged to defend his own perceived lack of principles. In his response to L'Estrange, Howell reminded his readers that their highest reward is yet to come as good Christians, and he defended the acts of indemnity as the mercy of a royal conscience itself guided by policy and common sense: if all were guilty of treason who had in any way contributed to the downfall of Charles I, would not the new king have to hang half of his subjects?[101] Howell was a born casuist to the end, and it was only after this rather hollow denial of personal ambition that he finally achieved his reward: a gift of £200 and the new position of Historiographer Royal.[102]

Howell died in 1666 with the literary and political success he had sought having largely eluded him. As Historiographer Royal he wrote little save a discourse on the order of precedence to be kept at meetings of European monarchs; like most of his other

[99] Cf. *FL* 375, wherein Howell states 'in the conduct of human affairs 'tis a rule, that a good conscience hath always within doors enough to reward itself, tho' the success fall not out according to the merit of the endeavour'; ibid. 599: 'A good conscience is a perpetual feast'.

[100] R. L'Estrange, *A Caveat to the Cavaliers or an Antidote against Mistaken Cordials: Dedicated to the Author of a Cordial for the Cavaliers* (1661), L1211, 3, 9, emphasis added.

[101] Howell, *Som Sober Inspections Made into those Ingredients that went to the Composition of a Late Cordial ... for the Satisfaction of som, who Misapprehended the Author* (1661), H3118, 1–14.

[102] *FL*, supp. 669 (Feb. 1662); D. Hay, 'The Historiographers Royal in England and Scotland', *Scottish Historical Review*, 30 (1951), 15–29.

works except the *Familiar Letters*, this has long been forgotten.[103] Howell was neither a great mind nor a man of principle in the modern sense; it is certainly difficult to see him as possessed of strong resolve. But he was true to his own convictions, which simply allowed more 'give' than most political moralists, then and since, usually think proper—this in an era which took seriously the notion that there were absolute goods and evils. I have suggested that the inconsistency and equivocation which mark his words and deeds can best be explained with reference to a particular philosophical outlook of the late Renaissance, that of neo-Stoicism; they also provide an index of the shift in political morality, from principle to prudence, which marks the seventeenth century in many parts of Europe. Howell's 'constancy' fell between the extremes of those who remained unflinchingly committed to one party or the other and the more glaring opportunism of those who more openly changed allegiance with the political winds. How many of Howell's numerous political statements were sincere, and how many mere posturing, we can never know: the techniques of dissimulation which he practised in most of his books were, in this sense, effective ones. But the failures and misfortunes of his career, so clearly reflected in his writings, do provide a suggestive case study of the problem of conscience and of the ways in which the conflicting demands of personal loyalty, public duty, and self-interest could be reconciled in word, if not in action.

---

[103] Howell, Προεδρια βασιλικη:-*Dissertatio de praecedentia* (1664), H31111, simultaneously published in an English edition, H3109.

14
Official Members in the Commons, 1660–1690:
A Study in Multiple Loyalties
JOHN FERRIS

REPRESENTATIVE institutions offer fertile breeding-grounds for split personalities. Even private citizens may at times be distracted by competing demands for their loyalty from the State, from society at large, from their neighbours, from their employers, from various interest groups, from their families, from their narrow self-interest. The representative shares all these pressures, to which he has to add the claims of his constituency, of his political allies, and of the assembly itself. In quiet times, priorities may be determined unconsciously; but few of those who were active in the turbulent political life of seventeenth-century England can have avoided conscious decision-making. Some, it is true, like Sir Gilbert Talbot, seem to have found the process easy. No backwoods squire, but an experienced diplomat and Master of the Jewel-house, he was forced, like all loyal churchmen in office in 1688, to choose between his God and his king. His response was unequivocal: 'If I be chosen a Member of Parliament when his Majesty shall call one, I will, as I have ever done in former Parliaments, be entirely governed and directed by his Majesty in my votes.' A younger son, 'not borne to a shilling', he held his office on a life patent; but this did not protect him when, faithful to his principles after the Revolution, he became a Non-juror. At the age of 84, he was thrown back on his family for support.[1]

If Edward Thurland (Solicitor-General to the Duke of York) was ever conscious of conflicting loyalties, they were not apparent to his executors, for his epitaph describes him as 'always faithful to his God, to his King (even in adversity), and to his friend'. Others saw him rather differently: 'a great promoter of the Act of Parliament whereby the poore Cavileers had the benefitt of all

---

[1] Sir G. Duckett, *Penal Laws and Test Act* (1882), 214; BL MS Harl. 7020, fo. 42ᵛ.

theire wine Lycences . . . given to the Duke of York'; and under the Cabal 'he dare not for his place mumble against the Court'. For him, silence proved golden; he was raised to the judicial bench at a time when political correctness was the overriding qualification, only to resign when the eddies of the Popish Plot made correctness almost impossible to achieve. Fortunate to the last, he died in 1683, before his former employer enjoyed the power to apply the ultimate test to his convictions, a test which might have produced a result different from Talbot's.[2]

John Hervey, Treasurer to Charles II's consort, provides a better-known case of elasticity of conscience. Derided contemptuously as 'a court cully' in 1671 by the same hostile source, he seems in fact to have done rather well out of the Court, adding to an ample income from his Suffolk estates a share in the profits of West End development. His servitude, unlike Talbot's, must have been voluntary; and he sat in the Cavalier Parliament as a government nominee in the Cinque Ports, affording the King double grounds for reproof when he voted against the Danby ministry. In the next division he was found in the other lobby. 'You were not against me to-day,' remarked the gratified monarch. 'No, Sire,' replied the honourable Member, 'I was against my conscience to-day.' This has been seen as no more than an example of courtly wit;[3] but, for the psychologist, wit may represent a last desperate externalization masking irresoluble conflicts within. This study will examine such conflicts in men like Talbot, Thurland, and Hervey, men who simultaneously occupied a seat in Parliament and received payments from the Crown at some time between 1660 and 1690, using for the most part the material in the relevant volumes of the *History of Parliament.*[4]

Co-operation between king and Commons, it has been said, could hardly exist without some devices 'to plant King's servants in the Commons, or to bestow crown offices on Members of the

[2] J. Aubrey, *The Natural History and Antiquities of the County of Surrey* (5 vols.; 1718), iv. 205; BL MS Harl. 7020, fo.39ᵛ; A. F. Havighurst, 'The Judiciary and Politics in the Reign of Charles II', *Law Quarterly Review*, 66 (1950), 229–30. Thurland was buried in his constituency; but his epitaph was trebly secure from the vulgar, being set in the chancel of Reigate parish church, high up, and in Latin. So little store was set by his service in Parliament that it was not even mentioned.

[3] *Burnet's History of My Own Time*, ed. O. Airy (2 vols.; Oxford, 1900), ii. 80–1; A. Browning, 'Parties and Party Organization in the Reign of Charles II', *TRHS* 4th ser., 30 (1948), 26.

[4] B. D. Henning, *The House of Commons 1660–1690* (1983).

Commons, so that some Members of the House looked to two masters'.[5] Nevertheless, concern over these 'placemen', as Gerald Aylmer has pointed out, was a recent phenomenon.[6] Before the Civil War, a distinction was drawn between minor officials and a small group of ministers, basically the Privy Councillors and the 'white staves' who headed the royal household administration. The latter were referred to by parliamentary convention as 'the honourable persons about the chair'—though their unity could be disrupted if peers' sons unfriendly to the government, like Sir Francis Hastings in the first Jacobean Parliament, chose to claim precedence.[7] Thus Denzil Holles was in a good strategic position to prevent the Speaker from leaving the chair on the eventful morning of 4 March 1629.[8] Minor household officials, as we have seen in Hervey's case, seem to have been expected to establish closer links of personal loyalty towards the monarch than, say, the Receiver-General for Hampshire, Gloucestershire, and Wiltshire. John Pym's attitude to the government changed radically during the 1620s, as Russell has shown; but, unlike John Birch in 1678, he could have felt no compulsion to cross the floor, or join the 'mutineers' in the gallery with the young Bulstrode Whitelocke.[9] Nor were the lines so clearly drawn as to affect his chances of re-election, or his relations with his patron, the Earl of Bedford. Privy Councillors, on the other hand, were marked men.[10] The career of Robert Naunton illustrates the peculiar difficulties that they faced. As Secretary of State, he fell victim to a Spanish intrigue between his election for Cambridge University and the assembly of Parliament in 1621. The King forbade him to take his seat, and he obeyed,

---

[5] B. Kemp, *King and Commons 1660–1832* (1957), 1.

[6] G. E. Aylmer, 'Place Bills and the Separation of Powers; Some Seventeenth-Century Origins of the "Non-Political" Civil Service', *TRHS* 5th ser., 15 (1965), 46.

[7] *Proceedings in Parliament 1614*, ed. M. Jansson (Philadelphia, Pa., 1988), 154. The seating of Hastings 'about the chair' is inferred from his consistent placing on committee lists immediately after the Privy Councillors.

[8] BL MS Lansdowne 93, fo. 138.

[9] *The Diary of Bulstrode Whitelocke*, ed. R. Spalding (British Academy Records of Social and Economic History, NS 13; Oxford, 1990), 53; A. Grey, *Debates of the House of Commons 1667–1694* (10 vols.; 1769), vi. 26. For Pym, see C. Russell, 'The Parliamentary Career of John Pym, 1621–1629', in P. Clark, A. G. R. Smith, and N. Tyacke (eds.), *The English Commonwealth 1547–1640* (Leicester, 1979), 147–65.

[10] D. H. Willson, *The Privy Councillors in the House of Commons 1604–1629* (Minneapolis, Minn., 1940), 89.

without a murmur.[11] After regaining office as Master of the Wards he stood for Suffolk in 1626; but his 'greatness' discouraged some of the electorate. 'He was tyed in so partickiuler an obligation to his magesty as if ther was ocasion to speak for the contry he wold be silent.'[12] In Essex in 1628 even the trickery of a complaisant sheriff could not secure the return of another Privy Councillor, Sir Thomas Edmondes, the Treasurer of the Household, and Sir Thomas Fanshawe, the Surveyor-General in the Exchequer.[13] In any case they would probably have lost their seats on petition, for in 1626 decisions on contested elections had left 'never a white staff in the House to beat a dog with'.[14] Sir Francis Bacon believed that he was 'never one hour out of credit with the House'; but he presumed too far in 1614 and provoked a resolution that in future no Attorney-General could be elected. This rule was enforced against Sir Thomas Coventry in 1621 and Sir Robert Heath in 1626,[15] thereby depriving the Crown of its most formidable spokesmen on matters of law.

It was, of course, the Long Parliament that first set about 'garbling' the House on a large scale, beginning with the expulsion of the 'monopolists' in 1641.[16] When all the Royalists had been disabled from sitting, political divergence was less feared than official incompetence, and the Self-Denying Ordinance aimed to separate place and membership by directly opposite means. Instead of officials losing their seats, MPs, with certain favoured exceptions, lost their posts. It was the increase in these exceptions that prompted the publication by Clement Walker in 1648 of the first 'black list' of placemen. But, with the author safely lodged in the Tower for the remainder of his days, the pamphlet could be ignored; and 'under the Rump there was the closest possible union between executive and legislative office'.[17] No longer required as assistants in the House of Lords, even judges could and did take their seats in the Commons.

[11] R. E. Schreiber, *The Political Career of Sir Robert Naunton 1589–1635* (Royal Historical Soc., 24; 1981), 84–5.

[12] *Winthrop Papers*, (Massachusetts Historical Soc.; 1929), 324, 326.

[13] HMC, *Buccleuch and Queensberry*, iii. 324.

[14] PRO C115/N5/8633 (James Palmer to Sir John Scudamore, 25 Mar. 1626).

[15] *The Letters and the Life of Francis Bacon* (7 vols.; 1861–74), iv. 280; T. L. Moir, *The Addled Parliament of 1614* (Oxford 1958), 85–7; Willson, *Privy Councillors*, 217.

[16] M. F. Keeler, *The Long Parliament 1640–1641* (Philadelphia, Pa., 1954), 10.

[17] Aylmer, 'Place Bills', 47–54.

Walker's vitriolic attack on the Long Parliament was posthumously republished in 1660 as *The Mystery of the Good Old Cause*, one sign of the general revulsion against Rumpers and Presbyterians that produced some of the most surprising election results of the century. This was a single-issue election: candidates in open constituencies who identified themselves with a conditional restoration of the Stuart monarchy were swept aside, even where their interests were as well established as those of Sir Dudley North in Cambridgeshire, Richard Knightley in Northamptonshire, and Sir Richard Onslow in Surrey. It was not a totally free election, for other traditional interests were excluded by the last Ordinance of the Long Parliament forbidding the candidature of Cavaliers or their sons.[18] Despite the slow progress of the necessary legislation, there seem to have been no complaints about placemen in the Convention, although presumably the private interests of the twenty-eight MPs who lost their offices during the session might have proved obstructive. This figure does not include those who had accepted temporary army commissions pending disbandment; but alongside them were a number of career officers like John Cloberry and Ralph Knight, who had played significant parts in the Restoration. They might perhaps have been expected to feel, not so much a sense of grievance, since they were for the most part personally well provided for, as a sense of compunction for their less fortunate subordinates. Knight played a courageous role in the Commons, defending some of the most unpopular Republican colonels.[19] But he had nothing to say for the subalterns or the rank and file, an absence of professional solidarity that well illustrates the horizontal divisions that had developed during the dying months of the Commonwealth.

But, as might be expected, there were more winners than losers in the Convention. Salaried office was obtained by fifty-eight sitting

---

[18] It is true that the Ordinance provided a let-out clause excepting those Royalists who had 'manifested their good affections to this Parliament' (C. H. Firth and R. S. Rait (eds.), *Acts and Ordinances of the Interregnum 1642–1660* (3 vols.; 1911), iii. 1472). No doubt this was liberally interpreted by the returning officers in many instances, just as they probably construed 'aiding, abetting, or assisting in any Warr against the Parliament' as narrowly as they dared. Hence the restrictions on candidature have been seen as nugatory; but this fails to explain why Sir Edward Seymour and Sir Frederick Cornwallis, for example, with normally safe borough seats, should have had to wait for by-elections held after the Restoration.

[19] *CJ* viii. 64; Bodl. MS dep. 9/3430, S. Bowman, diary, fo. 5ᵛ; *The Parliamentary or Constitutional History of England*, 22 (1760), 444.

Members, many of whom might fairly be classed as Cavaliers. A recent writer has asserted of their rewards at the Restoration: 'if Charles I had won Edgehill, the booty could not have been greater.'[20] But it would certainly not have been shared with Major-General Richard Browne, Sir Harbottle Grimston, Edward Montagu, Sir Robert Pye, Silius Titus, and Sir William Waller, to name only a few conspicuous examples of former Parliamentarians in the Convention who now gained or were restored to office. Grants made by Charles I had to be honoured,[21] and new grants, whether in possession or reversion, offered 'a convenient way of rewarding, at no direct cost to the crown, the many petitioners' who besieged the Court and any likely patron. Administrative capacity could not automatically be expected from those whose chief claims to office were their 'sufferings'; but the patents usually gave life tenure, which rendered them more readily transferable. With no danger of dismissal, even for negligence or misconduct, deputies or outright purchasers were easily found.[22] Whether these grants and transactions assisted in the management of the Convention cannot be determined. In theory, at least, Clarendon disapproved of rewards and promises for faithful service in Parliament. But the leadership of the Commons, both before and after his return from exile, seems to have been in the hands of Arthur Annesley and Sir Anthony Ashley Cooper, two adroit politicians generally credited with complete lack of scruple in public life, and it would be remarkable if they did not use whatever means they could command.[23]

The removal of both Annesley and Ashley Cooper to the Lords as Earl of Anglesey and Lord Ashley in the coronation honours, the re-establishment of traditional interests in the constituencies, and the contentious legislation in prospect obliged Clarendon to recognize, however reluctantly, that he must undertake some form of management in the next Parliament. The task was not suited to a temperament unapt 'to do any man any kindness of his own

[20] R. Hutton, *The Restoration* (Oxford, 1987), 137.
[21] Apparent exceptions, such as the displacement of a Royalist as clerk of the hanaper by Thomas Clarges, were temporary or conditional.
[22] J. C. Sainty, 'A Reform in the Tenure of Offices during the Reign of Charles II', *BIHR* 41 (1968), 152; 'The Tenure of Offices in the Exchequer', *EHR* 80 (1965), 473.
[23] P. Seaward, *The Cavalier Parliament and the Reconstruction of the Old Regime 1661–1667* (Cambridge, 1989), 258; H. C. Foxcroft, *A Supplement to Burnet's History of My Own Time* (Oxford, 1902), 59, 62.

nature'.²⁴ Sir Courtenay Pole took the responsibility for proposing the unpopular hearth-tax, 'for which he had the court thanks, but no snip, though damnably promised'; and he could never again 'be choosen Parliament man of any place where there are chimneys'.²⁵ Nevertheless Paul Seaward concludes that Clarendon employed his extensive patronage as Lord Chancellor to reward service in the Commons.²⁶ The apparently functionless excise appeals commission, for which Lord Treasurer Southampton must bear the responsibility, was a more flagrant example of jobbery, giving salaried employment to five MPs (out of a commission of six).²⁷

During the session, 'that the king might be the more vacant to those thoughts and divertisements which pleased him best', it fell to Clarendon and Southampton to hold daily conferences with 'some select persons of the house of commons that had always served the king' and determine 'in what method to proceed in disposing the house'. This small, secret, and probably elderly coterie was headed by Clarendon's old friend, Sir Hugh Pollard, who had 'a greater party in the house of commons willing to be disposed of by him than any man that ever sat there in my time'.²⁸ Indeed, as knight of the shire for Devon, he was well placed to influence the largest regional grouping in the Commons, the 124 MPs who sat for the south-western counties. His hospitality was legendary, ultimately ruinous; and his appointment as Comptroller of the Household gave him a footing at Court. On the other hand, his parliamentary record was almost comically defective; its best-known episode was his expulsion from the Long Parliament for involvement in the Army Plot, his activity in the Convention is almost untraceable, and for most of 1661 he was absent from Westminster in his governorship of Guernsey.²⁹ When he returned he found that, both at Court and in the Commons, his position had been undermined. During his absence Sir Henry Bennet had been appointed Privy Purse and by-elected for a Cornish borough. At Court Bennet participated in those 'divertisements' that Clar-

²⁴ *The Diary of Samuel Pepys*, ed. R. C. Latham and W. Matthews (11 vols.; 1970–83), viii. 418.
²⁵ BL MS Harl. 7020, fo. 42ᵛ; *Letters of Humphrey Prideaux*, ed. E. M. Thompson (Camden Soc., NS 15; 1875), 108–9.
²⁶ Seaward, *Cavalier Parliament*, 85.
²⁷ *Calendar of Treasury Books*, ed. W. A. Shaw (32 vols.; 1904–62), i. 75.
²⁸ E. Hyde, Earl of Clarendon, *Life* (3 vols.; Oxford, 1827), i. 361–2; ii. 205.
²⁹ Keeler, *Long Parliament*, 308.

endon scorned; in the Commons, though himself silent and inactive, he knew how to attract competent followers and to retain their loyalty. Amongst them were two of the west country Members on whom Pollard should have been able to rely, Winston Churchill and Thomas Clifford. Though only 'of ordinary conditions and mean fortunes', they were young men, who, even Clarendon had to admit, 'spoke confidently and often, and upon some occasions seemed to have credit in the house'.[30] By the King's command, they were added to the court managers in the Commons, and Churchill was intruded into the royal Household as Clerk-Comptroller of the Green Cloth.[31]

Conflict between Clarendon's followers and Bennet's in the 1663 session produced the chaotic situation among government supporters in the Commons described by Henry Coventry (Groom of the Bedchamber): 'I am for my own part as assiduous both at Court and in the House as I can be, and as inquisitive as my temper will give me leave; and yet I can neither tell you what the House intends, nor what we at Whitehall wish they should.'[32] In retrospect, Clarendon ascribed the breakdown of his management to by-elections, which brought into the Commons 'a very great number of men in all stations in the court, as well below stairs as above'.[33] There were certainly some disreputable characters among the new Members, such as the 'procurers' Edward Progers and Henry Brouncker (Grooms of the Bedchamber to the King and the Duke of York respectively); and, as head of the department responsible for the issue of by-election writs and the custody of the returns, Clarendon ought to have been well informed. In fact, throughout the period during which he held the great seal, twenty-two courtiers were returned in eighty-seven elections, and of these seven held only honorary appointments as Gentlemen of the Privy

---

[30] *Pepys Diary*, viii. 165; Clarendon, *Life*, ii. 204, 210. Churchill's failure to live up to his early prominence as a Parliament man prompted D. T. Witcombe to suggest (*Charles II and the Cavalier House of Commons 1663–1674* (Manchester, 1966), 21) that Clarendon must have intended to refer to Sir William Coventry, whom he had already bracketed with Bennet as a principal enemy. In any case, Clarendon would never have described a son of one of his most respected predecessors on the Woolsack as 'of ordinary conditions'. Omissions in the index to the *Calendar of State Papers Ireland* make it possible to underestimate Churchill's activity in the early sessions of the Cavalier Parliament, rightly asserted by A. L. Rowse in *The Early Churchills* (1956), 39, 43–4.

[31] HMC *Ormonde*, NS vii. 185.

[32] Ibid. iii. 52.

[33] Clarendon, *Life*, ii. 196.

Chamber, scarcely enough to account for all his troubles. Before he left office the description of 'courtier' had become sufficient in itself to guarantee electoral defeat.[34]

Meanwhile, for the 1664 session the King required the repeal of the Triennial Act. Clarendon and Bennet, now given government office as Secretary of State, had together to construct a majority. The list drawn up for this purpose survives among the papers of Lord Ashley, subsequently (as Lord Shaftesbury) the deadliest of list-makers, at least in intention.[35] Out of 507 Members, 166 were marked as Court supporters, and of these no less than 115 can be shown to have been holding gainful employment under the Crown, twenty-six had been rewarded in some other way (by royal bounty, pensions, or unpaid office), and only twenty-five had not yet been 'gratified'.[36] It was for them that the local prize commissions were reserved during the second Dutch War. As Sir William Coventry (secretary to the Duke of York) told an aspirant from outside Parliament, 'the King and the Duke had resolved to put in some Parliament men that had deserved well, and that would needs be obliged by putting them in'. Rewards for loyal supporters were a very different matter from buying off opponents, he observed, even so able and faithful a Member as William Garway; for, 'by bringing over one discontented man, you raise up three in his room'.[37]

Pollard was succeeded as government manager in the Commons by Sir Allen Brodrick, not mentioned by Clarendon in this capacity, probably because of his morals. He held no court appointment, and his other duties as Comptroller of the Pipe cannot have been exacting. In 1666 he reckoned, without naming them, some 140 MPs as 'all that depend on the Court', out of a total membership of 507. Nevertheless he believed there was no vote in the Commons that could not be carried, given clear directions from the government.[38] But with faction flourishing at Court they were not provided

[34] W. C. Abbott, 'The Long Parliament of Charles II', *EHR* 21 (1906), 40; *Pepys Diary*, vii. 337.

[35] *Memoirs of Thomas, Earl of Ailesbury*, ed. W. E. Buckley (2 vols.; Westminster, 1890), i. 64. The alleged category of 'men worthy' (i.e. to be hanged) does not in fact appear in the list as printed by J. R. Jones, 'Shaftesbury's Worthy Men', *BIHR* 30 (1957), 236–41. Here the Court supporters are more prosaically marked as base or vile.

[36] J. R. Jones, 'Court Dependents in 1664', *BIHR* 34 (1951), 81–91. Some additional office-holders have been found among the Members listed, chiefly at Court and in the army.

[37] *Pepys Diary*, v. 342; vii. 310–11.

[38] Seaward, *Cavalier Parliament*, 299.

and management again collapsed. It was the King's servants whom Sir George Carteret (Treasurer of the Navy) blamed for failure in the Commons. 'Instead of making the Parliament better, they rather play the rogue one with another.' Archbishop Sheldon concurred: 'all the disorders have arisen from the King's family and servants.'[39] Ironically, it was their discipline in a supply debate that was commended in *Last Instructions to a Painter*, the brilliant satire by Andrew Marvell, a Court dependant in 1664 as secretary of embassy, but now, and permanently, out of a job. Either from experience or observation, he knew a great deal about the controls over Members that the government could exert. The court officers, for example, he depicted as marshalled by Sir Stephen Fox (Clerk of the Green Cloth and Paymaster of the Forces). The 'expectants pale, with hope of spoil allur'd', were led by Robert Steward, who surely deserved a better reward for his services as Chairman of Ways and Means than the two minor offices that, years later, came his way. Thurland humbly brought up the rear of 'the lawyers Mercenary Band', headed by Heneage Finch (Solicitor-General). Others are shown as voting for the Court by reason of their dependence on parliamentary privilege to secure themselves from arrest by their creditors. The threat of prorogation or dissolution sufficed to bring them to heel, and also those who had private Bills to pass; while there were Members, like Pole, 'whose violent acts before (Their publick Acts) obliged them still to more'.[40]

Clarendon's fall was necessarily attended by some displacement of those most closely identified with him. Brodrick went out of office permanently, later to embarrass his patron's sons by the inflexibility of his opposition to the government of the day, and to become 'a strict and religious person'.[41] One placeman lost his seat in Parliament on a flimsy charge of corrupt practices, which might not have sufficed if courtiers had been less unpopular. John Ashburnham (Groom of the Bedchamber), it has been said, 'fell foul of the double standard of conduct which made the acceptance of bribes almost universal yet still a technical offence'.[42] It was

[39] *Pepys Diary*, vii. 370; Seaward, *Cavalier Parliament*, 398.

[40] *Poems and Letters of Andrew Marvell*, ed. H. M. Margoliouth (2 vols.; Oxford, 1927), i. 145.

[41] J. C. Sainty, *Officers of the Exchequer* (List and Index Soc., special ser., 18; 1983), 76; *The Correspondence of Henry Hyde, Earl of Clarendon and of his Brother Laurence Hyde, Earl of Rochester*, ed. S. W. Singer (2 vols.; 1828), i. 4; Foxcroft, *Supplement*, 138–9.

[42] Witcombe, *Cavalier House of Commons*, 73. Ashburnham is sometimes styled Sir John (*The Diary of John Milward*, ed. C. Robbins (Cambridge, 1938), 132); but he was never knighted,

claimed on his behalf that he had received £500 to obtain import licences, not as an MP, but as a courtier; but, unfortunately for him, he had taken a prominent part in supporting a petition from the same merchants to Parliament.

Direct inside information about the system of management ceases with the fall of Clarendon, and Pepys's diary also becomes less informative after Sir George Carteret and Sir William Coventry were driven from office. Clarendon's successors lacked the period of leisure consequent on enforced early retirement, and also, perhaps, the need for self-justification that produces political memoirs. Even Ashley is no exception, for he found the task of defending his tortuous career so difficult that he never resumed the autobiographical sketch composed during the Civil War.[43] We are left with the bitter comments of outsiders, sharpened by the increasing tension between Court and Country.[44] Otherwise, only one list survives from the next few years: 'the names of such Parliament men as are servants, or have dependence by offices or commands under his Majestie', drawn up by another compulsive list-maker, Sir Thomas Osborne (Treasurer of the Navy).[45] His criteria may have been stricter than Brodrick's, for the number of MPs in these categories has shrunk to ninety. Another 107 Members, Osborne reckoned, had usually voted for supply, while the adherents of the Dukes of York and Buckingham might furnish ninety-four more votes and provide a working majority, if a coalition could be formed. A great many more names of at least potential government supporters occur in hostile accounts, forming altogether, as Browning pointed out, a number considerably in excess of any actually mustered for the Court in any known division.[46] It is clear, therefore, that the new ministry, soon to be nicknamed the Cabal, had everything to lose, despite a handful of embittered Clarendonians, from a dissolution of the Parliament elected so long ago and under such different circumstances. But differences can be observed in the methods adopted by the new ministers. 'Other politicians', wrote Browning, 'had neither

---

though in the Sussex commission of the peace he was given the precedence of a Privy Councillor.

[43] W. D. Christie, *A Life of Anthony Ashley Cooper, 1st Earl of Shaftesbury* (2 vols.; 1871), i, p. xxxii.

[44] Aylmer, 'Place Bills', 56.

[45] A. Browning, *Thomas, Earl of Danby* (3 vols.; Glasgow, 1951), iii. 34–42.

[46] Browning, 'Parties', 25–6.

Clarendon's caution, his reverence for the past, or his honesty of purpose'.[47] Change was first experienced in the Treasury, where a board of 'rougher hands' took over on Southampton's death and a decision was made to grant no more life patents nor reversions.[48] 'Pleasure tenure', Sir John Sainty comments, 'for obvious reasons rendered officers, whether Members of the House of Commons or not, far more susceptible to political pressure . . . making it possible for them to be dismissed for reasons that had nothing to do with administrative efficiency'.[49] With better disciplinary weapons available, it became less hazardous to use office as a means of buying off opposition; and the new ministry practised taking off 'the great and leading men' in Parliament, leaving 'the herd as a despised company, who could do nothing because they had none to head them'.[50] Among the beneficiaries of the system was Sir Thomas Littleton, one of the new breed of professional politicians called into existence by the protracted life of the Cavalier Parliament, who could afford to neglect his Shropshire borough and live wholly in London, so that, while he was in opposition, 'matters were most in his hands during the intervals of Parliament'.[51] He became Osborne's colleague in the Navy Treasury, and was scathingly attacked in *The Alarum*, a pamphlet that may have targeted MPs like Garway who were believed to be vulnerable to similar offers.

Sir Thomas Littleton was an angry man against the Court until silenced by a good place, and is now content that everything should be let alone, having got what he grumbled for . . . . If anybody is disposed to betray trust and vote against conscience, he will think they do exceeding well in it.[52]

The 'five recanters of the Hous' stigmatized by Marvell in both verse and prose also gained well-paid posts after they 'openly took Leave of their former Party, and fell to head the King's Busyness'.[53] Sir Robert Howard became Secretary of the Treasury, Sir Richard

[47] Ibid. 22.
[48] H. Roseveare, *The Treasury 1660–1870* (1973), 20.
[49] Sainty, 'Reform in Tenure', 155.
[50] *Burnet's History*, ed. Airy, ii. 79; Aylmer, 'Place Bills', 56.
[51] *Burnet's History*, ed. Airy, ii. 92. As Littleton's next-door neighbour in Lincoln's Inn Fields, Burnet must have witnessed the comings and goings of the opposition leaders. It remains an open question whether it was their improved organization that spurred on the government or vice versa (Aylmer, 'Place Bills', 57).
[52] *Cal. SP Dom. 1668–9*, 542.
[53] *Poems and Letters of Andrew Marvell*, i. 169; ii. 305.

Temple Commissioner of Customs, Sir Robert Carr Chancellor of the Duchy of Lancaster, and Edward Seymour Navy Commissioner. Only Sir Frescheville Holles was less well provided for; all he got was an unpaid appointment in the Privy Chamber, the command of a warship in the third Dutch War, and a state funeral in Westminster Abbey. Perhaps he was merely unlucky; or perhaps his character was against him. He had already changed sides once, and lost his army commission in consequence; and in the Commons he was a less effective debater than the others. None of them seems to have been reckoned an efficient administrator, and Howard and Temple were both idle and incompetent. It is noteworthy that Carr was alone in receiving a life patent; but then, he had married Bennet's sister.[54]

It was believed that the policy of buying off the most formidable opposition speakers with office originated with Bennet, now removed to the Upper House as Lord Arlington, much to the relief of his constituents, whom he had neglected. As Secretary of State, also, he 'loves business no better than business loves him',[55] and the donkey-work of the office fell to his low-born undersecretary, Joseph Williamson. Returned to the Commons only at the fifth attempt, Williamson was as yet scarcely of the status required for managing his fellow Members.[56] This was the responsibility of the bold, industrious Clifford, who had succeeded Pollard as Comptroller of the Household, and retained a white stave for the rest of his time in the Commons, though he added to it a seat on the Treasury board. In the hostile accounts of the Court party that began to multiply under the Cabal,[57] he was styled 'the chief commissioner for the mannageing the bribe-money to buy votes in Parliament'.[58] The last phrase deserves emphasis, for it suggests a difference from Brodrick's methods, by which Members had been

---

[54] Sir R. Somerville, *Office-Holders in the Duchy and County Palatine of Lancaster* (Chichester, 1972), 3.

[55] *Cal. SP Dom. 1664–5*, 257; *1668–9*, 542. Arlington's biographer concludes with reference to his religion that 'Arlington's conscience could easily have accommodated itself to the necessity of bowing in the House of Rimmon, though for a lifetime' (V. Barbour, *Henry Bennet, Earl of Arlington* (Washington, DC, 1914), 262). Such disregard of the claims of God, as well as of office, constituency, and the House of Commons, clearly disqualifies him from inclusion in a study of multiple loyalties.

[56] BL MS Harl. 7020, fo. 36ᵛ; *Cal. SP Dom. 1670*, 452.

[57] D. Hayton and C. Jones, *A Register of Parliamentary Lists 1660–1761* (Leicester, 1979), 80–5.

[58] BL MS Harl. 7020, fo. 42ᵛ.

'bribed to be diligent in their business rather than to be false to their convictions'.[19] The reforms effected by Clifford and his colleagues in the Treasury may have made it possible for him to loosen the purse-strings a little; while the patronage at his disposal was limited by the rivalry between his master Arlington and Buckingham for the King's ear, and in any case supply of office could never hope to equal demand.[60] If it was on cash rather than on place that Clifford came to rely, it may explain why he seconded the apparently disinterested motion of Sir Jonathan Trelawny (Comptroller of the Household to the Duke of York) for a swingeing tax on office. 'It seemed to me unreasonable at first', wrote Sir Edward Dering, who had but recently obtained a modest place (Commissioner of the Privy Seal) and a seat in Parliament for a pocket borough, 'that offices, which most owe but for life, and three parts of four of them are but during his Majesty's pleasure, should pay double to estates of inheritance'. But 'most of the court party' could hardly ignore such clear indications of the official line, and the motion was carried.[61]

Money had two further advantages over place; it was less immediately visible, and it could be spread uncommonly thin. As indigence increased among the loyal Members elected in 1661, a quite modest degree of help with expenses (even £50 a session) might become acceptable.[62] 'With the increasing frequency and duration of sessions,' Browning pointed out, 'the burden imposed on the individual Member by attendance had greatly increased, and a considerable number . . . were too impoverished to bear it.'[63] So it was alleged that Arlington, 'besides promises of this or that place, tells out ready money to hirelings, who engage to betray their country for it. . . . His man Clifford . . . sets up to be generous, by being free of the King's wine at table and his money in the Treasury.'[64] He cannot be denied a very considerable success

[19] Browning, 'Parties', 26.

[60] M. D. Lee, *The Cabal* (Urbana, Ill., 1965), 123.

[61] *The Parliamentary Diary of Sir Edward Dering 1670–1673*, ed. B. D. Henning (New Haven, Conn., 1940), 39, 57. Dering's accounts reveal that the promotion to the customs and Treasury commissions earned by his unstinted loyalty in the Commons eventually brought him in considerably more than his estate (*The Diaries and Papers of Sir Edward Dering, 2nd Bt. 1644–1684*, ed. M. F. Bond (1976), 6).

[62] The cheapest Members appear to have been Thomas King (Harwich), a victualling agent, and Thomas Morrice (Haslemere), an exciseman; the two dearest were county Members, Carr (Lincolnshire) and Samuel Sandys (Worcestershire).

[63] Browning, 'Parties', 24–5.

[64] *Cal. SP Dom. 1668–9*, 541.

in the session of 1670–1, which produced unparalleled grants of supply for the maintenance of the Triple Alliance of Protestant powers to resist the expansion of France. But his personality and methods aroused alarm and resentment fully in proportion to his success,[65] provoking a sardonic analysis of the party he had created that became the basis for *Flagellum Parliamentarium* and later accounts. In the original version in the Harleian manuscripts, 162 Members are named, of whom 107 are said to hold office, fourteen 'had a lick of the bribe-pot', and another fourteen, like Pole, had been 'cullied' with promises.[66] Rather surprisingly only five Members are described as poor or beggarly, and only eight in debt. An interesting feature is the attempt to define the individual services rendered to the government in the Commons. Some of these details, as in the case of Pole, go back to the period of Clarendon's administration. Sir Job Charlton (a Welsh judge) had been 'a Roaring dragon against the Tryennial Act', and, like Thurland, 'a promoter for the Act that stript the poore Cavileere of theire Wine Lycences'; while Finch was 'the only contriver of the repeale of the Act for trieniall Parliaments'. But most of the activities described were of more recent date, and could only have been known to an MP who was at least tolerably regular in his attendance at committees. William Montagu (Attorney-General to the queen consort), who had been 'a perfect Enemye against the Triennial Act', was now 'a principall Committee man for money bills'. Ten other Members were also prominent in promoting supply. Finch was 'the great framer of all money Acts which he stuffs with Oathes and ruine'; Steward (no longer a mere expectant, but Master in Chancery and trustee for the sale of the fee-farm rents) had proved himself 'noe flinching committee man at money bills'; while Edmund Waller was 'a poet that can turn a Money bill into bad rime but never into good reason'.[67] The writer was especially indignant over the Law Duties Act, an alternative to increasing the burden on land at a time of falling rents that might be expected

---

[65] Lee, *Cabal*, 123.

[66] Pole held no gainful office after the dissolution of the prize commission at the end of the second Dutch War, and received no favours from the Cabal; but he was to be handsomely pensioned by Danby.

[67] The writer either believed, or affected to believe, that Marvell's *Last Instructions* (which is actually remarkable for the ingenuity of its rhymes) was written by Waller, whose panegyric on the Duke of York it parodies (Hutton, *Restoration*, 271, 368).

to reduce lawyers' income. Sir Robert Atkyns senior (Solicitor-General to the queen consort) was branded as 'an infamous bird that betrayed his own nest' (i.e. his profession) in steering the bill through committee; and indeed eyebrows might be raised at his acceptance of the post of Receiver-General under the Act, which he passed on to his son when he was himself raised to the judicial bench. One of Clifford's assistant whips can be identified from the list. Sir John Talbot (Sir Gilbert's nephew) is called 'one of the monitors in the Commons House', a description justified by his sixty tellerships. An army officer and a 'great huff', much in demand at duels, he would have made an excellent disciplinarian. Though he was a strong Protestant, Marvell implied that he had no objection to the command of papists, a positive recommendation at a time when Clifford was already suspected of 'a little warping to Rome'.[68]

To obtain an adequate supply for the third Dutch War, Clifford needed to buy over two more leading figures from the opposition. Garway's justified discontent was at last assuaged, and the suspicions of his political allies confirmed, by his appointment as customs commissioner, a post for which his City connections made him at least better qualified than Temple. Sir Thomas Lee had no administrative ambitions, and had to be bought outright. 'He valued himself upon artifice and cunning, in which he was a great master, without being out of countenance when it was discovered'. An observant coachman recognized him as he received his £6,000; but he told the House that he had earned it by his assiduous attendance. Garway and Lee had been hired for a single purpose, to divide the opposition over supply by speaking for double the sum on which they had agreed as necessary for the war effort; and, at the price of betraying their friends, they succeeded.[69]

This was Clifford's last parliamentary triumph before his political suicide over the Test Act. Because of the suspicions aroused over his aims and objectives, the historian of the Cabal regards his management as less than successful, and his influence over the Commons as illusory. Moreover, he failed to recognize the value of the excise pensions, and it was left to his successor as Lord

[68] *Poems and Letters of Andrew Marvell*, i. 144; *The Diary of John Evelyn*, ed. E. S. de Beer (6 vols.; Oxford, 1955), iii. 577.

[69] *Poems and Letters of Andrew Marvell*, i. 145; R. North, *Examen* (London, 1740), 456; *Burnet's History*, ed. Airy, ii. 16, 92.

Treasurer to earn for this Parliament the sobriquet of the 'Pensioners' Parliament'.[70] This successor was Osborne, soon to acquire his familiar title of Earl of Danby. On taking over the Treasury, he discovered that the excise farmers had '(to obtaine theire ends) oblidged themselves to soe many pensions to gentlemen of the Court and country as amounted to neare 20,000 *l*. a yeare'. With the cancellation of the farm, this substantial sum became available to purchase or reward fidelity in the Commons.[71]

At this juncture the death of Sir Robert Long (Auditor of the Exchequer) provided Danby with the opportunity of transferring Howard from his politically sensitive post at the Treasury. The replacement of a conscientious and experienced official by an incompetent idler was bad enough in itself, and made worse by the concession to Howard of a life tenure. Danby, it has been concluded, was indifferent, even hostile, to the reform of his department, and this is not the only instance during his administration of the relaxation of the insistence on pleasure tenures that had prevailed since the Restoration. He was justly punished when Howard, like Carr, became a thorn in the flesh of Danby's increasingly beleaguered followers in the Commons.[72] A counterweight to them might have been obtained if he had fulfilled expectations by giving the secretaryship of the Treasury to Sir Thomas Meres, 'who they say must be stopt with this or he will not be silent at the Parliaments meeting'.[73] Meres, a professional politician like Littleton, was not only a frequent speaker but the most active committeeman in the Cavalier Parliament. Unlike Littleton, he never lost touch with his constituency, representing Lincoln in eleven Parliaments on the cathedral interest. His estate was modest, only £300 a year, but as a moneyed man he could afford two residences, one in the Cathedral Close, the other in Bloomsbury Square. In London he took the chair in a political discussion club, and kept himself informed of continental developments, for instance the increasing pressure on the French Protestants at the hands of their intolerant monarch.[74] Politically, then,

[70] Lee, *Cabal*, 139, 143–4.

[71] Browning, *Danby*, iii. 28.

[72] Roseveare, *Treasury*, 30, 43; Sainty, 'Reform in Tenure', 160.

[73] *Letters Addressed from London to Sir Joseph Williamson*, ed. W. D. Christie (Camden Soc., NS 8; 1874), 108.

[74] *Herald and Genealogist*, 2 (1865), 123–4; Grey, *Debates*, iii. 5.

his attitude both to the Church and to France was in complete accord with Danby's. His failure to obtain the post must be attributed to the new minister's well-attested preference for medio-crity. Arlington was back at Court as Lord Chamberlain, and Danby could not be unaware how his Commons 'discoveries' had helped to undermine Clarendon's influence with the King. Moreover, he had doubtless already made his plans for the use of the excise pensions, which required a dependant of unquestionable fidelity at the Treasury; and for this purpose he selected his wife's brother, Charles Bertie, who was not yet even in Parliament.

The collapse of the Cabal had left the Court party in the Commons in confusion. 'Never more need for plausible, prudent managers', wrote Roger Whitley, the Postmaster-General, who 'means honestly but dare not show it'.[75] But Danby's second-raters were 'baffled in every debate', so that the most loyal courtiers felt ashamed of their votes. Competent, low-born administrators like Williamson and Samuel Pepys (secretary to the Admiralty) never caught the ear of the House, and bored the better-bred with their long-winded expositions. Danby hoped to atone for these deficiencies by good management. Discarding Clifford's methods, he 'reckoned that the major number was the surer game; so he neglected the great men, who he thought raised the price too high, and reckoned that he could gain ten ordinary men cheaper than one of these'.[76]

After so long a Parliament, attended with rival factions at Court and at least two radical changes of ministry, there were numbers of influential Members who had lost office for one reason or another and bore a grudge against their successful rivals. Giles Strangways, an independent adherent of Danby's, who informed the House that he desired no gainful office, might 'reflect' on Littleton and embarrass Waller, two of those recently displaced, with the observation: 'Some men were of one mind when in office, and another out of office.' But it was an earlier casualty of Court intrigue, Sir William Coventry, who decided that the time was now ripe for legislation. His Bill, supported by Marvell on its first reading, would have required MPs to resign their seats on receiving places but allowed them to stand for re-election, thus accom-

---

[75] *Letters to Williamson*, ed. W. D. Christie (Camden Soc., NS 9; 1874), 108; BL MS Harl. 7020, fo. 34.

[76] *Burnet's History*, ed. Airy, ii. 79.

modating their duties to King and constituency. He told the Commons:

This bill does not provide that great officers shall not serve the King. Those that have offices may be safer in them, and those that have no places shall not get them from them that have. The old way was, men were chosen into Parliament after they had been Privy Councillors . . . to be the better able to serve the country and place they are chosen for. . . . We have served here a great while, and it may be his corporation will not chuse him again because he has no office, that another may serve them better. Consider what may be the consequence, if qualifications change; and not only absence may make us ignorant of the affairs of the place we serve for, but our presence here may do it to the office also.

Coventry showed himself keenly aware of the problem of multiple loyalties; but he was too 'visionary' for the Commons, just as he had formerly been for the King, and his Bill was rejected by 145 votes to 113. Coventry and Lee acted as tellers on the one side, with two soldiers, Sir John Talbot and Sir John Hanmer, on the other.[77]

Thus ended the most serious attempt of the period to find a reasonable compromise over placemen, though Coventry rightly believed that, 'if the bill does not pass, it may revive in future Parliaments'. Such a revival did not happen at once, probably because it had become clear that other methods of management had been introduced. From Bertie's secret service accounts, fifty-six MPs have been identified as in receipt of excise pensions, while out of 215 Members named by the hostile author of *A Seasonable Argument* as many as sixty-five are said to have received money boons or pensions against 105 in office, a balance very different from earlier comparable accounts.[78] Management became more systematic and control tighter. Silent Members like Thomas Wyndham (Groom of the Bedchamber) were recruited to assist Talbot and Trelawny as tellers. The Secretaries of State, Henry Coventry and Williamson, kept elaborate lists of Members for Danby's edification, and wrote personally before every session to desire the attendance of reliable supporters. During sessions the Whips met regularly every evening at Danby's house. An obscure Essex Member, Sir Richard Wiseman, entertained splendidly with funds of mysterious origin, acquiring a wide acquaintance in the

---

[77] Grey, *Debates*, iii. 48, 69–73; Aylmer, 'Place Bills', 59; *Pepys Diary*, ix. 386.
[78] *English Historical Documents 1660–1714*, ed. A. Browning (1953), 237–49.

House that allowed him to supervise doubtful or wavering Members. His ignorance of the official life showed when he recommended the dismissal of Carr and John Birch (Auditor of Excise), both of whom held on life patents, though Carr could be, and was, punished for his unreliability by removal from the Privy Council.[79]

But the erosion of the Court party continued, especially in debate, and discipline gave way, even among the courtiers. The orders of the King and the Duke of York for their servants to attend the elections committee in support of Sir John Reresby were not obeyed, nor could the Duke of Monmouth (Captain-General) prevail with the officers under his command.[80] A more important reverse for the government occurred on 7 May 1678, when the address for the removal of Lauderdale was carried by a single vote. Henry Savile (Groom of the Bedchamber) had actually lobbied as well as voted against the Scottish minister. Believing that 'our measures now at court are so taken that it is esentiall to a mans succeeding there to be of the parliament', he had come in at great trouble and expense for the newly enfranchised borough of Newark. But his regard for his seat was less than his regard for his place; turned off by the King in an uncharacteristic fit of rage, he absented himself from the House until he was forgiven.[81] More significant defections followed in the division on the impeachment of Danby in December. Fox had already been compelled to surrender the Pay Office; he was now dismissed from the Board of Green Cloth 'in as severe terms as could be expressed'. Sir Francis Winnington (Attorney-General) followed him after the dissolution.[82] He remained in opposition, though not without hopes of a return to office. Fox's position was more complex. As one of Danby's victims, he won the popular constituency of Westminster at the next election, and he co-operated fully with the inquiry into the malpractices of the fallen minister. But, 'as the only instrument that has kept things afloat by his credit and supplies', he could not long be spared from the royal service, and he was appointed to the Treasury board.[83]

---

[79] *Correspondence of the Family of Hatton*, ed. E. M. Thompson (Camden Soc. NS 22; 1879), 166.

[80] *Memoirs of Sir John Reresby*, ed. A. Browning (Glasgow, 1936), 140.

[81] *The Lauderdale Papers*, ed O. Airy (Camden Soc. NS 38; 1885), 131, 140.

[82] HMC, *Ormonde*, NS iv. 290; *Cal. SP Dom. 1679–80*, 10.

[83] C. Clay, *Public Finance and Private Wealth: The Career of Sir Stephen Fox 1627–1716* (Oxford, 1978), 119–23. Grey, *Debates*, vii. 316–24; HMC, *Ormonde*, NS iv. 517–18, 538.

The inquiry, chaired by Winnington, met a stubborn resistance from those more closely identified with Danby's system. Bertie refused to reveal any official secrets without the King's permission, and was sent to the Tower. Sir John Talbot, named as a pensioner by Fox, defended himself brilliantly, and apparently with truth. His pension had been compensation for the excise farm which Danby had terminated. 'I never took one shilling as a gift or begging from the time the King came in. I do disown anything by way of secret service to influence my vote here.' His support for the government of the day had been so constant, and his readiness to fight in defence of his honour was so well known, that nobody was tempted to pursue the matter. Wiseman too was obdurate, if less convincing, and the inquiry petered out.[84]

Some opposition figures, including Meres, Littleton, and Lee, were given seats on the Admiralty board, at the same time as a bi-partisan Privy Council was formed. Neither experiment was a success. As Henry Coventry wrote out of his long experience: 'To be well heard at Court and well spoken of in Parliament is great good fortune, if our new ministers can acquire it.' They failed on both counts. 'The bare being preferred maketh some of them suspected' by the Commons, while the King was determined to exclude them from real power. Lee resigned, declaring with commendable honesty that 'at his age and under his inexperience he could never hope to arrive at any useful knowledge' of naval matters. The others clung on, to bear the undeserved odium of the neglect which lack of funds rendered inevitable.[85]

It may have been these appointments, as much as suspicions of Danby's methods, that prompted the motion for a place bill in the first Exclusion Parliament; but it was squeezed out by more urgent business. When the next Parliament met, rumour was soon rife that other opposition figures had accepted office; and Winnington, designated Attorney-General, felt compelled to move a resolution, backed by considerable historical insight, that no Member should accept any office under the Crown. Silius Titus, another venal politician, tried to laugh the rumours off. 'As I came to the House this morning, I heard myself to be a great man, and that I had a place at Court, and had so many compliments upon being a great

[84] Grey, *Debates*, vii. 228–9, 231–6, 329–30, 333–6.
[85] *Ailesbury*, i. 35; HMC, *Ormonde*, NS v. 57; *Samuel Pepys's Naval Minutes*, ed. J. R. Tanner (Navy Records Soc., 60; 1926), 259.

minister that I began to flatter myself that I was really so.' But the resolution was carried unanimously.[86]

The Treasury reorganization of 1683 helped to increase the resources of the Crown in both men and money; and the effect was visible in James II's Parliament. 'Such a landed Parliament was never seen,' wrote Lord Ailesbury;[87] but it also marked the first appearance at Westminster of a number of relatively obscure revenue officials, such as William Aldworth (Comptroller of the Hearth-Tax), Thomas Done (Auditor of Imprests), Richard Kent (Receiver-General of customs), and William Shaw (Treasury clerk). They gave no trouble to the government of the day, even when James's belligerent defence of his intrusion of Roman Catholic officers into the greatly expanded army pushed loyalty to its limits. The House still sent John Coke to the Tower for declaring that Englishmen 'ought not to be frighted by a few high words'; though the Queen Dowager, herself a Roman Catholic, either continued him in her service as gentleman usher or allowed him a pension.[88] Fox's son Charles, on the other hand, avoided the Tower, but lost his post as Paymaster. His friends were 'importunate with him to withdraw himself' from the division on redress before supply, but he was 'moved by the impulse of his conscience' to defend the Church, and was 'dismissed from his valuable employments'.[89] James Kendall, in the same division, told the Earl of Middleton (Secretary of State) that he could afford to lose his commission in the army because 'my brother died last night, and has left me £700 a year'.[90] With less substantial office-holders, pressure might be successfully applied. In 1688 the regulators reported that Henry Clerke was 'nott to be reconciled to your Majesties interest, except the feare of looseing his office in the Allination Office will engage him'; and at the next election he did not stand.[91]

The rival patronage claims of Danby and Halifax after the Revolution, and their importunate pressure for their clients and associates, obviously caused King William much annoyance.[92] Pensions had acquired such an ill name that offices became the only

[86] *CJ*, ix. 609, 695; Grey, *Debates*, viii. 222; Aylmer, 'Place Bills', 64.
[87] *Ailesbury*, i. 87.
[88] Reresby, 398; Duckett, *Penal Laws*, 440.
[89] *Memoirs of the Life of Sir Stephen Fox, Kt.* (1717), 77–8.
[90] Reresby, 403; *Burnet's History*, ed. M. J. Routh (6 vols.; Oxford, 1833), iii. 92.
[91] Duckett, *Penal Laws*, 226.
[92] H. C. Foxcroft, *The Life and Letters of Sir George Savile, Bart.* (2 vols.; 1898), ii. 210.

acceptable means of management; but, as usual, there were never enough to go round, even with Non-jurors like the Talbots to replace. Competition, not only between rival patrons, but between rival parties, was intense; and neither Whigs nor Tories were at a loss to find incompetence and corruption in the other camp. Debates on the situation in Ireland were wholly taken up with apportioning the responsibility for defective victualling between the Tory Shales and the Whig Harbord.[93] William Sacheverell decided that the coalition was unworkable, and resigned from the Admiralty board. As a private Member, he proposed legislation to exclude from municipal office those responsible for the surrender of charters, a first step towards driving the Tories out of public life. So bitter became the recriminations in Parliament that William was obliged to dissolve. The period under review thus ended with no practical steps taken to resolve the problem of undue numbers of government dependents in the Commons.

There had, however, been significant developments in the kind of office held by MPs, especially by managers. Access to the Court became less desirable; indeed, for Danby especially, any connection with the Lord Chamberlain, his dreaded rival Arlington, was to be avoided. Fear that subordinates might use Court influence to undermine ministers, as Arlington himself had done against Clarendon, may have underlain the harsh treatment of Fox, first by the intrusion of the politically negligible Brouncker over his head on to the Board of Green Cloth, then by the dissolution of 'the great undertaking' and his replacement as Paymaster by the modest Sir Henry Puckering, front man for a hopelessly inadequate financial syndicate.[94] Fox's double role illustrates this shift from courtiers to executives. At a higher level, no 'white stave' after Clifford sat in the Commons until Thomas Wharton became Comptroller of the Household after the Revolution; *persona non grata* to both sovereigns, in this capacity he represented no threat to ministers. His appointment merely recognized his unsurpassed interest in the constituencies.[95]

On the other hand, ready access to government funds became an increasingly important qualification. 'An office to a Parliament

[93] H. Horwitz, *Parliament, Policy, and Politics in the Reign of William III* (Manchester, 1977), 38, 41.
[94] Clay, *Public Finance*, 106, 112.
[95] Foxcroft, *Savile*, ii. 227; J. P. Carswell, *The Old Cause* (1954), 74.

man is but a safer and softer word for a pension,' declared an electioneering pamphlet in 1679;[96] but it was the safety enjoyed by such officials as Birch, Carr, and Howard that the government found intolerable. Money payments gave better control. 'If a pensioner went not well, slash! He was put out of his pension,' William Harbord told the first Exclusion Parliament.[97] As paymaster, Fox was not responsible for the selection of pensioners; but his ledgers revealed the issue of government funds to MPs on the recommendations of Bertie, Wiseman, and their assistants.[98] The Navy was the largest spending department, and between 1661 and 1681 its successive Treasurers (Carteret, Littleton, Osborne, Seymour) were seldom far removed from the highest counsels of the nation or uninvolved in parliamentary management. The power of the Treasury scarcely needs demonstration; even before the great reform of 1668, Southampton's conscientious and ultra-respectable secretary Sir Philip Warwick kept a little book with the names of fifty MPs in receipt of secret service money.[99] Of Bertie's activities no more need be said; and his successor Henry Guy was apparently unable to deny that he had introduced the practice of secret service pensions.[100] Less anxiety might have been felt about improper influence in the Commons had it contained more Members like Lee and Sacheverell, prepared to resign office if unable to perform their duties or subscribe to government policy. But we have also seen how Hervey and Savile, after a brief struggle with their consciences, valued their places at Court above their parliamentary responsibilities; and Harbord clung to his Irish secretaryship by voting against his reason or stealing away before divisions. 'And if that be found out, it gives offence also,' he lamented; and indeed Wiseman had his eye on him.[101] It is instructive to compare the responses of Ashburnham and Thomas Wancklyn (who held no office) to the threat of expulsion from the House. Secure in his place at Court, Ashburnham made no effort to retain his seat. But Wancklyn had no other income than

---

[96] J. R. Jones, *The First Whigs* (Oxford, 1961), 95.
[97] Grey, *Debates*, vii. 317. Harbord's office as auditor of the Duchy of Cornwall was secure, although, on Wiseman's report that he dis-served the King in Parliament, he lost the Irish secretaryship.
[98] Clay, *Public Finance*, 117, 121–2.
[99] Grey, *Debates*, vii. 317
[100] H. Roseveare, *The Treasury* (London, 1969), 66; Grey, *Debates*, ix. 177.
[101] *Essex Papers*, ed. C. E. Pike (Camden Soc. 3rd ser., 24, 1913), 4.

what he could derive from using his parliamentary privilege to protect debtors and litigants. After a strenuous but irrelevant defence, the old Cavalier 'received his sentence and went away weeping'.[102]

It has been calculated that the number of placemen in the Commons rose from 101 at the dissolution of 1690 to 132 at the death of William III. Their significance, Henry Horwitz considers, can easily be exaggerated: 'the bulk of these official Members . . . were returned to the Commons on their own or on private patrons' electoral interests', and the real threat to gentry predominance in the Commons came from the City. However, concern was high throughout the reign of William III; place bills were introduced, and revenue officials progressively disqualified. It was the House of Lords, perhaps under the influence of Sir William Coventry's nephew, the Marquess of Halifax, that reintroduced the provision for re-election after appointment to office, which at last made its way on to the statute book in 1707.[103]

[102] Grey, *Debates*, v. 58.
[103] Horwitz, *Parliament, Policy, and Politics*, 124, 211, 313, 314, 359; *English Historical Documents*, ed. Browning, 141.

15
William Penn's Odyssey: From Child of Light to Absentee Landlord

RICHARD S. DUNN

THERE are many ways of interpreting William Penn's complex and contradictory career in England and America, but perhaps the most instructive procedure is to focus on his lifelong effort to translate unconventional and unpopular personal convictions into purposeful and effective public action. As the circumstances of his career changed, Penn articulated his private beliefs in strikingly different ways. There were four distinct phases to his public life. Between 1667 and 1679, as a young Quaker idealist, he felt inspired by God to challenge the religious and political establishment in England openly and aggressively. Protesting repeatedly against religious persecution by Church and State, he insisted on his God-given right to liberty of conscience and on his ancestral English right to freedom of speech and action. But during the years 1680 to 1684, when he founded a colony in America, Penn abruptly reformulated this public posture. Seeing the chance to design a new and better environment in Pennsylvania, he stopped being adversarial and sought to draw settlers to his plantation with an irenic message of economic opportunity, religious liberty, social pluralism, and political harmony; and he assumed the paternalistic role of benevolent supervisor over his colonial experiment. This sunshine strategy worked very well during his first visit to Pennsylvania from 1682 to 1684, but after he returned to England he changed course yet again. From 1685 to 1688 Penn tried to promote religious toleration by a new method: serving as James II's confidential adviser and agent, he attempted to convert his bigoted sovereign into an apostle of religious liberty, and to cajole dissenting Protestants into endorsing a Catholic king. In pursuing this risky

I am delighted to write this essay for my dear friend Gerald Aylmer, with whom I have been discussing Anglo–American seventeenth-century history (and much else) for more than forty years.

tactic Penn isolated himself disastrously from almost all of the other political and religious reformers in England, and he also lost touch with his colonists in Pennsylvania. The Glorious Revolution, which destroyed Penn's power base and forced him into hiding as a purported Jacobite, initiated the final phase of his career. From 1689 onwards, he was generally on the defensive. His public pronouncements became more conventional, consisting mainly of moral advice on how to lead a virtuous life, and he spent most of his time trying to fend off his adversaries and to salvage his personal fortune both in England and in America. During the 1690s and 1700s his private interests and public goals were increasingly at odds. Well before he died in 1718, Penn had lost most of his inspired idealism. The public service he took up in 1667 had exacted a distressing private toll.

Regrettably little is known about Penn's youth, but the surviving record indicates that he was already searching in his early teens for his own personal definition of private conscience and public duty. He was born in 1644, three months after the Parliamentary army beat Charles I's army at Marston Moor. His father, an ambitious and expedient naval officer, became a classic trimmer, fighting first for Parliament and next for Cromwell and last for Charles II. Young Penn saw very little of his father as a child, and clearly began deviating from the parental model when he had his first mystical experience at the age of 12. He later said about himself: 'from 13 years of Age I have been a sedulous Pursuer after Religion; & of a retired Temper.'[1] One may, however, question just how 'retired' this man's temper ever was. Shortly after the Restoration the Admiral enrolled his son at Christ Church College, Oxford, at the age of 16, but young Penn publicly objected to the Anglican ritual and was sent down in 1662. For the next five years parent and son papered over their differences while young William toured and studied in France, read the law at Lincoln's Inn, and worked as his father's land agent in Ireland. But in 1667—at the age of 23—he dramatically foiled his father's worldly expectations by becoming a Quaker.[2]

[1] William Penn to William Burroughs, c.1675, *The Papers of William Penn*, ed. M. M. Dunn and R. S. Dunn (4 vols.; Philadelphia, Pa., 1981–7) i. 303. See also M. M. Dunn, 'The Personality of William Penn', in R. S. Dunn and M. M. Dunn (eds.), *The World of William Penn* (Philadelphia, Pa., 1986), 3–7.

[2] The chief surviving documentation for Penn's early years is printed in *Papers of William Penn*, i. 29–55. A full-scale biography of the man is much needed; the best available is by C. O. Pearce, *William Penn* (Philadelphia, Pa., 1956).

By entering this despised and persecuted sect, Penn was rebelling against the English religious, social, and political establishment as conspicuously as he possibly could. Certainly, the Quakers were no longer as messianic as they had been in the 1650s, but they were better organized for long-term survival, and completely out of step with the Restoration settlement. They still believed in the divine power of the inner light, in the potential perfectability of man, and in universal brotherhood and peace. They repudiated the standard Christian concept of the priesthood, and held that man-made temples such as Anglican 'steeplehouses' and Dissenter chapels profaned the spirit of God. These Children of the Light flouted social convention by refusing to acknowledge worldly rank and status, by refusing to use titles of honour, by refusing to doff the hat, or to swear oaths. Thousands of them were fined when they resisted paying tithes, or were gaoled when they gathered for religious meetings. Historians argue as to whether the Restoration Quakers were of predominantly humble or middling status, but no one claims that they drew much support from the gentlemanly élite.[3] By joining their ranks William Penn not merely rejected his father's code of conduct, but became a social and cultural pariah.

The young convert was very little troubled by any of these considerations, because he had entered a religious community that provided him with the inward solace he had long been searching for, and Quakerism also offered ample scope for public service. From the late 1660s through the 1670s he was an ardent apostle for the beleaguered Friends. He had terrible rows with his father, though the two men became reconciled shortly before the Admiral died in 1670. Between 1667 and 1671 young Penn was arrested four times, and spent over a year in prison.[4] By 1680 he had published more than fifty tracts, most of them in answer to writers who criticized Quakerism. As a pamphlet warrior he engaged in vituperative doctrinal quarrels with antagonists representing almost every shade of English religious opinion—from Catholics and Anglicans to Baptists and Presbyterians to Socinians and Muggletonians—and he also tangled in print with several apostate

---

[3] For differing assessments of Quaker social origins, see R. T. Vann, *The Social Development of English Quakerism* (Cambridge, Mass., 1969), and D. H. Fischer, *Albion's Seed: Four British Folkways in America* (Oxford, 1989), 434–8.

[4] For Penn's imprisonments and his stormy relations with his father, see *Papers of William Penn*, i. 49–59, 81–97, 148–52, 171–80, 191–212; v. 118–28.

Quakers.⁵ Furthermore, Penn used his father's connections at the Stuart Court to lobby for the release of Quaker prisoners, and he undertook extensive missionary travels in England, Ireland, Holland, and Germany to spread his religious message. Repeatedly he protested against religious persecution by Church and State in a notable series of pamphlets including *The Great Case of Liberty of Conscience* (1670), *England's Present Interest Discover'd* (1675), and *An Address to Protestants* (1679). In a famous trial that helped to strengthen English civil liberties, the Penn–Mead trial of 1670, he was acquitted by a jury that accepted his argument against the instructions of the prosecuting magistrate.⁶

Like other Quakers in the 1670s, Penn was not interested in fleeing from persecution, for the Quakers interpreted their sufferings as a test of their faith. Yet his personal appetite for suffering had its limits. In the 1670s he argued repeatedly that his fellow Friends were entitled to the ancient rights and liberties of freeborn Englishmen. He also pressed for the newer and far more controversial Protestant Reformation conception of individual liberty of conscience.⁷ His experience of prison life during 1667–71 led him to campaign both at Whitehall and at Parliament for release from oath-taking and other forms of discriminatory anti-Quaker legislation.⁸ Through these actions Penn helped to reshape the worldly objectives of the Quaker movement. He effectually abandoned the effort of the earliest Quakers to turn the world upside-down, and worked instead to preserve his community as a small minority living in uneasy propinquity with a large and hostile majority. He also supported George Fox's effort to shape Quaker meeting structure during the 1670s, and argued for the necessity

---

⁵ For background on Penn's religious thought, see W. B. Endy, *William Penn and Early Quakerism* (Princeton, NJ, 1973), especially ch. 3. E. B. Bronner and D. Fraser describe 55 tracts published between 1668 and 1680 in *William Penn's Published Writings, 1660–1726: An Interpretive Bibliography* (Philadelphia, Pa. 1986), which constitutes vol. v of *Papers of William Penn*. Only 3 of these tracts dealt with secular subjects. Of the others, 26 responded to religious critics of Quakerism: 9 to Baptists, 5 to Independents, 4 to Anglicans, 2 to Presbyterians, 2 to Socinians, 2 to apostate Quakers, 1 to Catholics, and 1 to Muggletonians. Another 13 urged religious toleration or relief from persecution; 8 were homilies addressed primarily to fellow Quakers; and 5 were general diatribes against non-Quakers.

⁶ Penn's missionary travels are documented in *Papers of William Penn*, i. 101–43, 241–8, 425–508; v. 420–3; the Penn–Mead trial is documented in ibid. i. 171–80; v. 118–25.

⁷ See M. M. Dunn, *Wiliam Penn: Politics and Conscience* (Princeton, NJ, 1967), ch. 2.

⁸ See *Papers of William Penn*, i. 219–22, 259–61, 353–4, 533–41; v. 201–5, 248–51, 258–9.

of internal community discipline.[9] But, apart from his role as a weighty Friend within the Quaker community, he held no public office and had no experience in public management. He never practised as a lawyer, and being a Quaker he was barred from service as a magistrate. As a political observer, he was an outsider who stood apart from the Whigs as well as from the Tories.

For one brief moment in 1679, amid the hysteria of the Popish Plot, Penn acted like a Whig partisan. When Charles II dissolved the Cavalier Parliament and called the first general election in eighteen years, Penn published his famous tract, *England's Great Interest in the Choice of this New Parliament*, in which he urged the electorate to choose sincere Protestants who would discover the plot, punish the King's evil counsellors, and secure frequent future Parliaments. Penn's tract has been called 'one of the first clear statements of party doctrine ever put before the English electorate'.[10] But this misconstrues his intentions. Even in 1679 Penn's priorities were not prime Whig priorities. Instead of calling for the exclusion of the Catholic Duke of York from the throne, he argued for the fundamental religious and civil rights of Englishmen. And the one parliamentary candidate he campaigned for ardently was the radical Republican Algernon Sidney, who was by no means a mainstream Whig politician.[11] When Sidney failed to obtain a seat, and the Whigs in Parliament spent all of their energies trying to block the succession of Charles II's brother, Penn rapidly lost whatever interest he had in English party politics, and resumed his familiar stance as a protester against secular authority.

Yet Penn the young Quaker activist never altogether abandoned the patrician outlook of an English gentleman. In 1670, on the death of his father, he inherited an extensive Irish estate in county Cork, and in 1672 he married Gulielma Springett, a Quaker heiress with even more valuable properties in Kent and Sussex. Penn was now a large landholder with a substantial annual income of about £2,000 in rents. In 1676 William and Gulielma bought Warminghurst Place in Sussex, a 350-acre estate with a very large

---

[9] See ibid. i. 327–37, 353–4, 363–5, 377–9.

[10] D. Ogg, *England in the Reign of Charles II* (Oxford, 1955), ii. 586. Penn's election tract is described in Bronner and Fraser, *William Penn's Published Writings*, 245–7.

[11] See M. M. Dunn, *William Penn: Politics and Conscience*, 27–40; J. R. Jones, 'A Representative of the Alternative Society of Restoration England?' in Dunn and Dunn (eds.), *The World of William Penn*, 60–3.

house which the local Quaker meeting used for worship. Penn lived handsomely, according to the meticulous accounts kept by his steward, Philip Ford.[12] But he also spent freely during the 1670s on Quaker causes. He published the fifty tracts he composed at his own expense. His mission travels and his efforts to rescue fellow Quakers from gaol and from persecution all cost plenty of money. Indeed, by 1680 Penn was seriously in debt. During the 1670s he seems to have spent about twice as much per annum as he received in landed income, and he contracted a series of loans totalling £8,700 which compounded his problems because he now had to pay interest charges of about £500 a year.[13]

Against this background of public service to Quakerism and private indebtedness, Penn took an action in 1680 that abruptly transformed him from an outsider to an insider. He asked Charles II to make him the proprietor of a new English colony in America. Since 1675 Penn had helped to supervise the Quaker settlement of West New Jersey,[14] and this experience undoubtedly triggered his interest in the possibilities of further colonization in the Delaware Valley. In May 1680 he petitioned the King to grant him a patent for a huge tract of land, bounded on the east by New Jersey and on the north and south by New York and Maryland. He grounded his petition on a claim that the Crown owed his father a debt of £16,000 for victualling expenses that the Admiral had incurred during the Dutch War of 1665–67. Penn's claim could certainly have been rejected, and the King's colonial advisers strongly disapproved of handing over strategic territory in the heart of English settlement to a Quaker agitator. But Penn's personal connections with the King and especially with the Duke of York (his neighbour in America) proved to be strong enough for him to be able to obtain a royal charter for the new colony of Pennsylvania in March 1681.[15]

Clearly Penn had both private and public reasons for wanting this American territory. By founding and operating a proprietary colony, he could greatly expand his real estate holdings and hope

[12] Ford's surviving accounts with Penn, 1672–80, are printed in *Papers of William Penn*, i. 574–645.
[13] See R. S. Dunn, 'Penny Wise and Pound Foolish: Penn as a Businessman', in Dunn and Dunn (eds.), *The World of William Penn*, 38–41.
[14] See *Papers of William Penn*, i. 383–421.
[15] Negotiation of the Pennsylvania charter is documented in ibid. ii. 21–78.

to solve his financial problems. But he was primarily motivated by altruistic considerations of public service. In part Penn wanted to rescue his fellow Quakers. Despite his efforts since 1667 to foster religious toleration, Friends throughout Britain were still being harassed by the Anglican Church and imprisoned by the secular authorities, and there was little prospect that this persecuting policy would change. Furthermore, Penn was well aware that many Quakers—especially those living in northern England and Wales— were trapped into a subsistence economy that frustrated all of their efforts to nurture and provide for their children.[16] With a second chance in America, these people could worship freely and support their families. And Penn had larger and loftier aims. While not expecting to remake the world, he did have utopian aspirations for Pennsylvania. He believed that his colonists would be morally regenerated by the religious freedom, political participation, and economic opportunity he offered them, and that they would learn to live together in brotherhood and peace.

On the day he received his charter in March 1681, Penn wrote to an Irish Friend: 'for my business here, know that after many waitings, watchings, solicitings & disputes in councel, this day my country was confirm'd to me.' He added, 'thou mayst communicate my graunt to Frds, & expect shortly my proposals; tis a cleer & just thing & my God that has given it me through many difficultys will I believe bless & make it the seed of a nation. I shall have a tender care to the Govern^t that it be well laid at first."[17] In a similar vein he told a Lancashire Quaker in August 1681, 'for my Country I see the lord in the obtaineing of it'. And he went on to observe that, since he had received this gift from God, he felt impelled to 'do that wch may answear his Kind providence & serve his truth & people; that an example may be Sett up to the nations. there may be room there [in America], tho not here [in England], for such an holy experiment."[18] These two letters contain memorable expressions of Penn's lofty intent: his vision of 'the seed of a nation' and 'an holy experiment'. In both letters, he saw his colony as a sacred trust, a gift from God rather than from Charles II. Yet

[16] See B. Levy, *Quakers and the American Family: British Settlement in the Delaware Valley* (New York, 1988), chs. 1–3.
[17] William Penn to Robert Turner, 5 Mar. 1681, *Papers of William Penn*, ii. 83. The royal charter was dated 4 Mar. 1681.
[18] William Penn to James Harrison, 25 Aug. 1681, ibid. ii. 108.

he also adopted a strikingly personal, patriarchal, and proprietary tone: 'my country' and 'my God'. In a few artless sentences Penn exposed the potential conflict between his altruism and his paternalism, a conflict that would quickly compromise his holy experiment.

Penn expected that Quakers would be particularly attracted to Pennsylvania, and during the eighteen months between his receipt of the charter in March 1681 and his departure for America in August 1682 he appealed directly to the leading Friends he knew in England, Ireland, Scotland, Wales, and Holland for help in recruiting investors and settlers. But he found that a good many Friends disapproved of the new colony, complaining that Penn was escaping his duty in England by enjoying his perquisites in America. This suspicious attitude helped to convince him that he needed to enlist non-Quakers as well. Because of his expansive belief in religious toleration and liberty of conscience, Penn was perfectly willing to make room in Pennsylvania for people who differed from him in opinion and in national origin. So he circulated a series of shrewdly calculated promotional pamphlets, describing his colony in realistic and attractive terms. He offered to sell land to large purchasers at 5,000 acres for £100, and to smaller purchasers in units scaled as low as 250 acres for £5. Penn's advertising brochures made no mention of his Quakerism and were far removed in spirit from the provocative tracts he had published between 1667 and 1680.[19]

Penn took particular pains with his colony's governmental system. 'For the matters of liberty & priviledge,' he announced in April 1681, 'I purpose that wch is extreordinary, & to leave myselfe & successors noe powr of doeing mischief, that the will of one man may not hinder the good of an whole Country.'[20] Indeed he and his advisers drafted a radically democratic plan known as the Fundamental Constitutions, in which the governor and his advisory council enjoyed minimal authority and the real political power emanated directly from the people, who elected and instructed an annual representative assembly, the chief organ of government. Here Penn echoed the arguments of the English Levellers back in

[19] Penn's promotional tracts for Pennsylvania are described in Bronner and Fraser, *William Penn's Published Writings*, 264–76, 282–4, 295–309, 320–9, 332–5.

[20] William Penn to Robert Turner, Anthony Sharp, and Roger Roberts, 12 Apr. 1681, *Papers of William Penn*, ii. 89.

the 1640s, but he was undoubtedly more directly influenced by the egalitarian structure of a Quaker meeting for worship. However, Penn had second thoughts about this plan, and settled instead on an alternative constitution known as the Frame of Government, which he proudly published in May 1682. The Frame of Government called for a bicameral system in which a very large council administered the colony and proposed legislation, to be accepted or rejected by an even more numerous assembly. This constitution clearly echoed the English Republican theorists from the 1650s— especially James Harrington, who was trying to find ways of guaranteeing legislative integrity by separating the power to draft a Bill from the power to vote on that Bill. And Penn was also influenced by the Quaker search for consensus, or unity achieved through a collective sense of the meeting.[21]

In retrospect, Penn's chief mistake as a constitution-maker was that he preserved a draft of the Fundamental Constitutions among his papers, because historians have generally chided him for rejecting the doctrine of popular sovereignty embedded in this scheme. The Fundamental Constitutions certainly gave more direct power to the people's representatives than did the Frame of Government. But it should be pointed out that the Frame of Government was in its own way an idealistic and liberal mechanism. Faithful to his word, Penn bestowed remarkably little power on the colony's governor in this constitution; he evidently expected to persuade the colonists via his personal style, not by prescriptive powers. By creating a huge seventy-two-member council and a two-hundred-member assembly, he was trying to involve as many people as possible in the governmental process. And, by institutionalizing collective consensus, he hoped to defuse the factionalism inherent in most representative systems of government and to build a spirit of political harmony in Pennsylvania.[22]

Penn's promotional efforts were highly successful. Between 1681 and 1685 some seven thousand people joined him in moving to Pennsylvania, which was a very large number considering that few Britons were emigrating to any of the other American colonies

---

[21] Penn's Fundamental Constitutions and Frame of Government are printed in ibid. ii. 140–56, 211–27.

[22] For a differing interpretation, see G. B. Nash, 'The Framing of Government in Pennsylvania: Ideas in Conflict with Reality', *William and Mary Quarterly*, 3rd ser. 23 (1966), 183–209.

during the 1670s and 1680s. Penn also distributed 715,000 acres of Pennsylvania land to nearly six hundred purchasers between 1681 and 1685, and received about £9,000 from these land sales. Some of his purchasers came from Holland, Germany, and France, but 88 per cent of them lived in England, mostly in the cities of London and Bristol, or in western and midland counties where Penn was personally well known.[23] By and large the people who accompanied Penn accepted the precepts of Quakerism. Despite his effort to recruit non-Quakers, the majority of the people who bought land from him or who migrated to his colony in the 1680s had either joined the Friends before they came or did so soon after arrival in America.[24] They had modest means and limited education, but were equipped with practical skills and rising expectations. They migrated in nucleated family groups, so that parents were able to guide and train their children and servants in a domestic setting. To Penn, such people must have seemed designed by God to help him build a model society in the new world.

The years 1682–84 marked the zenith of William Penn's career. On arrival in Pennsylvania, he undertook a series of actions that promoted the orderly development of the colony and shaped its character for decades to come. He made a lasting peace with the local Delaware Indians and bought their land on generous terms. He respected the rights of the few hundred Europeans already living in his territory before 1681. He permitted the incoming colonists to choose what land they wanted to stake out within reason, but surveyed and distributed it in such a way that settlement was systematic and contiguous. He laid out the capital city of Philadelphia—his city of brotherly love—on an expansive scale, and merchants and artisans flocked to live there. He helped to organize a network of Quaker meetings. He bore the full costs of the colony government, as a way of giving the new settlers some breathing room before they were required to pay taxes. He permitted the German and Welsh settlers to form separate

[23] A complete list of the First Purchasers of 1681–5 is printed in *Papers of William Penn*, ii. 630–64; for commentary, see G. B. Nash, *Quakers and Politics: Pennsylvania, 1681–1726* (Princeton, NJ, 1968), ch. 1. D. H. Fischer argues in *Albion's Seed*, 438–51, that the Quaker migrants to Pennsylvania came primarily from the northern midlands, but this was not Penn's home turf, and most of the colonists he personally recruited came—as he did—from southern England.

[24] See R. T. Vann, 'Quakerism: Made in America?', in Dunn and Dunn (eds.), *The World of William Penn*, 157–70.

communities in order to preserve their ethnic identity. And he persuaded the three lower counties (the present state of Delaware), dominated by non-Quakers, to join in political union with the three upper counties of Pennsylvania, dominated by Quakers. Thus he played the difficult role of benevolent patriarch with great success.[25]

Yet, even in these halcyon days, there were portents of trouble over Penn's dual status as patriarch-cum-landlord. His wife, Gulielma, stayed with their young children in England when Penn came to his colony in 1682, and, though he started to build a proprietary manor house for his family at Pennsbury on the Delaware River,[26] he showed no intention of selling his English and Irish properties and moving lock, stock, and barrel to Pennsylvania. Just before he left England, Penn learnt from his steward, Philip Ford, that his expenses as proprietor were running well ahead of his income from land sales: consequently he owed £2,851 to Ford, and had to sign a mortgage and a bond as security for payment of this debt.[27] At the time Penn was little troubled by these transactions, for he assumed that the debt would be liquidated when Ford sold more land for him. But in fact the proprietor continued to spend far more than he earned during his two-year stay in Pennsylvania. He maintained a retinue of colony officials and household servants, and found that the colonists were unwilling to pay quitrents or levy taxes, since they saw him as a rich man well able to shoulder all the costs of his administration. Some Quakers in the 1680s openly accused him of greed, and told him that by assuming the title of lord proprietor he was abandoning Quaker simplicity and equality and indulging his worldly pride.[28]

Penn's acquisitive propensities also led him into a colossal blunder in dealing with his southern neighbour, Lord Baltimore, the proprietor of Maryland. In 1681 Penn had circulated a map of Pennsylvania which indicated that the southern border of his colony—stipulated in his charter as the fortieth degree of latitude—

---

[25] There is a large literature on the initial settlement of Pennsylvania. For two contrasting interpretations, see E. B. Bronner, *William Penn's 'Holy Experiment': The Founding of Pennsylvania, 1681–1701* (New York, 1962), chs. 2–4; and Nash, *Quakers and Politics*, ch. 2.

[26] Penn lived at Pennsbury Manor (in Bucks County, north of Philadelphia) in 1699–1701, but after his death the house and outbuildings were abandoned and fell into ruin. Pennsbury was reconstructed in the 1930s, and is now open to the public.

[27] See *Papers of Willliam Penn*, ii. 290–5.

[28] See ibid. ii. 346–9, 361–2, 502–6.

ran along the latitude of the modern city of Baltimore, whereas in fact it runs nearly fifty miles further north. Acting on this erroneous supposition, Penn claimed jurisdiction over all the inhabitants in what is now the northern quarter of Maryland, and directed them to switch allegiance from the proprietor of Maryland to the proprietor of Pennsylvania. Naturally this vexed Lord Baltimore, especially when he discovered that the fortieth degree of latitude actually runs a few miles north of the city of Philadelphia. Lord Baltimore sent agents into Delaware (Penn's three lower counties), offering more generous land rights and tax rates than Penn had established in order to lure these people into accepting his jurisdiction. Some did so. By 1684 the two proprietors were hopelessly deadlocked, and both returned to England to argue their cases before the King.[29]

Before Penn's quarrel with Baltimore reached its climax, he had already encountered sharp criticism from Pennsylvania colonists who disliked his Frame of Government. They complained that the council and assembly he had designed were far too large, and they wanted a more conventional and adversarial arrangement of two rival legislative houses, where the assembly and the council could each propose and debate legislation—as in the English Parliament or in the other American colonial legislatures. Penn agreed to scale down both houses, thus abandoning the idea of a broadly participatory government, but he clung to his pet notion of separating the council's power to propose from the assembly's power to vote. Possibly he might have converted the colonists to his way of thinking had he stayed in Pennsylvania. But when he announced that he was leaving them in order to battle Lord Baltimore over boundary claims, he looked a lot less like a patriarch and a lot more like a landlord—and an absentee landlord to boot.

Penn's return to England undermined all of his plans for America, and severely damaged his reputation as a champion of political and religious liberalism. In February 1685, before the Quaker proprietor had presented his case against Lord Baltimore to the Lords of Trade, Charles II died and was succeeded by his Catholic brother James II, who, as Duke of York, had long been Penn's principal patron and benefactor at Court. The new king

---

[29] The Penn–Baltimore boundary dispute is documented in ibid. ii. esp. 111–14, 256–9, 381–5, 405–11, 494–500.

quickly demonstrated his continuing goodwill. In November 1685 the Lords of Trade judged that Penn's claim to Delaware was stronger than Lord Baltimore's, and in March 1686, at Penn's behest, James II suspended all legal proceedings against English Quakers.[30] By this time the King had quarrelled with the Anglicans and Tories who had been Charles II's chief supporters—and the Quakers' chief tormentors. Penn decided to remain in England a while longer; he saw a golden opportunity to counsel James and help shape policy at home, as he was doing in Pennsylvania. Obviously he opened himself to the charge of betraying his principles by currying the favour of a bigoted absolutist. But Penn did not see James in these terms. Both men stood outside of the standard Whig–Tory political spectrum. Both had been harassed for their religious beliefs. Penn had always been more critical of the Church of England than of the Roman Catholic Church because he had suffered repeatedly from Anglican persecution. And he trusted the King because James had consistently befriended him at Court.[31]

From 1686 to 1688 Penn had personal, confidential access to James II; he was often at Court and accompanied his sovereign on royal progresses. The exact nature of their dealings will always remain shadowy because almost all of the documentation has disappeared,[32] but it is clear that Penn wanted James to adopt somewhat the same benevolent and patriarchal religious policy in England that he himself was pursuing in Pennsylvania. Knowing that the King was determined to grant toleration to Catholics, Penn asked him to grant toleration to Protestant Dissenters as well. Simultaneously he tried to persuade the Quakers and other dissenting Protestants attacked by the Church of England to support James in return for religious liberty. This was a chancy tactic at best, since most Dissenters saw James II as a tyrannical zealot who intended to convert the Anglican state church into a popish state church. But Penn published ten tracts during James's reign arguing that Protestants should accept religious toleration as a gift from their Catholic monarch.[33] He also toured England

[30] See ibid. iii. 59–61, 68–70, 73, 83–4.

[31] See J. R. Jones, *The Revolution of 1688 in England* (1972), ch. 5.

[32] Penn seems to have destroyed any correspondence he had with James II or his agents; the editors of the *Papers of William Penn* found practically no paper trail of his activities during 1685–91.

[33] Penn's tracts from 1685–8 are described in Bronner and Fraser, *William Penn's Published Writings*, 312–61; see also M. M. Dunn, *William Penn: Politics and Conscience*, chs. 4–5.

preaching this message, and he acted as the King's private emissary in trying to negotiate with the Prince of Orange and with Whig exiles in Holland. He even supported James's effort to manipulate the electorate in order to obtain a Parliament that would repeal the penal laws against Catholics and Dissenters.[34] In allying himself so closely with an unpopular and isolated king, Penn was adopting a public posture far removed from his anti-establishment protests of 1667–80.

The Glorious Revolution proved to be a personal disaster for Penn. After James II was ignominiously driven from the throne, his Quaker ally was arrested and questioned four times between December 1688 and July 1690 by William's and Mary's government as a suspected Jacobite.[35] In 1691 Viscount Sidney reported to Penn that, when he tried to intercede with William III on his behalf, the King's 'answer to me is, that you have been one of his greatest enemies [and] that you have done him all the harme you could'.[36] Very likely William believed that Penn was actively plotting for James's restoration to power—a charge that has never been substantiated. No convincing evidence has yet been discovered to link the Quaker with other Jacobite conspirators during the 1690s.[37] It is quite possible that Penn kept in some sort of touch with his exiled king, whom he still regarded favourably; in several autobiographical fragments dating from the early 1690s, Penn describes how the Duke of York was the only influential figure at Court who listened to his pleas for religious toleration in 1674 and 1684.[38] Unfortunately, he left no autobiographical record of his activities in the wake of the Glorious Revolution; on the contrary, between 1690 and 1694 he went into hiding for much of the time to avoid further harassment on charges of treason.

The Revolution of 1688–89 affected Penn in other ways as well. To a large extent the great public causes he had been agitating since 1667—liberty of conscience, civil rights, and representative government—were now resolved. Penn played no role whatsoever in drafting or articulating the 1689 Settlement, but the Toleration

---

[34] See *Papers of William Penn*, iii. 153–7, 172–7.
[35] See ibid. iii. 211–14, 217, 251–2, 275–8, 283–4, 293–4.
[36] Viscount Sidney to William Penn, 7 Nov. [1691], ibid. iii. 332.
[37] A number of Jacobite letters allegedly written by a 'Mr. Pen' have been produced, but they are not in his hand nor in his epistolary style. See e.g., the purported letter from Penn to Monsieur de Gassis in France, ibid. iii. 663–6.
[38] See ibid. iii. 335–44.

Act permitted Quakers to worship publicly, while the Bill of Rights enumerated the elementary civil liberties of Englishmen and affirmed that Parliament shared power with the Crown. Much of Penn's reforming agenda from the 1670s and 1680s was suddenly out of date. And the Revolution also affected his position as lord proprietor of Pennsylvania. From 1689 onwards William III was engaged in a major international war with France, and he saw the pacifist Penn and his Quaker colonists as unfit to govern a strategic American outpost in wartime. Accordingly, in 1692 the King directed the royal governor of New York to take charge of Pennsylvania.[39] Penn regained the management of his colony in 1694, but he never regained an insider's role at Whitehall, and for the remainder of his proprietorship Pennsylvania was regarded as an ill-managed colony by the bureaucrats in the Colonial Office.

Penn had private sorrows to add to his distress: his wife, Gulielma, died in 1694 and his favourite son, Springett, in 1696. But he was a resilient man, and he gradually adapted quite remarkably to his changed circumstances. During the 1690s Penn significantly altered his public persona, presenting himself as an elder statesman with a ready supply of sententious moral advice. He had frequently offered prudential counsel before, as in a farewell letter of 1682 to his wife and children, full of Polonius-like instructions on how to lead a virtuous life.[40] In similar vein, his second version of *No Cross, No Crown* (1682) stressed the practical as well as the spiritual disadvantages of pride, avarice, and luxury and the countervailing benefits of modesty, temperance, and simplicity. But Penn hit his stride as a public moralist in a little volume of maxims entitled *Some Fruits of Solitude* (1693), which he followed with *More Fruits of Solitude* (1702) and *Fruits of a Father's Love* (published posthumously in 1726).[41] In these advice books Penn offered pithy precepts on such topics as marriage and love, family management, and the perils of worldliness. His greatest imperative was social harmony, and he tried to establish guidelines for avoiding and composing damaging disputes.[42] He wrote for a general audi-

---

[39] See ibid. iii. 347, 358–64.

[40] William Penn to Gulielma Penn and their children, ibid. ii. 269–77. This letter, first published in 1761, was reprinted frequently in the late eighteenth and early nineteenth centuries.

[41] See Bronner and Fraser, *William Penn's Published Writings*, 287–94, 401–9, 493–4, 514–16.

[42] In another effort at social harmony, Penn argued for the establishment of a European Parliament in his *Essay towards the Present and Future Peace of Europe* (1693).

ence rather than a specifically Quaker one, and *Some Fruits of Solitude* proved to be his most popular and enduring work.

The author's injunctions to avoid luxury and avarice take on an ironiç twist when one considers that Penn himself was in worse financial shape in the 1690s than he had been in the 1680s. His debt to his steward, Philip Ford, climbed from £2,851 in 1682 to £4,293 in 1685 to £12,714 in 1697. Between 1685 and 1699 the two men made a series of contractual agreements in which Penn kept renewing his obligations to Ford on increasingly stringent terms, first mortgaging, then leasing, then selling his colony to his steward. From 1697 onwards, Ford allowed Penn to rent Pennsylvania from him for £630 per annum. Ford never attempted to exercise direct control over the colony, but when he died in 1702 the debt was unsettled and the title to the proprietorship was unresolved.[43]

By the mid-1690s Penn himself had almost no control over Pennsylvania. When he had left the colony in 1684, intending to return speedily, he divided the responsibilities of government among eleven prominent colonists, hoping to foster a spirit of collective harmony among them. But the opposite occurred. As early as 1685 he wrote in distress to the Pennsylvania Council: 'I am sorry at heart for y^r Anemositys. . . . For the love of god, me & the poor Country, be not so Governmentish, so Noisy & open in y^r dissatisfactions.'[44] Penn's pleas went unheard. During his long absence the Pennsylvania Quakers refused to display even nominal obedience to orders from the home government. They quarrelled with the deputy-governors Penn sent out as his substitutes. They quarrelled with the non-Quakers, who soon formed a numerical majority within the colony. And they quarrelled among themselves. In part these people were inexperienced at government; in part they were hostile to government. But they clung tenaciously to power. During the 1680s and 1690s the Pennsylvania Quakers adopted an extraordinarily fractious and confrontational political style, which was completely at odds with the loving harmony that Penn had tried to foster in his plans for the colony and in his moral advice literature.[45]

[43] See the Penn–Ford contractual agreements, 1685–99, in *Papers of William Penn*, iii. 656–63.

[44] William Penn to Thomas Lloyd and others, 15 Aug. 1685, ibid. iii. 50.

[45] See Nash, *Quakers and Politics*, chs. 3–5.

Finally in 1699 Penn returned to Pennsylvania, accompanied by his second wife, Hannah Callowhill Penn, to discover that the colonists were by no means altogether pleased to see him again. Penn was not merely older and less vigorous than in 1682; he had lost his ability to shape events in America. He had to accept a permanent division between Pennsylvania and Delaware, because the Quakers in Pennsylvania refused to share power any longer with the non-Quakers in Delaware. He could extract little money in quitrents or taxes. And, most important in the long run, he was forced to discard the Frame of Government that he had established in 1682 and accept a new constitution, the Charter of Privileges, drawn up by his chief critics in the colony, in which the governor (aided by his council) had the executive authority and a unicameral assembly had the legislative authority. Under this new arrangement the governor was considerably more powerful than in 1682 because he had veto power; the council was far less powerful than in 1682 because it was stripped of law-making authority; and the assembly combined full drafting and voting powers and became the most potent legislative body in America.[46]

In some ways the Charter of Privileges of 1701 was a new version of the Fundamental Constitutions that Penn had rejected in 1681, but it omitted the idealized democracy of that earlier plan by locating power in the legislature rather than in the citizenry. The Quakers who drew up this new constitution did not care to experiment with popular sovereignty, because the majority of Pennsylvania citizens were by now non-Quakers. Instead, they focused on holding as many seats in the assembly as possible, and in fact controlled the assembly into the 1750s. Penn lost very heavily in 1701. His holy experiment in politics was gone, because the Charter of Privileges invited conflict between the executive and legislative branches of government. Penn had tried to ameliorate conflict and achieve harmony by providing an open forum in which rival opinions and interests could be tempered and balanced through active community participation, but after 1701 there was less chance of a Quaker-style consensus in Pennsylvania than in most other colonies. And the irony is that Penn's defeat has always been interpreted as a victory of political liberty over proprietary authority. Thus, although Penn was a liberal political thinker, he

[46] The Charter of Privileges is printed in *Papers of William Penn*, iv. 104–10.

is identified as being on the conservative side in the American contest between liberty and authority.

In 1701 William Penn returned to England because Crown agents were trying to strip him of his charter. He had the bad luck to be the most conspicuous chartered proprietor in America at a time when the Board of Trade was trying vigorously to impose direct royal rule over all of the proprietary colonies. Although Penn managed to beat off this challenge,[47] he was soon embroiled with the heirs to his steward, Philip Ford, who sued him for £20,000, and forced him into debtor's prison in 1708, to the scandal and embarrassment of the English Quaker community. Eventually the Fords extracted £7,600 from him—a sum that Penn could raise only by borrowing from a circle of wealthy English Quakers, for he had already sold his house at Warminghurst Place to pay off other debts.[48] In the end he became so worn down by the burden of managing his colony that he agreed to sell his governmental rights to Queen Anne. He had just about completed negotiations in 1712 for the surrender of Pennsylvania to the Crown on payment of £12,000 when he suffered a series of disabling strokes that ended his active career and preserved Pennsylvania as a proprietary colony until the American Revolution. Penn lived on as a hapless invalid for another six years until he died in 1718.[49]

In sum, this remarkable man was never a total rebel against his father's privileged world, nor did his ardent belief in the Inner Light ever eradicate an instinctive enjoyment of wealth and status. It seems likely that William Penn found it impossible to face the deepest problem about his way of life, that his Quakerism conflicted with his worldly desires and attainments. This may explain why he lived in a state of continuous whirlwind activity, always travelling, or preaching, or lobbying, or composing one of his 134 books and pamphlets, or writing one of his many thousand letters—because 'he had to keep on the move to avoid meeting even himself'.[50] But, if Penn had something of a split personality, for many years he managed to hold his worldly and spiritual values in splendidly

---

[47] Penn's battle with the Board of Trade in 1702 is detailed in ibid. iv. 139–200.
[48] The Penn–Ford lawsuits of 1705–8 are documented in ibid. iv. 399–508, 769–73.
[49] See ibid. iv. 707–54.
[50] M. M. Dunn, 'The Personality of William Penn', in Dunn and Dunn (eds.), *The World of William Penn*, 11.

productive creative tension. And when he translated his unpopular private beliefs into purposeful action, he accomplished vastly more in the public arena than he could possibly have achieved as a conventional landed squire—or even as a pure Child of Light.

For more than forty years and with great versatility Penn employed his inner spiritual resources together with his outer worldly assets for public ends. As a young Quaker agitator he drew upon his father's Court connections and his father's and wife's private fortunes to fight against religious persecution. As the benevolent founder of Pennsylvania, he combined lofty altruism with shrewd entrepreneurship to draw thousands of colonists to his holy experiment in America. Then, cultivating his own Court connections, he tried to persuade James II to grant religious liberty to all Englishmen. And even in his final years, when he was besieged by adversaries in England and Pennsylvania, he continued to speak out as a public moralist and an advocate of social harmony. It is painful to trace the downward slope of Penn's career in the 1690s and 1700s, to see him hounded by creditors, badgered by Colonial Office officials, and dismissed by the inhabitants of Pennsylvania as a greedy landlord with impractical ideas. The old man had little space left for the visions that had inspired his younger self back in the 1670s and 1680s. But, in fact, one of his visions had largely come true. Just as Penn hoped when he founded his colony, the people who flocked to Pennsylvania felt exhilarated and regenerated by the religious freedom, political participation, and economic opportunity he offered them. Penn's colonists refused to live together in brotherly love, and rejected his holy experiment. But they did plant the seeds of a nation.

16
A Select Bibliography
of the Writings of
G. E. Aylmer, 1957–1990
WILLIAM SHEILS

1957

'The Last Years of Purveyance, 1610–1660', *Ec. Hist. Rev.* 2nd ser.,
10: 81–93.
'Attempts at Administrative Reform, 1625–1640', *EHR* 72: 229–
59.

Review

C. D. Bowen, *The Lion and the Throne: The Life and Times of Sir
Edward Coke* (1957), and H. Hulme, *The Life of Sir John Eliot,
1592–1632: The Struggle for Parliamentary Freedom* (1957), in *History*,
42: 238–40.

1958

'Charles I's Commission on Fees, 1627–1640', *BIHR* 31: 58–67.
'Montacute: A Great House of the Landed Gentry', *Times Educational
Supplement*, 31 Oct., 1592.

1959

'Office Holding as a Factor in English History, 1625–42', *History*,
44: 228–40.

Review

G. Yule, *The Independents in the English Civil War* (Cambridge, 1958),
in *History*, 44: 61–3.

1961

(ed.), *The Diary of William Lawrence, Covering Periods between 1662 and 1681* (Beaminster).

The King's Servants: The Civil Service of Charles I, 1625–1642 (rev. edn., 1974).

'The Officers of the Exchequer, 1625–1642', in F. J. Fisher (ed.), *Essays in the Economic and Social History of Tudor and Stuart England in Honour of R. H. Tawney* (Cambridge), 164–81.

Reviews

R. Ashton, *The Crown and the Money Market, 1603–1640* (Oxford, 1960), in *Ec. Hist. Rev.* 2nd ser., 14: 145–7.

V. Pearl, *London and the Outbreak of the Puritan Revolution: City Government and National Politics, 1625–43* (1961), in *Ec. Hist. Rev.* 2nd ser., 14: 346–9.

1962

Review

W. K. Jordan, *The Charities of Rural England 1480–1640: The Aspirations and the Achievement of the Rural Society* (1961), in *Ec. Hist. Rev.* 2nd ser., 15: 155–6.

1963

The Struggle for the Constitution, 1603–89: England in the Seventeenth Century (2nd edn., 1968; 3rd edn., 1972; 4th edn., 1975).

Review

T. G. Barnes, *Somerset 1625–1640: A County's Government during the 'Personal Rule'* (Cambridge, Mass., 1961), in *EHR* 78: 330–3.

1965

'Place Bills and the Separation of Powers: Some Seventeenth-Century Origins of the "Non-Political" Civil Service', *TRHS* 5th ser. 15: 45–69.

'The Crisis of the Aristocracy 1558–1641 (Review Article)', *P&P* 32: 113–25.

Review

H. E. Bell and R. C. Ollard (eds.), *Historical Essays 1600–1750, presented to David Ogg* (1963), in *EHR* 80: 124–5.

1966

Review

C. Hill, *The Intellectual Origins of the English Civil War* (Oxford, 1965), in *EHR* 81: 783–9.

1967

'Britain Transformed: Crown, Conscience and Commonwealth', in H. R. Trevor-Roper (ed.), *The Age of Expansion*, 209–40.
'Americans and Seventeenth-Century Parliament-Men (Review Article)', *History*, 52: 287–92.

Reviews

A. Clarke, *The Old English in Ireland 1625–42* (1966), in *History*, 52: 209–11.
H. R. Trevor-Roper, *Religion, the Reformation and Social Change* (1967), in *TLS* 19 Oct., 973–4.

1968

' "England's Spirit unfoulded, or an incouragement to take the engagement": A Newly Discovered Pamphlet by Gerrard Winstanley', *P&P* 40: 3–15.
'Caste, ordre (ou statut) et classe dans les premiers temps de l'Angleterre moderne', in R. Mousnier (ed.), *Problèmes de stratification sociale* (Paris), 137–57.

Review

M. Prestwich, *Cranfield: Politics and Profits under the Early Stuarts* (Oxford, 1966), in *EHR* 83: 348–51.

1970

'The King's Debts', *Purnell's History of the English Speaking Peoples*, 1479–87.
'Gentlemen Levellers?', *P&P* 49: 120–5.
(with W. Lamont), *Charles I* (Sussex Tapes).
(with W. Lamont), *Puritanism* (Sussex Tapes).

1971

'Was Oliver Cromwell a member of the army in 1646–47 or not?', *History* 56: 183–8.

Reviews

H. F. Kearney, *Scholars and Gentlemen: Universities and Society in Preindustrial Britain, 1500–1700* (1970), in *History*, 56: 95–6.
J. T. Cliffe, *The Yorkshire Gentry from the Reformation to the Civil War* (1969), in *EHR* 86: 363–4.

1972

'Who was ruling in Herefordshire from 1645 to 1661?', *Transactions of the Woolhope Club*, 40: 373–87.
(ed.), *The Interregnum: The Quest for Settlement 1646–1660.*

'Introduction', in Aylmer (ed.), *The Interregnum*, 1–28.
Irish Resistance (York, Audiocassette).

Review

W. Notestein, *The House of Commons 1604–1610* (New Haven, Conn., 1971), in *EHR* 87: 363–5.

1973

The State's Servants: The Civil Service of the English Republic, 1649–1660.
'St. Patrick's Day 1628, in Witham, Essex', *P&P* 61: 139–48.
'Commissions for Crown Revenues and Land Sales in the Early Seventeenth Century', *BIHR* 46: 208–9.

1974

Reviews

G. R. Elton, *Reform and Renewal: Thomas Cromwell and the Common Weal* (Cambridge, 1974), in *Journal of Ecclesiastical History*, 25: 217–18

J. P. Cooper (ed.), *The Wentworth Papers 1597–1628* (Camden Soc. 4th ser., 12; 1973), in *EHR* 89: 387–9.

1975

(ed.), *The Levellers in the English Revolution.*

(with J. R. Jones), *The Restoration* (Sussex Tapes, Brighton).

(with C. S. R. Russell), *Parliament in the Seventeenth Century* (Sussex Tapes, Brighton).

1976

Review

C. G. C. Tite, *Impeachment and Parliamentary Judicature in Early Stuart England* (1974), in *EHR* 91: 130.

1977

(ed. with R. Cant), *A History of York Minster* (Oxford).

'Funeral Monuments and Other Post-Medieval Sculpture', in Aylmer and Cant (eds.), *A History of York Minster*, 430–86.

Review

A. Macfarlane (ed.), *The Diary of Ralph Josselin 1616–83* (Oxford, 1977), in *TLS* 18 Mar., 324.

1978

'Unbelief in Seventeenth-Century England', in D. Pennington and K. Thomas (eds.), *Puritans and Revolutionaries: Essays in Seventeenth Century History Presented to Christopher Hill* (Oxford), 22–46.

'Office-Holding, Wealth, and Social Structure in England *c.*1580–*c.*1720', *Domanda e consumi* (Florence), 247–59.

Reviews

C. Hill, *Milton and the English Revolution* (1977), in *History*, 63: 456–8.

T. W. Moody, F. X. Martin, and F. J. Byrne (eds.), *A New History of Ireland*, iii, *Early Modern Ireland 1534–1691* (Oxford, 1976), in *EHR* 93: 117–21.

1979

'The "Ormée" and the Popular Movement in the English Revolution', in P. Budel (ed.), *Sociétés et groupes sociaux en Acquitaine et en Angleterre* (Bordeaux), 95–103.

(with J. S. Morrill), *The Civil War and Interregnum: Sources for Local Historians*.

'The Council in the North: A Note on the Location of the Secretary's Office', *York Historian*, 2: 21–3.

'Bureaucracy', in P. Burke (ed.), *The New Cambridge Modern History*, xiii. *Companion Volume* (Cambridge), 104–20.

'Introduction', *The Clarke Manuscripts at Worcester College, Oxford* (Harvester Microform, Brighton).

Review

J. G. A. Pocock (ed.), *The Political Works of James Harrington* (Cambridge, 1977), in *EHR* 94: 129–32.

1980

'Crisis and Regrouping in the Political Élites: England from the 1630s to the 1660s', in J. G. A. Pocock (ed.), *Three British Revolutions: 1641, 1688, 1776* (Princeton, NJ), 140–62.

'The Historical Background', in C. A. Patrides and C. B. Waddington (eds.), *The Age of Milton* (Manchester), 1–33.

'From Office-Holding to Civil Service: The Genesis of Modern Bureaucracy', *TRHS* 5th ser. 30: 91–108.

'The Meaning and Definition of "Property" in Seventeenth-Century England', *P&P* 86: 87–97 (with further note in ibid. 89 (1981), 143).

Reviews

B. Sharp, *In Contempt of All Authority, Rural Artisans and Riot in the West of England, 1586–1660* (Los Angeles, Calif., 1980), in *TLS* 26 Dec., 1486

Q. Skinner, *The Foundations of Modern Political Thought*, i. *The Renaissance*, ii. *The Age of Reformation* (Cambridge, 1978), in *EHR* 95: 839–42.

1981

Review

S. S. Webb, *The Governors-General: The English Army and the Definition of Empire, 1569–1681* (Chapel Hill, NC, 1979), in *EHR* 96: 398–400.

1982

'Seventeenth-Century Wykehamists', in R. Custance (ed.), *Winchester College: Sixth Centenary Essays* (Oxford), 281–311.

Review

C. C. Weston and J. R. Greenberg, *Subjects and Sovereigns: The Grand Controversy over Legal Sovereignty in Stuart England*, in *EHR* 97: 371–4.

1983

(ed., with J. S. Morrill), *Land Men and Beliefs: Studies in Early Modern History by J. P. Cooper*.

'English Perceptions of Scandinavia in the Seventeenth Century', in G. Rystad (ed.), *Europe and Scandinavia: Aspects of the Process of Integration in the 17th Century* (Lund), 181–93.

Review

A. Fletcher, *The Outbreak of the English Civil War* (1981), in *EHR* 98: 155–8.

1984

'The Religion of Gerrard Winstanley', in B. Reay and J. F. McGregor (eds.), *Radical Religion in the English Revolution* (Oxford), 91–119.

Reviews

E. Read Foster, *The House of Lords 1603–1649* (Chapel Hill, NC, 1984), in *TLS* 23 Mar., 308

B. Reay, C. Hill, and W. Lamont, *The World of the Muggletonians* (1983), and B. R. White, *The English Baptists of the Seventeenth Century* (Baptists' Historical Society, 1983), in *Journal of Ecclesiastical History*, 35: 283–5.

J. F. Larkin (ed.), *Stuart Royal Proclamations*, ii. *Royal Proclamations of King Charles I, 1625–1646* (Oxford, 1983), in *EHR* 99: 574–6.

1986

'Collective Mentalities in Mid-Seventeenth-Century England, i. The Puritan Outlook', *TRHS* 5th ser. 36: 1–25.

'The Economics and the Finances of the Colleges and University *c*.1530–1640', in J. McConica (ed.), *The History of the University of Oxford*, iii. *The Collegiate University* (Oxford), 521–58.

Rebellion or Revolution? England 1640–1660 (Oxford).

Review

S. S. Webb, *1676: The End of American Independence* (Cambridge, Mass., 1985), in *EHR* 101: 946–9.

1987

'Did the Ranters exist?' *P&P* 117: 208–19.

'Collective Mentalities in Mid-Seventeenth-Century England, ii. Royalist Attitudes', *TRHS* 5th ser. 37: 1–30.

1988

'Collective Mentalities in Mid-Seventeenth-Century England, iii. Varieties of Radicalism', *TRHS* 5th ser. 38: 1–25.

1989

'Collective Mentalities in Mid-Seventeenth-Century England, iv. Cross Currents: Neutrals, Trimmers, and Others', *TRHS* 5th ser. 39: 1–22.

The Personal Rule of Charles I, 1629–40 (Historical Association, New Appreciations in History, 14).

Review

P. Clark and D. Souden (eds.), *Migration and Society in Early Modern England* (1987), and D. Cressy, *Coming Over, Migration and Communication between England and New England in the Seventeenth Century* (Cambridge, 1987), in *EHR* 104: 127–9.

1990

'The Peculiarities of the English State', *Journal of Historical Sociology*, 3: 91–108.

'Buckingham as an Administrative Reformer', *EHR* 105: 355–62.

INDEX